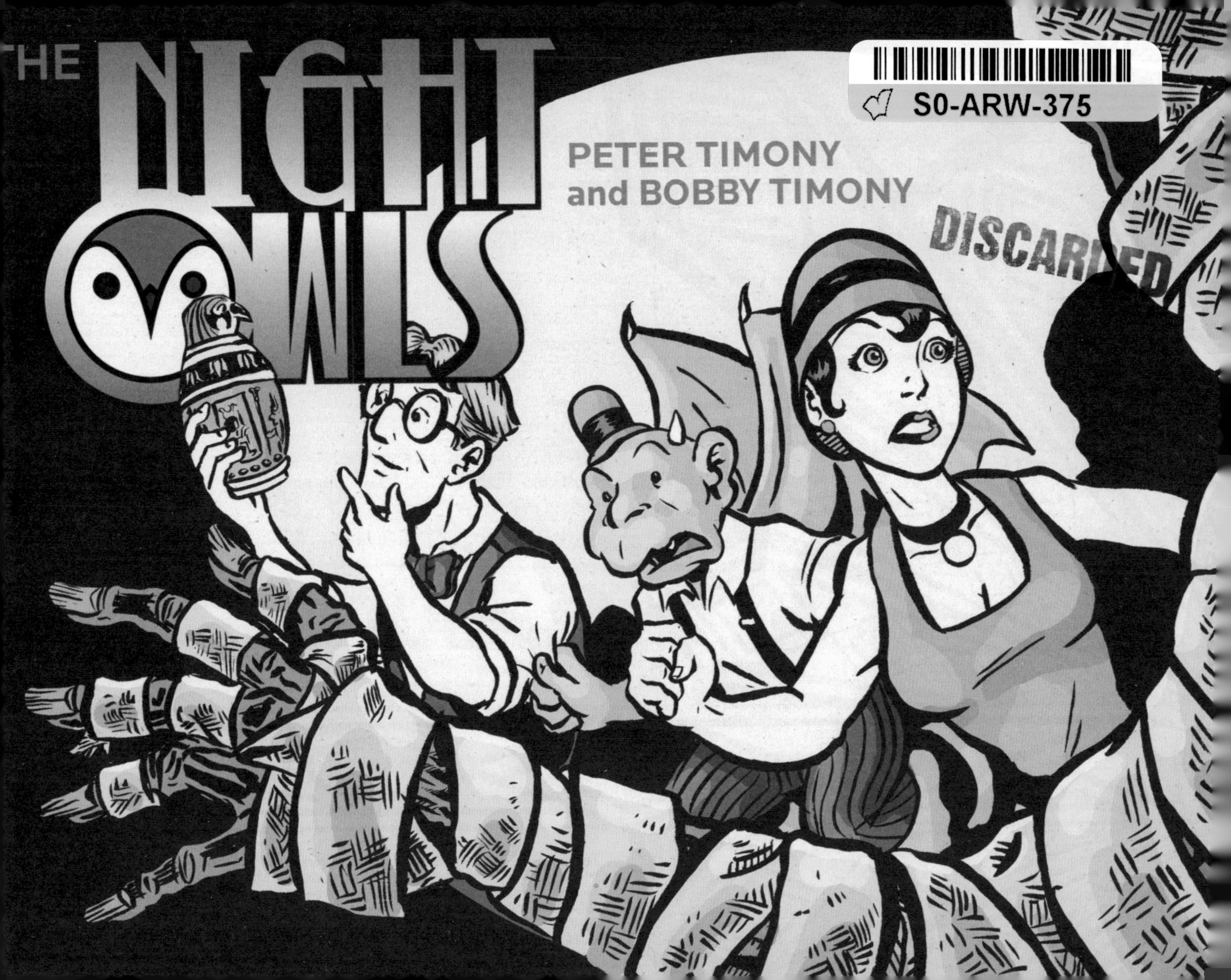
THE NIGHT OWLS
PETER TIMONY
and BOBBY TIMONY

RON PERAZZA Editorial Director–Zuda Comics

KWANZA JOHNSON Editor

NIKA DENOYELLE Assistant Editor

JESSICA NUMSUWANKIJKUL Assistant Editor (Book Edition)

BOB HARRAS Consulting Editor

MARIA P. CABARDO Art Director

RICHARD BRUNING SVP–Creative Director

PAUL LEVITZ President & Publisher

PATRICK CALDON EVP–Finance & Operations

AMY GENKINS SVP–Business & Legal Affairs

JIM LEE Editorial Director–WildStorm

GREGORY NOVECK SVP–Creative Affairs

STEVE ROTTERDAM SVP–Sales & Marketing

CHERYL RUBIN SVP–Brand Management

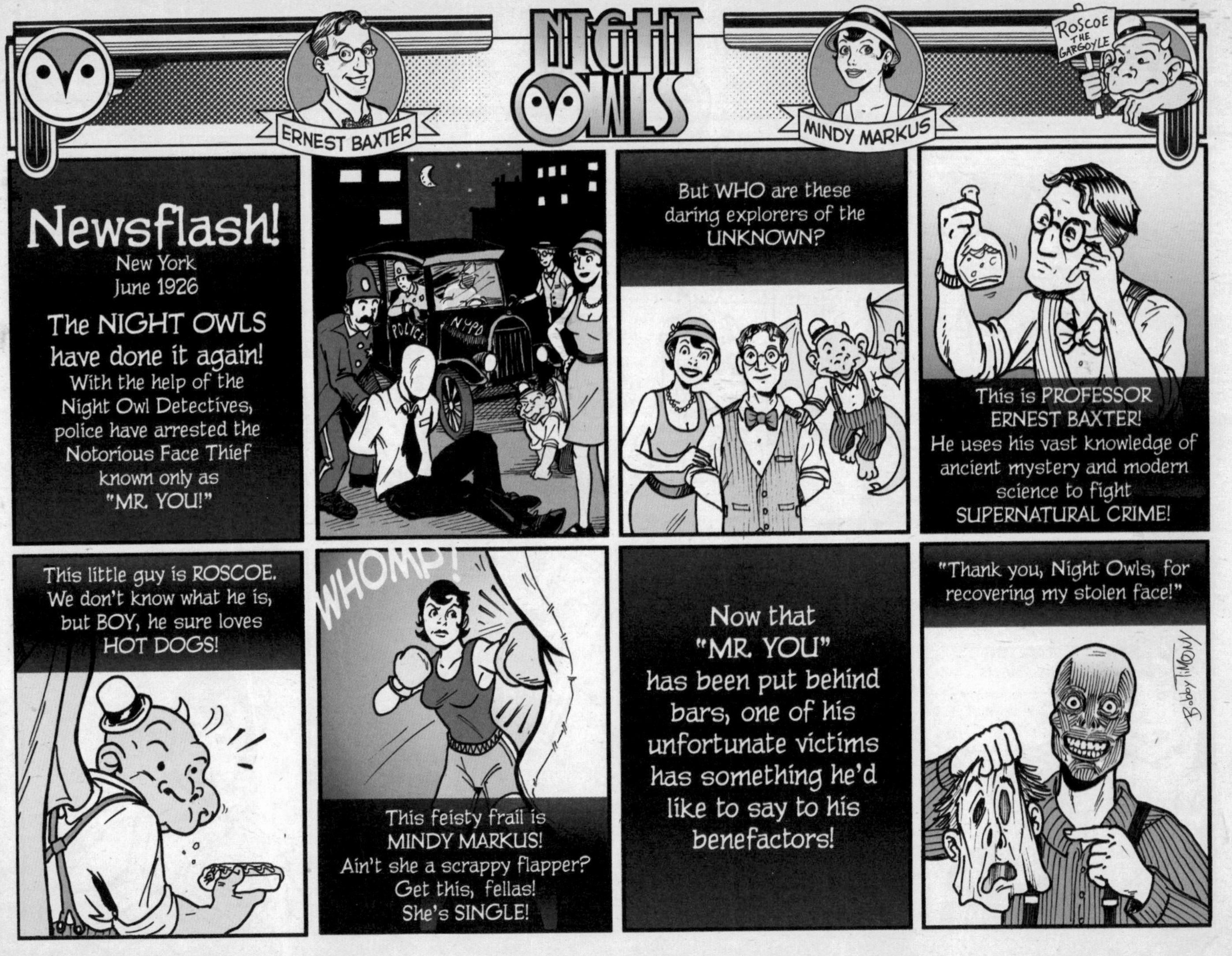
NIGHT OWLS
ERNEST BAXTER
MINDY MARKUS
ROSCOE THE GARGOYLE
Newsflash!
New York
June 1926
The NIGHT OWLS have done it again!
With the help of the Night Owl Detectives, police have arrested the Notorious Face Thief known only as "MR. YOU!"
POLICE
NYPD
But WHO are these daring explorers of the UNKNOWN?
This is PROFESSOR ERNEST BAXTER!
He uses his vast knowledge of ancient mystery and modern science to fight SUPERNATURAL CRIME!
This little guy is ROSCOE. We don't know what he is, but BOY, he sure loves HOT DOGS!
WHOMP!
This feisty frail is MINDY MARKUS! Ain't she a scrappy flapper? Get this, fellas! She's SINGLE!
Now that "MR. YOU" has been put behind bars, one of his unfortunate victims has something he'd like to say to his benefactors!
"Thank you, Night Owls, for recovering my stolen face!"
Bobby Timony

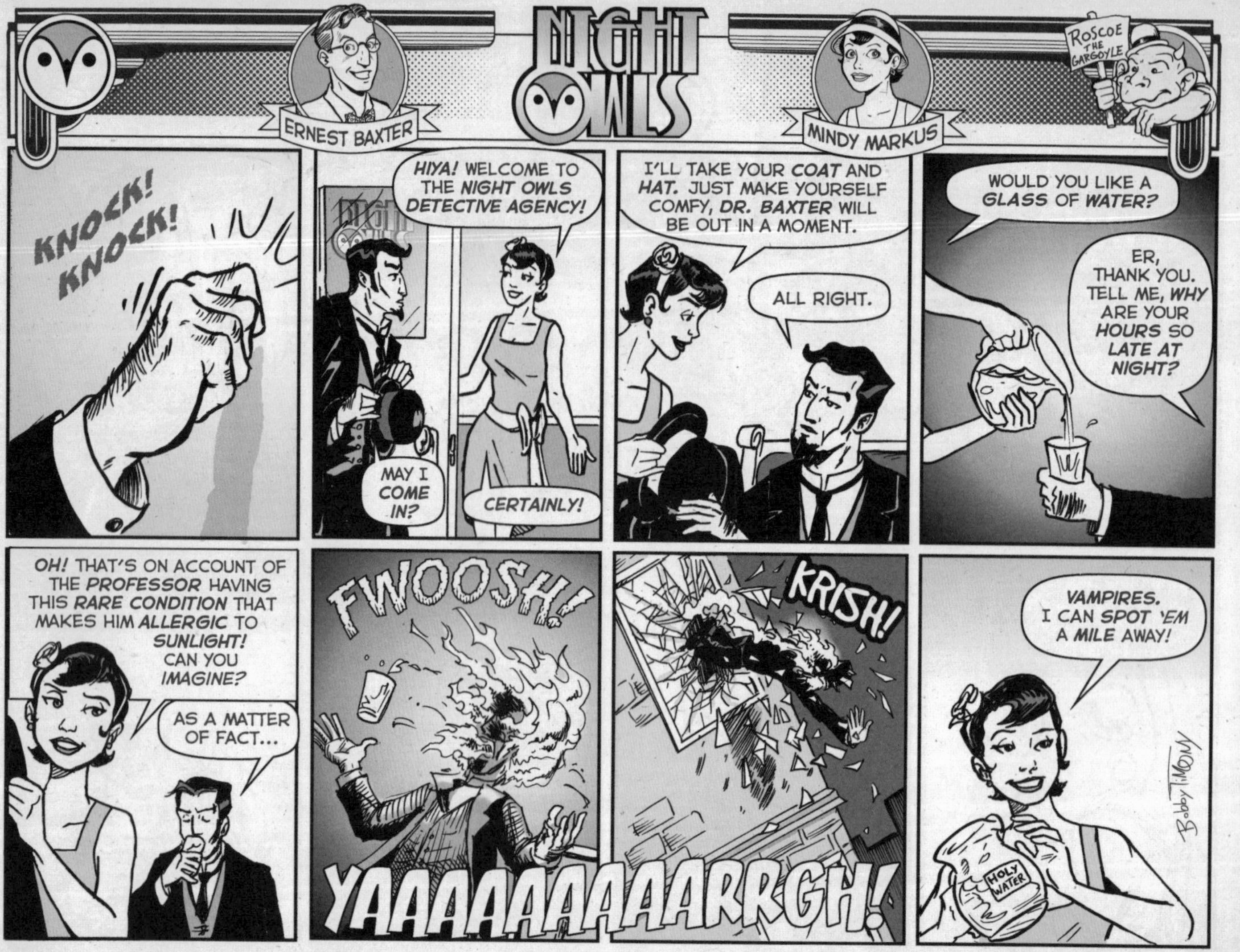
NIGHT OWLS
ERNEST BAXTER
MINDY MARKUS
ROSCOE THE GARGOYLE
KNOCK! KNOCK!
HIYA! WELCOME TO THE NIGHT OWLS DETECTIVE AGENCY!
MAY I COME IN?
CERTAINLY!
I'LL TAKE YOUR COAT AND HAT. JUST MAKE YOURSELF COMFY, DR. BAXTER WILL BE OUT IN A MOMENT.
ALL RIGHT.
WOULD YOU LIKE A GLASS OF WATER?
ER, THANK YOU. TELL ME, WHY ARE YOUR HOURS SO LATE AT NIGHT?
OH! THAT'S ON ACCOUNT OF THE PROFESSOR HAVING THIS RARE CONDITION THAT MAKES HIM ALLERGIC TO SUNLIGHT! CAN YOU IMAGINE?
AS A MATTER OF FACT...
FWOOSH!
KRISH!
YAAAAAAAAAAARRGH!
VAMPIRES. I CAN SPOT 'EM A MILE AWAY!
HOLY WATER
Bobby Timony

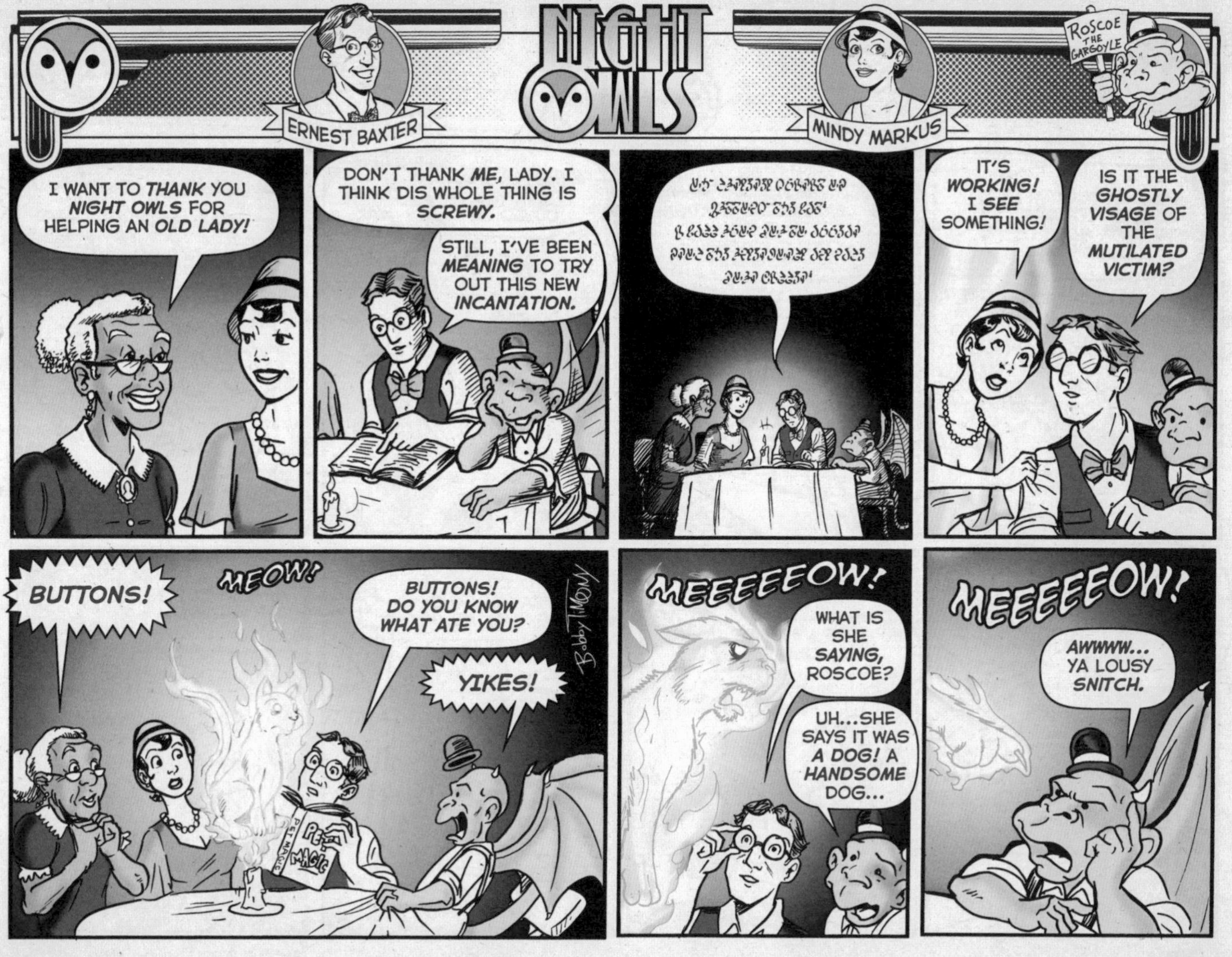
NIGHT OWLS
ERNEST BAXTER
MINDY MARKUS
ROSCOE THE GARGOYLE
I WANT TO THANK YOU NIGHT OWLS FOR HELPING AN OLD LADY!
DON'T THANK ME, LADY. I THINK DIS WHOLE THING IS SCREWY.
STILL, I'VE BEEN MEANING TO TRY OUT THIS NEW INCANTATION.
IT'S WORKING! I SEE SOMETHING!
IS IT THE GHOSTLY VISAGE OF THE MUTILATED VICTIM?
BUTTONS!
MEOW!
BUTTONS! DO YOU KNOW WHAT ATE YOU?
YIKES!
PET MAGIC
Bobby Timony
MEEEEEEOW!
WHAT IS SHE SAYING, ROSCOE?
UH...SHE SAYS IT WAS A DOG! A HANDSOME DOG...
MEEEEEEOW!
AWWWW... YA LOUSY SNITCH.

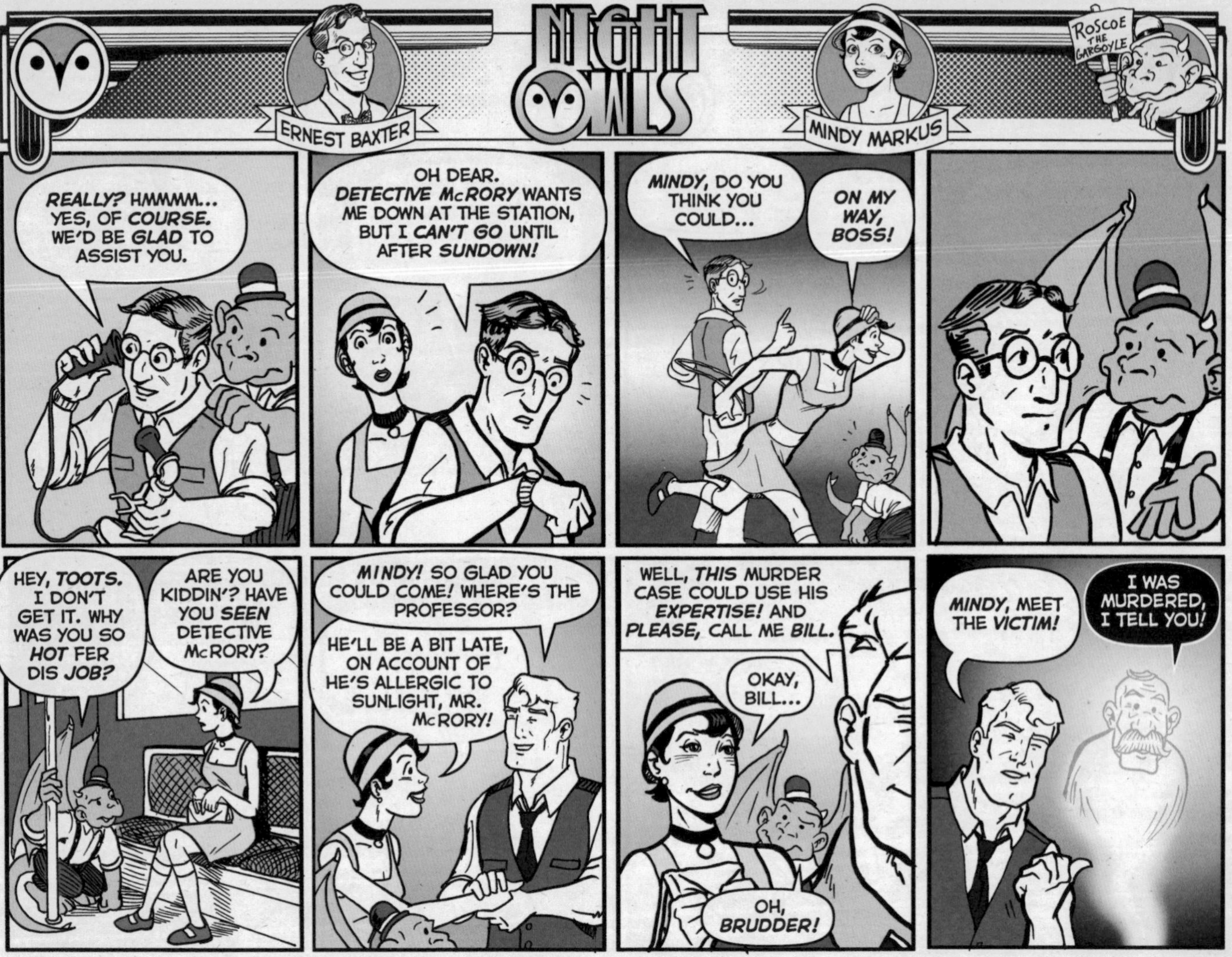
NIGHT OWLS
ERNEST BAXTER
MINDY MARKUS
ROSCOE THE GARGOYLE
REALLY? HMMMM... YES, OF COURSE. WE'D BE GLAD TO ASSIST YOU.
OH DEAR. DETECTIVE McRORY WANTS ME DOWN AT THE STATION, BUT I CAN'T GO UNTIL AFTER SUNDOWN!
MINDY, DO YOU THINK YOU COULD...
ON MY WAY, BOSS!
HEY, TOOTS. I DON'T GET IT. WHY WAS YOU SO HOT FER DIS JOB?
ARE YOU KIDDIN'? HAVE YOU SEEN DETECTIVE McRORY?
MINDY! SO GLAD YOU COULD COME! WHERE'S THE PROFESSOR?
HE'LL BE A BIT LATE, ON ACCOUNT OF HE'S ALLERGIC TO SUNLIGHT, MR. McRORY!
WELL, THIS MURDER CASE COULD USE HIS EXPERTISE! AND PLEASE, CALL ME BILL.
OKAY, BILL...
OH, BRUDDER!
MINDY, MEET THE VICTIM!
I WAS MURDERED, I TELL YOU!

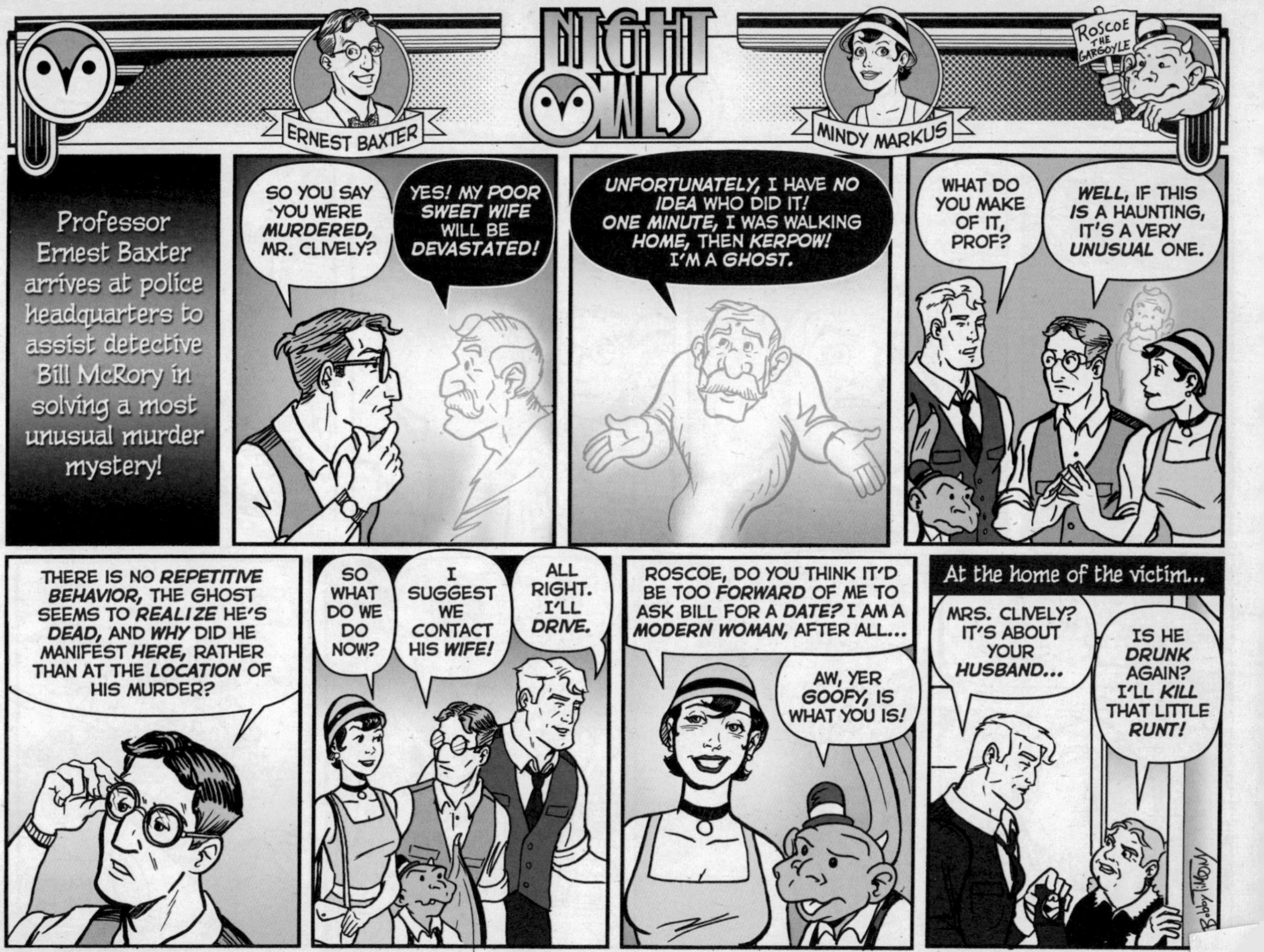
NIGHT OWLS
ERNEST BAXTER
MINDY MARKUS
ROSCOE THE GARGOYLE
Professor Ernest Baxter arrives at police headquarters to assist detective Bill McRory in solving a most unusual murder mystery!
SO YOU SAY YOU WERE MURDERED, MR. CLIVELY?
YES! MY POOR SWEET WIFE WILL BE DEVASTATED!
UNFORTUNATELY, I HAVE NO IDEA WHO DID IT! ONE MINUTE, I WAS WALKING HOME, THEN KERPOW! I'M A GHOST.
WHAT DO YOU MAKE OF IT, PROF?
WELL, IF THIS IS A HAUNTING, IT'S A VERY UNUSUAL ONE.
THERE IS NO REPETITIVE BEHAVIOR, THE GHOST SEEMS TO REALIZE HE'S DEAD, AND WHY DID HE MANIFEST HERE, RATHER THAN AT THE LOCATION OF HIS MURDER?
SO WHAT DO WE DO NOW?
I SUGGEST WE CONTACT HIS WIFE!
ALL RIGHT. I'LL DRIVE.
ROSCOE, DO YOU THINK IT'D BE TOO FORWARD OF ME TO ASK BILL FOR A DATE? I AM A MODERN WOMAN, AFTER ALL...
AW, YER GOOFY, IS WHAT YOU IS!
At the home of the victim...
MRS. CLIVELY? IT'S ABOUT YOUR HUSBAND...
IS HE DRUNK AGAIN? I'LL KILL THAT LITTLE RUNT!
Bobby Timony

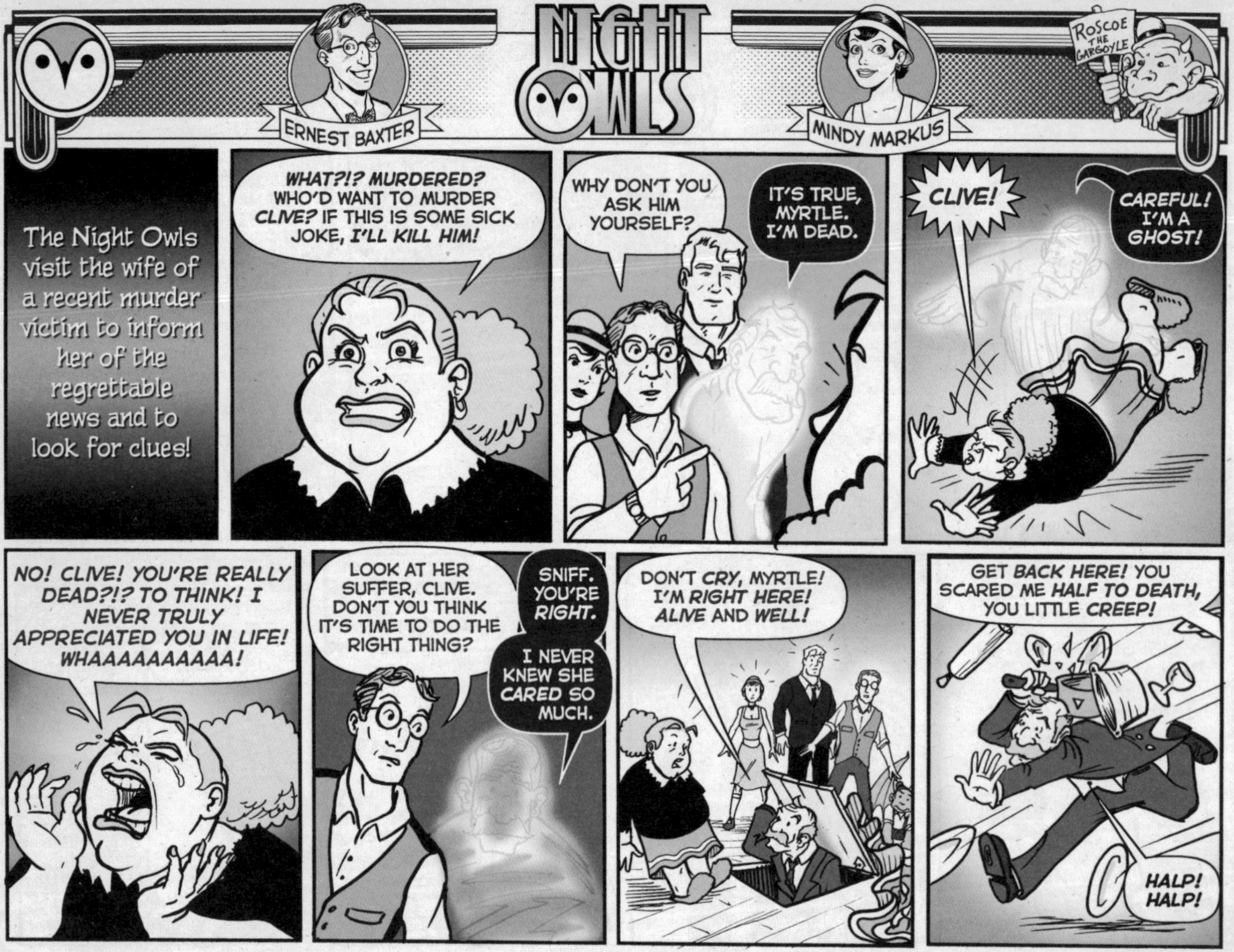
NIGHT OWLS
ERNEST BAXTER
MINDY MARKUS
ROSCOE THE GARGOYLE
The Night Owls visit the wife of a recent murder victim to inform her of the regrettable news and to look for clues!
WHAT?!? MURDERED? WHO'D WANT TO MURDER CLIVE? IF THIS IS SOME SICK JOKE, I'LL KILL HIM!
WHY DON'T YOU ASK HIM YOURSELF?
IT'S TRUE, MYRTLE. I'M DEAD.
CLIVE!
CAREFUL! I'M A GHOST!
NO! CLIVE! YOU'RE REALLY DEAD?!? TO THINK! I NEVER TRULY APPRECIATED YOU IN LIFE! WHAAAAAAAAAA!
LOOK AT HER SUFFER, CLIVE. DON'T YOU THINK IT'S TIME TO DO THE RIGHT THING?
SNIFF. YOU'RE RIGHT.
I NEVER KNEW SHE CARED SO MUCH.
DON'T CRY, MYRTLE! I'M RIGHT HERE! ALIVE AND WELL!
GET BACK HERE! YOU SCARED ME HALF TO DEATH, YOU LITTLE CREEP!
HALP! HALP!

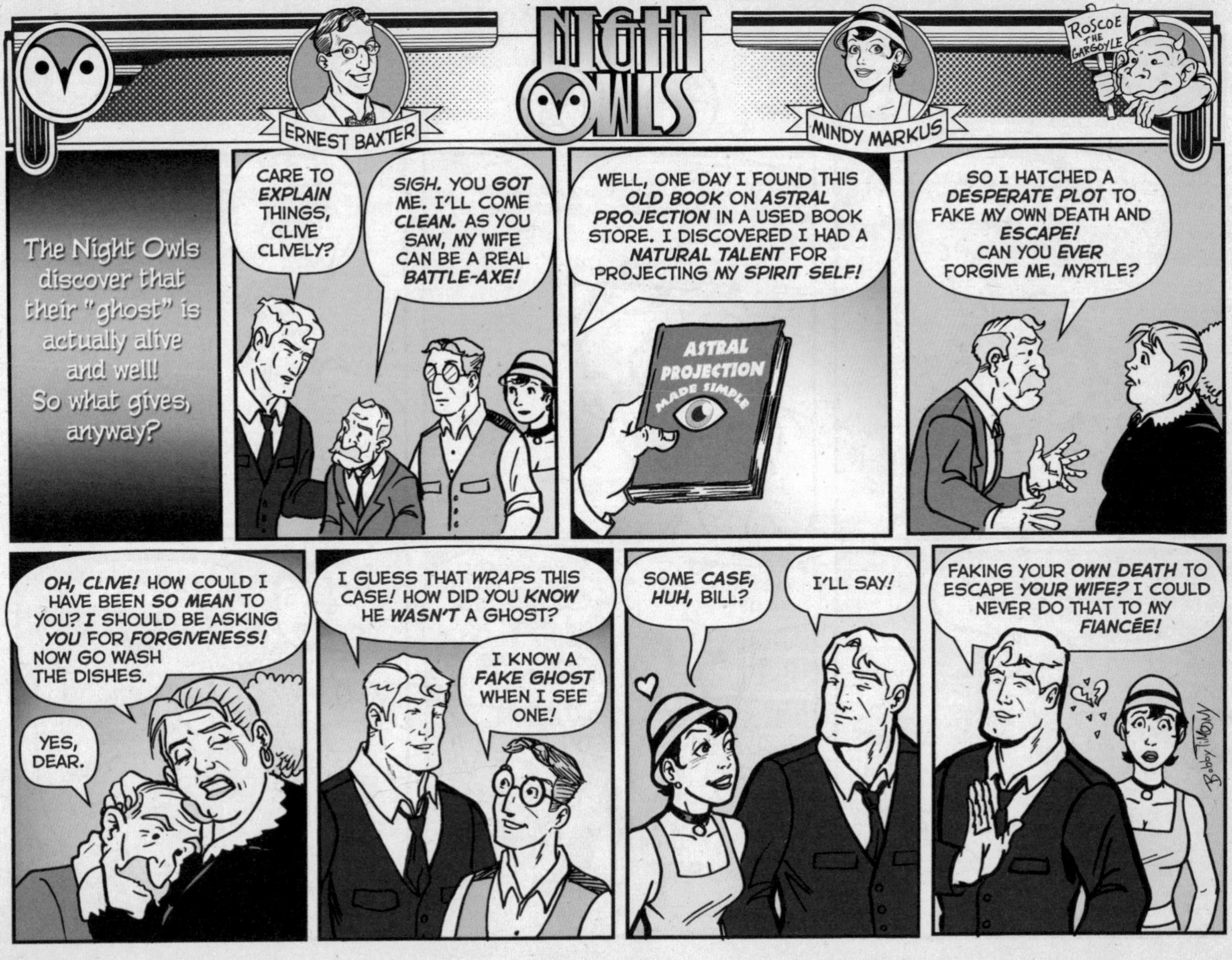
NIGHT OWLS
ERNEST BAXTER
MINDY MARKUS
ROSCOE THE GARGOYLE
The Night Owls discover that their "ghost" is actually alive and well! So what gives, anyway?
CARE TO EXPLAIN THINGS, CLIVE CLIVELY?
SIGH. YOU GOT ME. I'LL COME CLEAN. AS YOU SAW, MY WIFE CAN BE A REAL BATTLE-AXE!
WELL, ONE DAY I FOUND THIS OLD BOOK ON ASTRAL PROJECTION IN A USED BOOK STORE. I DISCOVERED I HAD A NATURAL TALENT FOR PROJECTING MY SPIRIT SELF!
ASTRAL PROJECTION MADE SIMPLE
SO I HATCHED A DESPERATE PLOT TO FAKE MY OWN DEATH AND ESCAPE! CAN YOU EVER FORGIVE ME, MYRTLE?
OH, CLIVE! HOW COULD I HAVE BEEN SO MEAN TO YOU? I SHOULD BE ASKING YOU FOR FORGIVENESS! NOW GO WASH THE DISHES.
YES, DEAR.
I GUESS THAT WRAPS THIS CASE! HOW DID YOU KNOW HE WASN'T A GHOST?
I KNOW A FAKE GHOST WHEN I SEE ONE!
SOME CASE, HUH, BILL?
I'LL SAY!
FAKING YOUR OWN DEATH TO ESCAPE YOUR WIFE? I COULD NEVER DO THAT TO MY FIANCÉE!
Bobby Timony

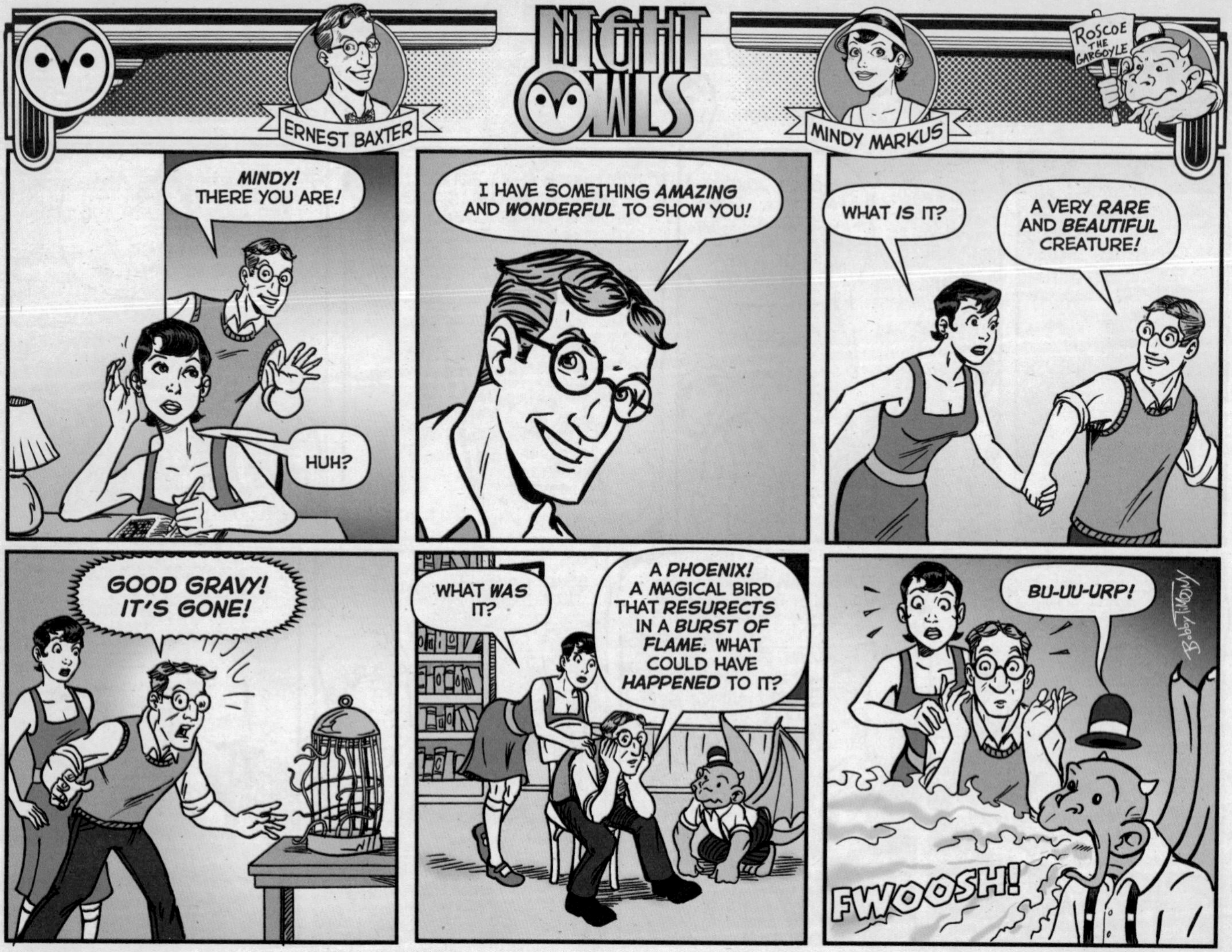
NIGHT OWLS
ERNEST BAXTER
MINDY MARKUS
ROSCOE THE GARGOYLE
MINDY! THERE YOU ARE!
HUH?
I HAVE SOMETHING AMAZING AND WONDERFUL TO SHOW YOU!
WHAT IS IT?
A VERY RARE AND BEAUTIFUL CREATURE!
GOOD GRAVY! IT'S GONE!
WHAT WAS IT?
A PHOENIX! A MAGICAL BIRD THAT RESURECTS IN A BURST OF FLAME. WHAT COULD HAVE HAPPENED TO IT?
BU-UU-URP!
FWOOSH!
Bobby Timony

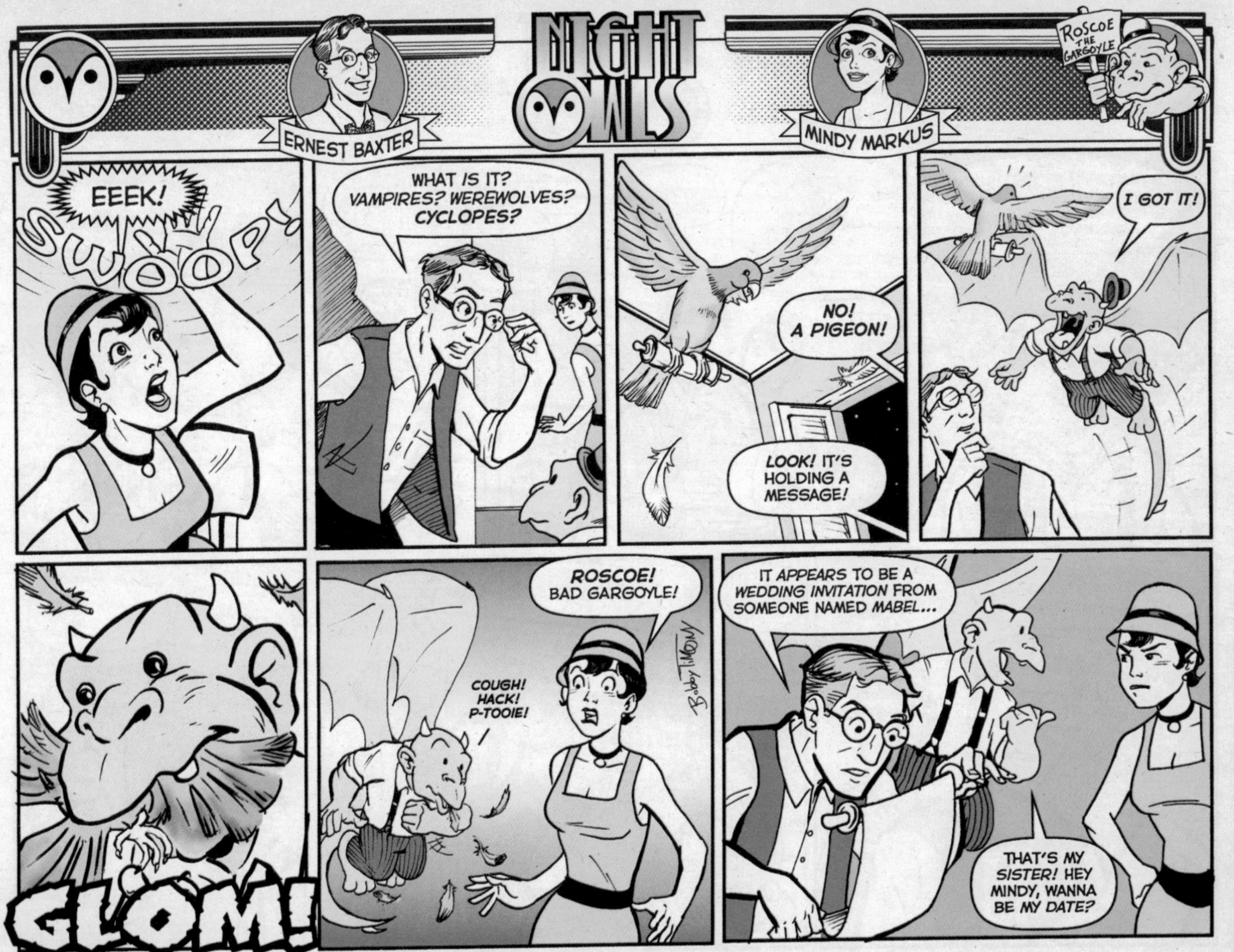
NIGHT OWLS
ERNEST BAXTER
MINDY MARKUS
ROSCOE THE GARGOYLE
EEEK!
SWOOP!
WHAT IS IT? VAMPIRES? WEREWOLVES? CYCLOPES?
NO! A PIGEON!
LOOK! IT'S HOLDING A MESSAGE!
I GOT IT!
GLOM!
ROSCOE! BAD GARGOYLE!
COUGH! HACK! P-TOOIE!
IT APPEARS TO BE A WEDDING INVITATION FROM SOMEONE NAMED MABEL...
THAT'S MY SISTER! HEY MINDY, WANNA BE MY DATE?

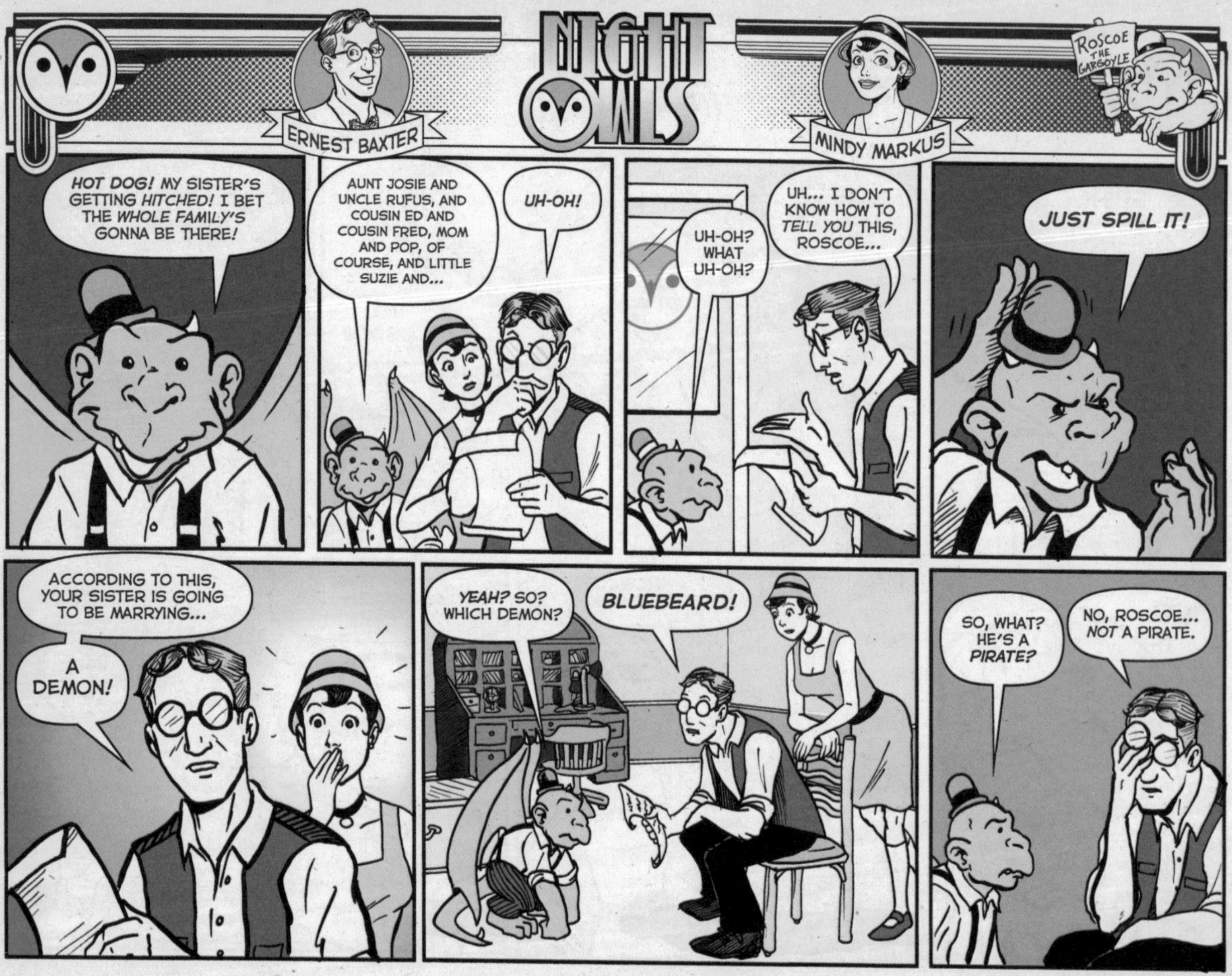
NIGHT OWLS
ERNEST BAXTER
MINDY MARKUS
ROSCOE THE GARGOYLE
HOT DOG! MY SISTER'S GETTING HITCHED! I BET THE WHOLE FAMILY'S GONNA BE THERE!
AUNT JOSIE AND UNCLE RUFUS, AND COUSIN ED AND COUSIN FRED, MOM AND POP, OF COURSE, AND LITTLE SUZIE AND...
UH-OH!
UH-OH? WHAT UH-OH?
UH... I DON'T KNOW HOW TO TELL YOU THIS, ROSCOE...
JUST SPILL IT!
ACCORDING TO THIS, YOUR SISTER IS GOING TO BE MARRYING...
A DEMON!
YEAH? SO? WHICH DEMON?
BLUEBEARD!
SO, WHAT? HE'S A PIRATE?
NO, ROSCOE... NOT A PIRATE.

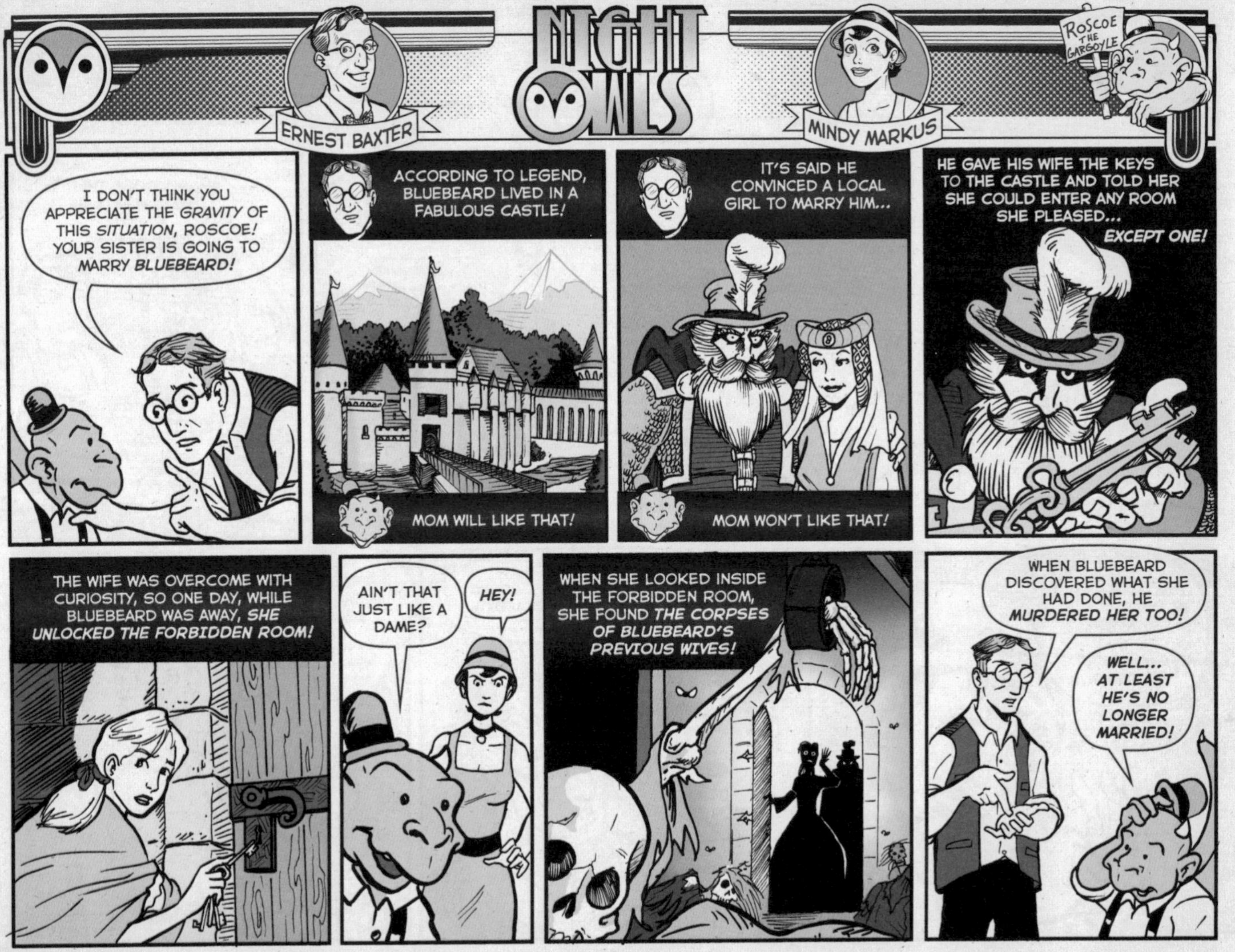
NIGHT OWLS
ERNEST BAXTER
MINDY MARKUS
ROSCOE THE GARGOYLE
I DON'T THINK YOU APPRECIATE THE GRAVITY OF THIS SITUATION, ROSCOE! YOUR SISTER IS GOING TO MARRY BLUEBEARD!
ACCORDING TO LEGEND, BLUEBEARD LIVED IN A FABULOUS CASTLE!
MOM WILL LIKE THAT!
IT'S SAID HE CONVINCED A LOCAL GIRL TO MARRY HIM...
MOM WON'T LIKE THAT!
HE GAVE HIS WIFE THE KEYS TO THE CASTLE AND TOLD HER SHE COULD ENTER ANY ROOM SHE PLEASED...
EXCEPT ONE!
THE WIFE WAS OVERCOME WITH CURIOSITY, SO ONE DAY, WHILE BLUEBEARD WAS AWAY, SHE UNLOCKED THE FORBIDDEN ROOM!
AIN'T THAT JUST LIKE A DAME?
HEY!
WHEN SHE LOOKED INSIDE THE FORBIDDEN ROOM, SHE FOUND THE CORPSES OF BLUEBEARD'S PREVIOUS WIVES!
WHEN BLUEBEARD DISCOVERED WHAT SHE HAD DONE, HE MURDERED HER TOO!
WELL... AT LEAST HE'S NO LONGER MARRIED!

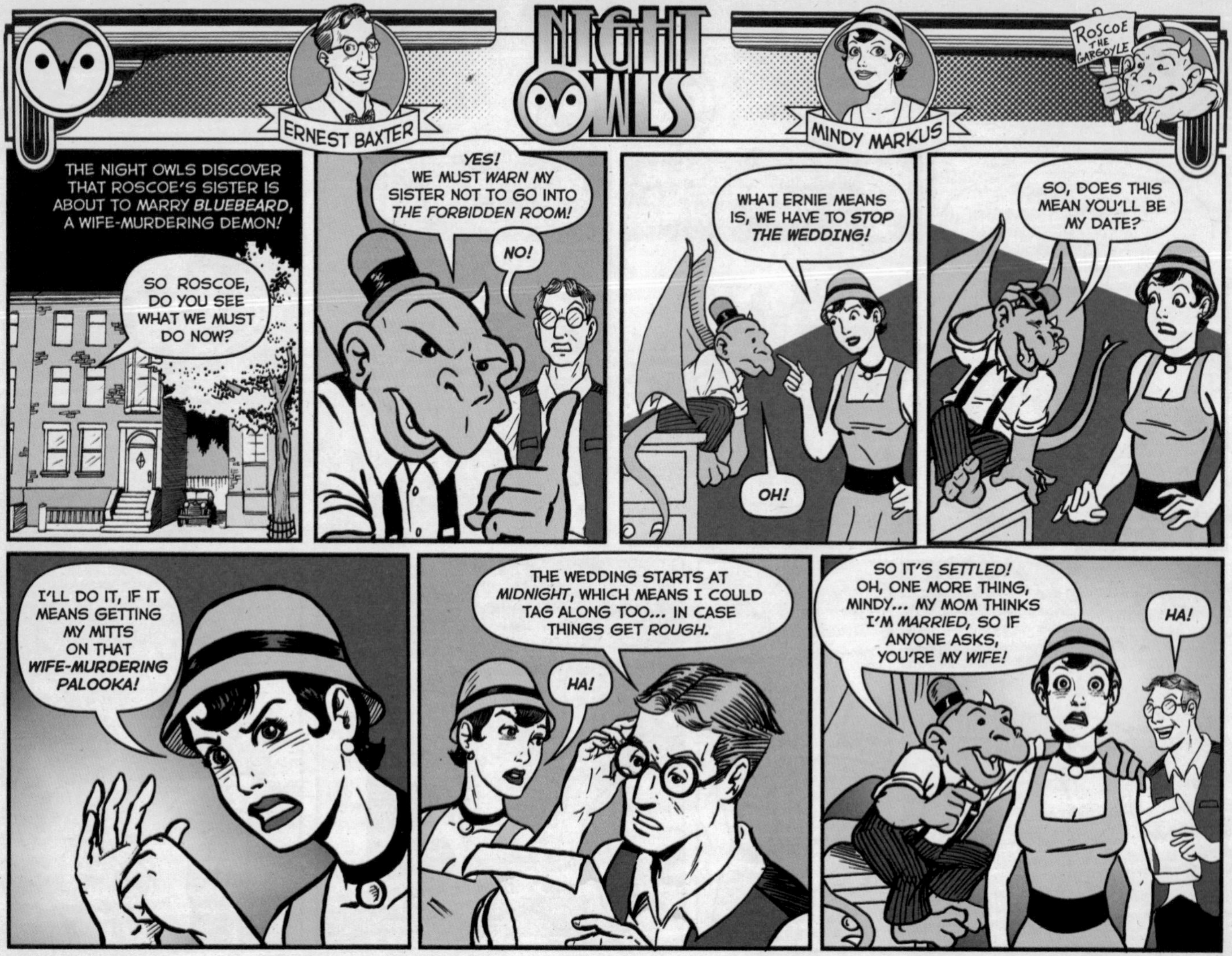
NIGHT OWLS
ERNEST BAXTER
MINDY MARKUS
ROSCOE THE GARGOYLE
THE NIGHT OWLS DISCOVER THAT ROSCOE'S SISTER IS ABOUT TO MARRY *BLUEBEARD*, A WIFE-MURDERING DEMON!
SO ROSCOE, DO YOU SEE WHAT WE MUST DO NOW?
YES! WE MUST *WARN* MY SISTER NOT TO GO INTO *THE FORBIDDEN ROOM!*
NO!
WHAT ERNIE MEANS IS, WE HAVE TO *STOP THE WEDDING!*
OH!
SO, DOES THIS MEAN YOU'LL BE MY DATE?
I'LL DO IT, IF IT MEANS GETTING MY MITTS ON THAT *WIFE-MURDERING PALOOKA!*
THE WEDDING STARTS AT *MIDNIGHT*, WHICH MEANS I COULD TAG ALONG TOO... IN CASE THINGS GET *ROUGH.*
HA!
SO IT'S *SETTLED!* OH, ONE MORE THING, MINDY... MY MOM THINKS I'M *MARRIED*, SO IF ANYONE ASKS, YOU'RE *MY WIFE!*
HA!

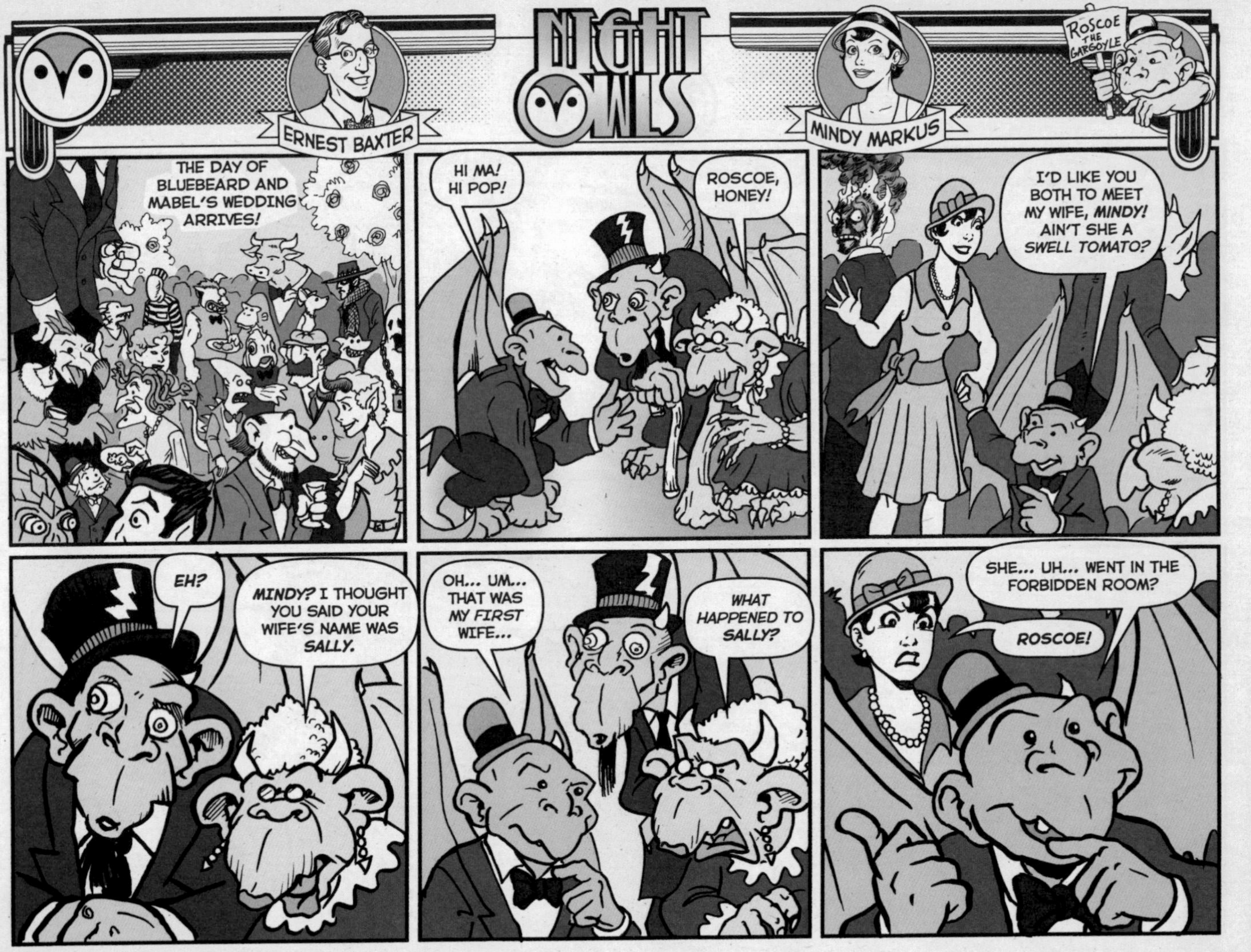
NIGHT OWLS
ERNEST BAXTER
MINDY MARKUS
ROSCOE THE GARGOYLE
THE DAY OF BLUEBEARD AND MABEL'S WEDDING ARRIVES!
HI MA! HI POP!
ROSCOE, HONEY!
I'D LIKE YOU BOTH TO MEET MY WIFE, MINDY! AIN'T SHE A SWELL TOMATO?
EH?
MINDY? I THOUGHT YOU SAID YOUR WIFE'S NAME WAS SALLY.
OH... UM... THAT WAS MY FIRST WIFE...
WHAT HAPPENED TO SALLY?
SHE... UH... WENT IN THE FORBIDDEN ROOM?
ROSCOE!

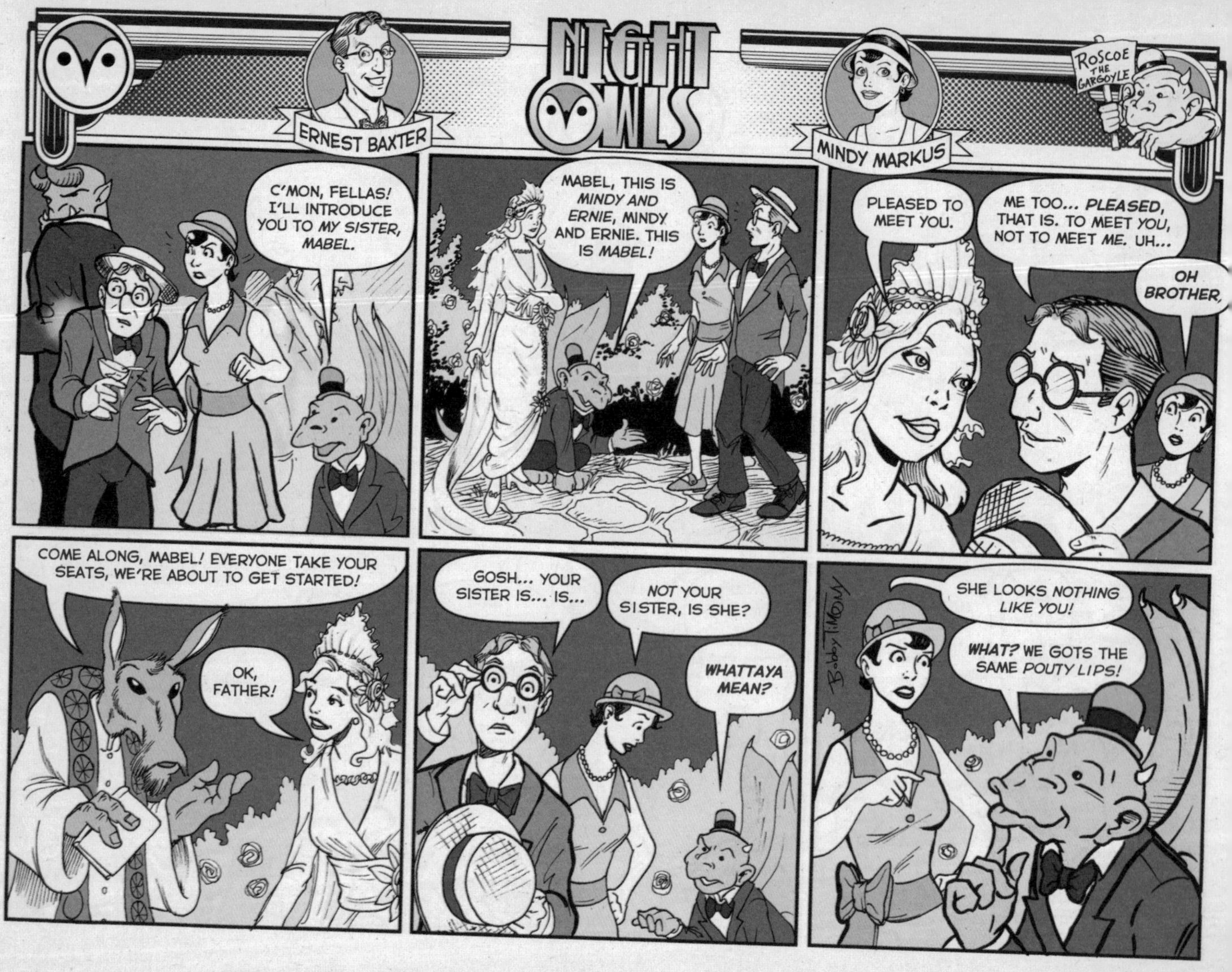
NIGHT OWLS
ERNEST BAXTER
MINDY MARKUS
ROSCOE THE GARGOYLE
C'MON, FELLAS! I'LL INTRODUCE YOU TO MY SISTER, MABEL.
MABEL, THIS IS MINDY AND ERNIE, MINDY AND ERNIE. THIS IS MABEL!
PLEASED TO MEET YOU.
ME TOO... PLEASED, THAT IS. TO MEET YOU, NOT TO MEET ME. UH...
OH BROTHER,
COME ALONG, MABEL! EVERYONE TAKE YOUR SEATS, WE'RE ABOUT TO GET STARTED!
OK, FATHER!
GOSH... YOUR SISTER IS... IS...
NOT YOUR SISTER, IS SHE?
WHATTAYA MEAN?
Bobby Timony
SHE LOOKS NOTHING LIKE YOU!
WHAT? WE GOTS THE SAME POUTY LIPS!

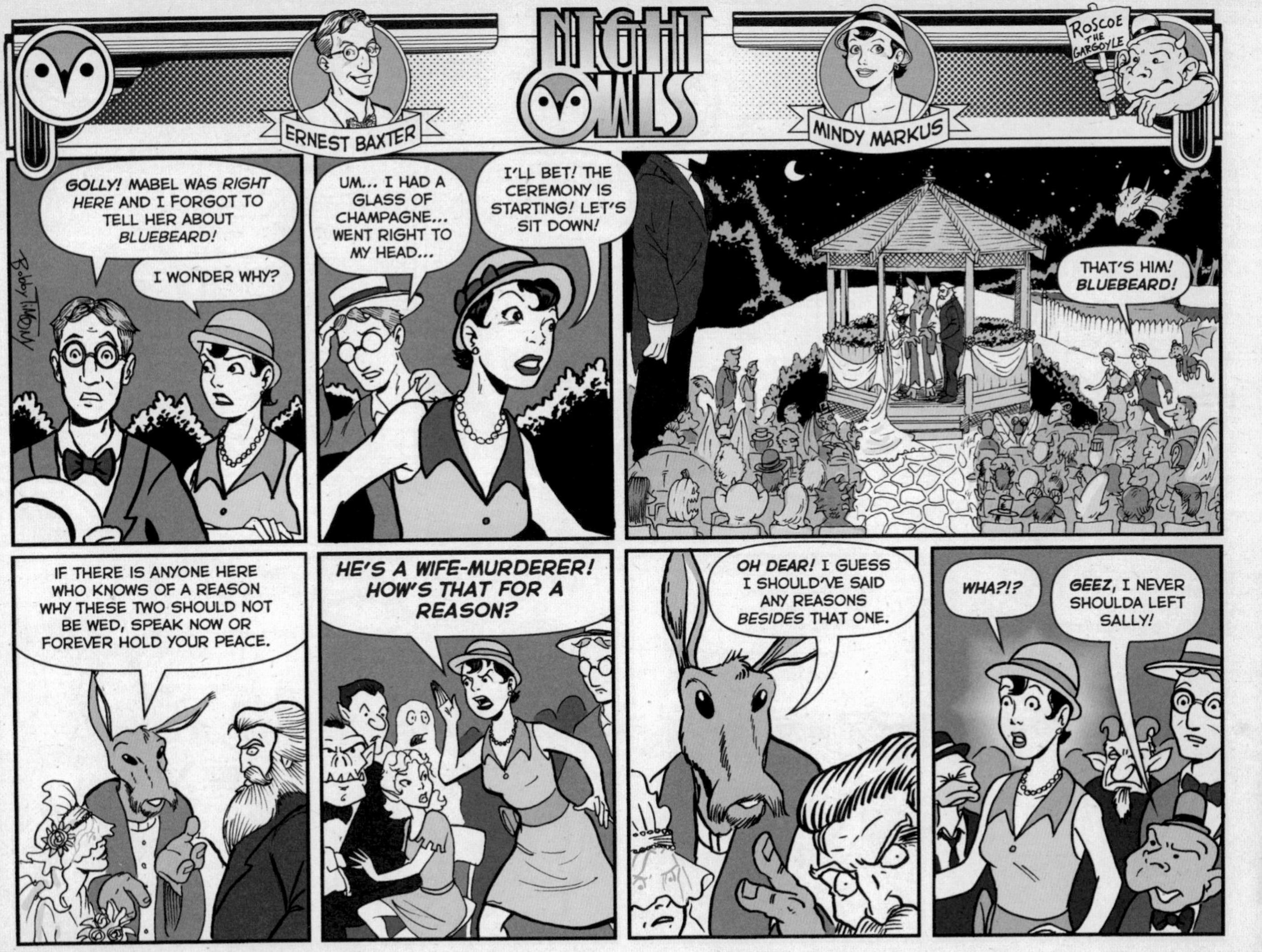
NIGHT OWLS
ERNEST BAXTER
MINDY MARKUS
ROSCOE THE GARGOYLE
Bobby Timony
GOLLY! MABEL WAS RIGHT HERE AND I FORGOT TO TELL HER ABOUT BLUEBEARD!
I WONDER WHY?
UM... I HAD A GLASS OF CHAMPAGNE... WENT RIGHT TO MY HEAD...
I'LL BET! THE CEREMONY IS STARTING! LET'S SIT DOWN!
THAT'S HIM! BLUEBEARD!
IF THERE IS ANYONE HERE WHO KNOWS OF A REASON WHY THESE TWO SHOULD NOT BE WED, SPEAK NOW OR FOREVER HOLD YOUR PEACE.
HE'S A WIFE-MURDERER! HOW'S THAT FOR A REASON?
OH DEAR! I GUESS I SHOULD'VE SAID ANY REASONS BESIDES THAT ONE.
WHA?!?
GEEZ, I NEVER SHOULDA LEFT SALLY!

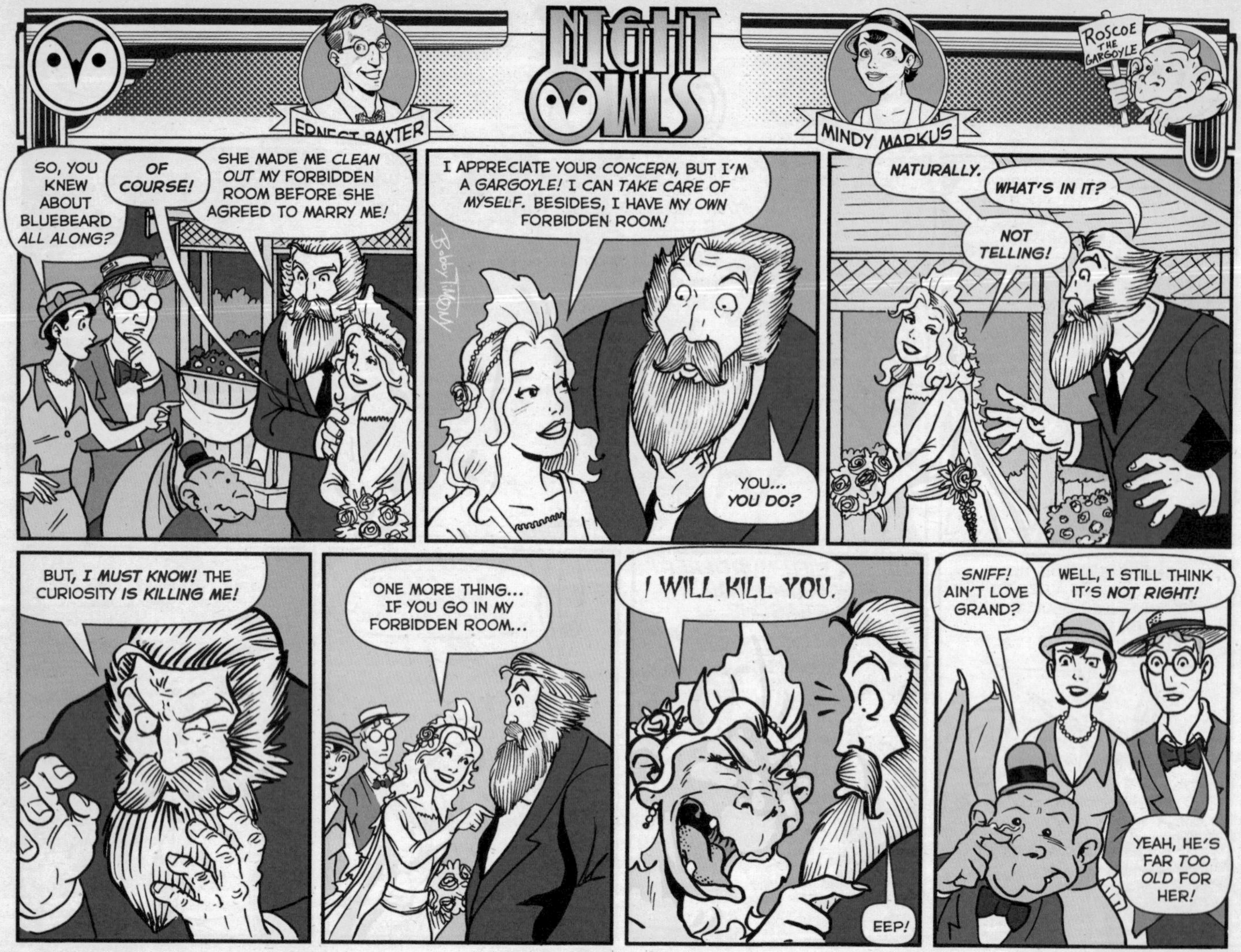

NIGHT OWLS
ERNEST BAXTER
MINDY MARKUS
ROSCOE THE GARGOYLE
SO, YOU KNEW ABOUT BLUEBEARD ALL ALONG?
OF COURSE!
SHE MADE ME CLEAN OUT MY FORBIDDEN ROOM BEFORE SHE AGREED TO MARRY ME!
I APPRECIATE YOUR CONCERN, BUT I'M A GARGOYLE! I CAN TAKE CARE OF MYSELF. BESIDES, I HAVE MY OWN FORBIDDEN ROOM!
YOU... YOU DO?
NATURALLY.
WHAT'S IN IT?
NOT TELLING!
BUT, I MUST KNOW! THE CURIOSITY IS KILLING ME!
ONE MORE THING... IF YOU GO IN MY FORBIDDEN ROOM...
I WILL KILL YOU.
EEP!
SNIFF! AIN'T LOVE GRAND?
WELL, I STILL THINK IT'S NOT RIGHT!
YEAH, HE'S FAR TOO OLD FOR HER!

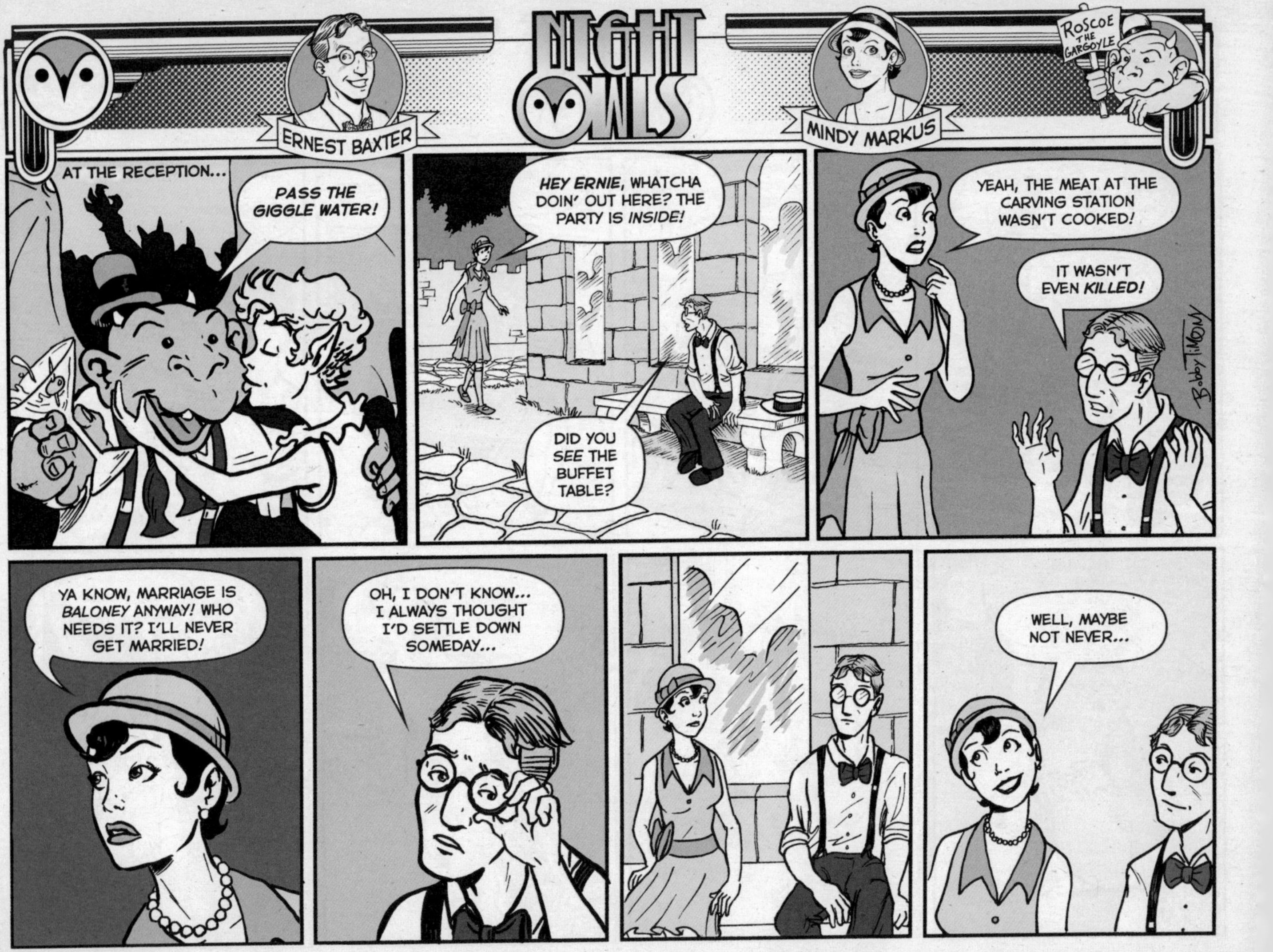
NIGHT OWLS
ERNEST BAXTER
MINDY MARKUS
ROSCOE THE GARGOYLE
AT THE RECEPTION...
PASS THE GIGGLE WATER!
HEY ERNIE, WHATCHA DOIN' OUT HERE? THE PARTY IS INSIDE!
DID YOU SEE THE BUFFET TABLE?
YEAH, THE MEAT AT THE CARVING STATION WASN'T COOKED!
IT WASN'T EVEN KILLED!
Bobby Timony
YA KNOW, MARRIAGE IS BALONEY ANYWAY! WHO NEEDS IT? I'LL NEVER GET MARRIED!
OH, I DON'T KNOW... I ALWAYS THOUGHT I'D SETTLE DOWN SOMEDAY...
WELL, MAYBE NOT NEVER...

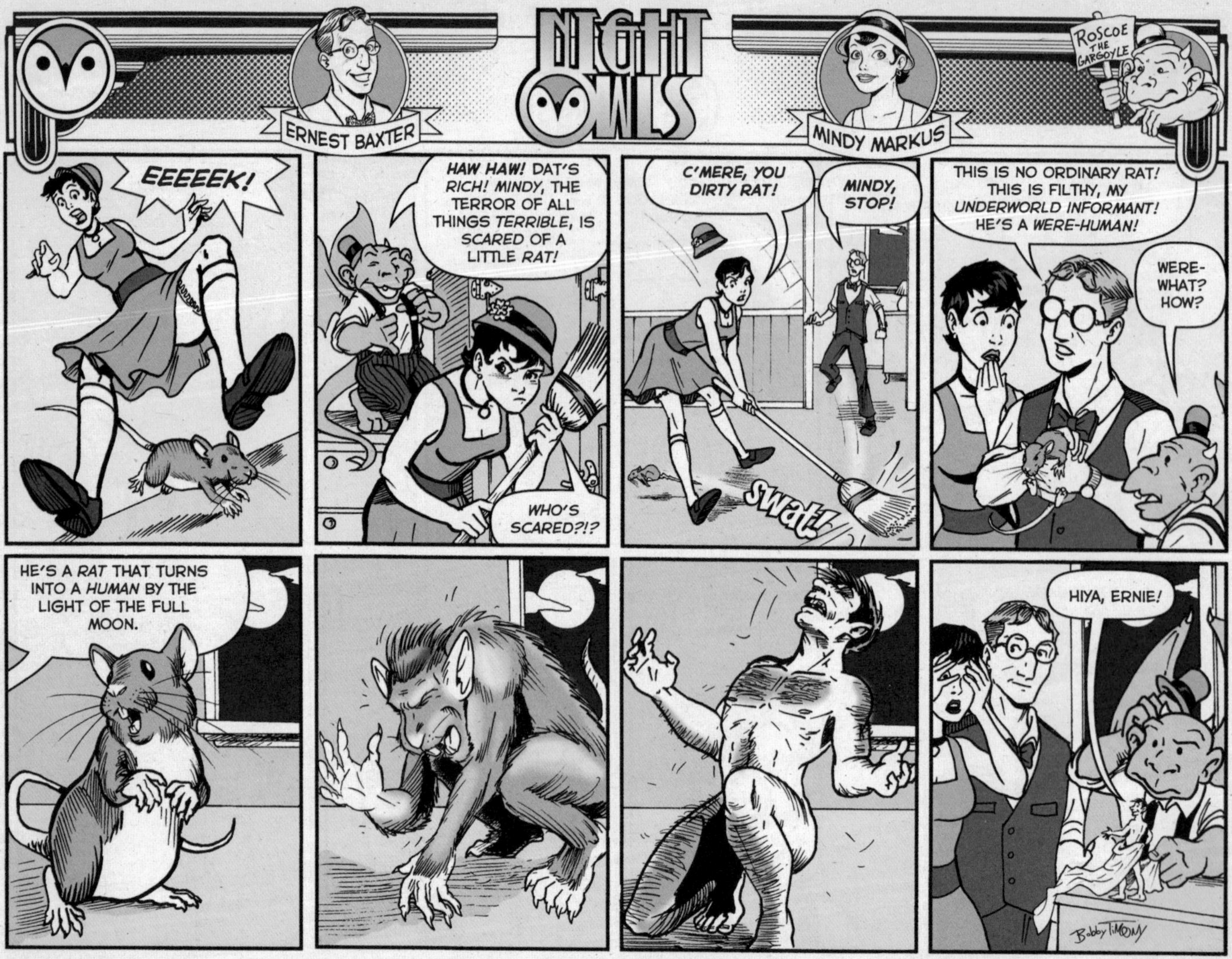
NIGHT OWLS
ERNEST BAXTER
MINDY MARKUS
ROSCOE THE GARGOYLE
EEEEEK!
HAW HAW! DAT'S RICH! MINDY, THE TERROR OF ALL THINGS TERRIBLE, IS SCARED OF A LITTLE RAT!
WHO'S SCARED?!?
C'MERE, YOU DIRTY RAT!
MINDY, STOP!
SWAT!
THIS IS NO ORDINARY RAT! THIS IS FILTHY, MY UNDERWORLD INFORMANT! HE'S A WERE-HUMAN!
WERE-WHAT? HOW?
HE'S A RAT THAT TURNS INTO A HUMAN BY THE LIGHT OF THE FULL MOON.
HIYA, ERNIE!
Bobby Timony

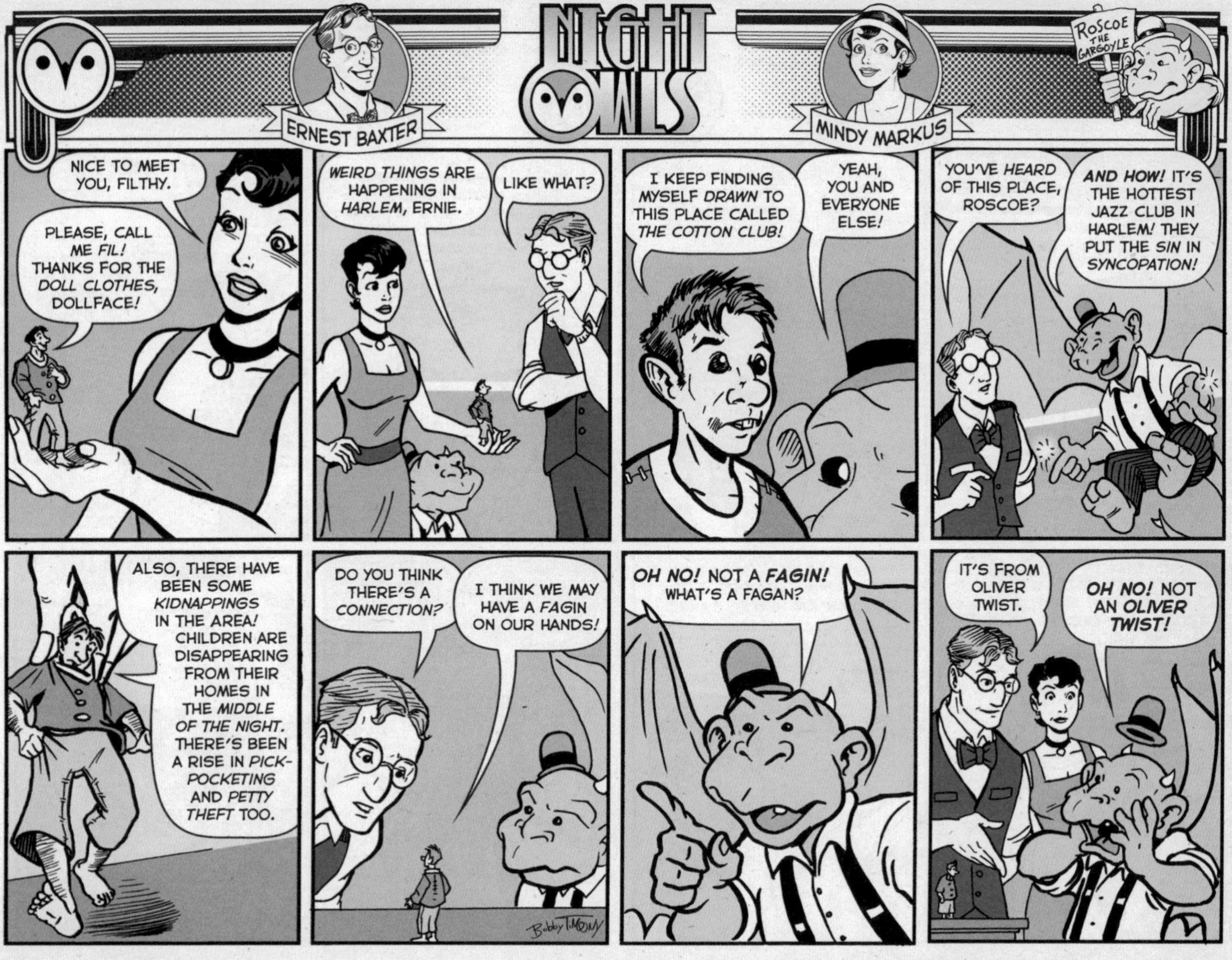
NIGHT OWLS
ERNEST BAXTER
MINDY MARKUS
ROSCOE THE GARGOYLE
NICE TO MEET YOU, FILTHY.
PLEASE, CALL ME FIL! THANKS FOR THE DOLL CLOTHES, DOLLFACE!
WEIRD THINGS ARE HAPPENING IN HARLEM, ERNIE.
LIKE WHAT?
I KEEP FINDING MYSELF DRAWN TO THIS PLACE CALLED THE COTTON CLUB!
YEAH, YOU AND EVERYONE ELSE!
YOU'VE HEARD OF THIS PLACE, ROSCOE?
AND HOW! IT'S THE HOTTEST JAZZ CLUB IN HARLEM! THEY PUT THE SIN IN SYNCOPATION!
ALSO, THERE HAVE BEEN SOME KIDNAPPINGS IN THE AREA! CHILDREN ARE DISAPPEARING FROM THEIR HOMES IN THE MIDDLE OF THE NIGHT. THERE'S BEEN A RISE IN PICK-POCKETING AND PETTY THEFT TOO.
DO YOU THINK THERE'S A CONNECTION?
I THINK WE MAY HAVE A FAGIN ON OUR HANDS!
OH NO! NOT A FAGIN! WHAT'S A FAGAN?
IT'S FROM OLIVER TWIST.
OH NO! NOT AN OLIVER TWIST!
Bobby TIMONY

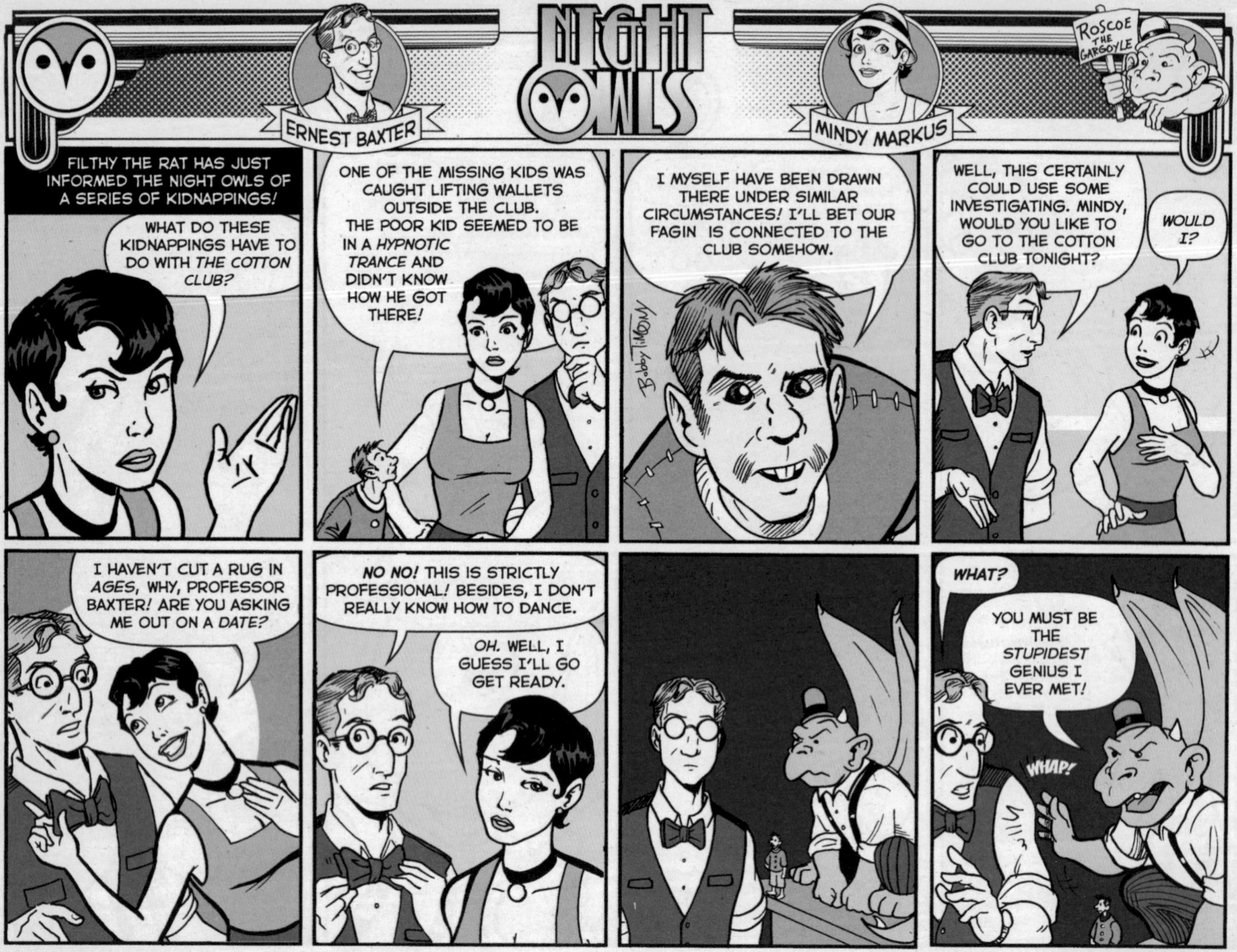
NIGHT OWLS
ROSCOE THE GARGOYLE
ERNEST BAXTER
MINDY MARKUS
FILTHY THE RAT HAS JUST INFORMED THE NIGHT OWLS OF A SERIES OF KIDNAPPINGS!
WHAT DO THESE KIDNAPPINGS HAVE TO DO WITH THE COTTON CLUB?
ONE OF THE MISSING KIDS WAS CAUGHT LIFTING WALLETS OUTSIDE THE CLUB. THE POOR KID SEEMED TO BE IN A HYPNOTIC TRANCE AND DIDN'T KNOW HOW HE GOT THERE!
I MYSELF HAVE BEEN DRAWN THERE UNDER SIMILAR CIRCUMSTANCES! I'LL BET OUR FAGIN IS CONNECTED TO THE CLUB SOMEHOW.
Bobby Timony
WELL, THIS CERTAINLY COULD USE SOME INVESTIGATING. MINDY, WOULD YOU LIKE TO GO TO THE COTTON CLUB TONIGHT?
WOULD I?
I HAVEN'T CUT A RUG IN AGES, WHY, PROFESSOR BAXTER! ARE YOU ASKING ME OUT ON A DATE?
NO NO! THIS IS STRICTLY PROFESSIONAL! BESIDES, I DON'T REALLY KNOW HOW TO DANCE.
OH. WELL, I GUESS I'LL GO GET READY.
WHAT?
YOU MUST BE THE STUPIDEST GENIUS I EVER MET!
WHAP!

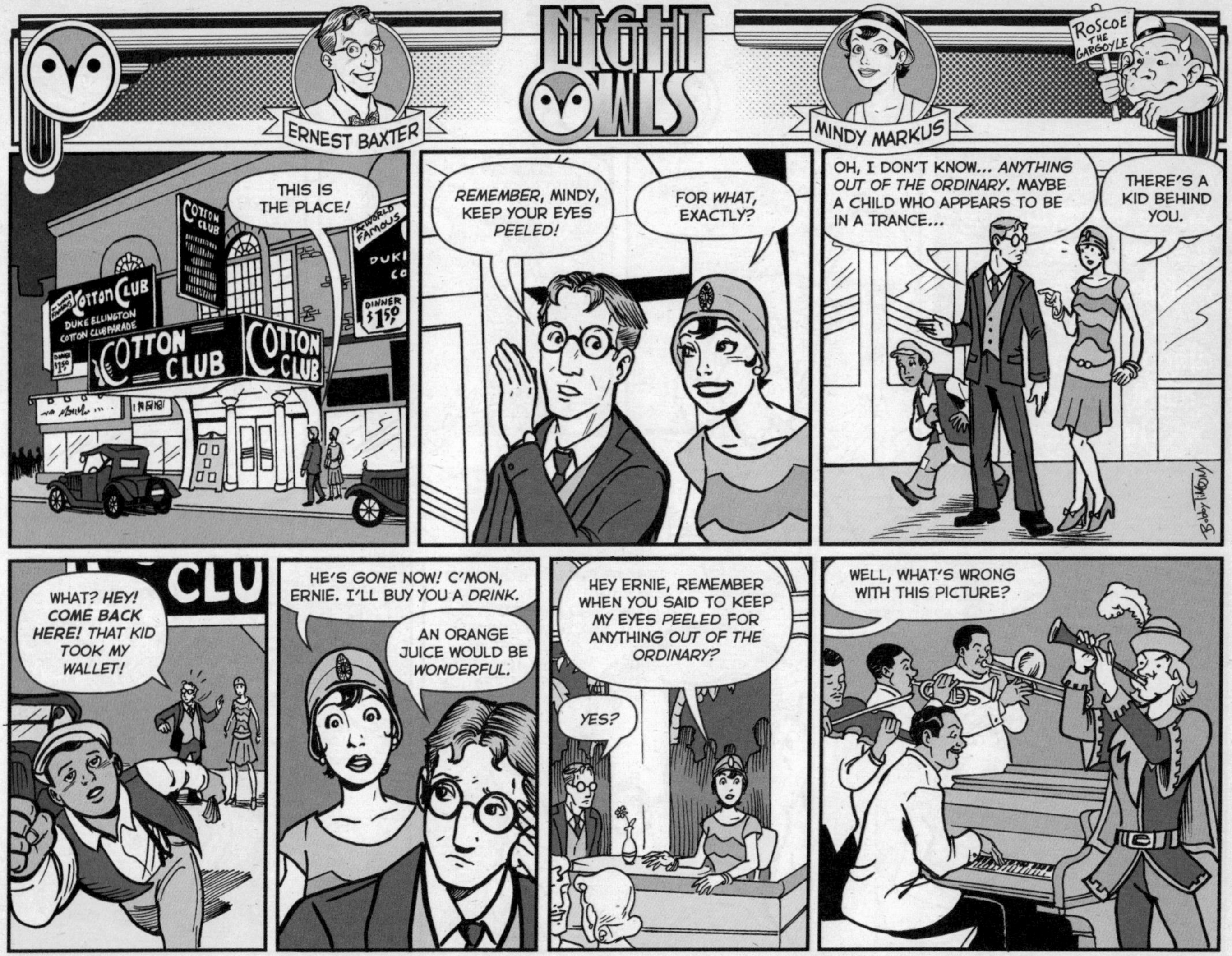
NIGHT OWLS
ERNEST BAXTER
MINDY MARKUS
ROSCOE THE GARGOYLE
THIS IS THE PLACE!
COTTON CLUB
DUKE ELLINGTON
COTTON CLUB PARADE
THE WORLD FAMOUS
DINNER $1.50
REMEMBER, MINDY, KEEP YOUR EYES PEELED!
FOR WHAT, EXACTLY?
OH, I DON'T KNOW... ANYTHING OUT OF THE ORDINARY. MAYBE A CHILD WHO APPEARS TO BE IN A TRANCE...
THERE'S A KID BEHIND YOU.
Bobby Timony
CLU
WHAT? HEY! COME BACK HERE! THAT KID TOOK MY WALLET!
HE'S GONE NOW! C'MON, ERNIE. I'LL BUY YOU A DRINK.
AN ORANGE JUICE WOULD BE WONDERFUL.
HEY ERNIE, REMEMBER WHEN YOU SAID TO KEEP MY EYES PEELED FOR ANYTHING OUT OF THE ORDINARY?
YES?
WELL, WHAT'S WRONG WITH THIS PICTURE?

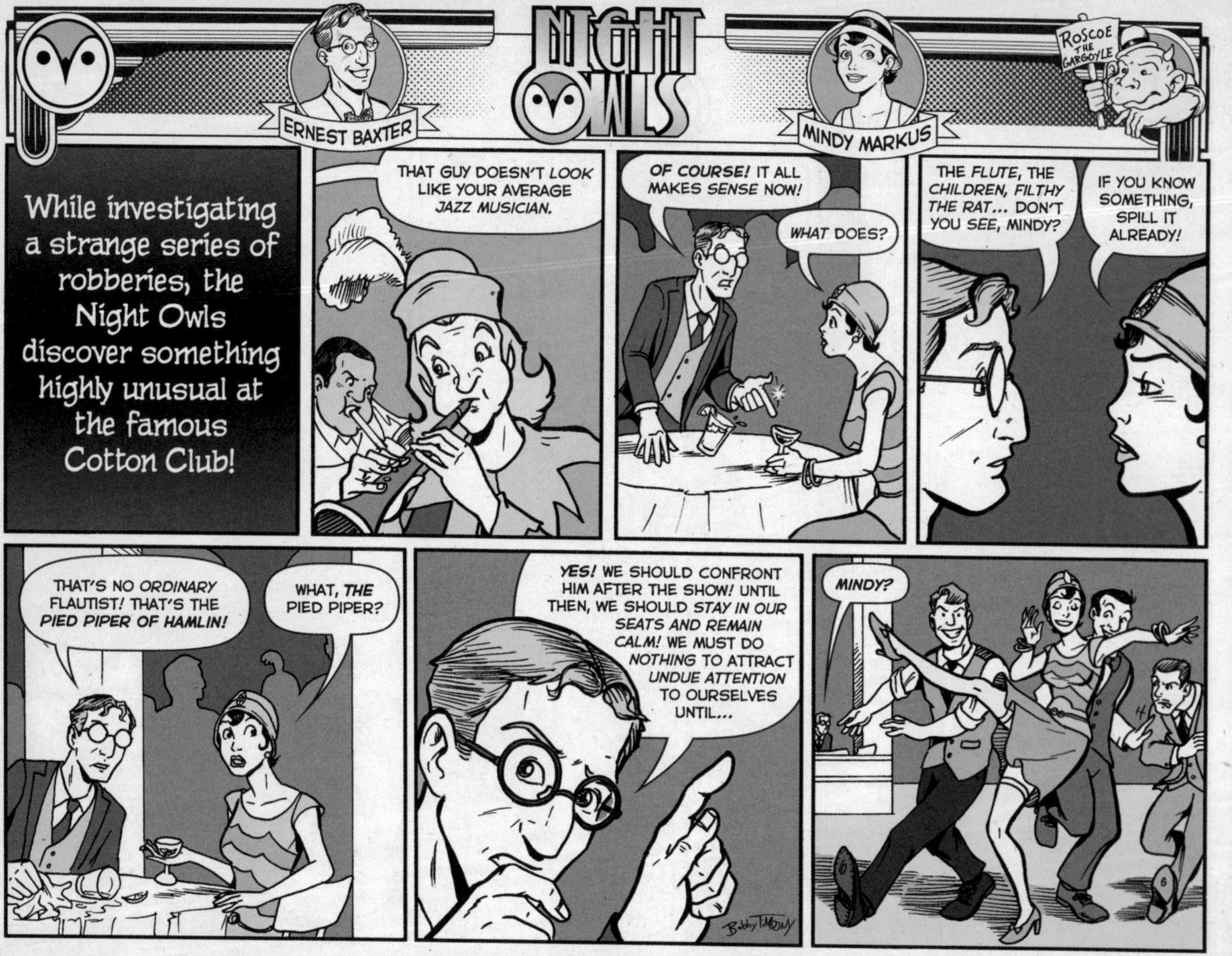
NIGHT OWLS
ERNEST BAXTER
MINDY MARKUS
ROSCOE THE GARGOYLE
While investigating a strange series of robberies, the Night Owls discover something highly unusual at the famous Cotton Club!
THAT GUY DOESN'T LOOK LIKE YOUR AVERAGE JAZZ MUSICIAN.
OF COURSE! IT ALL MAKES SENSE NOW!
WHAT DOES?
THE FLUTE, THE CHILDREN, FILTHY THE RAT... DON'T YOU SEE, MINDY?
IF YOU KNOW SOMETHING, SPILL IT ALREADY!
THAT'S NO ORDINARY FLAUTIST! THAT'S THE PIED PIPER OF HAMLIN!
WHAT, THE PIED PIPER?
YES! WE SHOULD CONFRONT HIM AFTER THE SHOW! UNTIL THEN, WE SHOULD STAY IN OUR SEATS AND REMAIN CALM! WE MUST DO NOTHING TO ATTRACT UNDUE ATTENTION TO OURSELVES UNTIL...
Bobby Timony
MINDY?

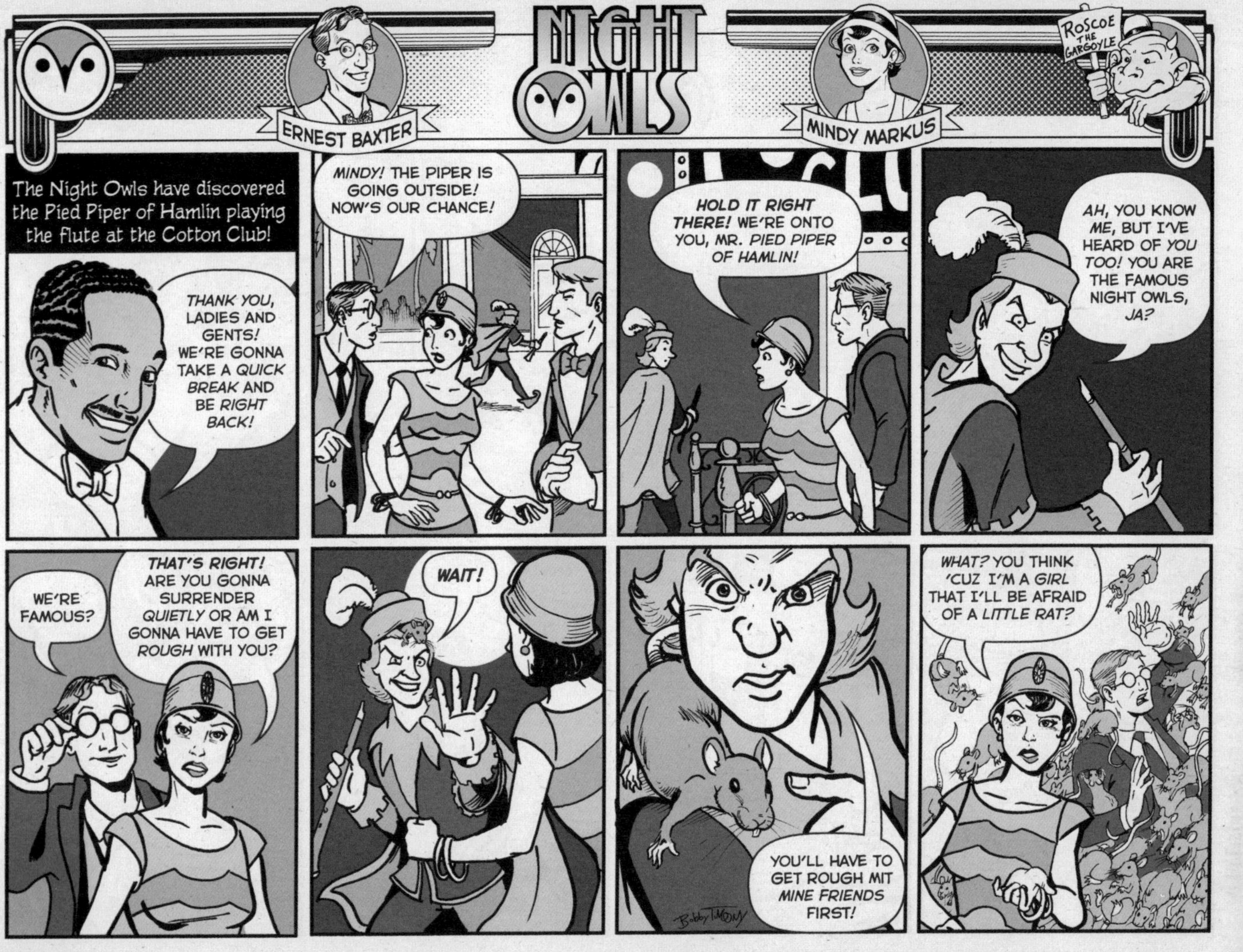
NIGHT OWLS
ERNEST BAXTER
MINDY MARKUS
ROSCOE THE GARGOYLE
The Night Owls have discovered the Pied Piper of Hamlin playing the flute at the Cotton Club!
THANK YOU, LADIES AND GENTS! WE'RE GONNA TAKE A QUICK BREAK AND BE RIGHT BACK!
MINDY! THE PIPER IS GOING OUTSIDE! NOW'S OUR CHANCE!
HOLD IT RIGHT THERE! WE'RE ONTO YOU, MR. PIED PIPER OF HAMLIN!
AH, YOU KNOW ME, BUT I'VE HEARD OF YOU TOO! YOU ARE THE FAMOUS NIGHT OWLS, JA?
WE'RE FAMOUS?
THAT'S RIGHT! ARE YOU GONNA SURRENDER QUIETLY OR AM I GONNA HAVE TO GET ROUGH WITH YOU?
WAIT!
YOU'LL HAVE TO GET ROUGH MIT MINE FRIENDS FIRST!
WHAT? YOU THINK 'CUZ I'M A GIRL THAT I'LL BE AFRAID OF A LITTLE RAT?

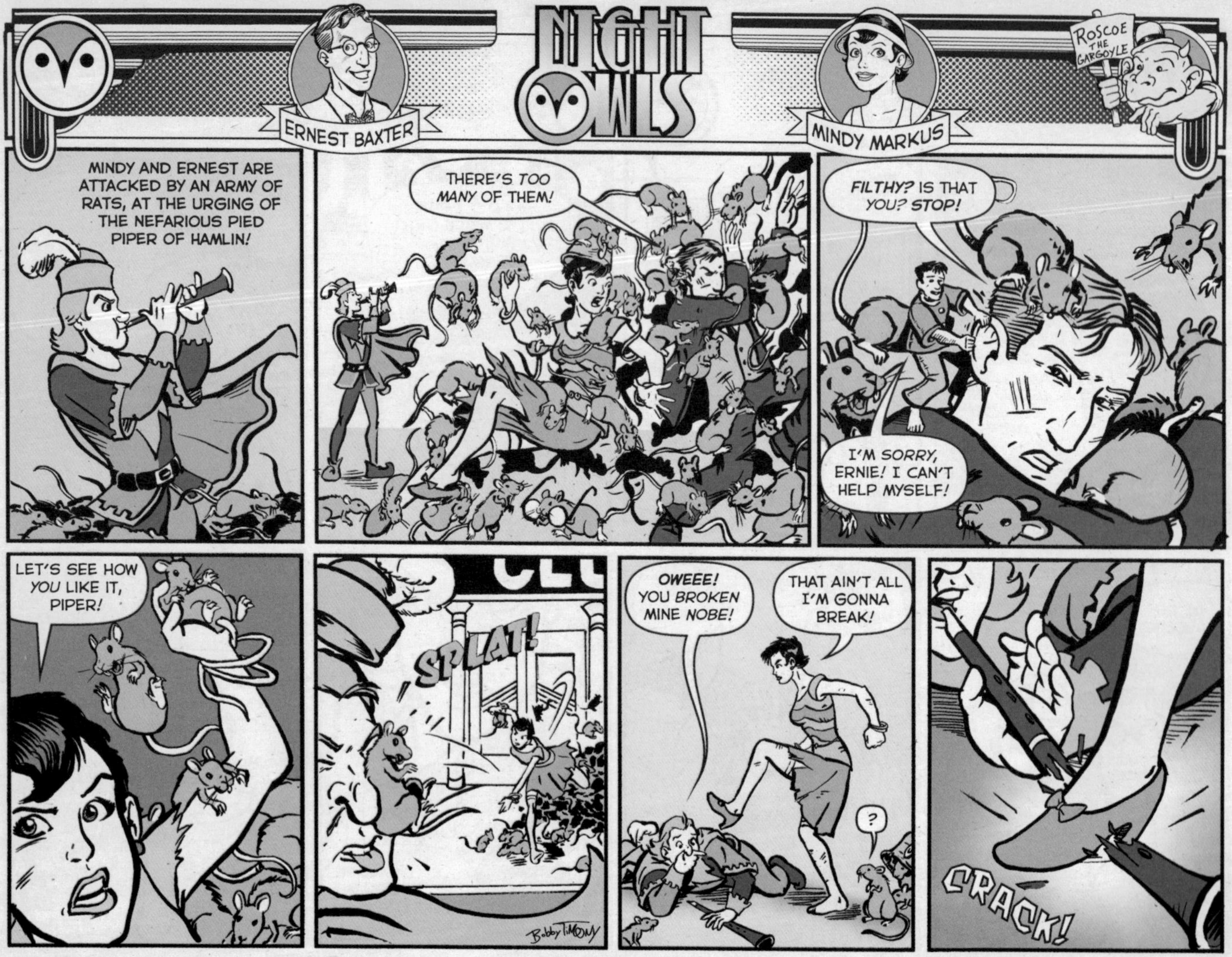
NIGHT OWLS
ERNEST BAXTER
MINDY MARKUS
ROSCOE THE GARGOYLE
MINDY AND ERNEST ARE ATTACKED BY AN ARMY OF RATS, AT THE URGING OF THE NEFARIOUS PIED PIPER OF HAMLIN!
THERE'S TOO MANY OF THEM!
FILTHY? IS THAT YOU? STOP!
I'M SORRY, ERNIE! I CAN'T HELP MYSELF!
LET'S SEE HOW YOU LIKE IT, PIPER!
SPLAT!
OWEEE! YOU BROKEN MINE NOBE!
THAT AIN'T ALL I'M GONNA BREAK!
?
CRACK!
Bobby Timony

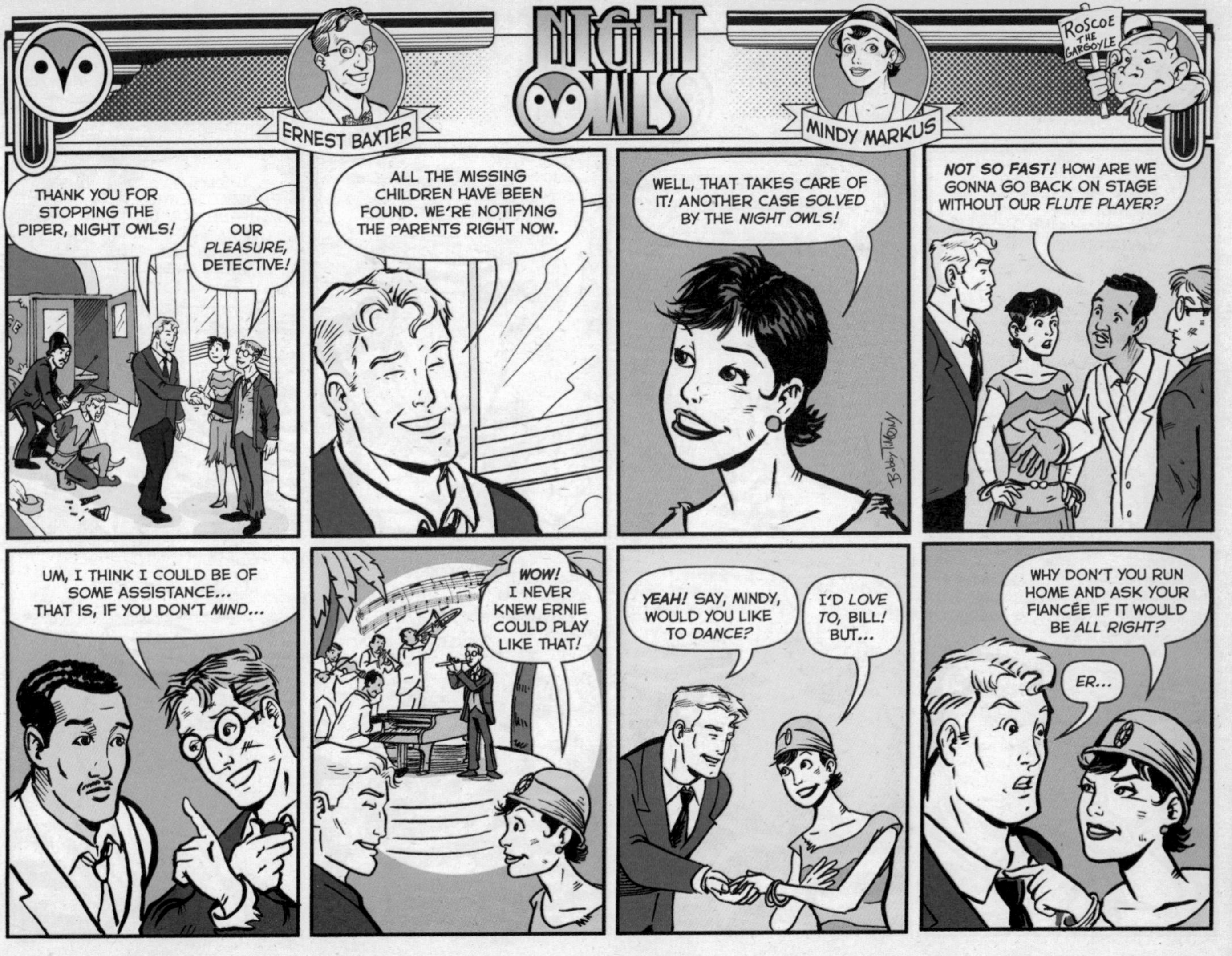
NIGHT OWLS
ERNEST BAXTER
MINDY MARKUS
ROSCOE THE GARGOYLE
THANK YOU FOR STOPPING THE PIPER, NIGHT OWLS!
OUR *PLEASURE*, DETECTIVE!
ALL THE MISSING CHILDREN HAVE BEEN FOUND. WE'RE NOTIFYING THE PARENTS RIGHT NOW.
WELL, THAT TAKES CARE OF IT! ANOTHER CASE *SOLVED* BY THE *NIGHT OWLS!*
NOT SO FAST! HOW ARE WE GONNA GO BACK ON STAGE WITHOUT OUR *FLUTE PLAYER?*
UM, I THINK I COULD BE OF SOME ASSISTANCE... THAT IS, IF YOU DON'T *MIND*...
WOW! I NEVER KNEW ERNIE COULD PLAY LIKE THAT!
YEAH! SAY, MINDY, WOULD YOU LIKE TO *DANCE?*
I'D *LOVE TO*, BILL! BUT...
WHY DON'T YOU RUN HOME AND ASK YOUR FIANCÉE IF IT WOULD BE *ALL RIGHT?*
ER...

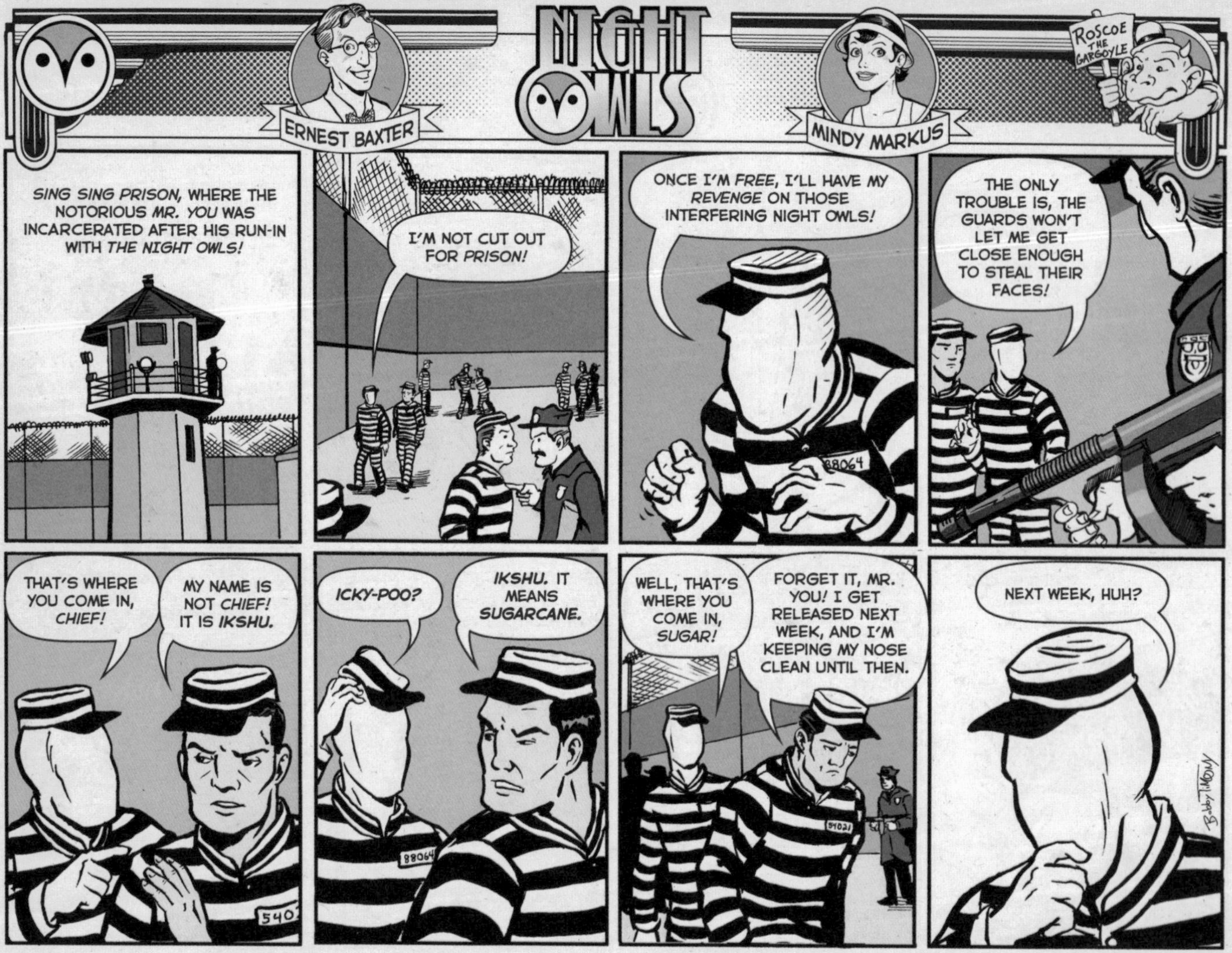
NIGHT OWLS
ERNEST BAXTER
MINDY MARKUS
ROSCOE THE GARGOYLE
SING SING PRISON, WHERE THE NOTORIOUS MR. YOU WAS INCARCERATED AFTER HIS RUN-IN WITH THE NIGHT OWLS!
I'M NOT CUT OUT FOR PRISON!
ONCE I'M FREE, I'LL HAVE MY REVENGE ON THOSE INTERFERING NIGHT OWLS!
88064
THE ONLY TROUBLE IS, THE GUARDS WON'T LET ME GET CLOSE ENOUGH TO STEAL THEIR FACES!
THAT'S WHERE YOU COME IN, CHIEF!
MY NAME IS NOT CHIEF! IT IS IKSHU.
ICKY-POO?
IKSHU. IT MEANS SUGARCANE.
88064
WELL, THAT'S WHERE YOU COME IN, SUGAR!
FORGET IT, MR. YOU! I GET RELEASED NEXT WEEK, AND I'M KEEPING MY NOSE CLEAN UNTIL THEN.
54021
NEXT WEEK, HUH?
Bobby Timony

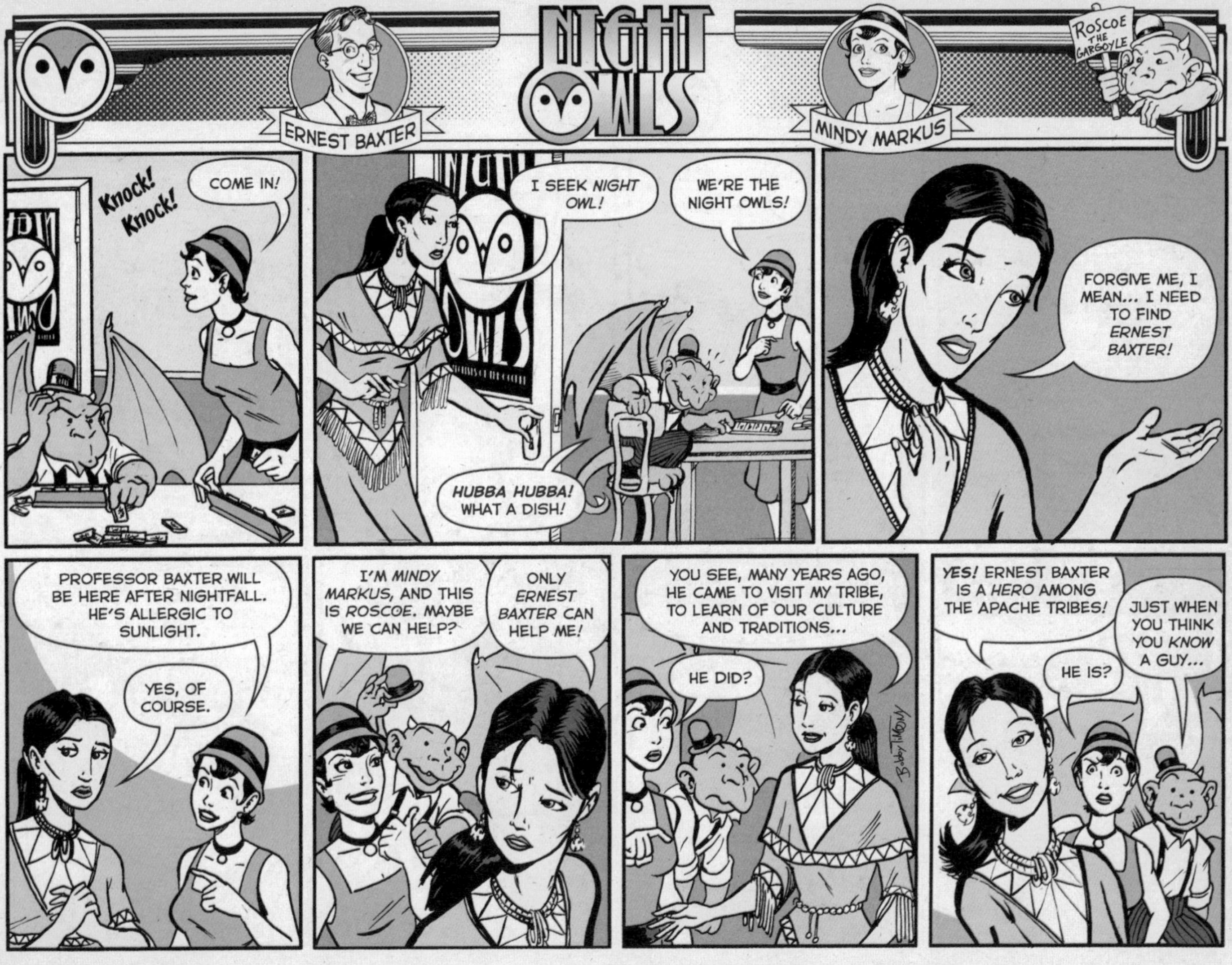
NIGHT OWLS
ERNEST BAXTER
MINDY MARKUS
ROSCOE THE GARGOYLE
Knock! Knock!
COME IN!
I SEEK NIGHT OWL!
WE'RE THE NIGHT OWLS!
HUBBA HUBBA! WHAT A DISH!
FORGIVE ME, I MEAN... I NEED TO FIND ERNEST BAXTER!
PROFESSOR BAXTER WILL BE HERE AFTER NIGHTFALL. HE'S ALLERGIC TO SUNLIGHT.
YES, OF COURSE.
I'M MINDY MARKUS, AND THIS IS ROSCOE. MAYBE WE CAN HELP?
ONLY ERNEST BAXTER CAN HELP ME!
YOU SEE, MANY YEARS AGO, HE CAME TO VISIT MY TRIBE, TO LEARN OF OUR CULTURE AND TRADITIONS...
HE DID?
YES! ERNEST BAXTER IS A HERO AMONG THE APACHE TRIBES!
HE IS?
JUST WHEN YOU THINK YOU KNOW A GUY...

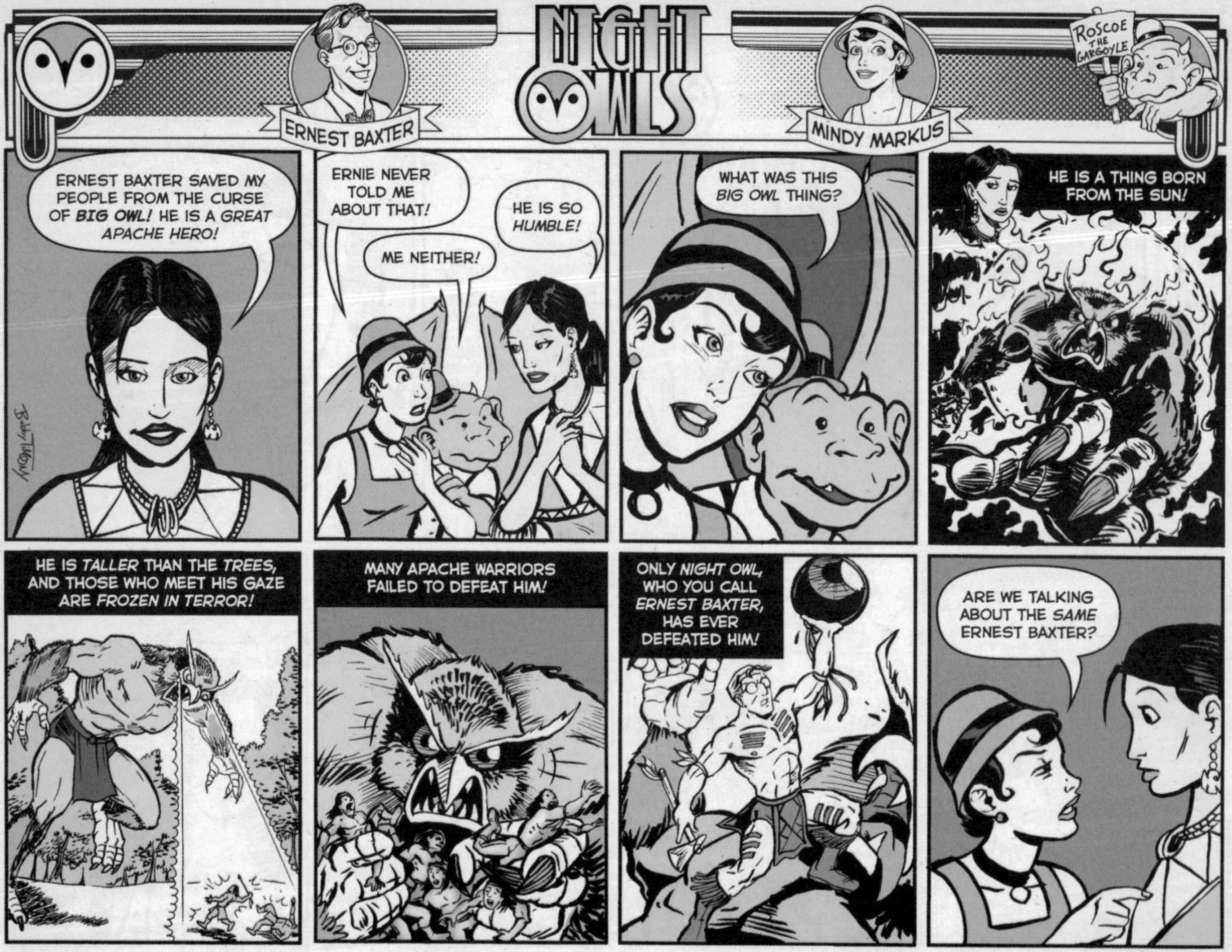
NIGHT OWLS
ERNEST BAXTER
MINDY MARKUS
ROSCOE THE GARGOYLE
ERNEST BAXTER SAVED MY PEOPLE FROM THE CURSE OF BIG OWL! HE IS A GREAT APACHE HERO!
ERNIE NEVER TOLD ME ABOUT THAT!
ME NEITHER!
HE IS SO HUMBLE!
WHAT WAS THIS BIG OWL THING?
HE IS A THING BORN FROM THE SUN!
HE IS TALLER THAN THE TREES, AND THOSE WHO MEET HIS GAZE ARE FROZEN IN TERROR!
MANY APACHE WARRIORS FAILED TO DEFEAT HIM!
ONLY NIGHT OWL, WHO YOU CALL ERNEST BAXTER, HAS EVER DEFEATED HIM!
ARE WE TALKING ABOUT THE SAME ERNEST BAXTER?

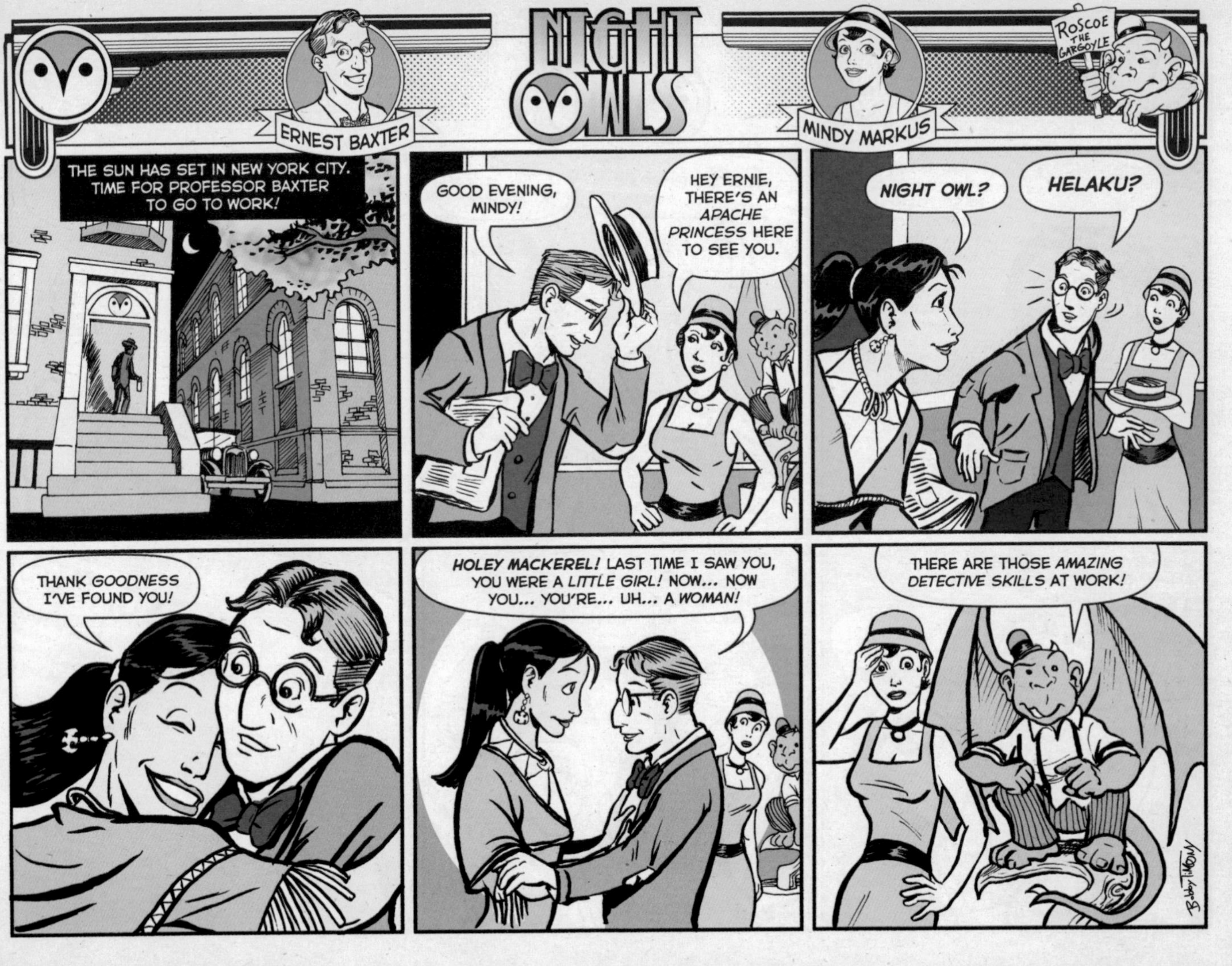
NIGHT OWLS
ERNEST BAXTER
MINDY MARKUS
ROSCOE THE GARGOYLE
THE SUN HAS SET IN NEW YORK CITY. TIME FOR PROFESSOR BAXTER TO GO TO WORK!
GOOD EVENING, MINDY!
HEY ERNIE, THERE'S AN APACHE PRINCESS HERE TO SEE YOU.
NIGHT OWL?
HELAKU?
THANK GOODNESS I'VE FOUND YOU!
HOLEY MACKEREL! LAST TIME I SAW YOU, YOU WERE A LITTLE GIRL! NOW... NOW YOU... YOU'RE... UH... A WOMAN!
THERE ARE THOSE AMAZING DETECTIVE SKILLS AT WORK!
Bobby Timony

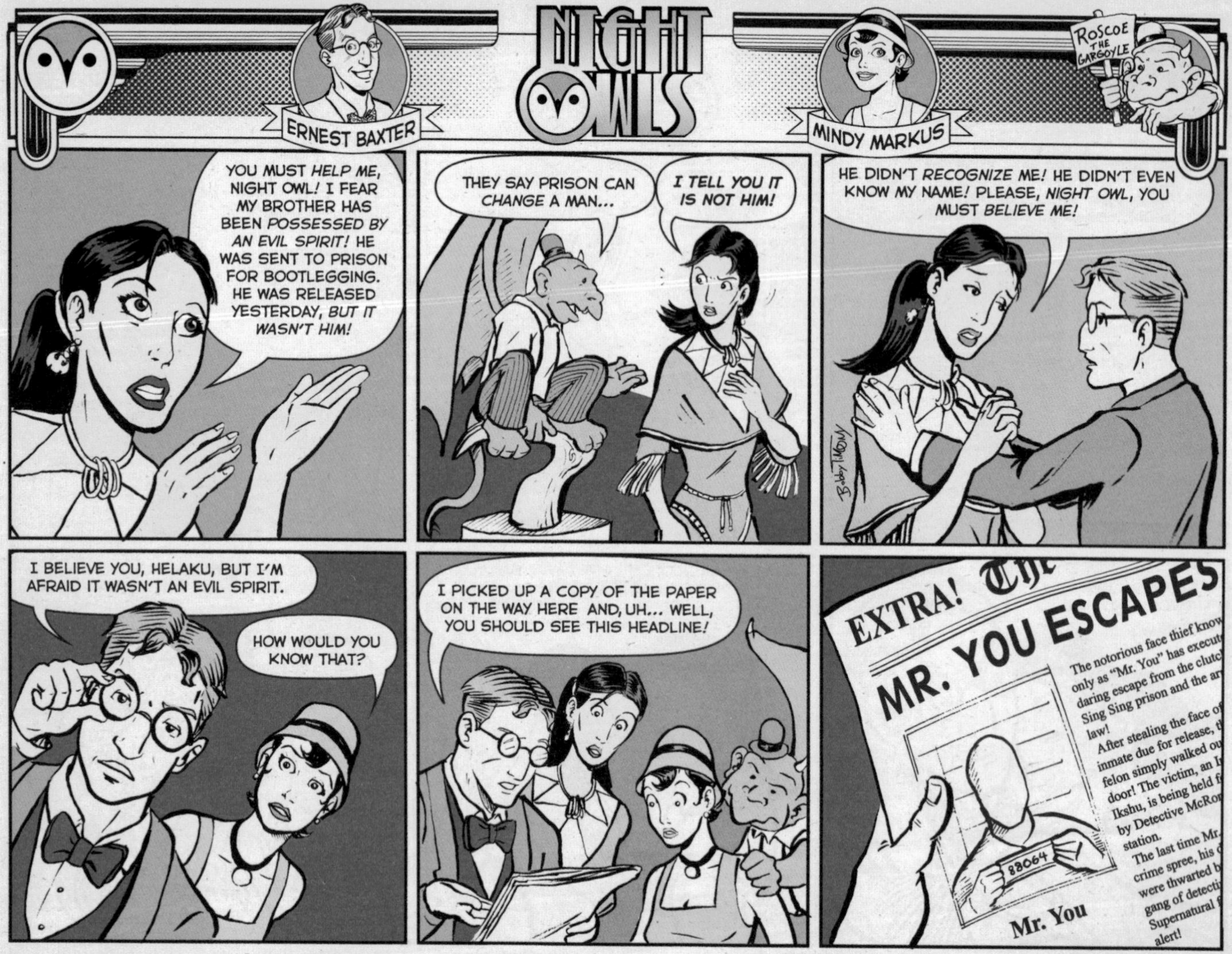
NIGHT OWLS
ERNEST BAXTER
MINDY MARKUS
ROSCOE THE GARGOYLE
YOU MUST *HELP ME*, NIGHT OWL! I FEAR MY BROTHER HAS BEEN *POSSESSED BY AN EVIL SPIRIT!* HE WAS SENT TO PRISON FOR BOOTLEGGING. HE WAS RELEASED YESTERDAY, *BUT IT WASN'T HIM!*
THEY SAY PRISON CAN *CHANGE* A MAN...
I TELL YOU IT IS NOT HIM!
HE DIDN'T *RECOGNIZE ME!* HE DIDN'T EVEN KNOW MY NAME! PLEASE, *NIGHT OWL*, YOU MUST *BELIEVE ME!*
Bobby Timony
I BELIEVE YOU, HELAKU, BUT I'M AFRAID IT WASN'T AN EVIL SPIRIT.
HOW WOULD YOU KNOW THAT?
I PICKED UP A COPY OF THE PAPER ON THE WAY HERE AND, UH... WELL, YOU SHOULD SEE THIS HEADLINE!
EXTRA!
MR. YOU ESCAPES
The notorious face thief
only as "Mr. You" has
daring escape from the
Sing Sing prison and the
law!
After stealing the face of
inmate due for release,
felon simply walked
door! The victim, an
Ikshu, is being held
by Detective
station.
The last time Mr.
crime spree, his
were thwarted
gang of
Supernatural
alert!
88064
Mr. You

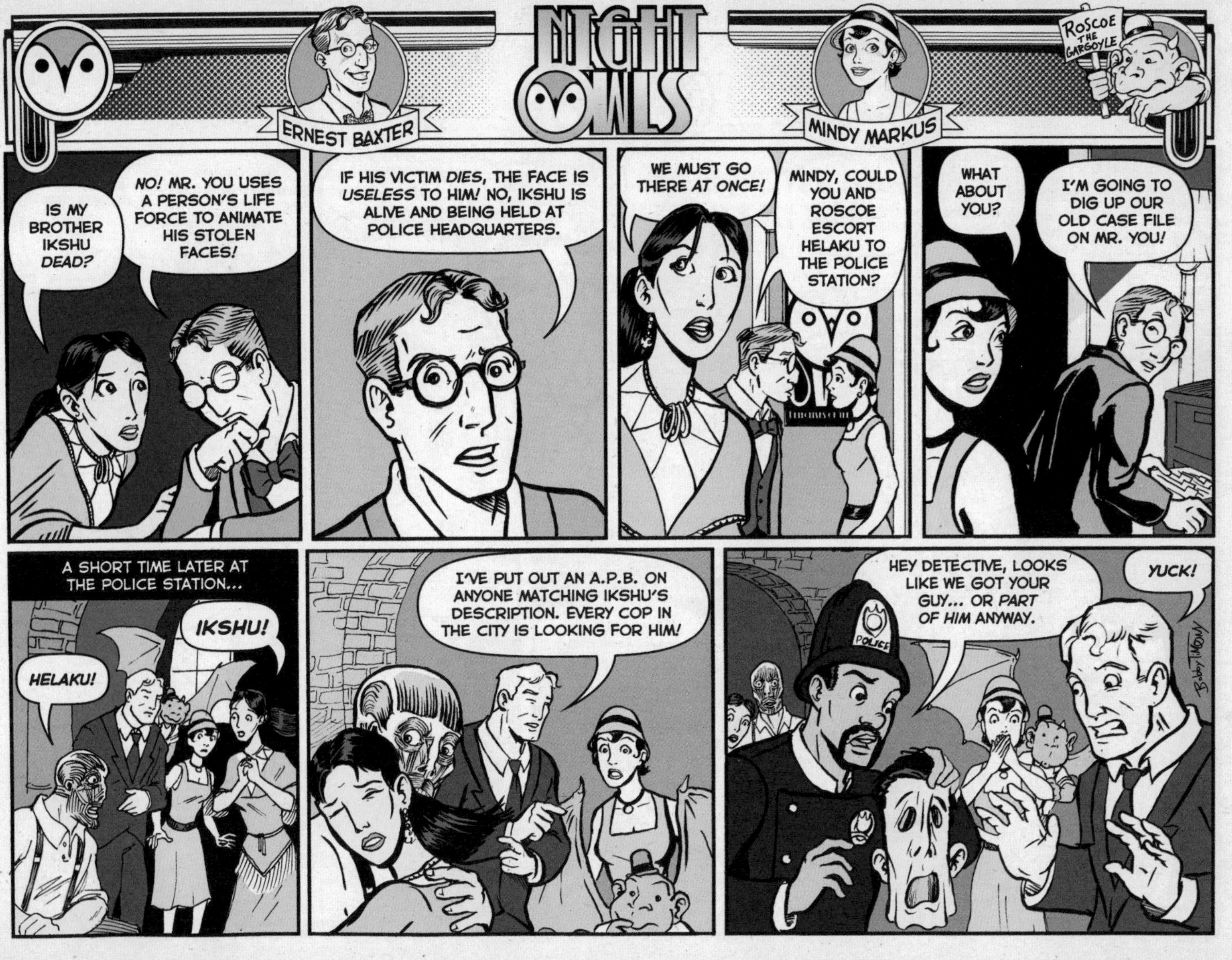

NIGHT OWLS
ERNEST BAXTER
MINDY MARKUS
ROSCOE THE GARGOYLE
IS MY BROTHER IKSHU *DEAD?*
NO! MR. YOU USES A PERSON'S LIFE FORCE TO ANIMATE HIS STOLEN FACES!
IF HIS VICTIM *DIES*, THE FACE IS *USELESS* TO HIM! NO, IKSHU IS ALIVE AND BEING HELD AT POLICE HEADQUARTERS.
WE MUST GO THERE *AT ONCE!*
MINDY, COULD YOU AND ROSCOE ESCORT HELAKU TO THE POLICE STATION?
WHAT ABOUT YOU?
I'M GOING TO DIG UP OUR OLD CASE FILE ON MR. YOU!
A SHORT TIME LATER AT THE POLICE STATION...
IKSHU!
HELAKU!
I'VE PUT OUT AN A.P.B. ON ANYONE MATCHING IKSHU'S DESCRIPTION. EVERY COP IN THE CITY IS LOOKING FOR HIM!
HEY DETECTIVE, LOOKS LIKE WE GOT YOUR GUY... OR *PART* OF *HIM* ANYWAY.
YUCK!
POLICE
Bobby Timony

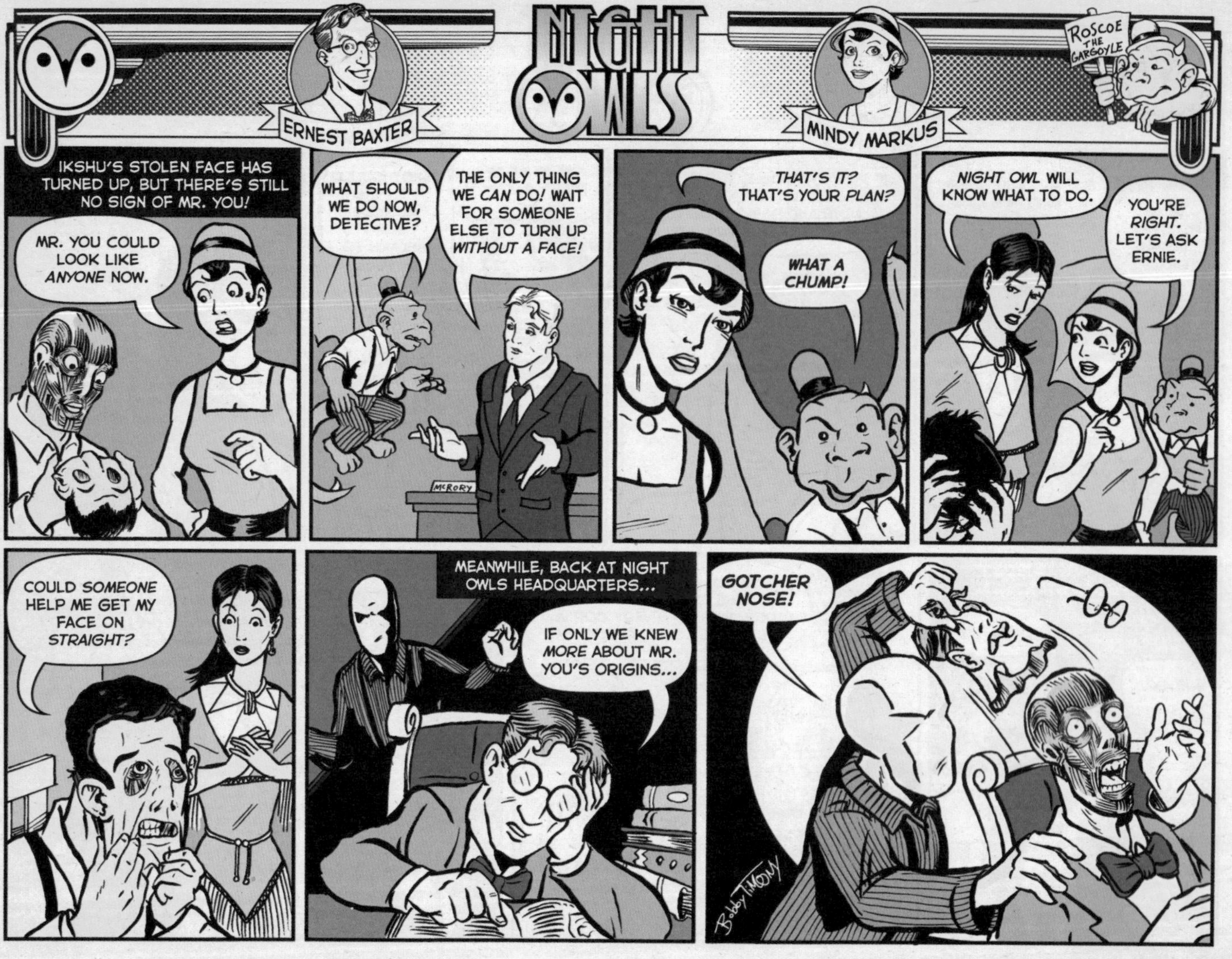
NIGHT OWLS
ERNEST BAXTER
MINDY MARKUS
ROSCOE THE GARGOYLE
IKSHU'S STOLEN FACE HAS TURNED UP, BUT THERE'S STILL NO SIGN OF MR. YOU!
MR. YOU COULD LOOK LIKE ANYONE NOW.
WHAT SHOULD WE DO NOW, DETECTIVE?
THE ONLY THING WE CAN DO! WAIT FOR SOMEONE ELSE TO TURN UP WITHOUT A FACE!
MCRORY
THAT'S IT? THAT'S YOUR PLAN?
WHAT A CHUMP!
NIGHT OWL WILL KNOW WHAT TO DO.
YOU'RE RIGHT. LET'S ASK ERNIE.
COULD SOMEONE HELP ME GET MY FACE ON STRAIGHT?
MEANWHILE, BACK AT NIGHT OWLS HEADQUARTERS...
IF ONLY WE KNEW MORE ABOUT MR. YOU'S ORIGINS...
GOTCHER NOSE!
Bobby Timony

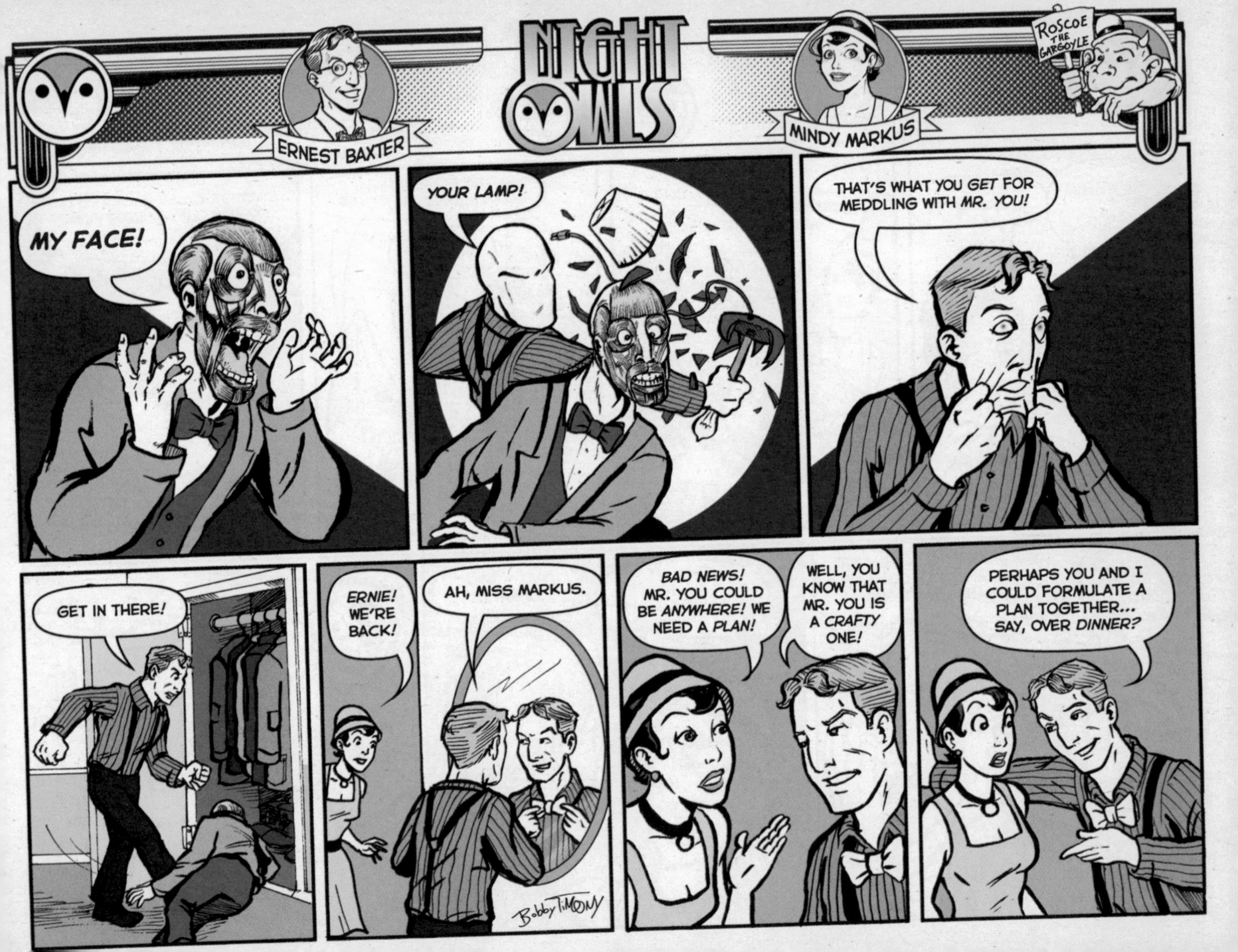
NIGHT OWLS
ERNEST BAXTER
MINDY MARKUS
ROSCOE THE GARGOYLE
MY FACE!
YOUR LAMP!
THAT'S WHAT YOU GET FOR MEDDLING WITH MR. YOU!
GET IN THERE!
ERNIE! WE'RE BACK!
AH, MISS MARKUS.
BAD NEWS! MR. YOU COULD BE ANYWHERE! WE NEED A PLAN!
WELL, YOU KNOW THAT MR. YOU IS A CRAFTY ONE!
PERHAPS YOU AND I COULD FORMULATE A PLAN TOGETHER... SAY, OVER DINNER?
Bobby TiMONY

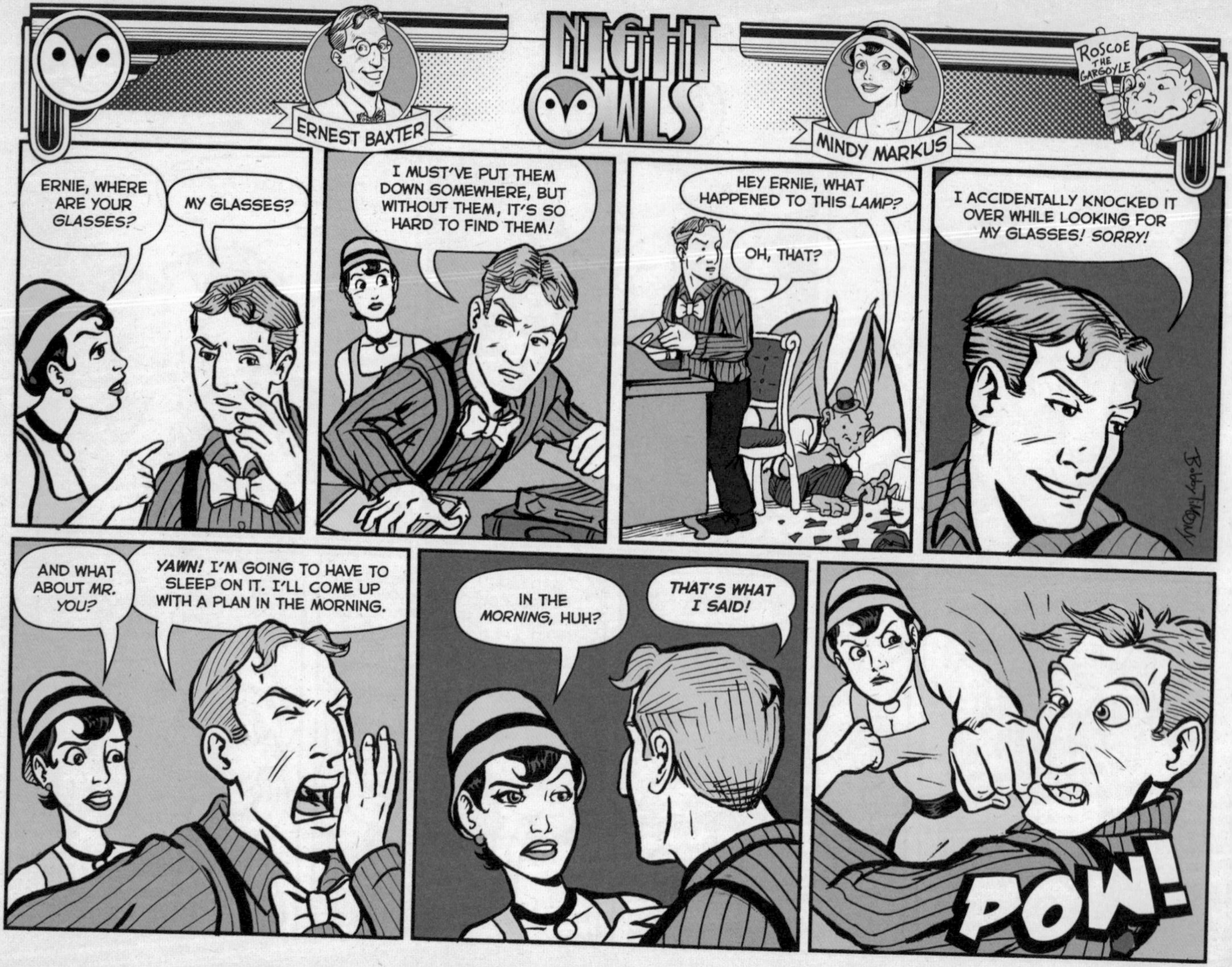
NIGHT OWLS
ERNEST BAXTER
MINDY MARKUS
ROSCOE THE GARGOYLE
ERNIE, WHERE ARE YOUR GLASSES?
MY GLASSES?
I MUST'VE PUT THEM DOWN SOMEWHERE, BUT WITHOUT THEM, IT'S SO HARD TO FIND THEM!
HEY ERNIE, WHAT HAPPENED TO THIS LAMP?
OH, THAT?
I ACCIDENTALLY KNOCKED IT OVER WHILE LOOKING FOR MY GLASSES! SORRY!
AND WHAT ABOUT MR. YOU?
YAWN! I'M GOING TO HAVE TO SLEEP ON IT. I'LL COME UP WITH A PLAN IN THE MORNING.
IN THE MORNING, HUH?
THAT'S WHAT I SAID!
POW!

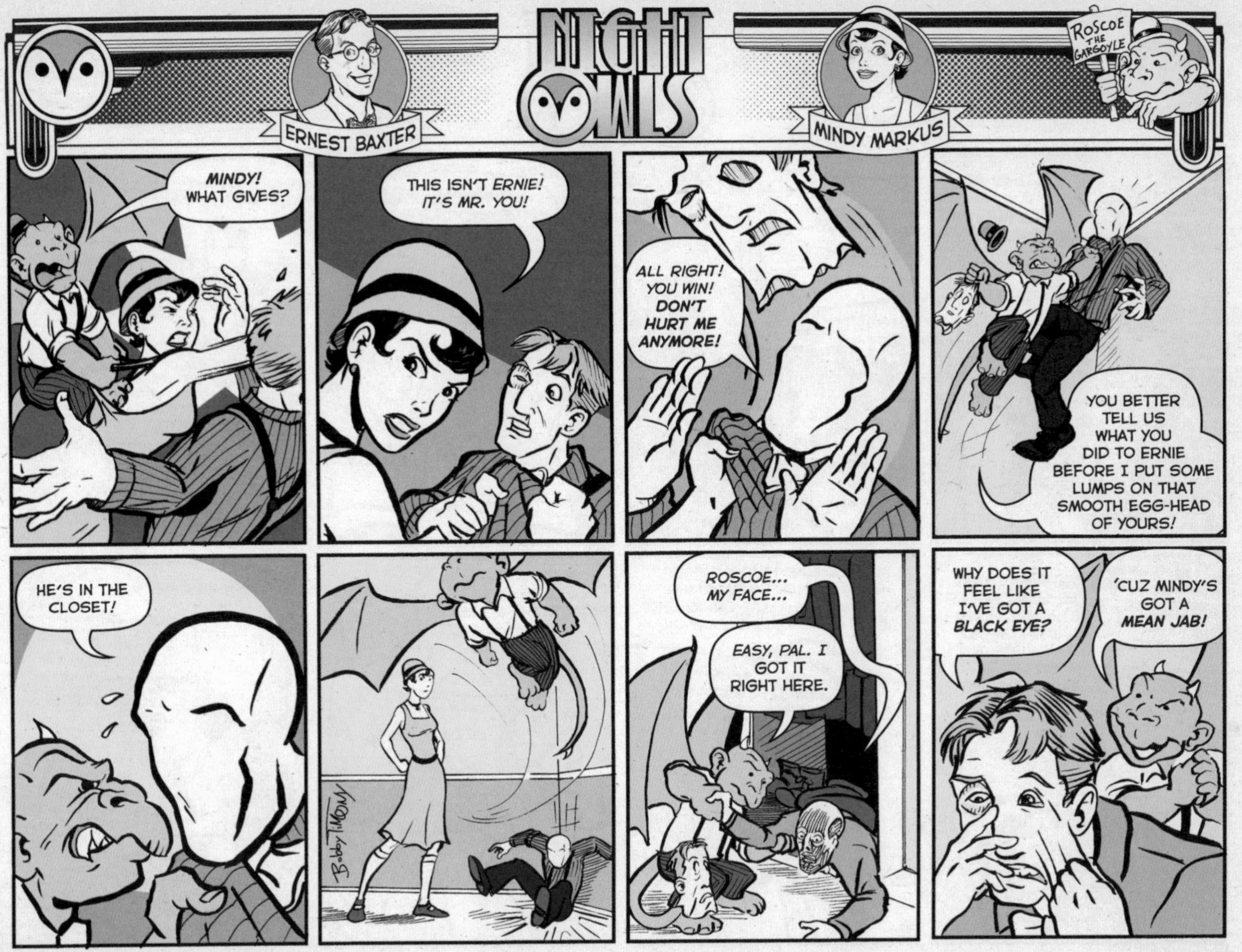
NIGHT OWLS
ERNEST BAXTER
MINDY MARKUS
ROSCOE THE GARGOYLE
MINDY! WHAT GIVES?
THIS ISN'T ERNIE! IT'S MR. YOU!
ALL RIGHT! YOU WIN! DON'T HURT ME ANYMORE!
YOU BETTER TELL US WHAT YOU DID TO ERNIE BEFORE I PUT SOME LUMPS ON THAT SMOOTH EGG-HEAD OF YOURS!
HE'S IN THE CLOSET!
Bobby T. Moony
ROSCOE... MY FACE...
EASY, PAL. I GOT IT RIGHT HERE.
WHY DOES IT FEEL LIKE I'VE GOT A BLACK EYE?
'CUZ MINDY'S GOT A MEAN JAB!

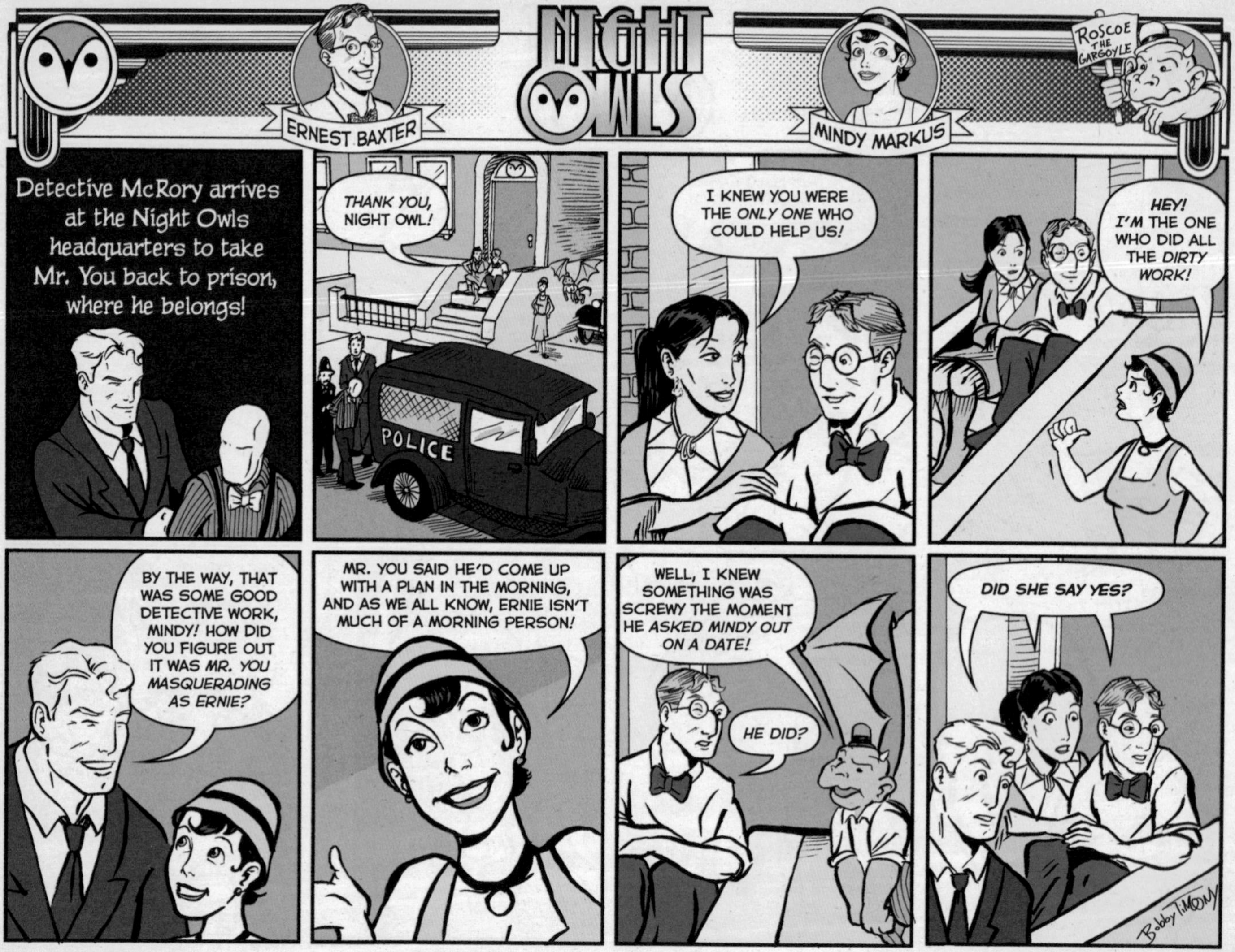
NIGHT OWLS
ERNEST BAXTER
MINDY MARKUS
ROSCOE THE GARGOYLE
Detective McRory arrives at the Night Owls headquarters to take Mr. You back to prison, where he belongs!
THANK YOU, NIGHT OWL!
POLICE
I KNEW YOU WERE THE ONLY ONE WHO COULD HELP US!
HEY! I'M THE ONE WHO DID ALL THE DIRTY WORK!
BY THE WAY, THAT WAS SOME GOOD DETECTIVE WORK, MINDY! HOW DID YOU FIGURE OUT IT WAS MR. YOU MASQUERADING AS ERNIE?
MR. YOU SAID HE'D COME UP WITH A PLAN IN THE MORNING, AND AS WE ALL KNOW, ERNIE ISN'T MUCH OF A MORNING PERSON!
WELL, I KNEW SOMETHING WAS SCREWY THE MOMENT HE ASKED MINDY OUT ON A DATE!
HE DID?
DID SHE SAY YES?
Bobby Timony

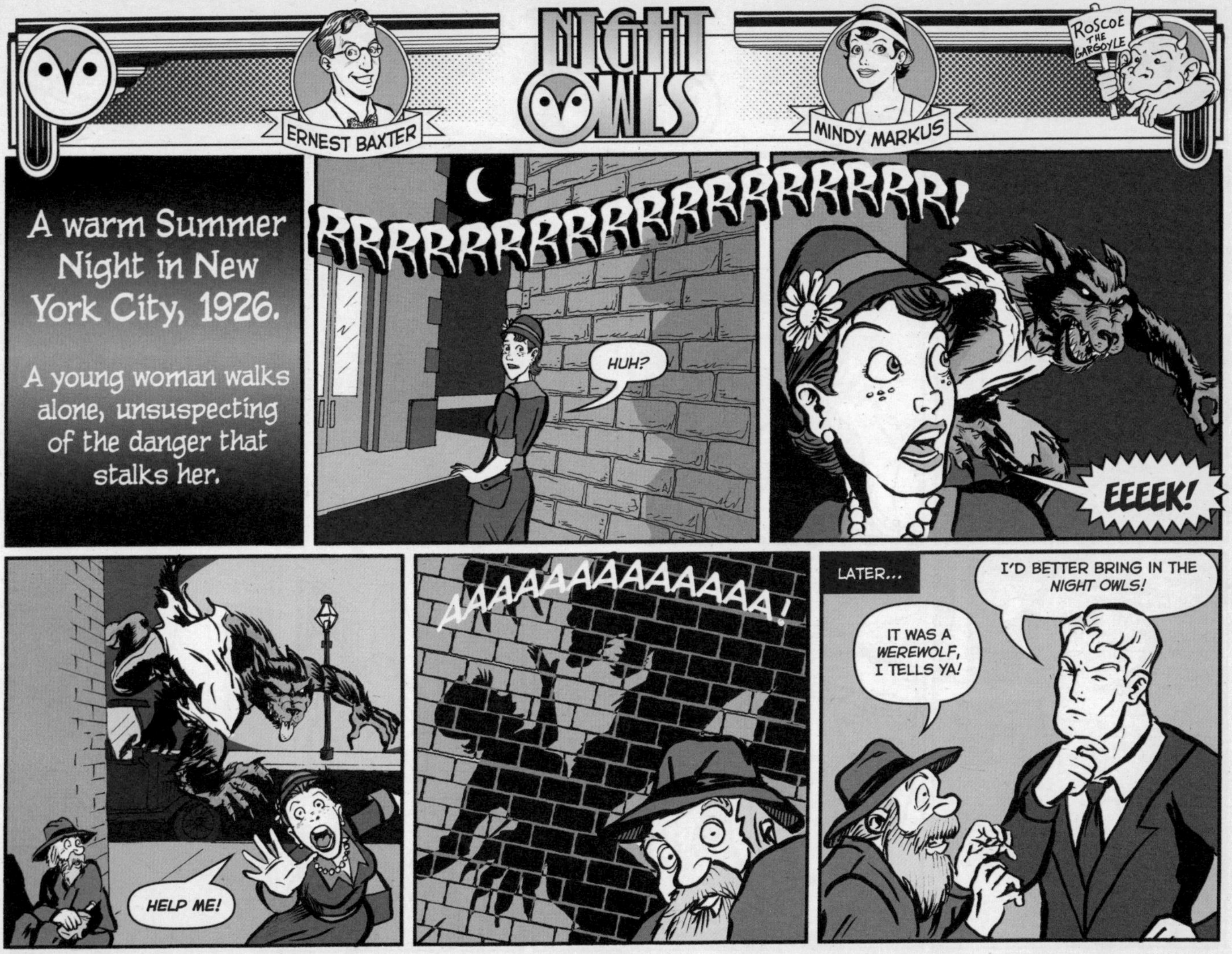
NIGHT OWLS
ERNEST BAXTER
MINDY MARKUS
ROSCOE THE GARGOYLE
A warm Summer Night in New York City, 1926.
A young woman walks alone, unsuspecting of the danger that stalks her.
RRRRRRRRRRRRRRRRRRRRRRR!
HUH?
EEEEK!
HELP ME!
AAAAAAAAAAAAAA!
LATER...
IT WAS A WEREWOLF, I TELLS YA!
I'D BETTER BRING IN THE NIGHT OWLS!

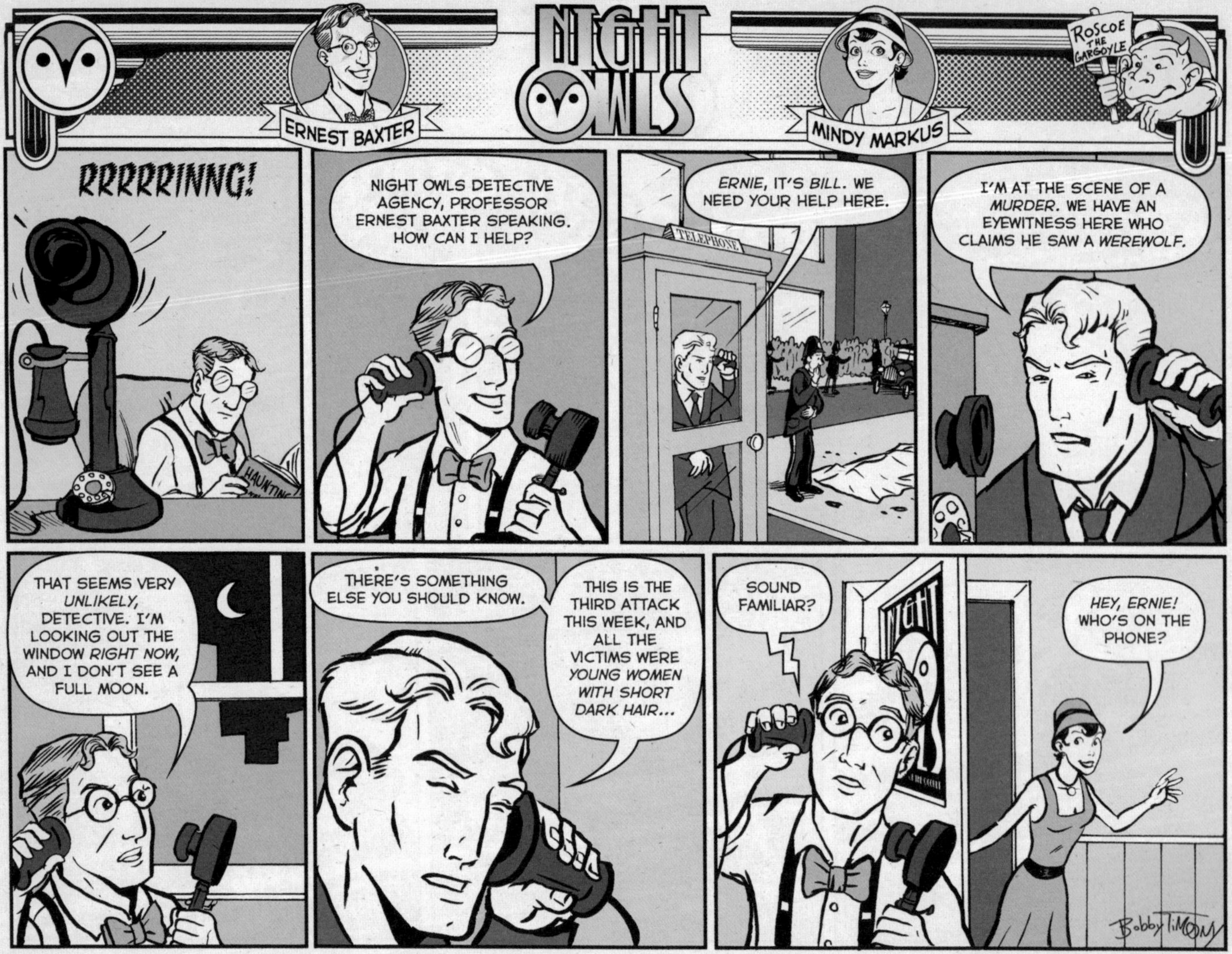
NIGHT OWLS
ERNEST BAXTER
MINDY MARKUS
ROSCOE THE GARGOYLE
RRRRRINNG!
HAUNTING
NIGHT OWLS DETECTIVE AGENCY, PROFESSOR ERNEST BAXTER SPEAKING. HOW CAN I HELP?
TELEPHONE
ERNIE, IT'S *BILL*. WE NEED YOUR HELP HERE.
I'M AT THE SCENE OF A *MURDER*. WE HAVE AN EYEWITNESS HERE WHO CLAIMS HE SAW A *WEREWOLF*.
THAT SEEMS VERY *UNLIKELY*, DETECTIVE. I'M LOOKING OUT THE WINDOW *RIGHT NOW*, AND I DON'T SEE A FULL MOON.
THERE'S SOMETHING ELSE YOU SHOULD KNOW.
THIS IS THE THIRD ATTACK THIS WEEK, AND ALL THE VICTIMS WERE *YOUNG WOMEN WITH SHORT DARK HAIR*...
SOUND FAMILIAR?
HEY, ERNIE! WHO'S ON THE PHONE?
Bobby Timony

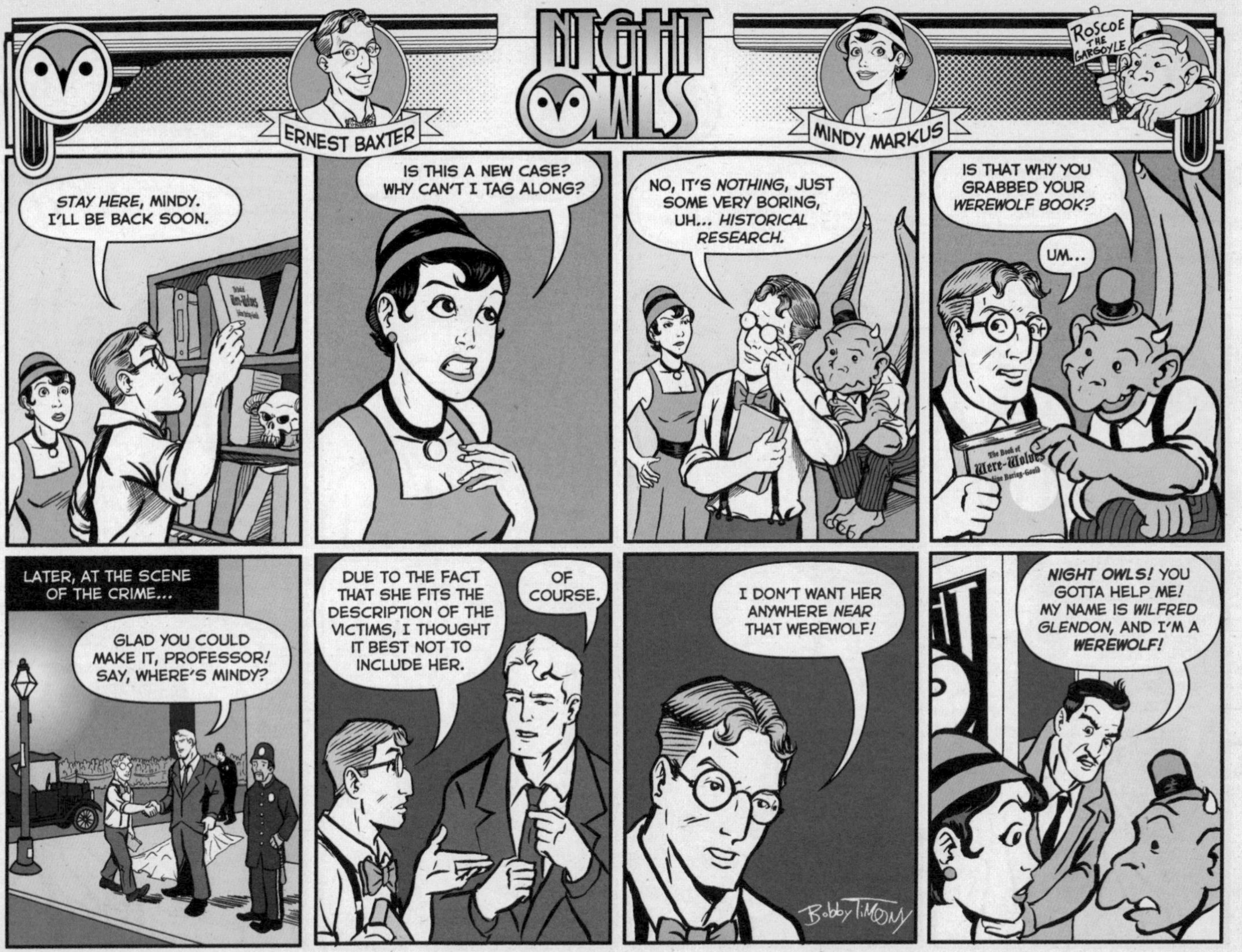
NIGHT OWLS
ERNEST BAXTER
MINDY MARKUS
ROSCOE THE GARGOYLE
STAY HERE, MINDY. I'LL BE BACK SOON.
IS THIS A NEW CASE? WHY CAN'T I TAG ALONG?
NO, IT'S NOTHING, JUST SOME VERY BORING, UH... HISTORICAL RESEARCH.
IS THAT WHY YOU GRABBED YOUR WEREWOLF BOOK?
UM...
The Book of Were-Wolves
LATER, AT THE SCENE OF THE CRIME...
GLAD YOU COULD MAKE IT, PROFESSOR! SAY, WHERE'S MINDY?
DUE TO THE FACT THAT SHE FITS THE DESCRIPTION OF THE VICTIMS, I THOUGHT IT BEST NOT TO INCLUDE HER.
OF COURSE.
I DON'T WANT HER ANYWHERE NEAR THAT WEREWOLF!
Bobby Timony
NIGHT OWLS! YOU GOTTA HELP ME! MY NAME IS WILFRED GLENDON, AND I'M A WEREWOLF!

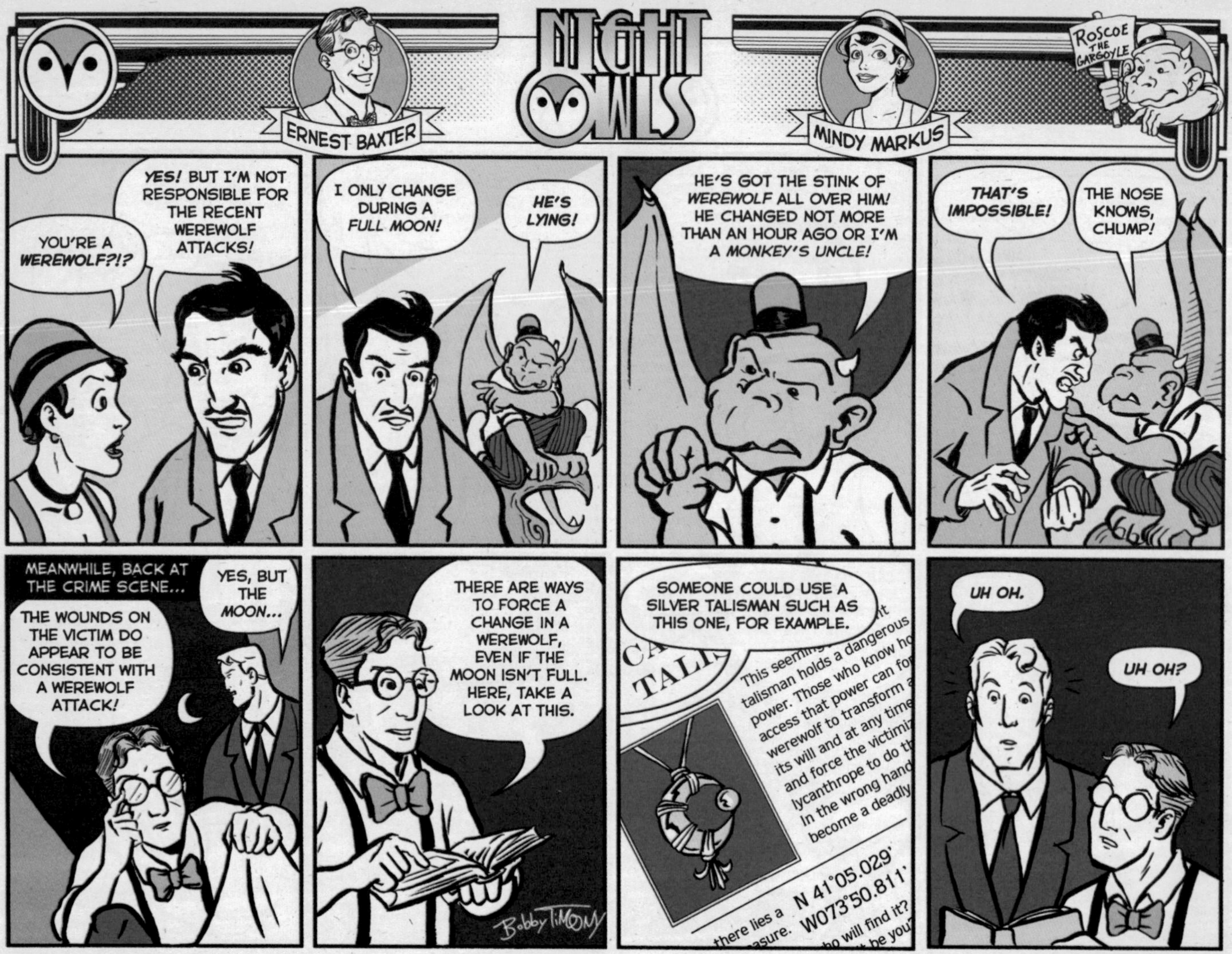
NIGHT OWLS
ERNEST BAXTER
MINDY MARKUS
ROSCOE THE GARGOYLE
YOU'RE A *WEREWOLF?!?*
YES! BUT I'M NOT RESPONSIBLE FOR THE RECENT WEREWOLF ATTACKS!
I ONLY CHANGE DURING A *FULL MOON!*
HE'S LYING!
HE'S GOT THE STINK OF *WEREWOLF* ALL OVER HIM! HE CHANGED NOT MORE THAN AN HOUR AGO OR I'M A *MONKEY'S UNCLE!*
THAT'S IMPOSSIBLE!
THE NOSE KNOWS, CHUMP!
MEANWHILE, BACK AT THE CRIME SCENE...
THE WOUNDS ON THE VICTIM DO APPEAR TO BE CONSISTENT WITH A WEREWOLF ATTACK!
YES, BUT THE *MOON...*
THERE ARE WAYS TO FORCE A CHANGE IN A WEREWOLF, EVEN IF THE MOON ISN'T FULL. HERE, TAKE A LOOK AT THIS.
Bobby Timony
SOMEONE COULD USE A SILVER TALISMAN SUCH AS THIS ONE, FOR EXAMPLE.
N 41°05.029'
W073°50.811'
UH OH.
UH OH?

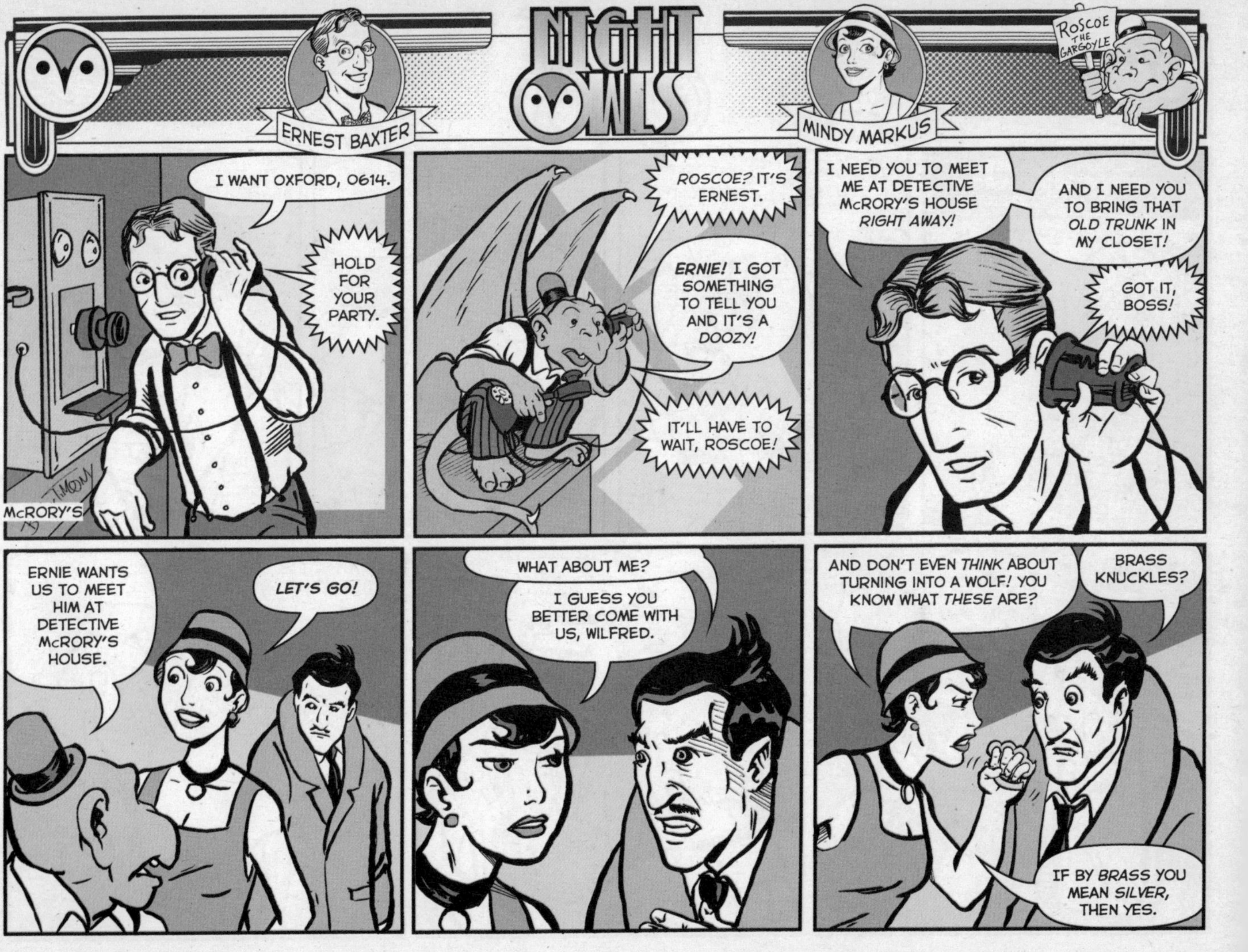
NIGHT OWLS
ERNEST BAXTER
MINDY MARKUS
ROSCOE THE GARGOYLE
I WANT OXFORD, 0614.
HOLD FOR YOUR PARTY.
McRORY'S
ROSCOE? IT'S ERNEST.
ERNIE! I GOT SOMETHING TO TELL YOU AND IT'S A DOOZY!
IT'LL HAVE TO WAIT, ROSCOE!
I NEED YOU TO MEET ME AT DETECTIVE McRORY'S HOUSE RIGHT AWAY!
AND I NEED YOU TO BRING THAT OLD TRUNK IN MY CLOSET!
GOT IT, BOSS!
ERNIE WANTS US TO MEET HIM AT DETECTIVE McRORY'S HOUSE.
LET'S GO!
WHAT ABOUT ME?
I GUESS YOU BETTER COME WITH US, WILFRED.
AND DON'T EVEN THINK ABOUT TURNING INTO A WOLF! YOU KNOW WHAT THESE ARE?
BRASS KNUCKLES?
IF BY BRASS YOU MEAN SILVER, THEN YES.

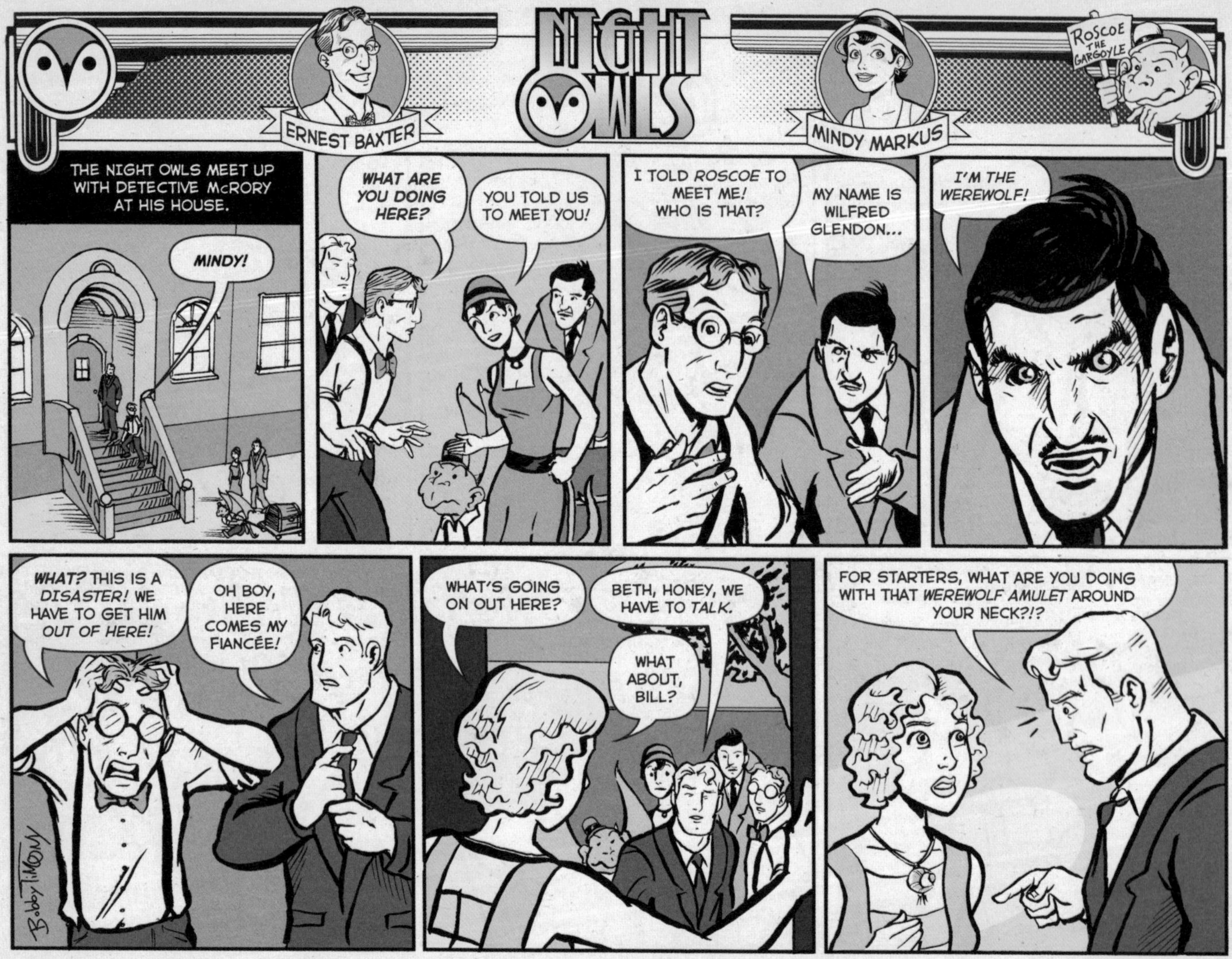
ERNEST BAXTER
NIGHT OWLS
MINDY MARKUS
ROSCOE THE GARGOYLE
THE NIGHT OWLS MEET UP WITH DETECTIVE McRORY AT HIS HOUSE.
MINDY!
WHAT ARE YOU DOING HERE?
YOU TOLD US TO MEET YOU!
I TOLD ROSCOE TO MEET ME! WHO IS THAT?
MY NAME IS WILFRED GLENDON...
I'M THE WEREWOLF!
WHAT? THIS IS A DISASTER! WE HAVE TO GET HIM OUT OF HERE!
OH BOY, HERE COMES MY FIANCÉE!
WHAT'S GOING ON OUT HERE?
BETH, HONEY, WE HAVE TO TALK.
WHAT ABOUT, BILL?
FOR STARTERS, WHAT ARE YOU DOING WITH THAT WEREWOLF AMULET AROUND YOUR NECK?!?
Bobby Timony

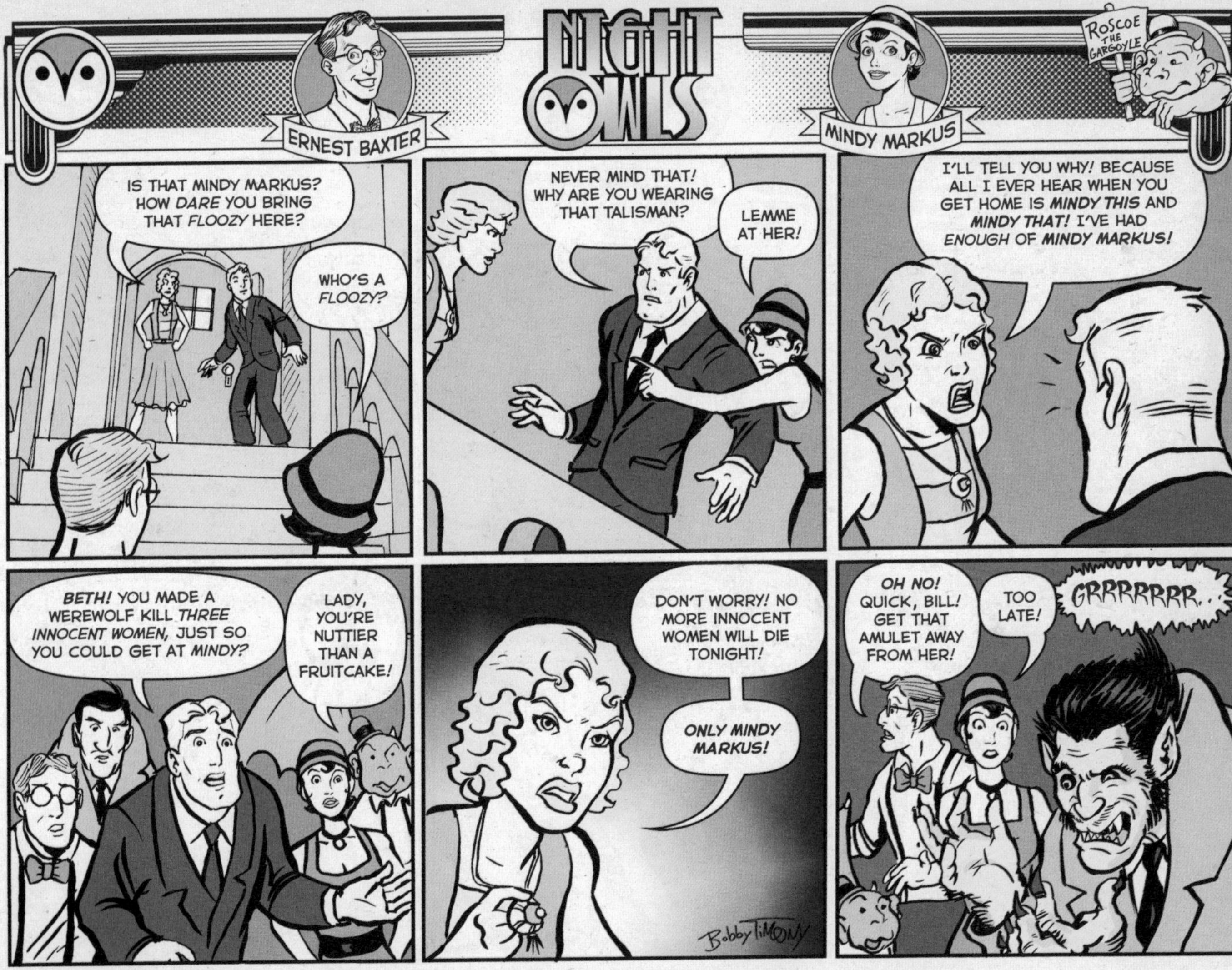
NIGHT OWLS
ERNEST BAXTER
MINDY MARKUS
ROSCOE THE GARGOYLE
IS THAT MINDY MARKUS? HOW *DARE* YOU BRING THAT *FLOOZY* HERE?
WHO'S A *FLOOZY?*
NEVER MIND THAT! WHY ARE YOU WEARING THAT TALISMAN?
LEMME AT HER!
I'LL TELL YOU WHY! BECAUSE ALL I EVER HEAR WHEN YOU GET HOME IS ***MINDY THIS*** AND ***MINDY THAT!*** I'VE HAD *ENOUGH* OF ***MINDY MARKUS!***
BETH! YOU MADE A WEREWOLF KILL *THREE INNOCENT WOMEN,* JUST SO YOU COULD GET AT *MINDY?*
LADY, YOU'RE NUTTIER THAN A FRUITCAKE!
DON'T WORRY! NO MORE INNOCENT WOMEN WILL DIE TONIGHT!
ONLY MINDY MARKUS!
OH NO! QUICK, BILL! GET THAT AMULET AWAY FROM HER!
TOO LATE!
GRRRRRRR...
Bobby Timony

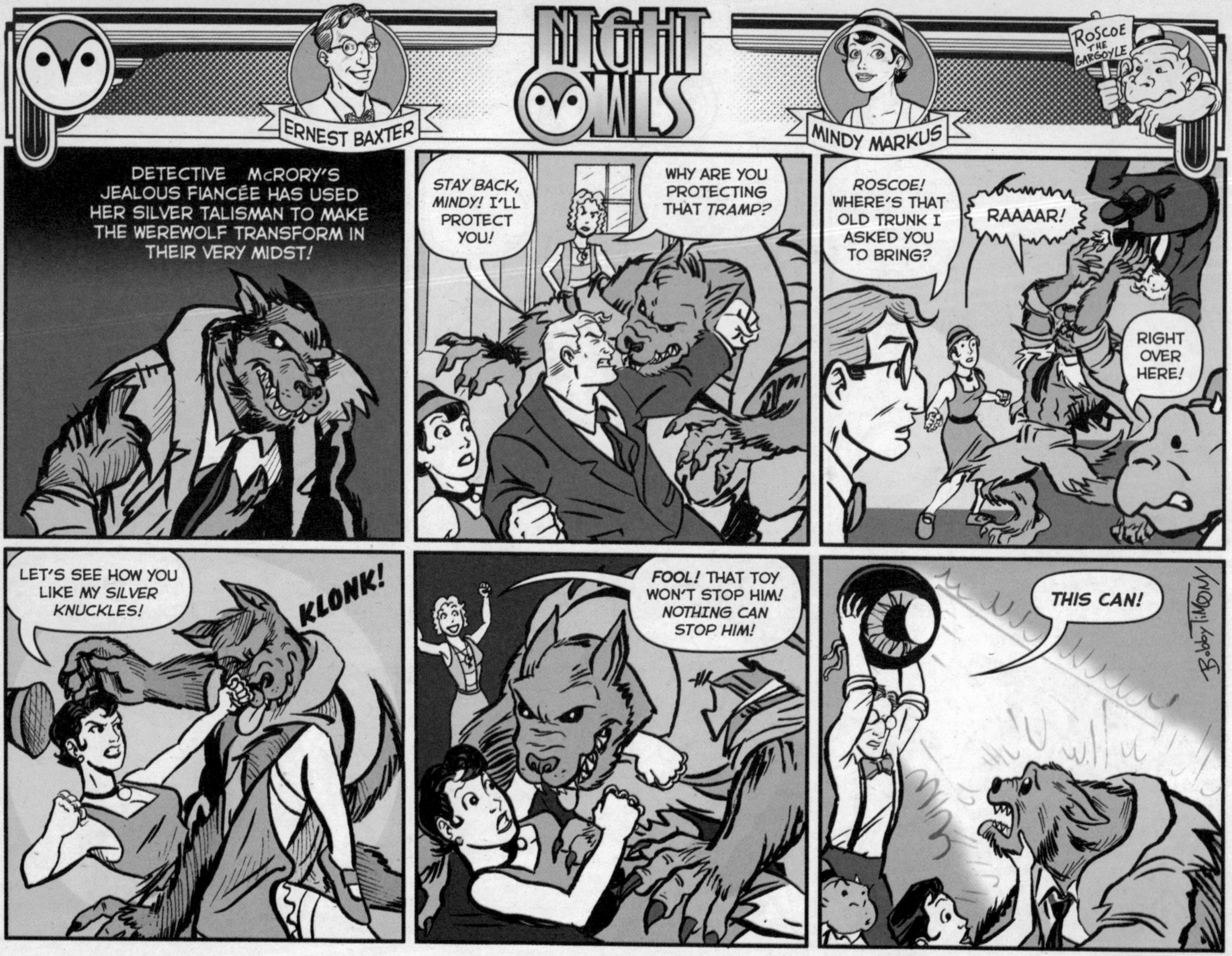
NIGHT OWLS
ERNEST BAXTER
MINDY MARKUS
ROSCOE THE GARGOYLE
DETECTIVE McRORY'S JEALOUS FIANCÉE HAS USED HER SILVER TALISMAN TO MAKE THE WEREWOLF TRANSFORM IN THEIR VERY MIDST!
STAY BACK, MINDY! I'LL PROTECT YOU!
WHY ARE YOU PROTECTING THAT TRAMP?
ROSCOE! WHERE'S THAT OLD TRUNK I ASKED YOU TO BRING?
RAAAAR!
RIGHT OVER HERE!
LET'S SEE HOW YOU LIKE MY SILVER KNUCKLES!
KLONK!
FOOL! THAT TOY WON'T STOP HIM! NOTHING CAN STOP HIM!
THIS CAN!
Bobby Timony

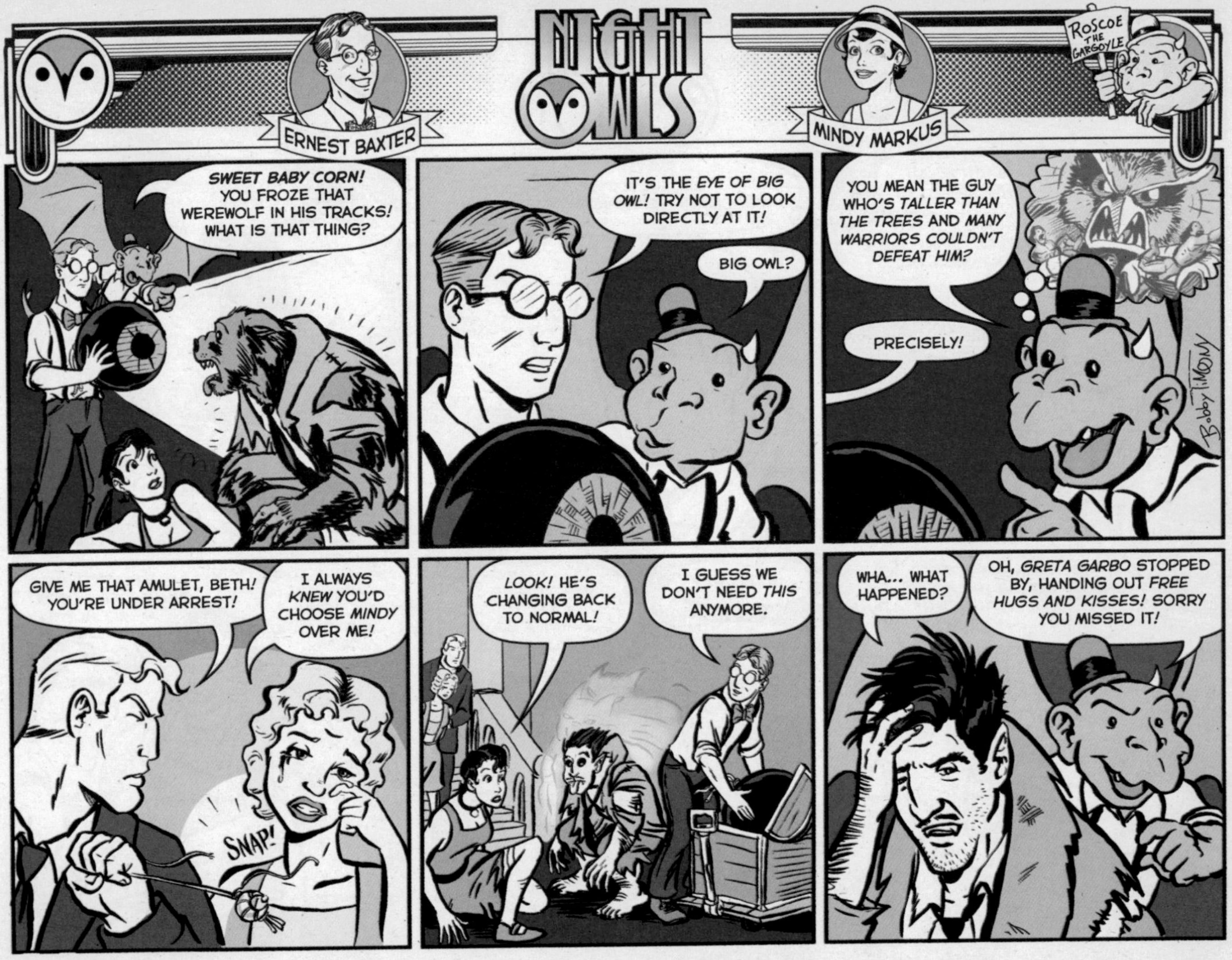
NIGHT OWLS
ERNEST BAXTER
MINDY MARKUS
ROSCOE THE GARGOYLE
SWEET BABY CORN! YOU FROZE THAT WEREWOLF IN HIS TRACKS! WHAT IS THAT THING?
IT'S THE EYE OF BIG OWL! TRY NOT TO LOOK DIRECTLY AT IT!
BIG OWL?
YOU MEAN THE GUY WHO'S TALLER THAN THE TREES AND MANY WARRIORS COULDN'T DEFEAT HIM?
PRECISELY!
Bobby Timony
GIVE ME THAT AMULET, BETH! YOU'RE UNDER ARREST!
I ALWAYS KNEW YOU'D CHOOSE MINDY OVER ME!
SNAP!
LOOK! HE'S CHANGING BACK TO NORMAL!
I GUESS WE DON'T NEED THIS ANYMORE.
WHA... WHAT HAPPENED?
OH, GRETA GARBO STOPPED BY, HANDING OUT FREE HUGS AND KISSES! SORRY YOU MISSED IT!

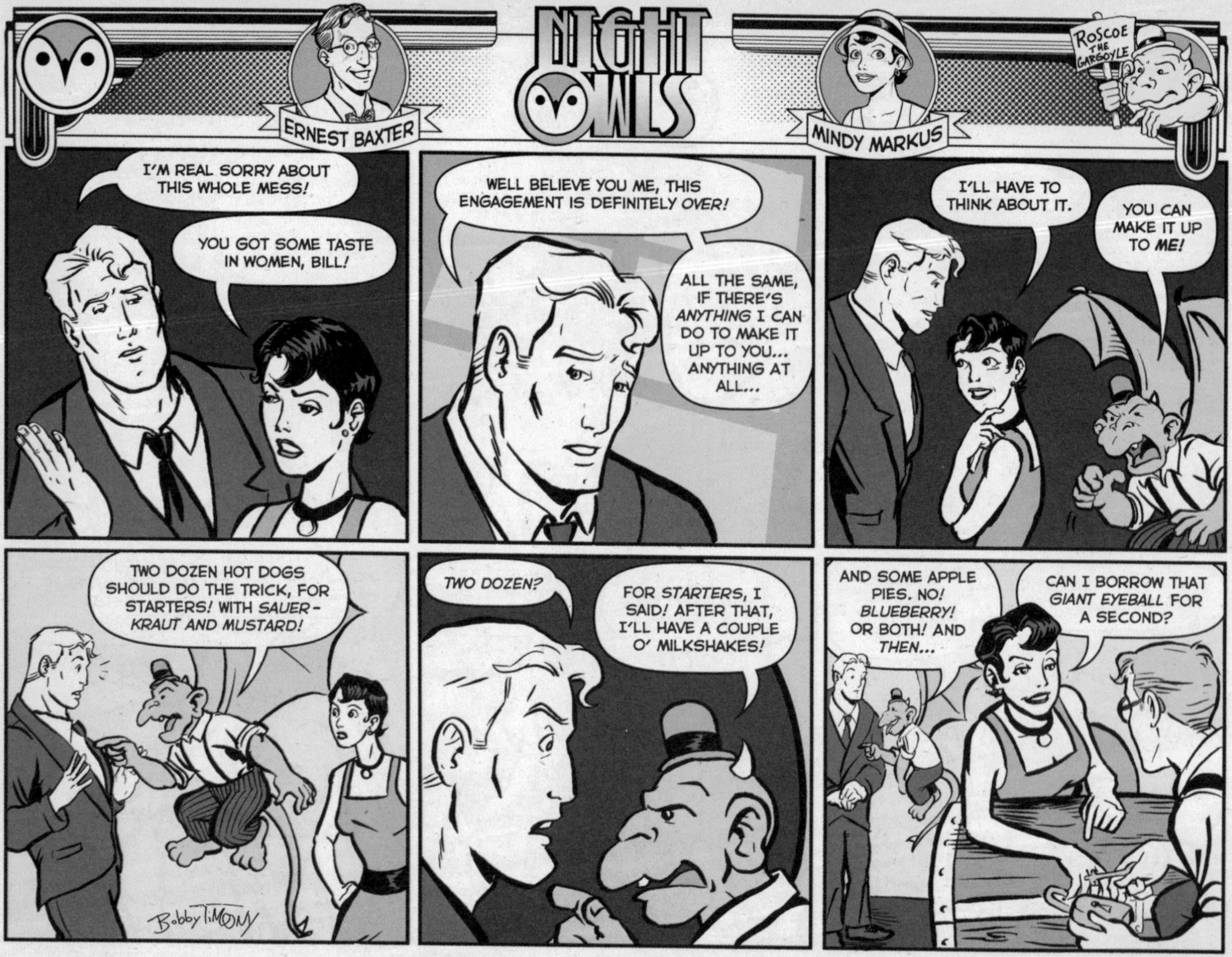
NIGHT OWLS
ERNEST BAXTER
MINDY MARKUS
ROSCOE THE GARGOYLE
I'M REAL SORRY ABOUT THIS WHOLE MESS!
YOU GOT SOME TASTE IN WOMEN, BILL!
WELL BELIEVE YOU ME, THIS ENGAGEMENT IS DEFINITELY *OVER!*
ALL THE SAME, IF THERE'S *ANYTHING* I CAN DO TO MAKE IT UP TO YOU... ANYTHING AT ALL...
I'LL HAVE TO THINK ABOUT IT.
YOU CAN MAKE IT UP TO *ME!*
TWO DOZEN HOT DOGS SHOULD DO THE TRICK, FOR STARTERS! WITH *SAUER-KRAUT AND MUSTARD!*
Bobby Timony
TWO DOZEN?
FOR *STARTERS*, I SAID! AFTER THAT, I'LL HAVE A COUPLE O' MILKSHAKES!
AND SOME APPLE PIES. NO! *BLUEBERRY!* OR BOTH! AND *THEN...*
CAN I BORROW THAT *GIANT EYEBALL* FOR A SECOND?

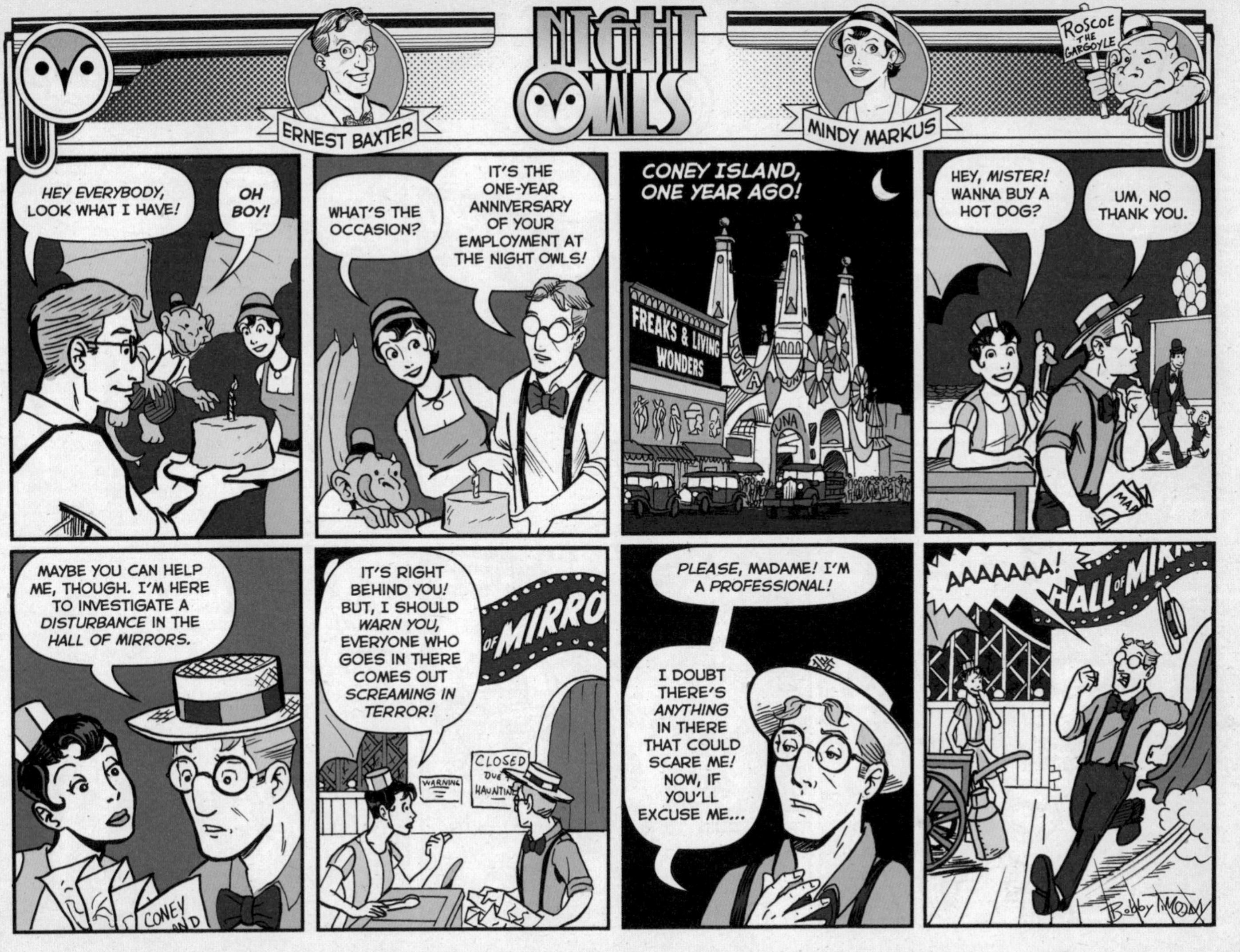
NIGHT OWLS
ERNEST BAXTER
MINDY MARKUS
ROSCOE THE GARGOYLE
HEY EVERYBODY, LOOK WHAT I HAVE!
OH BOY!
WHAT'S THE OCCASION?
IT'S THE ONE-YEAR ANNIVERSARY OF YOUR EMPLOYMENT AT THE NIGHT OWLS!
CONEY ISLAND, ONE YEAR AGO!
FREAKS & LIVING WONDERS
LUNA
HEY, MISTER! WANNA BUY A HOT DOG?
UM, NO THANK YOU.
MAYBE YOU CAN HELP ME, THOUGH. I'M HERE TO INVESTIGATE A DISTURBANCE IN THE HALL OF MIRRORS.
IT'S RIGHT BEHIND YOU! BUT, I SHOULD WARN YOU, EVERYONE WHO GOES IN THERE COMES OUT SCREAMING IN TERROR!
CLOSED DUE TO HAUNTING
WARNING
PLEASE, MADAME! I'M A PROFESSIONAL!
I DOUBT THERE'S ANYTHING IN THERE THAT COULD SCARE ME! NOW, IF YOU'LL EXCUSE ME...
AAAAAAA!
HALL OF MIRRORS
Bobby Timony

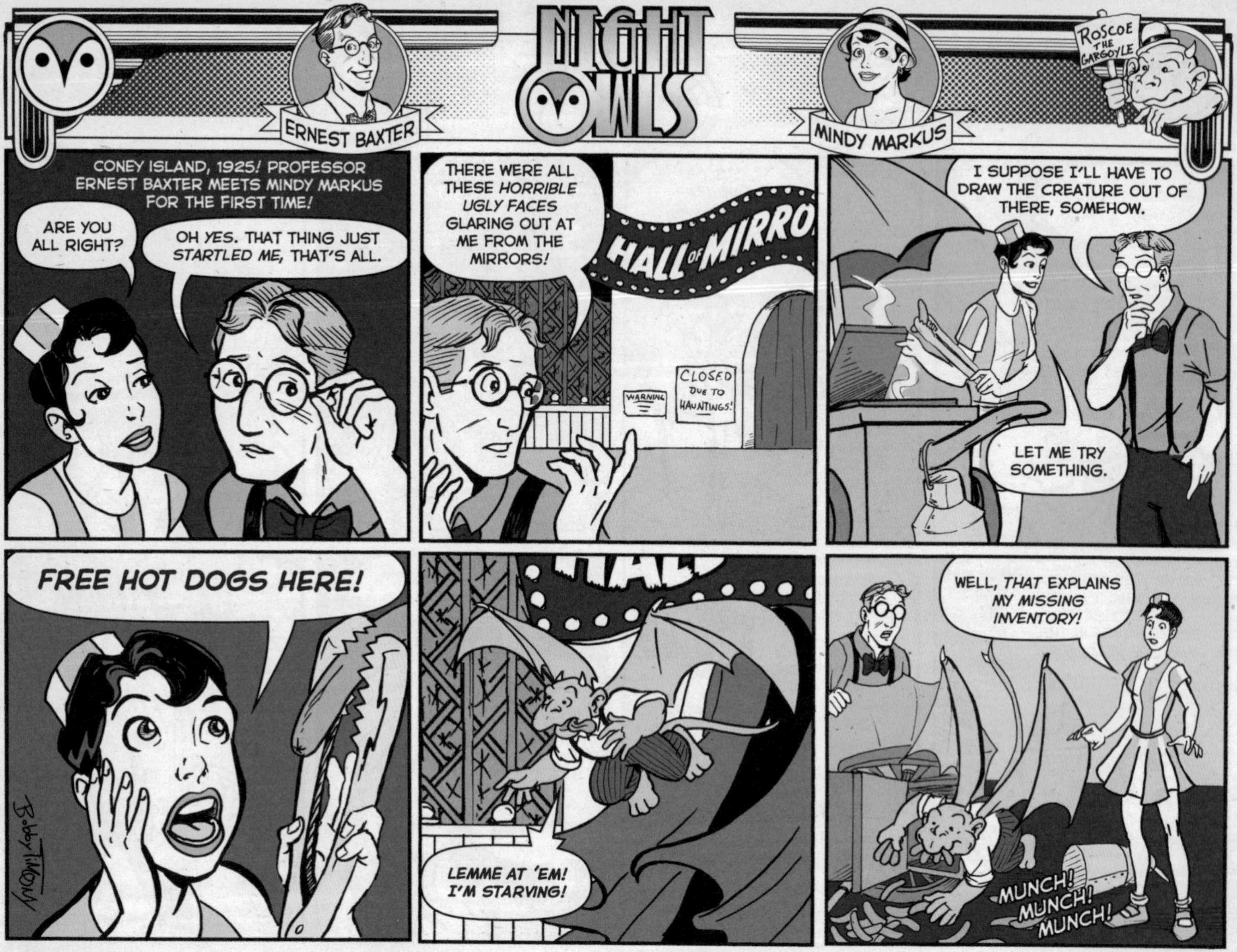
NIGHT OWLS
ERNEST BAXTER
MINDY MARKUS
ROSCOE THE GARGOYLE
CONEY ISLAND, 1925! PROFESSOR ERNEST BAXTER MEETS MINDY MARKUS FOR THE FIRST TIME!
ARE YOU ALL RIGHT?
OH YES. THAT THING JUST STARTLED ME, THAT'S ALL.
THERE WERE ALL THESE HORRIBLE UGLY FACES GLARING OUT AT ME FROM THE MIRRORS!
HALL OF MIRRO
WARNING
CLOSED DUE TO HAUNTINGS!
I SUPPOSE I'LL HAVE TO DRAW THE CREATURE OUT OF THERE, SOMEHOW.
LET ME TRY SOMETHING.
FREE HOT DOGS HERE!
LEMME AT 'EM! I'M STARVING!
WELL, THAT EXPLAINS MY MISSING INVENTORY!
MUNCH! MUNCH! MUNCH!
Bobby Timony

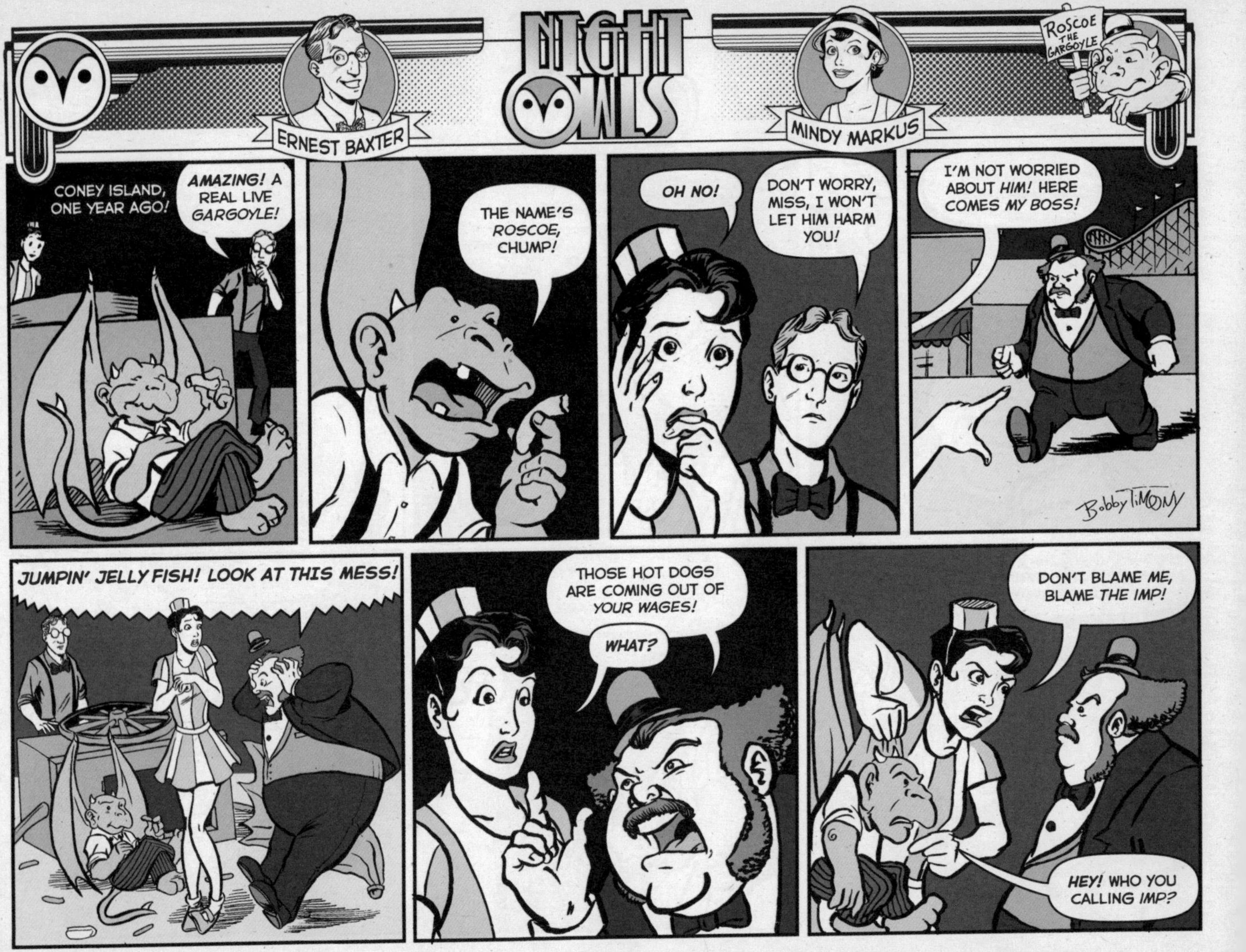
NIGHT OWLS
ERNEST BAXTER
MINDY MARKUS
ROSCOE THE GARGOYLE
CONEY ISLAND, ONE YEAR AGO!
AMAZING! A REAL LIVE GARGOYLE!
THE NAME'S ROSCOE, CHUMP!
OH NO!
DON'T WORRY, MISS, I WON'T LET HIM HARM YOU!
I'M NOT WORRIED ABOUT HIM! HERE COMES MY BOSS!
Bobby Timony
JUMPIN' JELLY FISH! LOOK AT THIS MESS!
THOSE HOT DOGS ARE COMING OUT OF YOUR WAGES!
WHAT?
DON'T BLAME ME, BLAME THE IMP!
HEY! WHO YOU CALLING IMP?

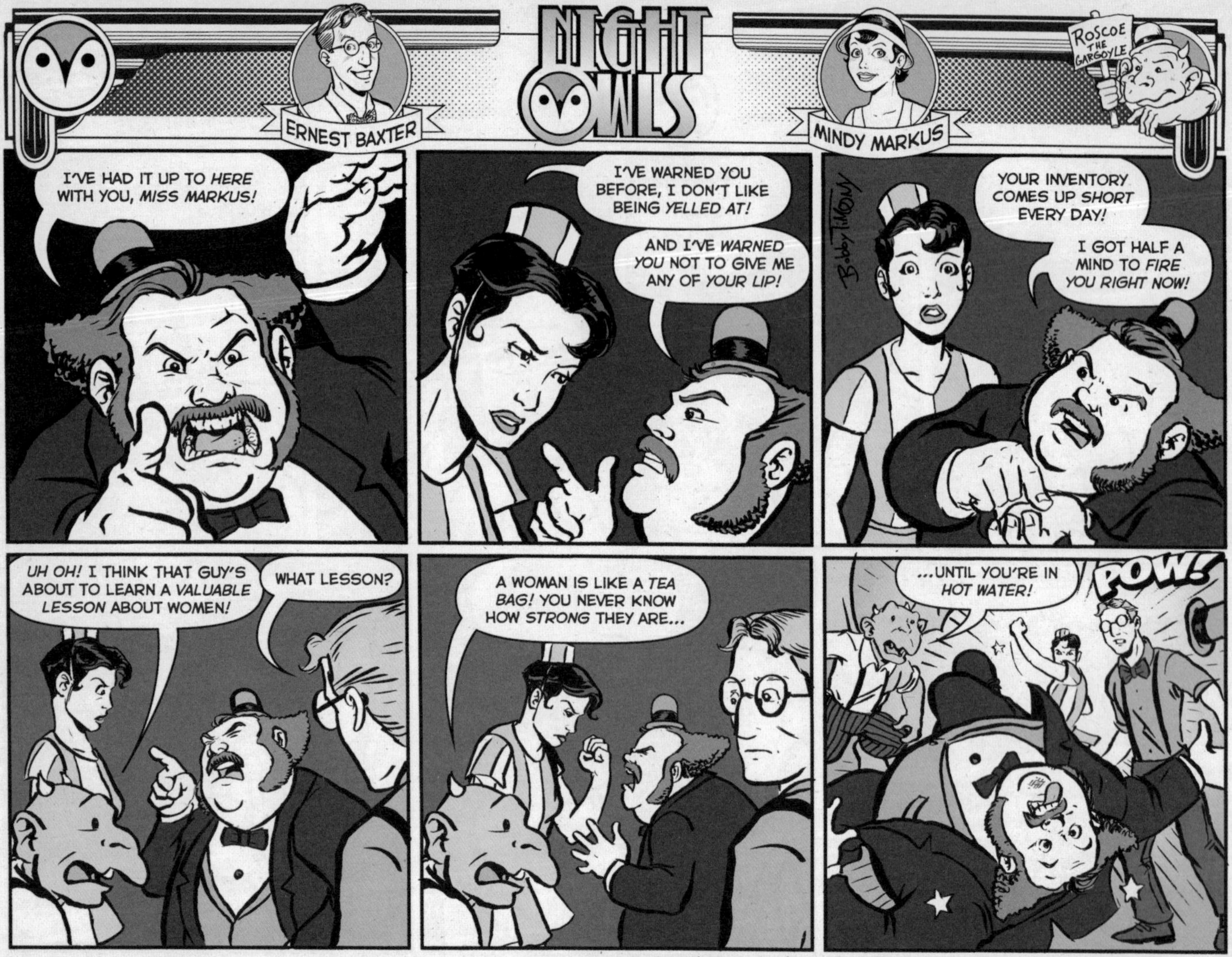
NIGHT OWLS
ERNEST BAXTER
MINDY MARKUS
ROSCOE THE GARGOYLE
Bobby Timony
I'VE HAD IT UP TO HERE WITH YOU, MISS MARKUS!
I'VE WARNED YOU BEFORE, I DON'T LIKE BEING YELLED AT!
AND I'VE WARNED YOU NOT TO GIVE ME ANY OF YOUR LIP!
YOUR INVENTORY COMES UP SHORT EVERY DAY!
I GOT HALF A MIND TO FIRE YOU RIGHT NOW!
UH OH! I THINK THAT GUY'S ABOUT TO LEARN A VALUABLE LESSON ABOUT WOMEN!
WHAT LESSON?
A WOMAN IS LIKE A TEA BAG! YOU NEVER KNOW HOW STRONG THEY ARE...
...UNTIL YOU'RE IN HOT WATER!
POW!

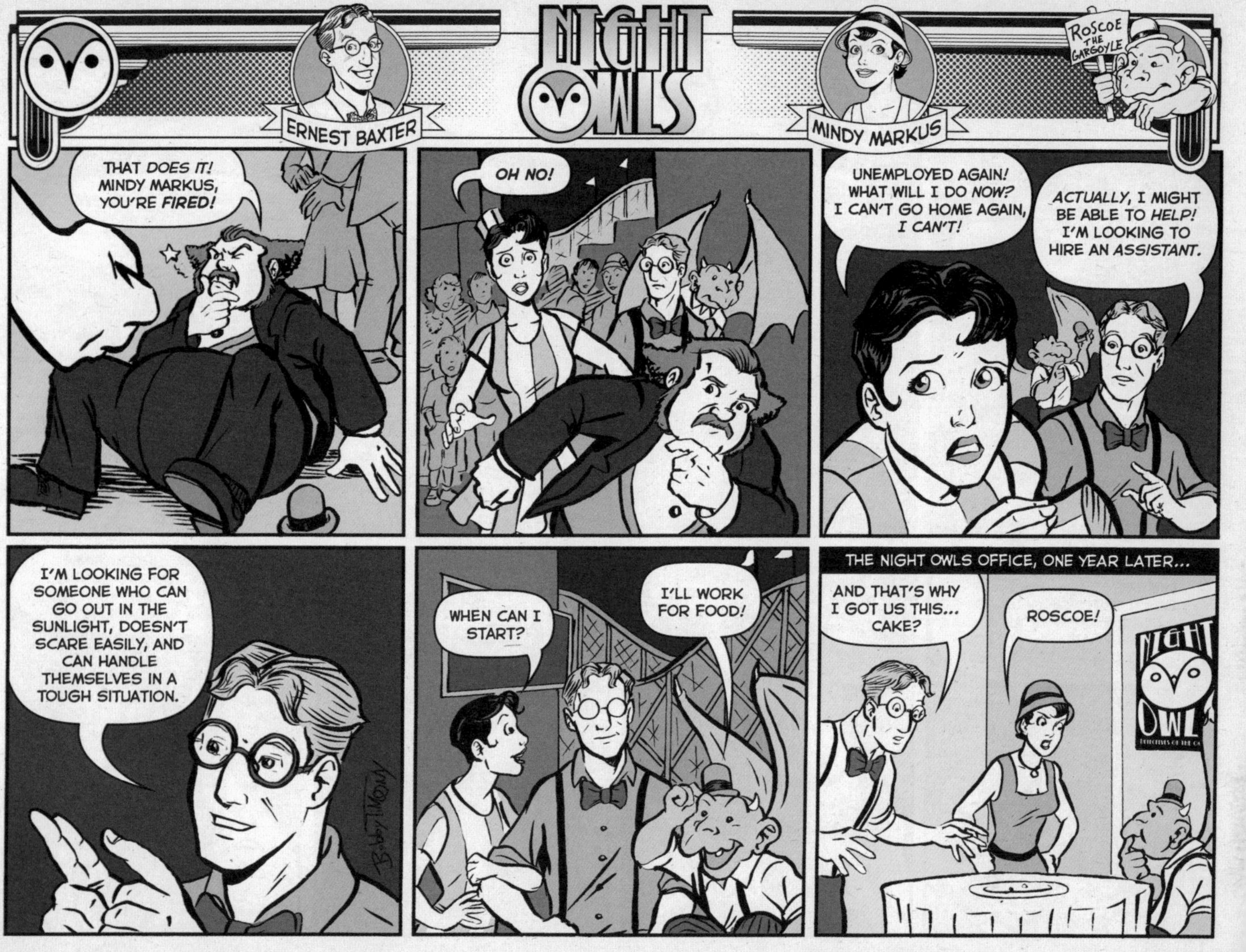
NIGHT OWLS
ERNEST BAXTER
MINDY MARKUS
ROSCOE THE GARGOYLE
THAT DOES IT! MINDY MARKUS, YOU'RE FIRED!
OH NO!
UNEMPLOYED AGAIN! WHAT WILL I DO NOW? I CAN'T GO HOME AGAIN, I CAN'T!
ACTUALLY, I MIGHT BE ABLE TO HELP! I'M LOOKING TO HIRE AN ASSISTANT.
I'M LOOKING FOR SOMEONE WHO CAN GO OUT IN THE SUNLIGHT, DOESN'T SCARE EASILY, AND CAN HANDLE THEMSELVES IN A TOUGH SITUATION.
WHEN CAN I START?
I'LL WORK FOR FOOD!
THE NIGHT OWLS OFFICE, ONE YEAR LATER...
AND THAT'S WHY I GOT US THIS... CAKE?
ROSCOE!
NIGHT OWL

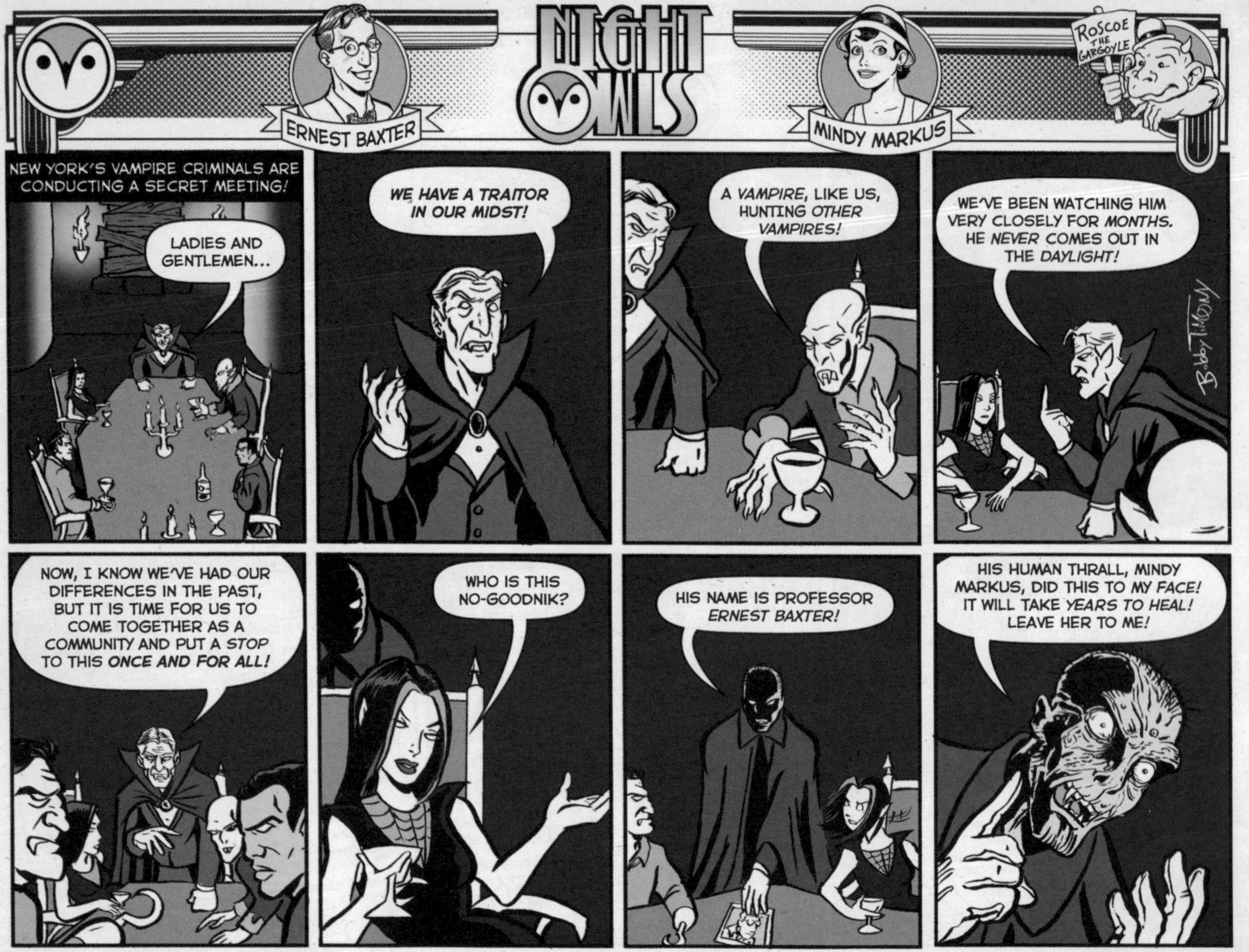
NIGHT OWLS
ERNEST BAXTER
MINDY MARKUS
ROSCOE THE GARGOYLE
NEW YORK'S VAMPIRE CRIMINALS ARE CONDUCTING A SECRET MEETING!
LADIES AND GENTLEMEN...
WE HAVE A TRAITOR IN OUR MIDST!
A VAMPIRE, LIKE US, HUNTING OTHER VAMPIRES!
WE'VE BEEN WATCHING HIM VERY CLOSELY FOR MONTHS. HE NEVER COMES OUT IN THE DAYLIGHT!
Bobby Timony
NOW, I KNOW WE'VE HAD OUR DIFFERENCES IN THE PAST, BUT IT IS TIME FOR US TO COME TOGETHER AS A COMMUNITY AND PUT A STOP TO THIS ONCE AND FOR ALL!
WHO IS THIS NO-GOODNIK?
HIS NAME IS PROFESSOR ERNEST BAXTER!
HIS HUMAN THRALL, MINDY MARKUS, DID THIS TO MY FACE! IT WILL TAKE YEARS TO HEAL! LEAVE HER TO ME!

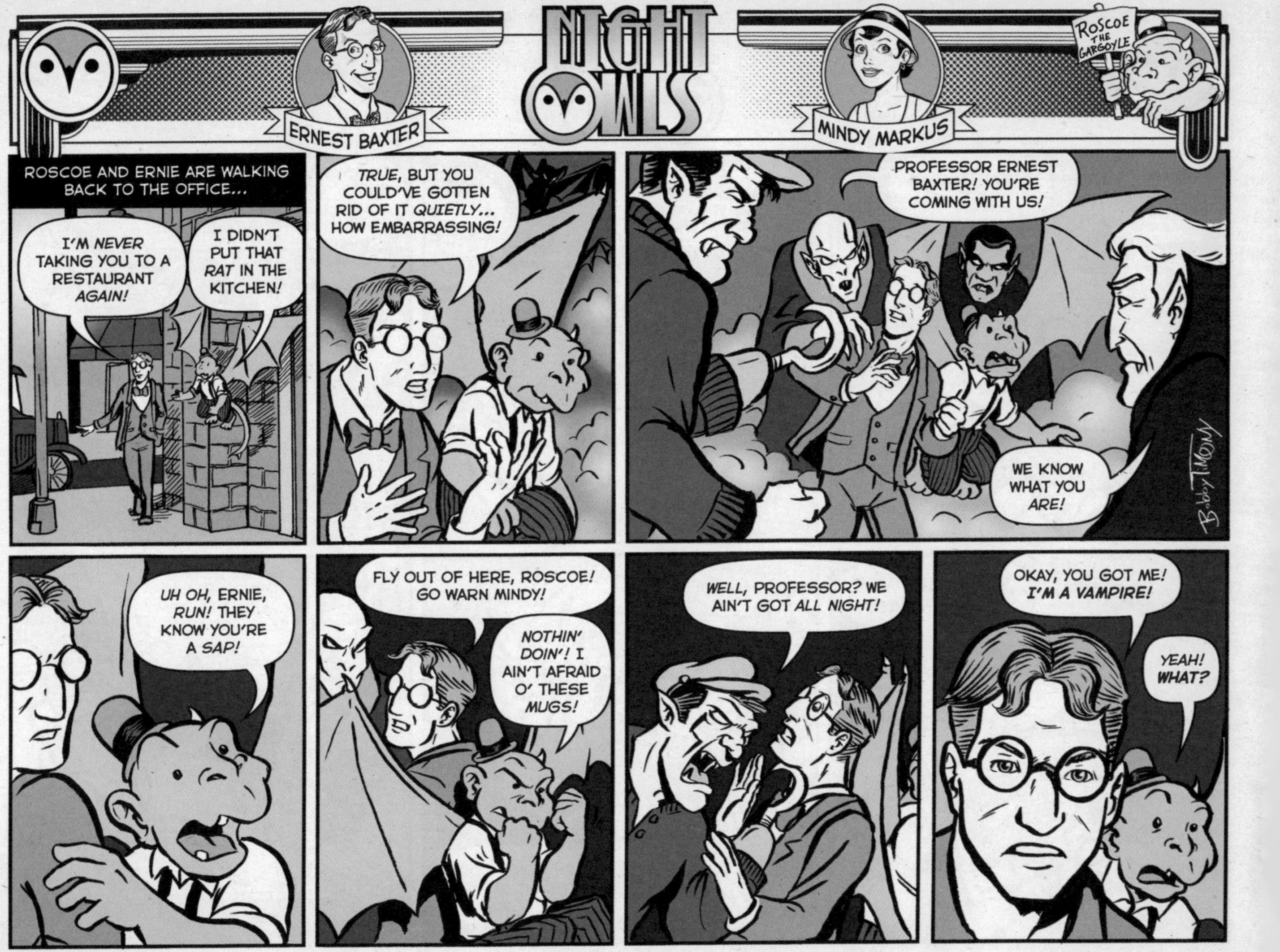
ERNEST BAXTER
NIGHT OWLS
MINDY MARKUS
ROSCOE THE GARGOYLE
ROSCOE AND ERNIE ARE WALKING BACK TO THE OFFICE...
I'M NEVER TAKING YOU TO A RESTAURANT AGAIN!
I DIDN'T PUT THAT RAT IN THE KITCHEN!
TRUE, BUT YOU COULD'VE GOTTEN RID OF IT QUIETLY... HOW EMBARRASSING!
PROFESSOR ERNEST BAXTER! YOU'RE COMING WITH US!
WE KNOW WHAT YOU ARE!
Bobby Timony
UH OH, ERNIE, RUN! THEY KNOW YOU'RE A SAP!
FLY OUT OF HERE, ROSCOE! GO WARN MINDY!
NOTHIN' DOIN'! I AIN'T AFRAID O' THESE MUGS!
WELL, PROFESSOR? WE AIN'T GOT ALL NIGHT!
OKAY, YOU GOT ME! I'M A VAMPIRE!
YEAH! WHAT?

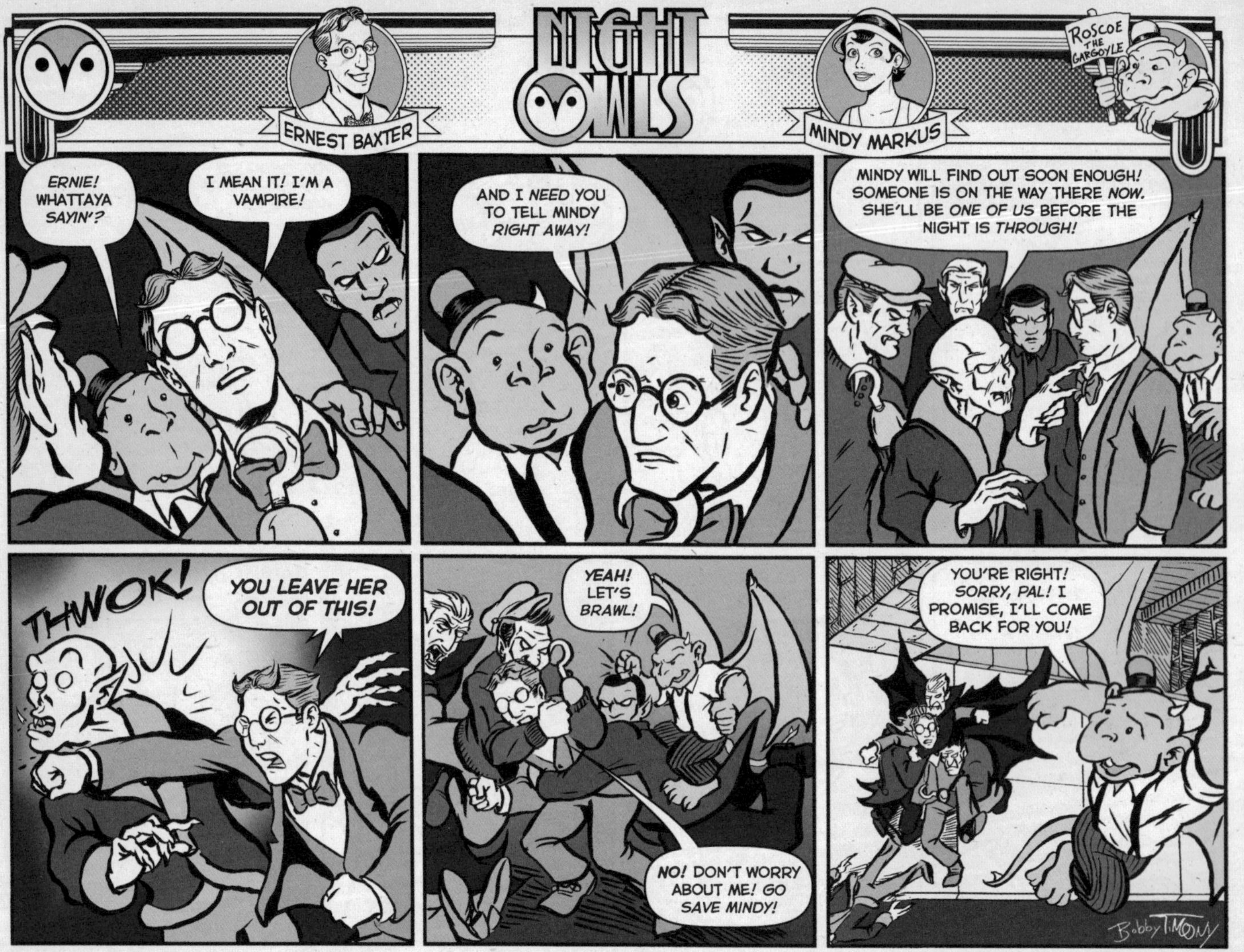
NIGHT OWLS
ERNEST BAXTER
MINDY MARKUS
ROSCOE THE GARGOYLE
ERNIE! WHATTAYA SAYIN'?
I MEAN IT! I'M A VAMPIRE!
AND I NEED YOU TO TELL MINDY RIGHT AWAY!
MINDY WILL FIND OUT SOON ENOUGH! SOMEONE IS ON THE WAY THERE NOW. SHE'LL BE ONE OF US BEFORE THE NIGHT IS THROUGH!
THWOK!
YOU LEAVE HER OUT OF THIS!
YEAH! LET'S BRAWL!
NO! DON'T WORRY ABOUT ME! GO SAVE MINDY!
YOU'RE RIGHT! SORRY, PAL! I PROMISE, I'LL COME BACK FOR YOU!
Bobby Timony

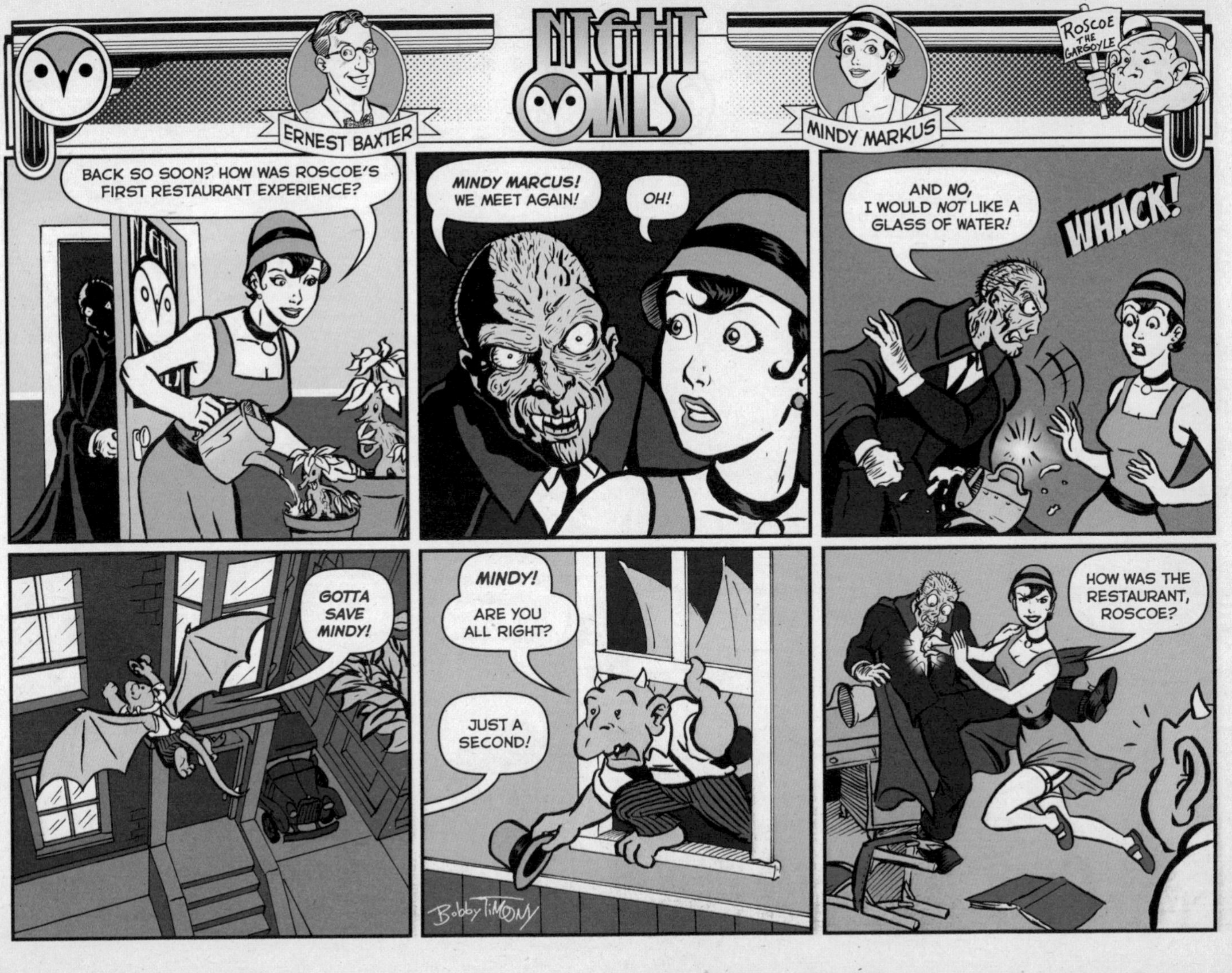
NIGHT OWLS
ERNEST BAXTER
MINDY MARKUS
ROSCOE THE GARGOYLE
BACK SO SOON? HOW WAS ROSCOE'S FIRST RESTAURANT EXPERIENCE?
MINDY MARCUS! WE MEET AGAIN!
OH!
AND NO, I WOULD NOT LIKE A GLASS OF WATER!
WHACK!
GOTTA SAVE MINDY!
MINDY!
ARE YOU ALL RIGHT?
JUST A SECOND!
HOW WAS THE RESTAURANT, ROSCOE?
Bobby Timony

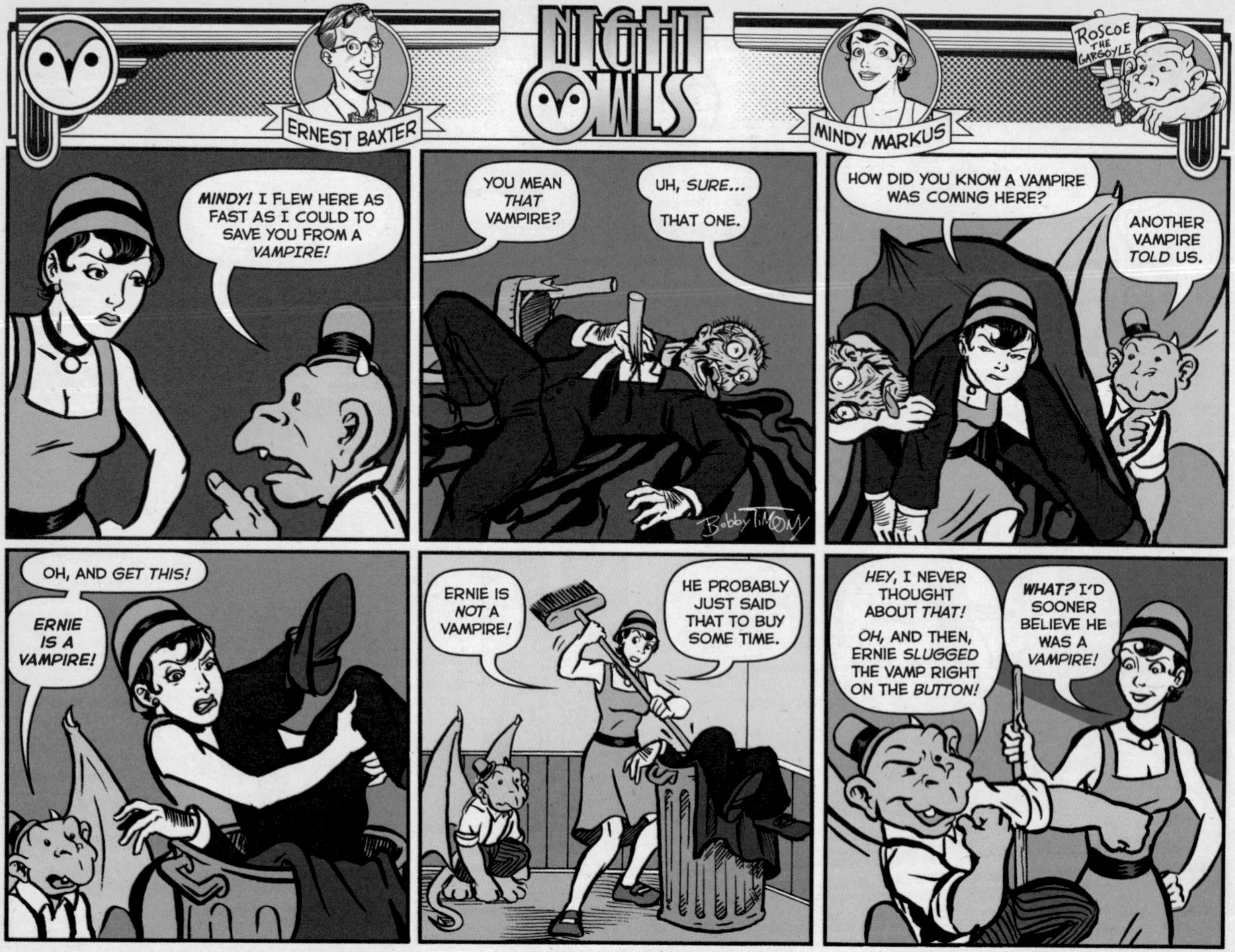
NIGHT OWLS
ERNEST BAXTER
MINDY MARKUS
ROSCOE THE GARGOYLE
MINDY! I FLEW HERE AS FAST AS I COULD TO SAVE YOU FROM A VAMPIRE!
YOU MEAN THAT VAMPIRE?
UH, SURE... THAT ONE.
HOW DID YOU KNOW A VAMPIRE WAS COMING HERE?
ANOTHER VAMPIRE TOLD US.
OH, AND GET THIS!
ERNIE IS A VAMPIRE!
ERNIE IS NOT A VAMPIRE!
HE PROBABLY JUST SAID THAT TO BUY SOME TIME.
HEY, I NEVER THOUGHT ABOUT THAT! OH, AND THEN, ERNIE SLUGGED THE VAMP RIGHT ON THE BUTTON!
WHAT? I'D SOONER BELIEVE HE WAS A VAMPIRE!

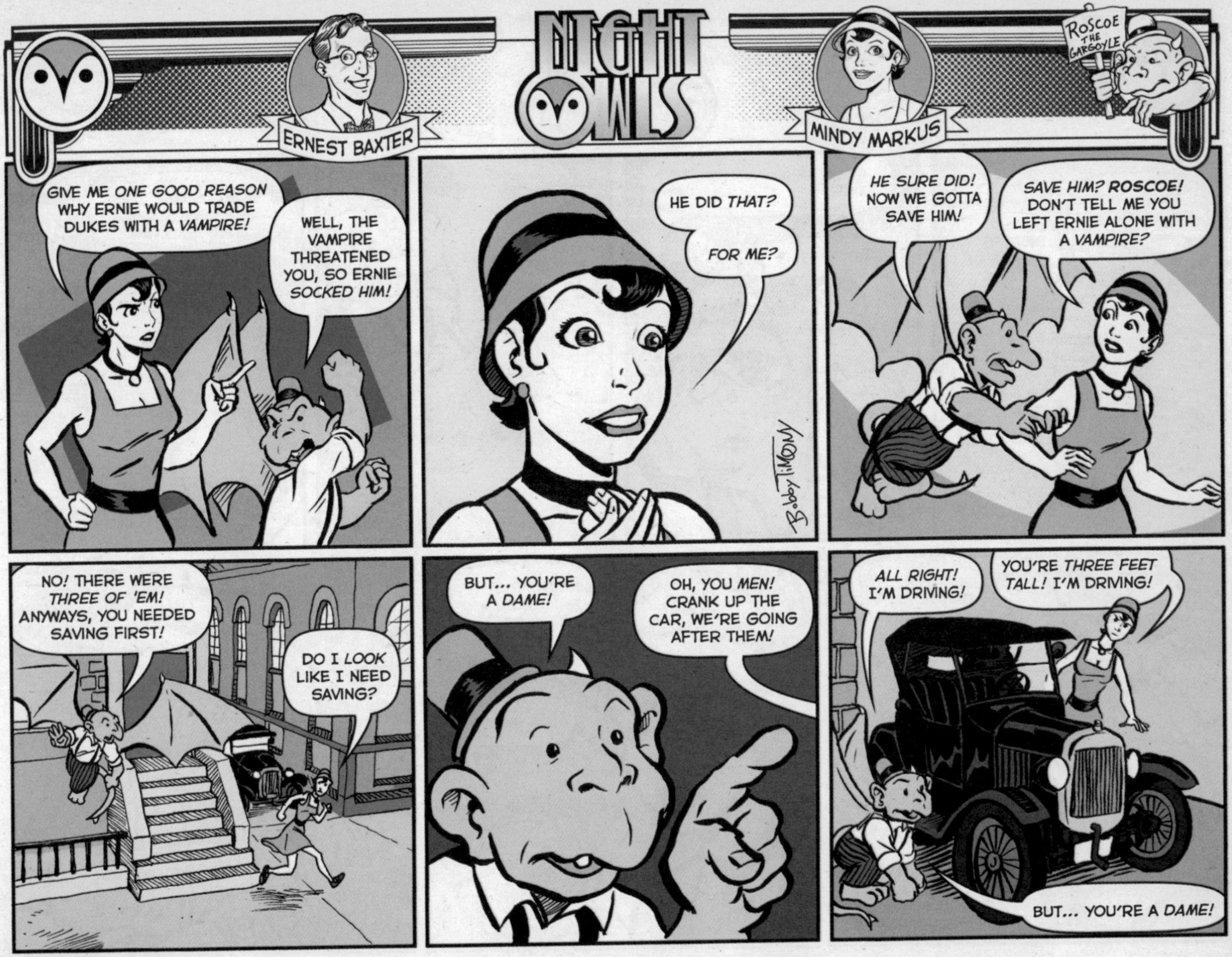
NIGHT OWLS
ERNEST BAXTER
MINDY MARKUS
ROSCOE THE GARGOYLE
GIVE ME *ONE GOOD REASON* WHY ERNIE WOULD TRADE DUKES WITH A *VAMPIRE!*
WELL, THE VAMPIRE THREATENED YOU, SO ERNIE *SOCKED HIM!*
HE DID *THAT?*
FOR ME?
Bobby Timony
HE SURE DID! NOW WE GOTTA SAVE HIM!
SAVE HIM? **ROSCOE!** DON'T TELL ME YOU LEFT ERNIE ALONE WITH A *VAMPIRE?*
NO! THERE WERE *THREE OF 'EM!* ANYWAYS, YOU NEEDED SAVING FIRST!
DO I *LOOK* LIKE I NEED SAVING?
BUT... YOU'RE A *DAME!*
OH, YOU *MEN!* CRANK UP THE CAR, WE'RE GOING AFTER THEM!
ALL RIGHT! I'M DRIVING!
YOU'RE *THREE FEET TALL!* I'M DRIVING!
BUT... YOU'RE A *DAME!*

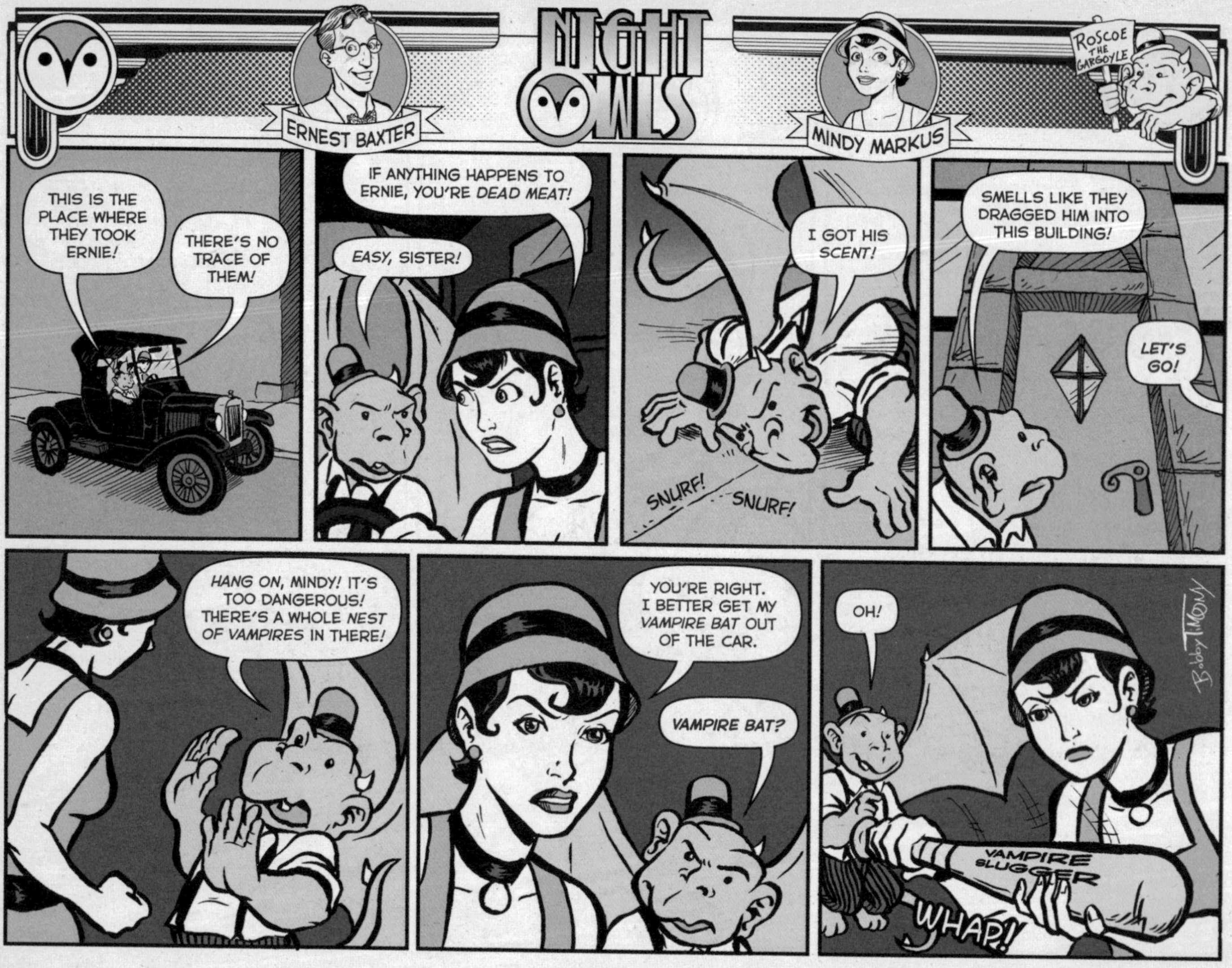
NIGHT OWLS
ERNEST BAXTER
MINDY MARKUS
ROSCOE THE GARGOYLE
THIS IS THE PLACE WHERE THEY TOOK ERNIE!
THERE'S NO TRACE OF THEM!
IF ANYTHING HAPPENS TO ERNIE, YOU'RE *DEAD MEAT!*
EASY, SISTER!
I GOT HIS SCENT!
SNURF! SNURF!
SMELLS LIKE THEY DRAGGED HIM INTO THIS BUILDING!
LET'S GO!
HANG ON, MINDY! IT'S TOO DANGEROUS! THERE'S A WHOLE *NEST OF VAMPIRES* IN THERE!
YOU'RE RIGHT. I BETTER GET MY *VAMPIRE BAT* OUT OF THE CAR.
VAMPIRE BAT?
OH!
VAMPIRE SLUGGER
WHAP!
Bobby Timony

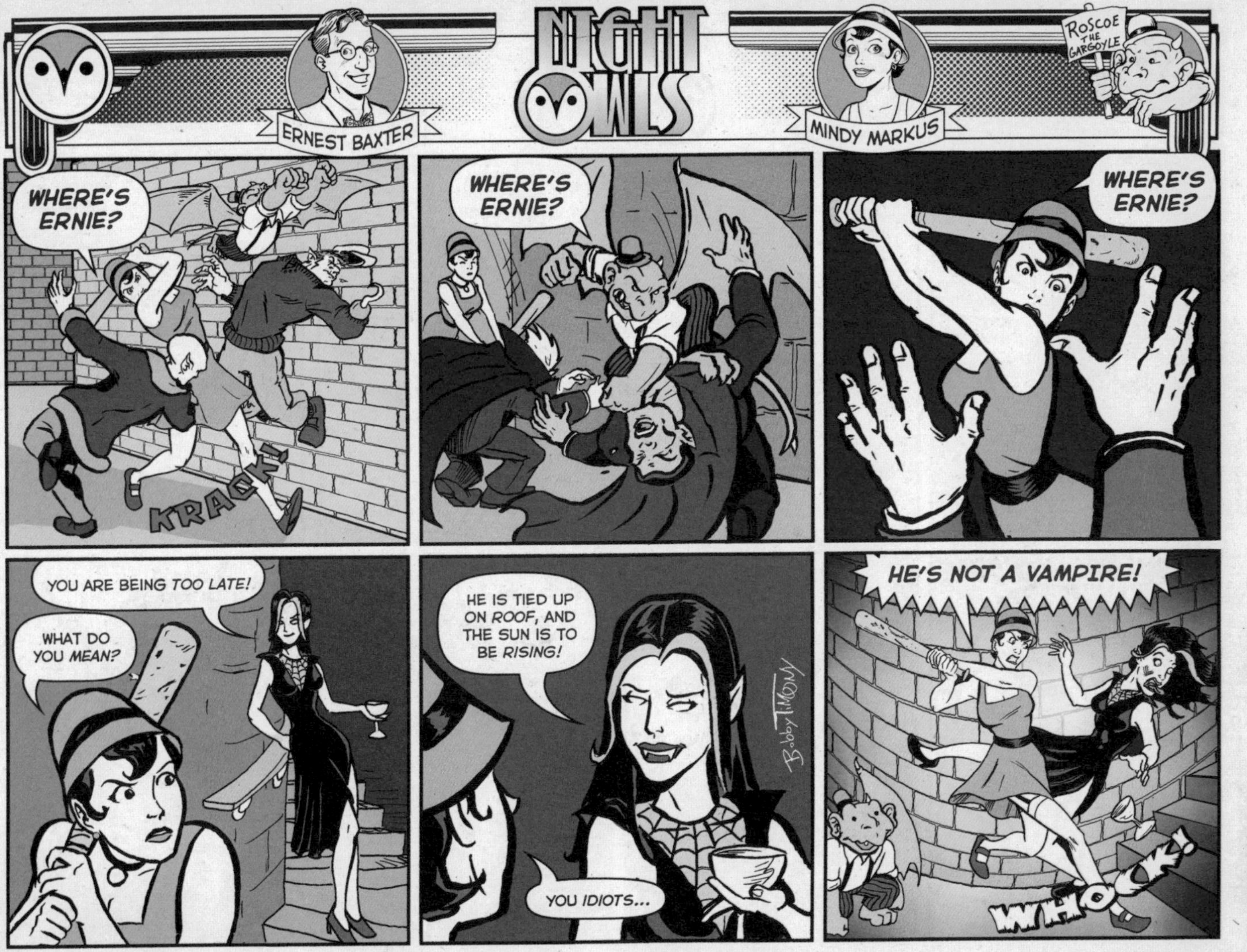
NIGHT OWLS
ERNEST BAXTER
MINDY MARKUS
ROSCOE THE GARGOYLE
WHERE'S ERNIE?
KRACK
WHERE'S ERNIE?
WHERE'S ERNIE?
YOU ARE BEING TOO LATE!
WHAT DO YOU MEAN?
HE IS TIED UP ON ROOF, AND THE SUN IS TO BE RISING!
YOU IDIOTS...
Bobby Timony
HE'S NOT A VAMPIRE!
WHOCK!

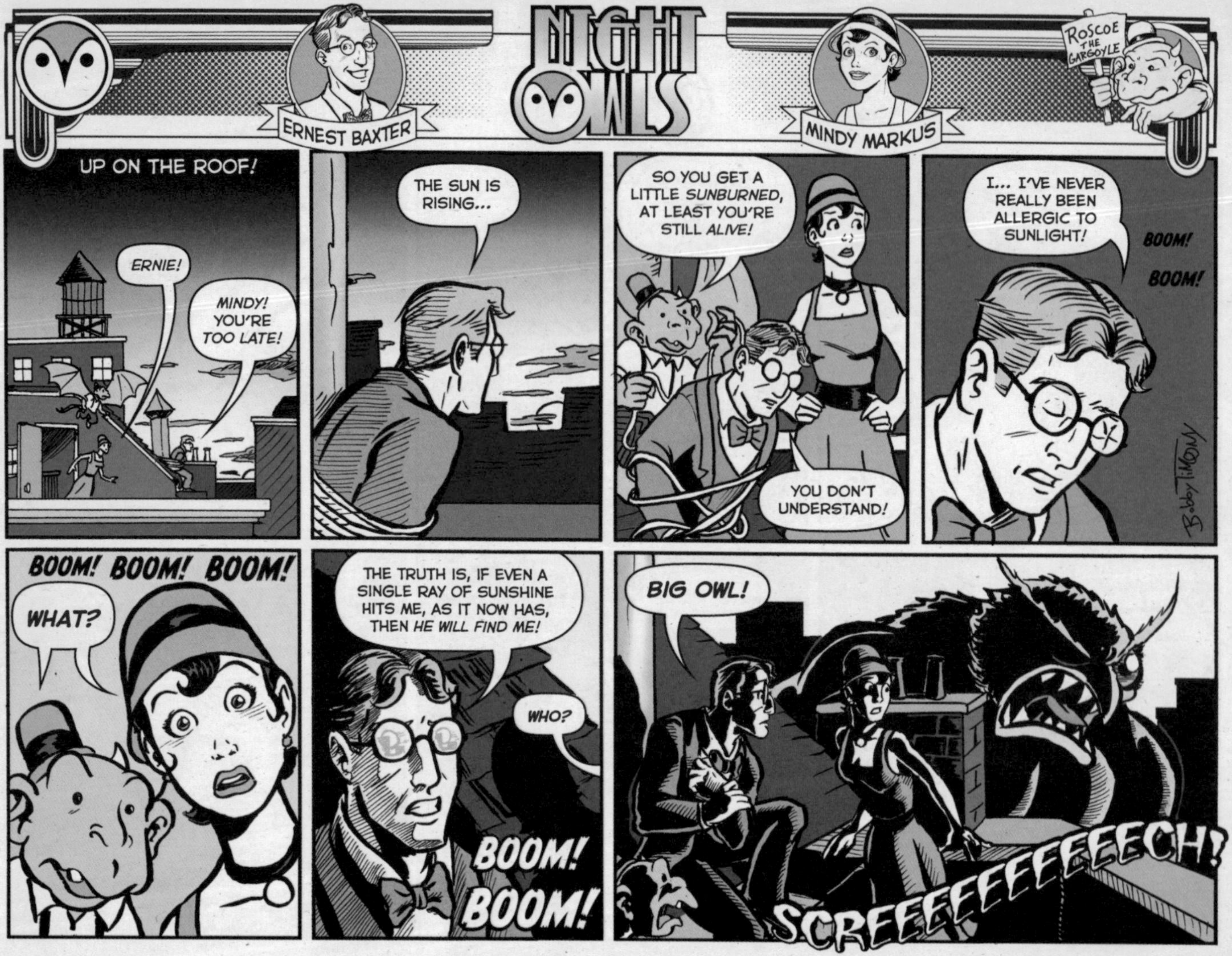

ERNEST BAXTER
NIGHT OWLS
MINDY MARKUS
ROSCOE THE GARGOYLE
UP ON THE ROOF!
ERNIE!
MINDY! YOU'RE TOO LATE!
THE SUN IS RISING...
SO YOU GET A LITTLE SUNBURNED, AT LEAST YOU'RE STILL ALIVE!
YOU DON'T UNDERSTAND!
I... I'VE NEVER REALLY BEEN ALLERGIC TO SUNLIGHT!
BOOM!
BOOM!
BOOM! BOOM! BOOM!
WHAT?
THE TRUTH IS, IF EVEN A SINGLE RAY OF SUNSHINE HITS ME, AS IT NOW HAS, THEN HE WILL FIND ME!
WHO?
BOOM!
BOOM!
BIG OWL!
SCREEEEEEEEEEEEECH!

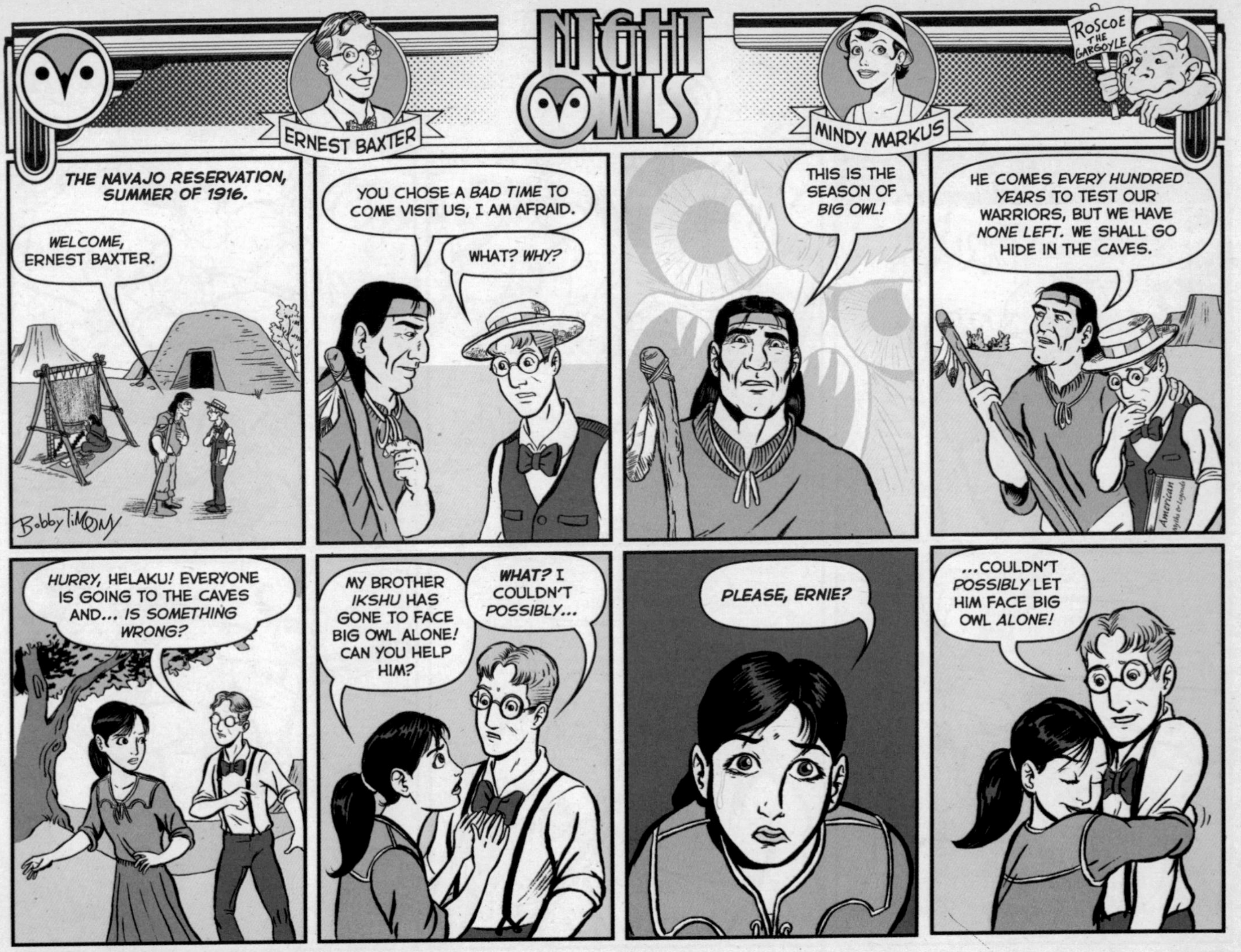
NIGHT OWLS
ERNEST BAXTER
MINDY MARKUS
ROSCOE THE GARGOYLE
THE NAVAJO RESERVATION, SUMMER OF 1916.
WELCOME, ERNEST BAXTER.
Bobby Timony
YOU CHOSE A BAD TIME TO COME VISIT US, I AM AFRAID.
WHAT? WHY?
THIS IS THE SEASON OF BIG OWL!
HE COMES EVERY HUNDRED YEARS TO TEST OUR WARRIORS, BUT WE HAVE NONE LEFT. WE SHALL GO HIDE IN THE CAVES.
American Myths & Legends
HURRY, HELAKU! EVERYONE IS GOING TO THE CAVES AND... IS SOMETHING WRONG?
MY BROTHER IKSHU HAS GONE TO FACE BIG OWL ALONE! CAN YOU HELP HIM?
WHAT? I COULDN'T POSSIBLY...
PLEASE, ERNIE?
...COULDN'T POSSIBLY LET HIM FACE BIG OWL ALONE!

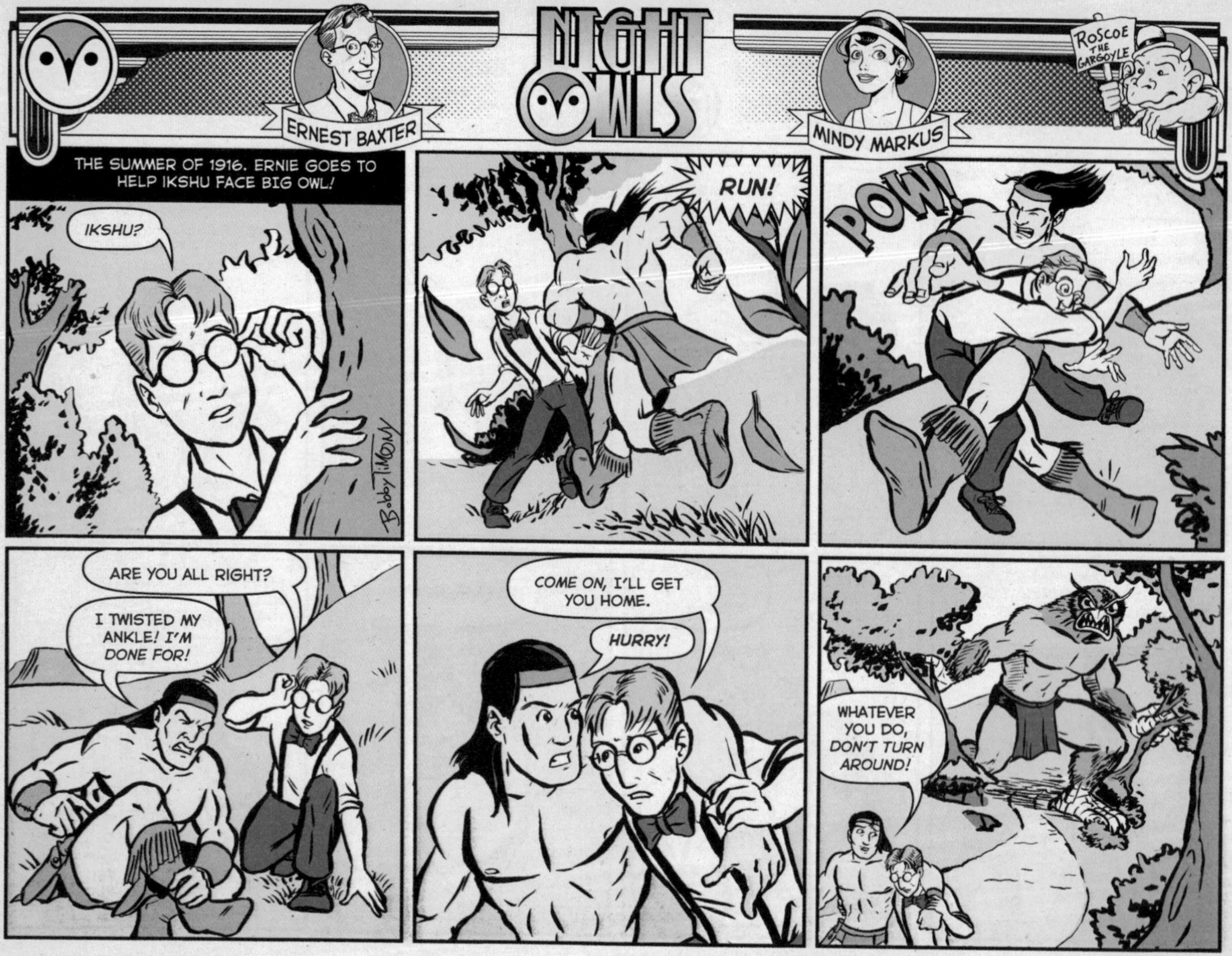
NIGHT OWLS
ERNEST BAXTER
MINDY MARKUS
ROSCOE THE GARGOYLE
THE SUMMER OF 1916. ERNIE GOES TO HELP IKSHU FACE BIG OWL!
IKSHU?
Bobby Timony
RUN!
POW!
ARE YOU ALL RIGHT?
I TWISTED MY ANKLE! I'M DONE FOR!
COME ON, I'LL GET YOU HOME.
HURRY!
WHATEVER YOU DO, DON'T TURN AROUND!

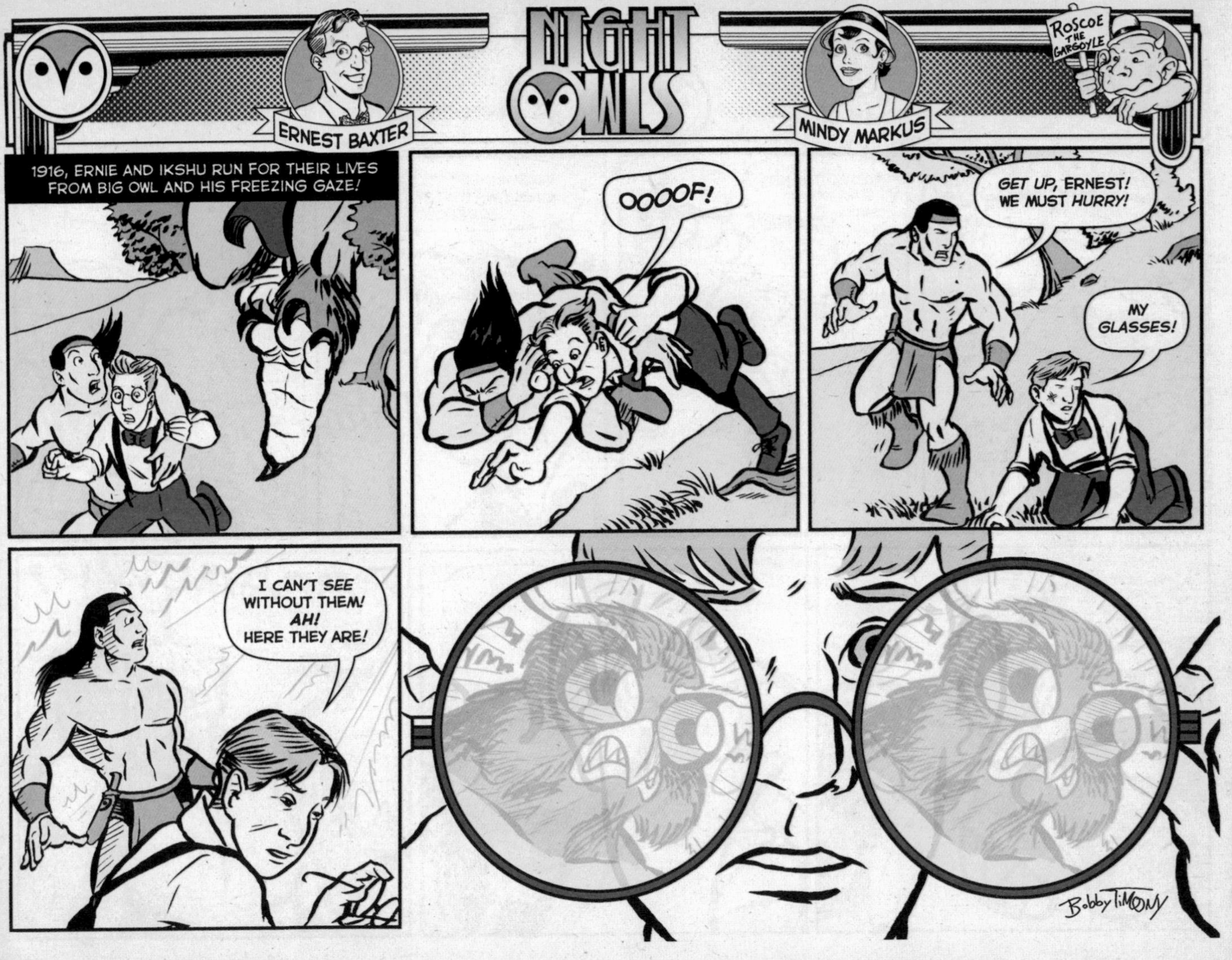
NIGHT OWLS
ERNEST BAXTER
MINDY MARKUS
ROSCOE THE GARGOYLE
1916, ERNIE AND IKSHU RUN FOR THEIR LIVES FROM BIG OWL AND HIS FREEZING GAZE!
OOOOF!
GET UP, ERNEST! WE MUST HURRY!
MY GLASSES!
I CAN'T SEE WITHOUT THEM! AH! HERE THEY ARE!
Bobby Timony

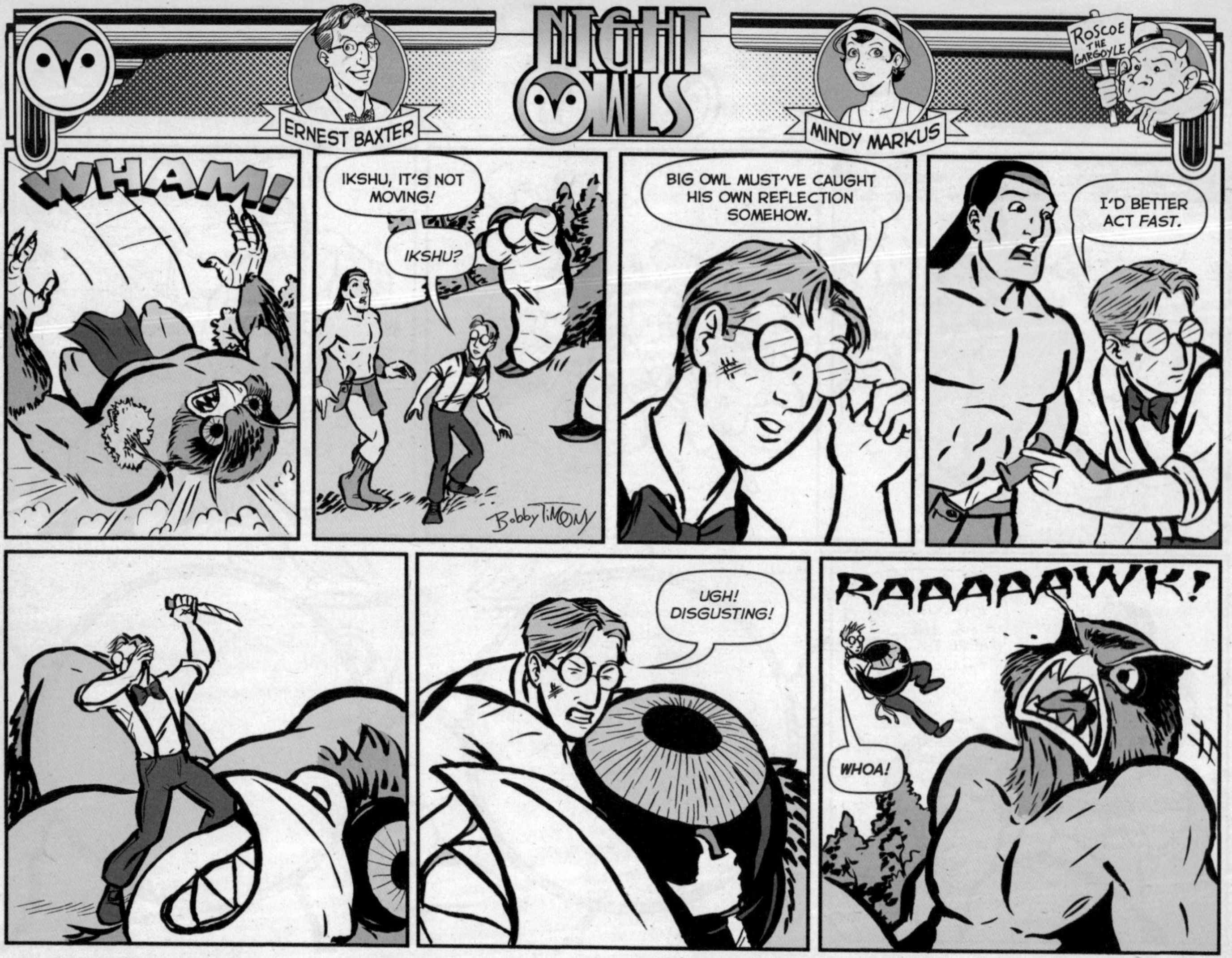
NIGHT OWLS
ERNEST BAXTER
MINDY MARKUS
ROSCOE THE GARGOYLE
WHAM!
IKSHU, IT'S NOT MOVING!
IKSHU?
Bobby Timony
BIG OWL MUST'VE CAUGHT HIS OWN REFLECTION SOMEHOW.
I'D BETTER ACT FAST.
UGH! DISGUSTING!
RAAAAAWK!
WHOA!

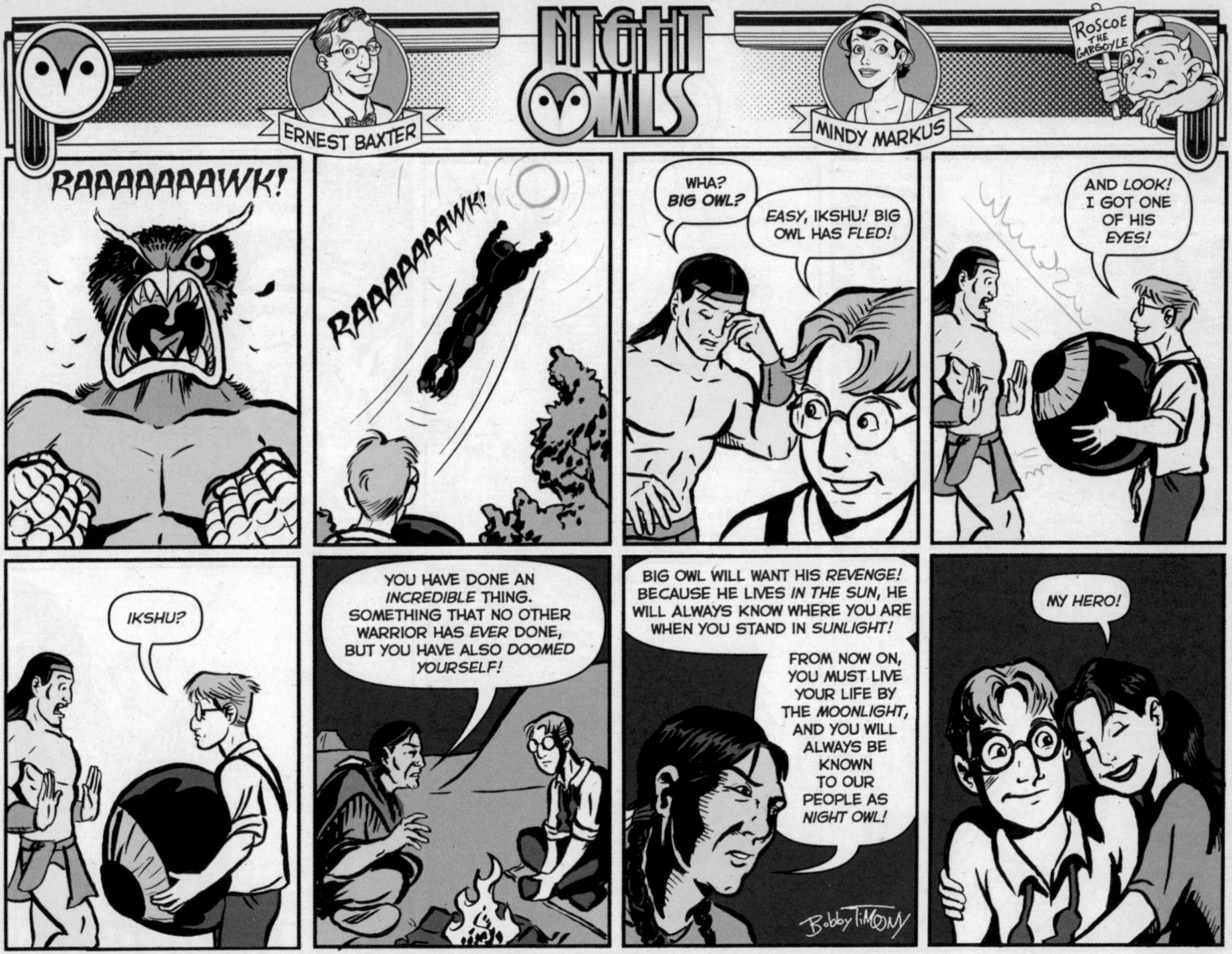
NIGHT OWLS
ERNEST BAXTER
MINDY MARKUS
ROSCOE THE GARGOYLE
RAAAAAAAAWK!
RAAAAAAAAWK!
WHA? BIG OWL?
EASY, IKSHU! BIG OWL HAS FLED!
AND LOOK! I GOT ONE OF HIS EYES!
IKSHU?
YOU HAVE DONE AN INCREDIBLE THING. SOMETHING THAT NO OTHER WARRIOR HAS EVER DONE, BUT YOU HAVE ALSO DOOMED YOURSELF!
BIG OWL WILL WANT HIS REVENGE! BECAUSE HE LIVES IN THE SUN, HE WILL ALWAYS KNOW WHERE YOU ARE WHEN YOU STAND IN SUNLIGHT!
FROM NOW ON, YOU MUST LIVE YOUR LIFE BY THE MOONLIGHT, AND YOU WILL ALWAYS BE KNOWN TO OUR PEOPLE AS NIGHT OWL!
MY HERO!
Bobby Timony

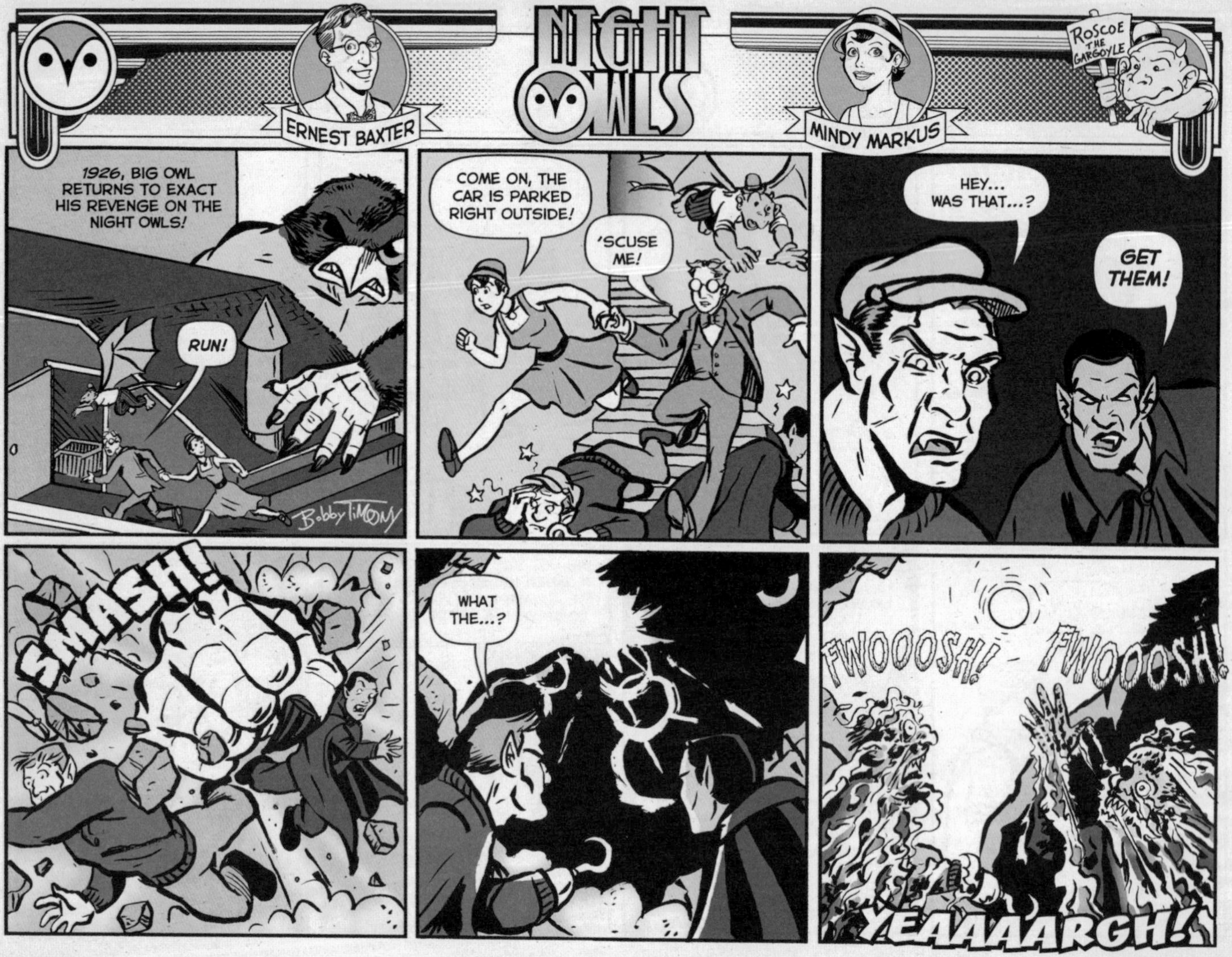
NIGHT OWLS
ERNEST BAXTER
MINDY MARKUS
ROSCOE THE GARGOYLE
1926, BIG OWL RETURNS TO EXACT HIS REVENGE ON THE NIGHT OWLS!
RUN!
Bobby Timony
COME ON, THE CAR IS PARKED RIGHT OUTSIDE!
'SCUSE ME!
HEY... WAS THAT...?
GET THEM!
SMASH!
WHAT THE...?
FWOOOSH!
FWOOOSH!
YEAAAAARGH!

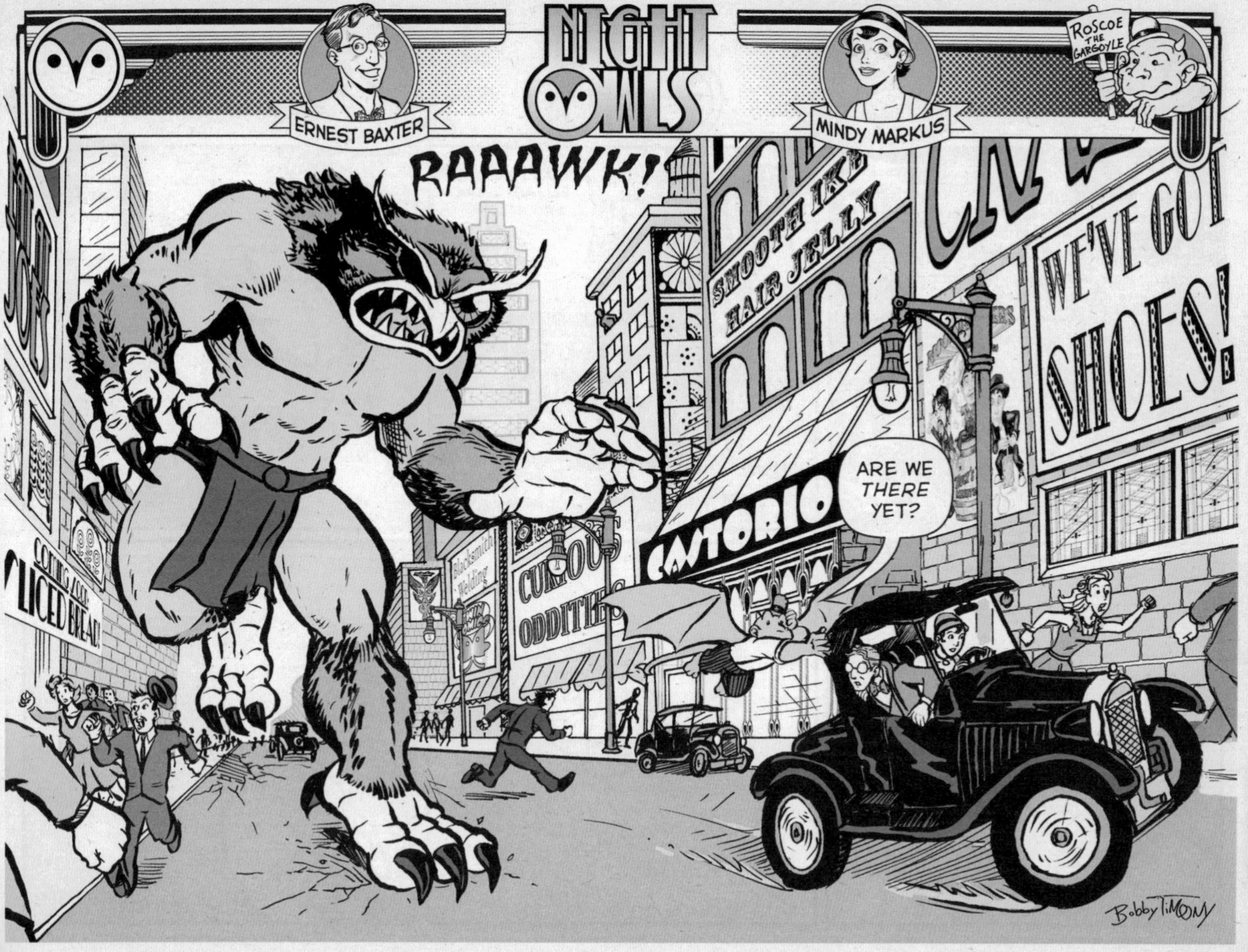

NIGHT OWLS
ERNEST BAXTER
MINDY MARKUS
ROSCOE THE GARGOYLE
RAAAWK!
SMOOTH IKE HAIR JELLY
WE'VE GOT SHOES!
ARE WE THERE YET?
CASTORIO
ODDITIES
Blacksmith Welding
Bobby Timony

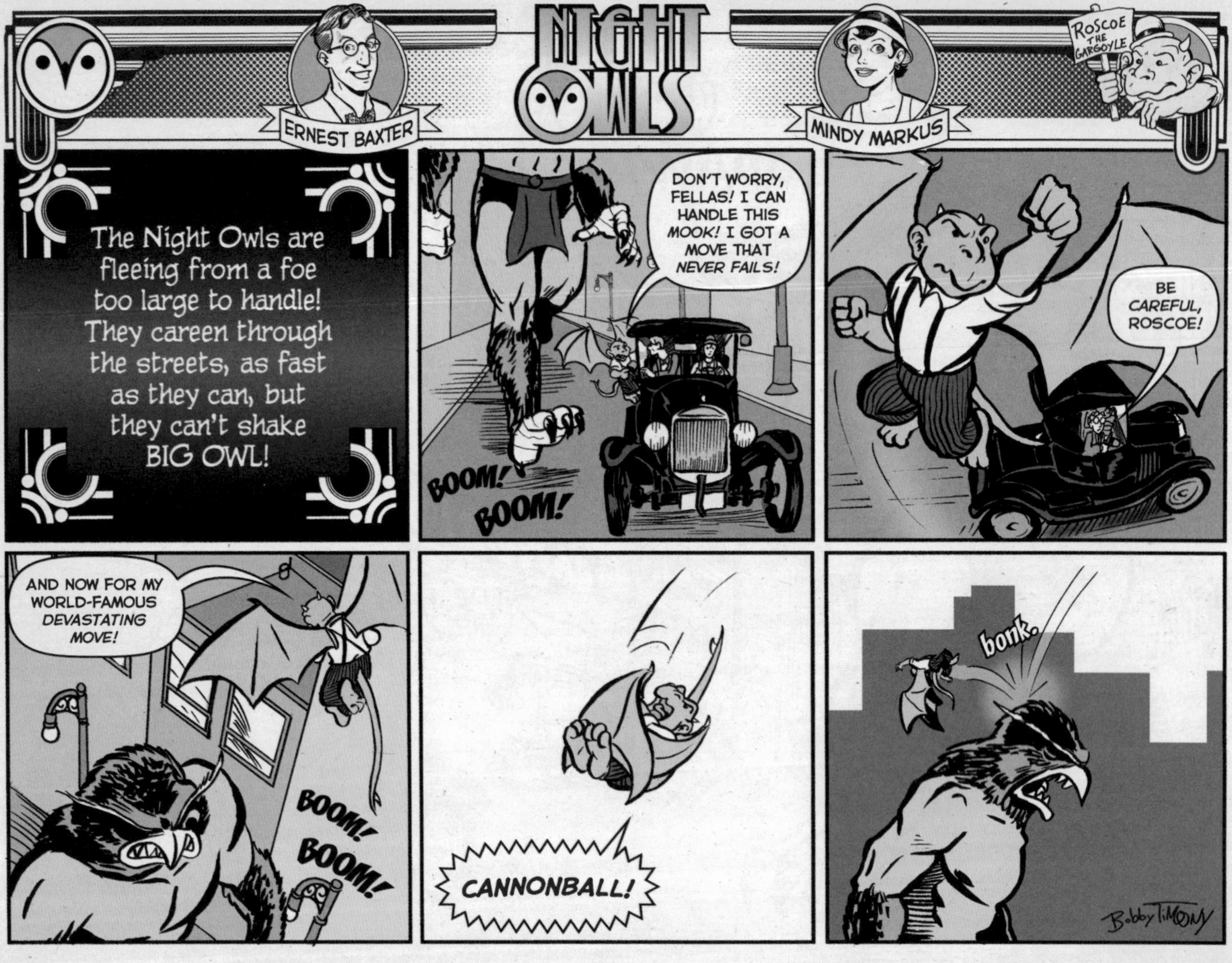
NIGHT OWLS
ERNEST BAXTER
MINDY MARKUS
ROSCOE THE GARGOYLE
The Night Owls are fleeing from a foe too large to handle! They careen through the streets, as fast as they can, but they can't shake BIG OWL!
DON'T WORRY, FELLAS! I CAN HANDLE THIS MOOK! I GOT A MOVE THAT NEVER FAILS!
BOOM! BOOM!
BE CAREFUL, ROSCOE!
AND NOW FOR MY WORLD-FAMOUS DEVASTATING MOVE!
BOOM! BOOM!
CANNONBALL!
bonk.
Bobby Timony

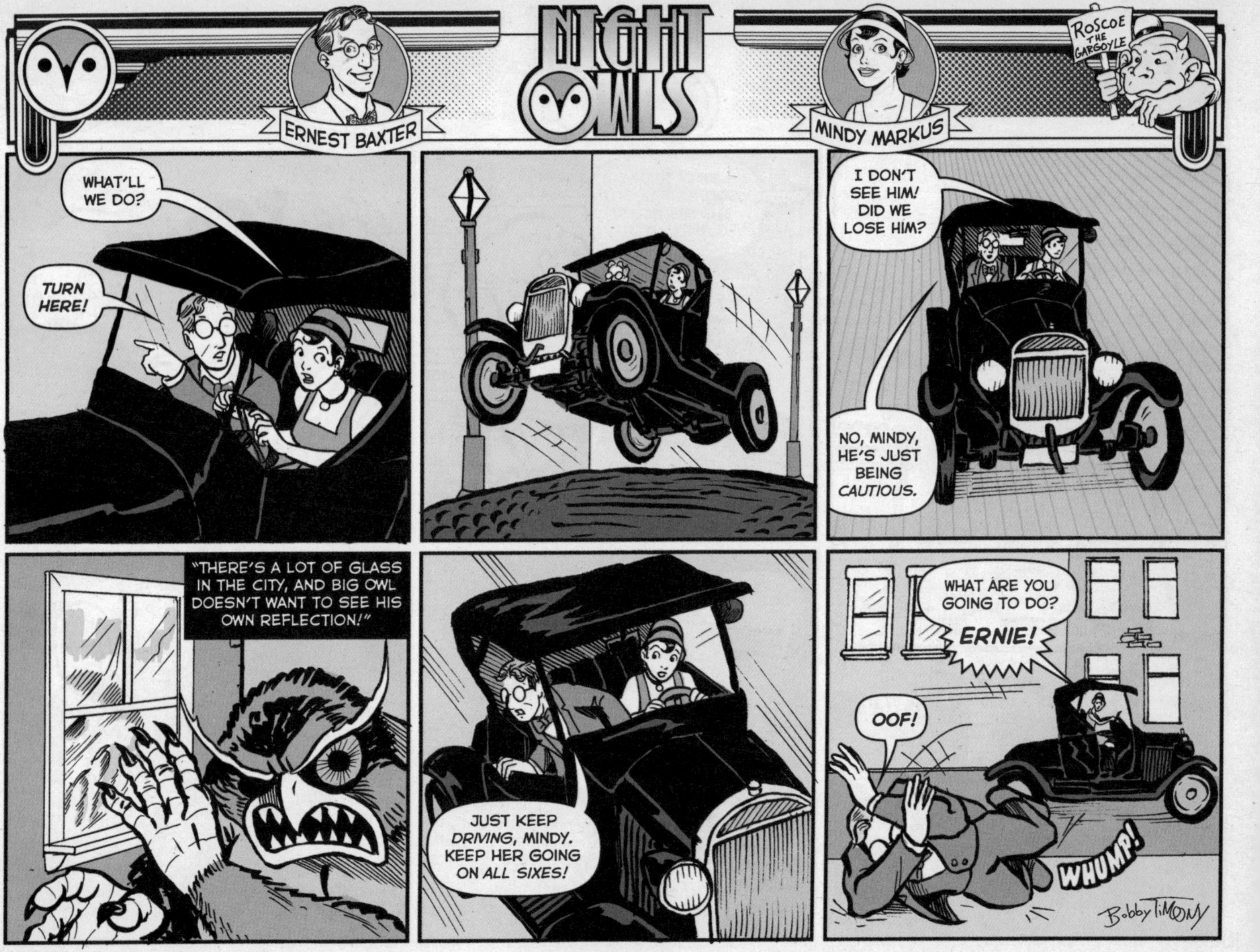
NIGHT OWLS
ERNEST BAXTER
MINDY MARKUS
ROSCOE THE GARGOYLE
WHAT'LL WE DO?
TURN HERE!
I DON'T SEE HIM! DID WE LOSE HIM?
NO, MINDY, HE'S JUST BEING CAUTIOUS.
"THERE'S A LOT OF GLASS IN THE CITY, AND BIG OWL DOESN'T WANT TO SEE HIS OWN REFLECTION!"
JUST KEEP DRIVING, MINDY. KEEP HER GOING ON ALL SIXES!
WHAT ARE YOU GOING TO DO?
ERNIE!
OOF!
WHUMP!
Bobby Timony

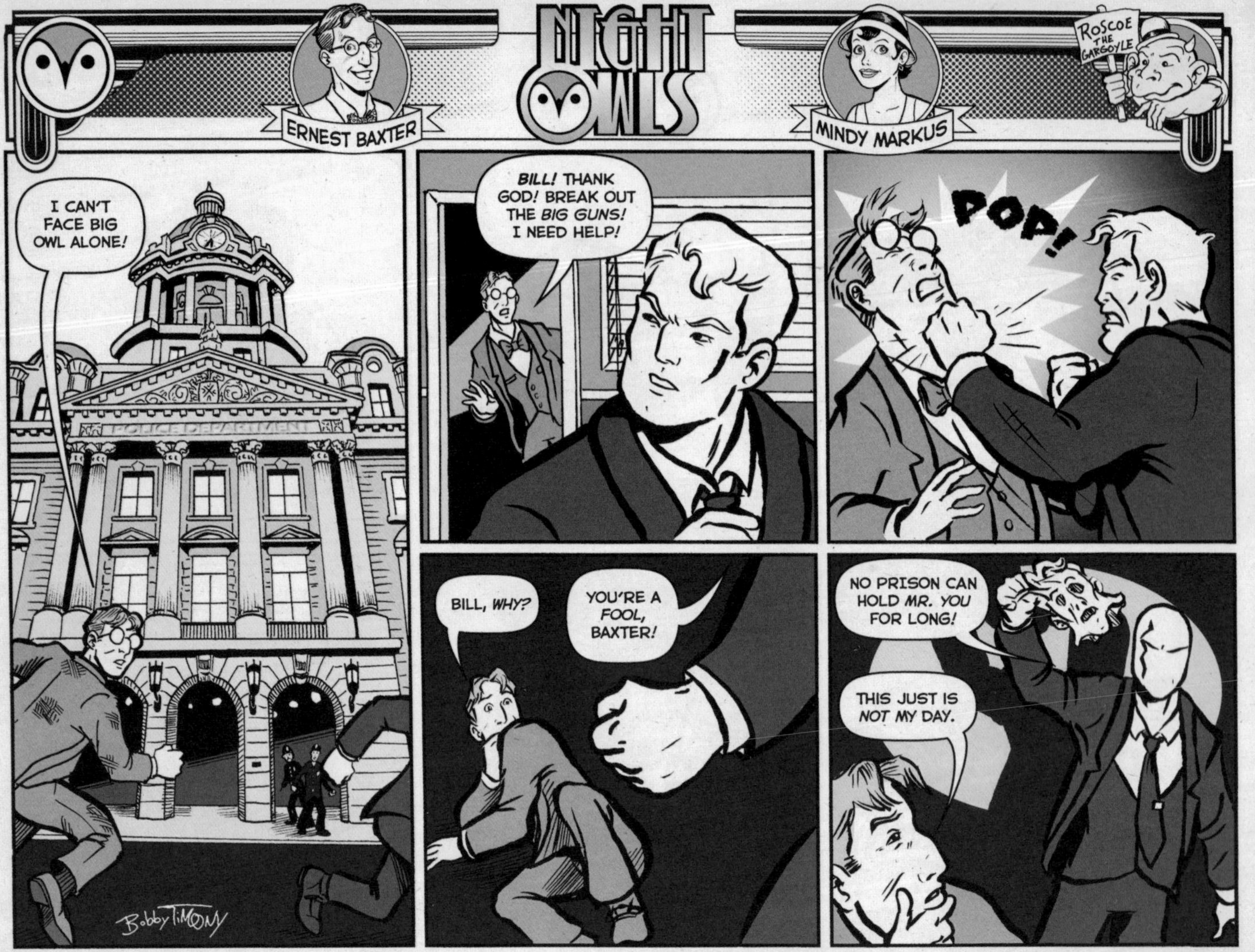
NIGHT OWLS
ERNEST BAXTER
MINDY MARKUS
ROSCOE THE GARGOYLE
POLICE DEPARTMENT
I CAN'T FACE BIG OWL ALONE!
BILL! THANK GOD! BREAK OUT THE BIG GUNS! I NEED HELP!
POP!
BILL, WHY?
YOU'RE A FOOL, BAXTER!
NO PRISON CAN HOLD MR. YOU FOR LONG!
THIS JUST IS NOT MY DAY.
Bobby Timony

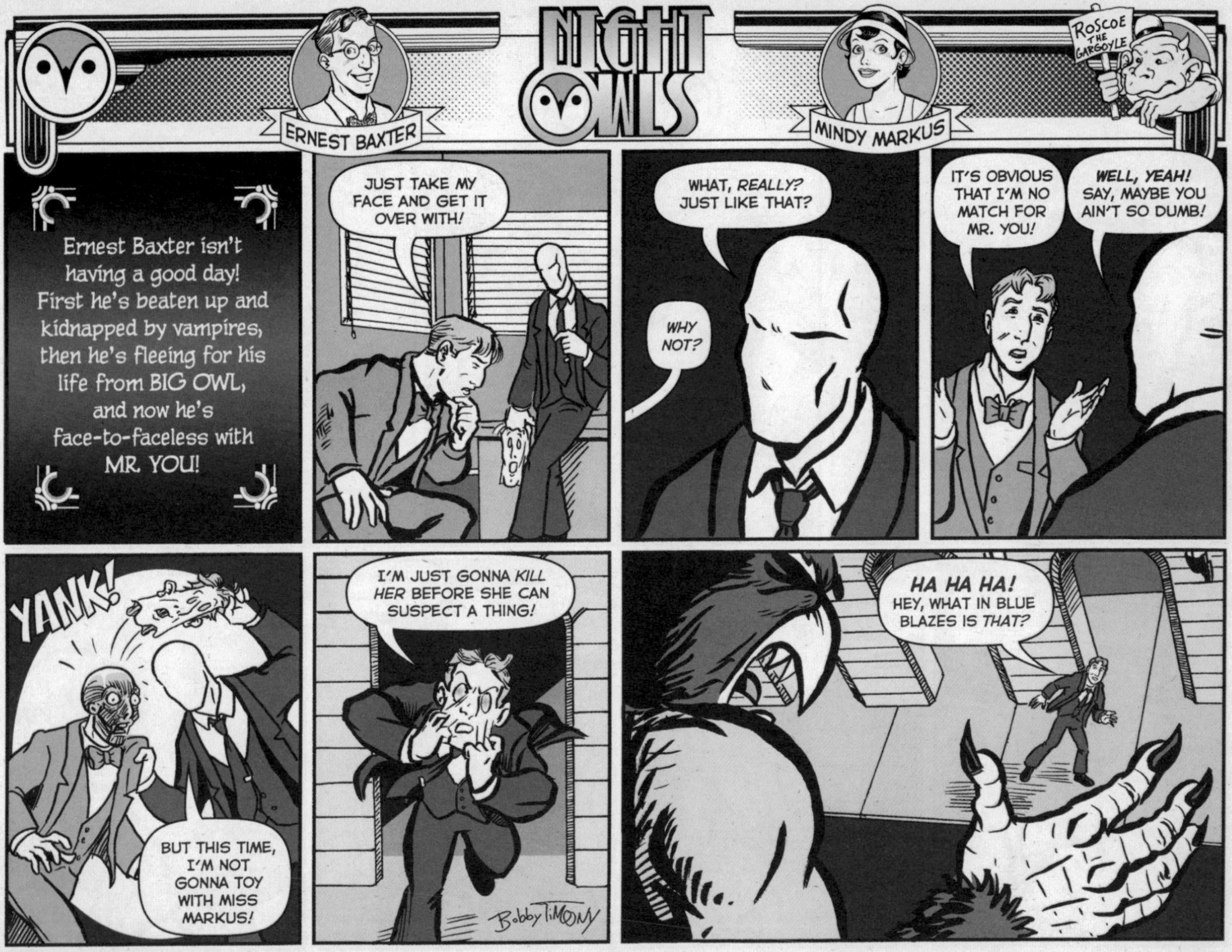

NIGHT OWLS
ERNEST BAXTER
MINDY MARKUS
ROSCOE THE GARGOYLE
Ernest Baxter isn't having a good day! First he's beaten up and kidnapped by vampires, then he's fleeing for his life from BIG OWL, and now he's face-to-faceless with MR. YOU!
JUST TAKE MY FACE AND GET IT OVER WITH!
WHAT, *REALLY?* JUST LIKE THAT?
WHY NOT?
IT'S OBVIOUS THAT I'M NO MATCH FOR MR. YOU!
WELL, YEAH! SAY, MAYBE YOU AIN'T SO DUMB!
YANK!
BUT THIS TIME, I'M NOT GONNA TOY WITH MISS MARKUS!
I'M JUST GONNA *KILL HER* BEFORE SHE CAN SUSPECT A THING!
Bobby Timony
HA HA HA! HEY, WHAT IN BLUE BLAZES IS *THAT?*

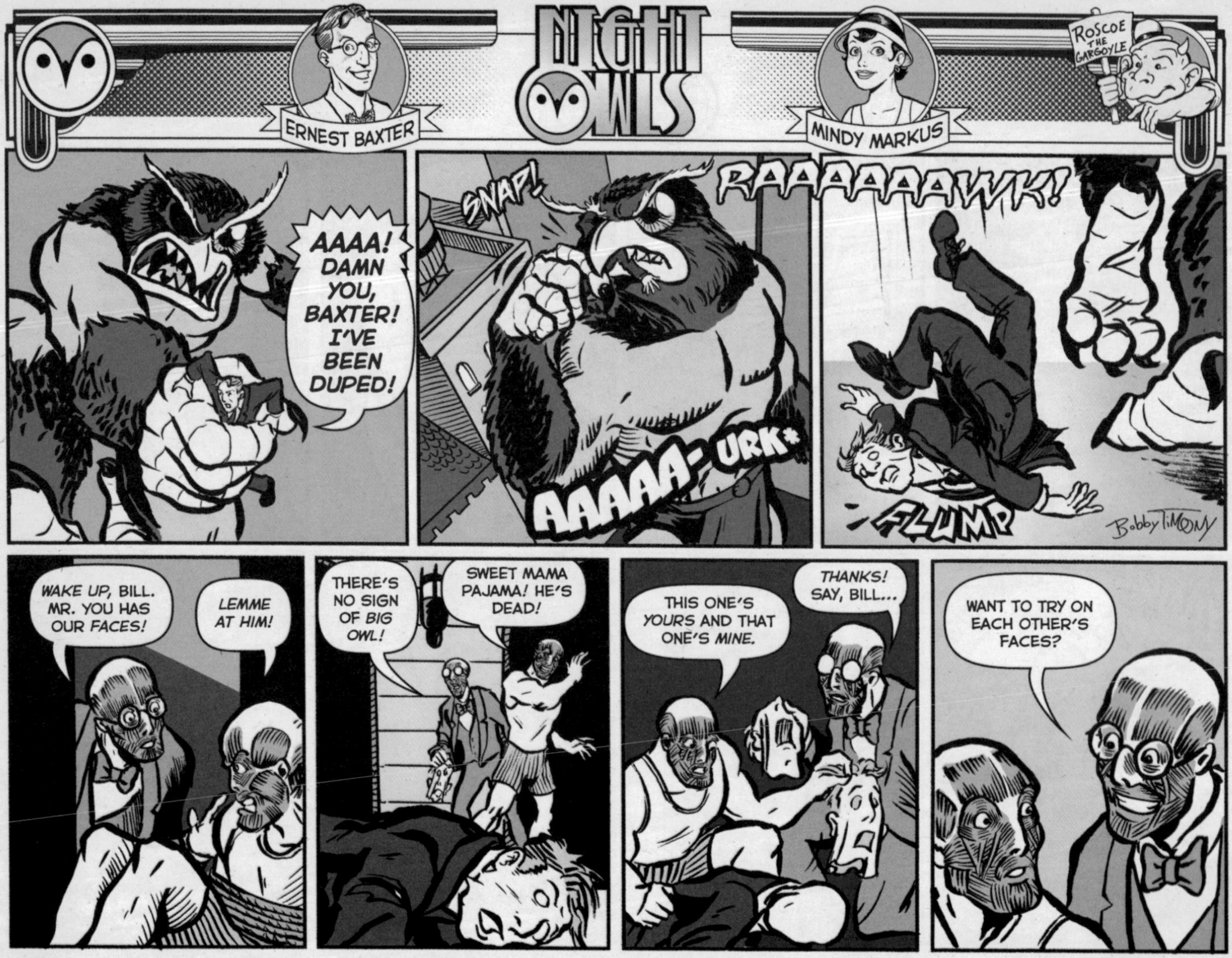
NIGHT OWLS
ERNEST BAXTER
MINDY MARKUS
ROSCOE THE GARGOYLE
AAAA! DAMN YOU, BAXTER! I'VE BEEN DUPED!
SNAP!
AAAAA- URK*
RAAAAAAAWK!
FLUMP
Bobby Timony
WAKE UP, BILL. MR. YOU HAS OUR FACES!
LEMME AT HIM!
THERE'S NO SIGN OF BIG OWL!
SWEET MAMA PAJAMA! HE'S DEAD!
THIS ONE'S YOURS AND THAT ONE'S MINE.
THANKS! SAY, BILL...
WANT TO TRY ON EACH OTHER'S FACES?

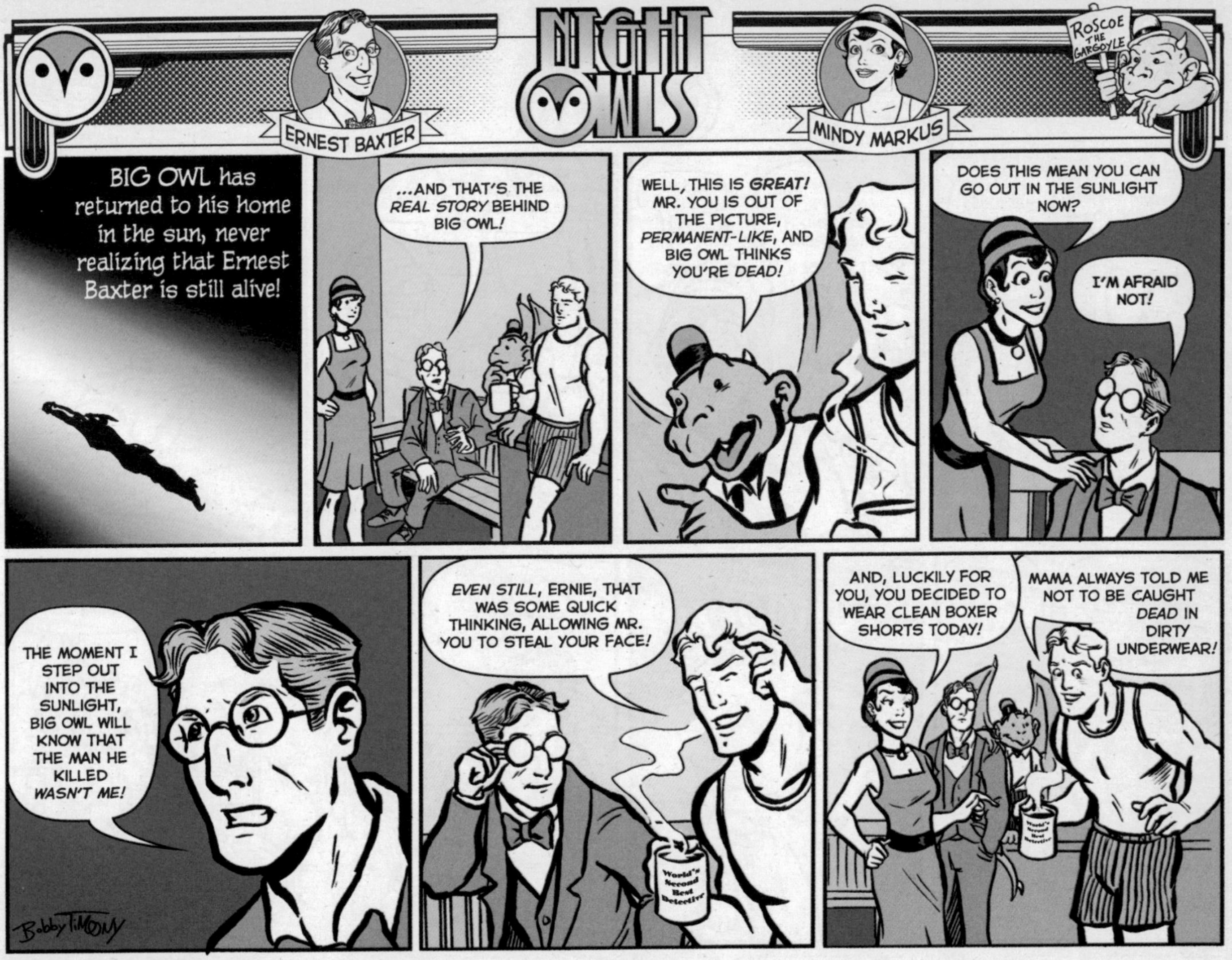
NIGHT OWLS
ERNEST BAXTER
MINDY MARKUS
ROSCOE THE GARGOYLE
BIG OWL has returned to his home in the sun, never realizing that Ernest Baxter is still alive!
...AND THAT'S THE REAL STORY BEHIND BIG OWL!
WELL, THIS IS GREAT! MR. YOU IS OUT OF THE PICTURE, PERMANENT-LIKE, AND BIG OWL THINKS YOU'RE DEAD!
DOES THIS MEAN YOU CAN GO OUT IN THE SUNLIGHT NOW?
I'M AFRAID NOT!
THE MOMENT I STEP OUT INTO THE SUNLIGHT, BIG OWL WILL KNOW THAT THE MAN HE KILLED WASN'T ME!
EVEN STILL, ERNIE, THAT WAS SOME QUICK THINKING, ALLOWING MR. YOU TO STEAL YOUR FACE!
World's Second Best Detective
AND, LUCKILY FOR YOU, YOU DECIDED TO WEAR CLEAN BOXER SHORTS TODAY!
MAMA ALWAYS TOLD ME NOT TO BE CAUGHT DEAD IN DIRTY UNDERWEAR!
Bobby Timony

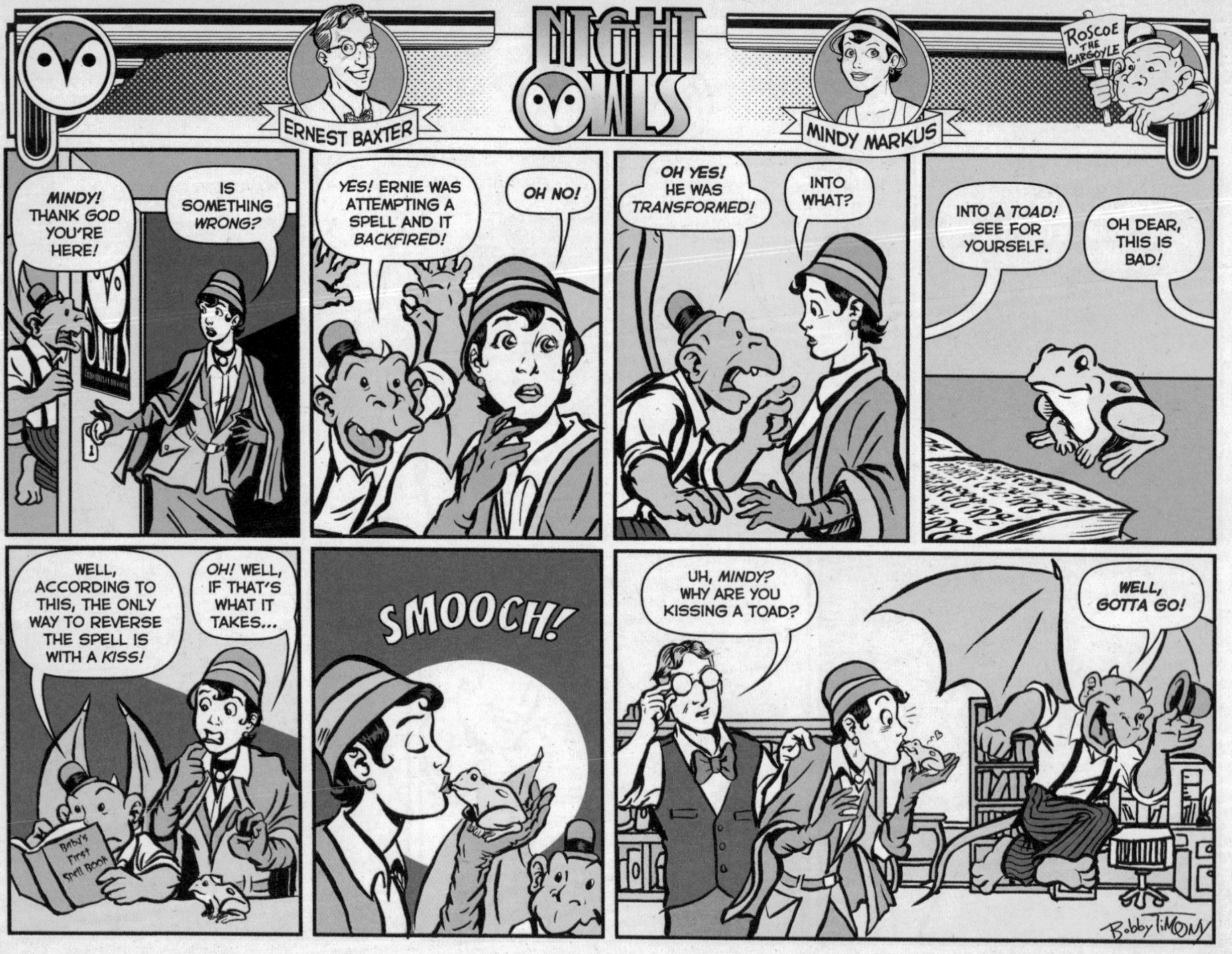
NIGHT OWLS
ERNEST BAXTER
MINDY MARKUS
ROSCOE THE GARGOYLE
MINDY! THANK GOD YOU'RE HERE!
IS SOMETHING WRONG?
YES! ERNIE WAS ATTEMPTING A SPELL AND IT BACKFIRED!
OH NO!
OH YES! HE WAS TRANSFORMED!
INTO WHAT?
INTO A TOAD! SEE FOR YOURSELF.
OH DEAR, THIS IS BAD!
WELL, ACCORDING TO THIS, THE ONLY WAY TO REVERSE THE SPELL IS WITH A KISS!
OH! WELL, IF THAT'S WHAT IT TAKES...
Baby's First Spell Book
SMOOCH!
UH, MINDY? WHY ARE YOU KISSING A TOAD?
WELL, GOTTA GO!
Bobby Timony

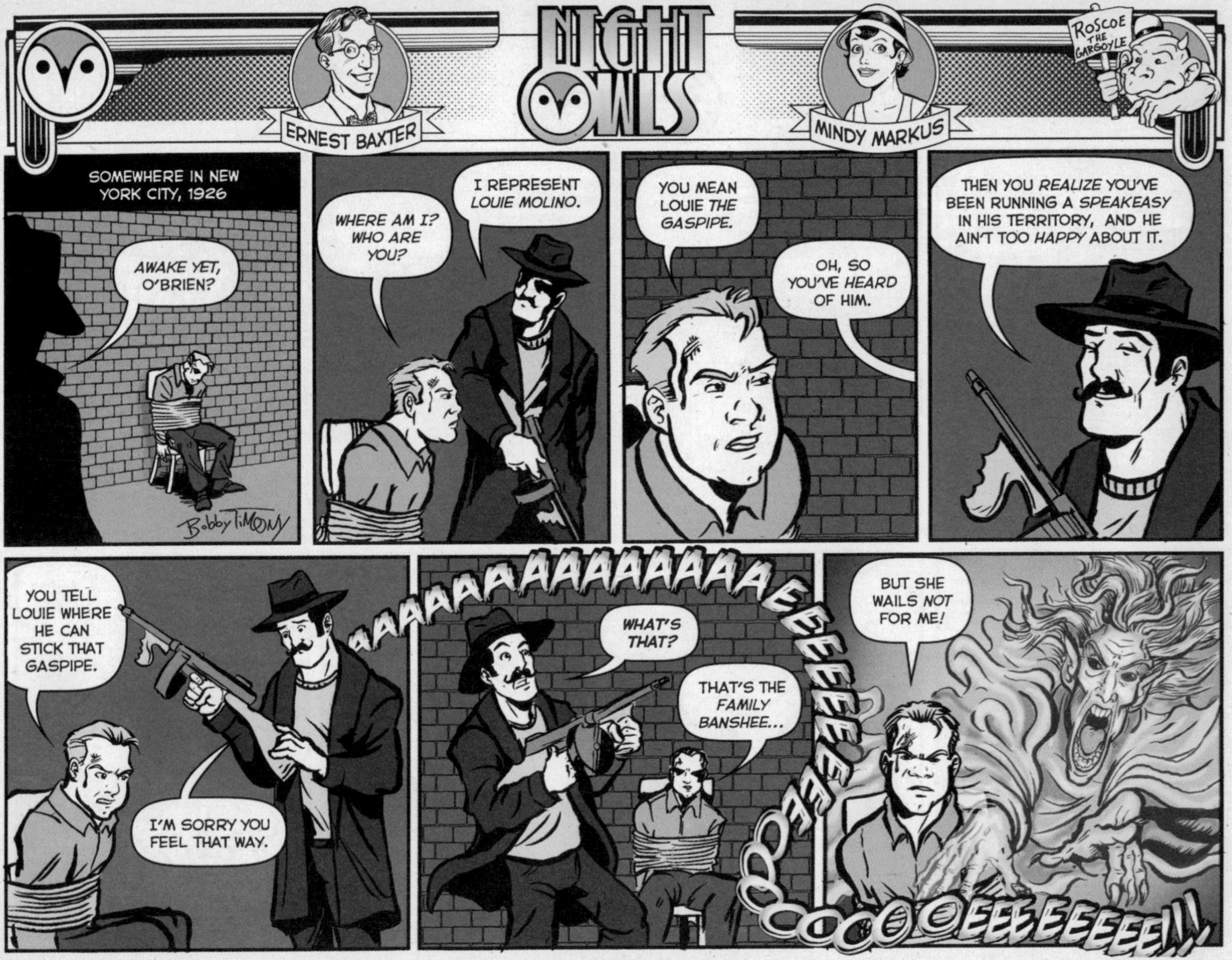
NIGHT OWLS
ERNEST BAXTER
MINDY MARKUS
ROSCOE THE GARGOYLE
SOMEWHERE IN NEW YORK CITY, 1926
AWAKE YET, O'BRIEN?
Bobby Timony
WHERE AM I? WHO ARE YOU?
I REPRESENT LOUIE MOLINO.
YOU MEAN LOUIE THE GASPIPE.
OH, SO YOU'VE HEARD OF HIM.
THEN YOU REALIZE YOU'VE BEEN RUNNING A SPEAKEASY IN HIS TERRITORY, AND HE AIN'T TOO HAPPY ABOUT IT.
YOU TELL LOUIE WHERE HE CAN STICK THAT GASPIPE.
I'M SORRY YOU FEEL THAT WAY.
AAAAAAAAAAAAAAAAAAAAEEEEEEE
WHAT'S THAT?
THAT'S THE FAMILY BANSHEE...
BUT SHE WAILS NOT FOR ME!
OOOOOOEEEEEEEEE!!!

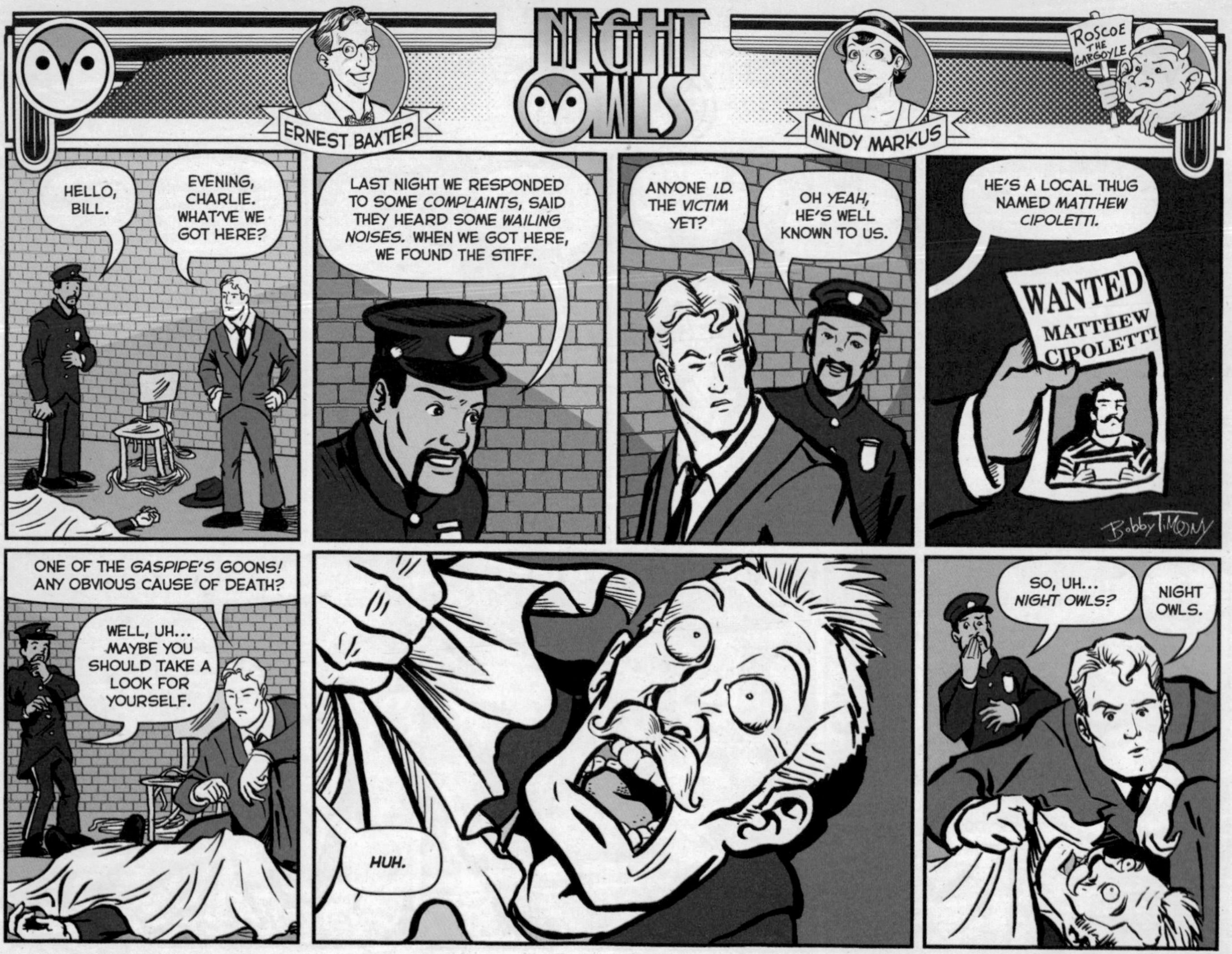
NIGHT OWLS
ERNEST BAXTER
MINDY MARKUS
ROSCOE THE GARGOYLE
HELLO, BILL.
EVENING, CHARLIE. WHAT'VE WE GOT HERE?
LAST NIGHT WE RESPONDED TO SOME *COMPLAINTS*, SAID THEY HEARD SOME *WAILING NOISES.* WHEN WE GOT HERE, WE FOUND THE STIFF.
ANYONE *I.D.* THE *VICTIM* YET?
OH *YEAH,* HE'S WELL KNOWN TO US.
HE'S A LOCAL THUG NAMED *MATTHEW CIPOLETTI.*
WANTED
MATTHEW CIPOLETTI
Bobby Timony
ONE OF THE *GASPIPE'S* GOONS! ANY OBVIOUS CAUSE OF DEATH?
WELL, UH... MAYBE YOU SHOULD TAKE A LOOK FOR YOURSELF.
HUH.
SO, UH... *NIGHT OWLS?*
NIGHT OWLS.

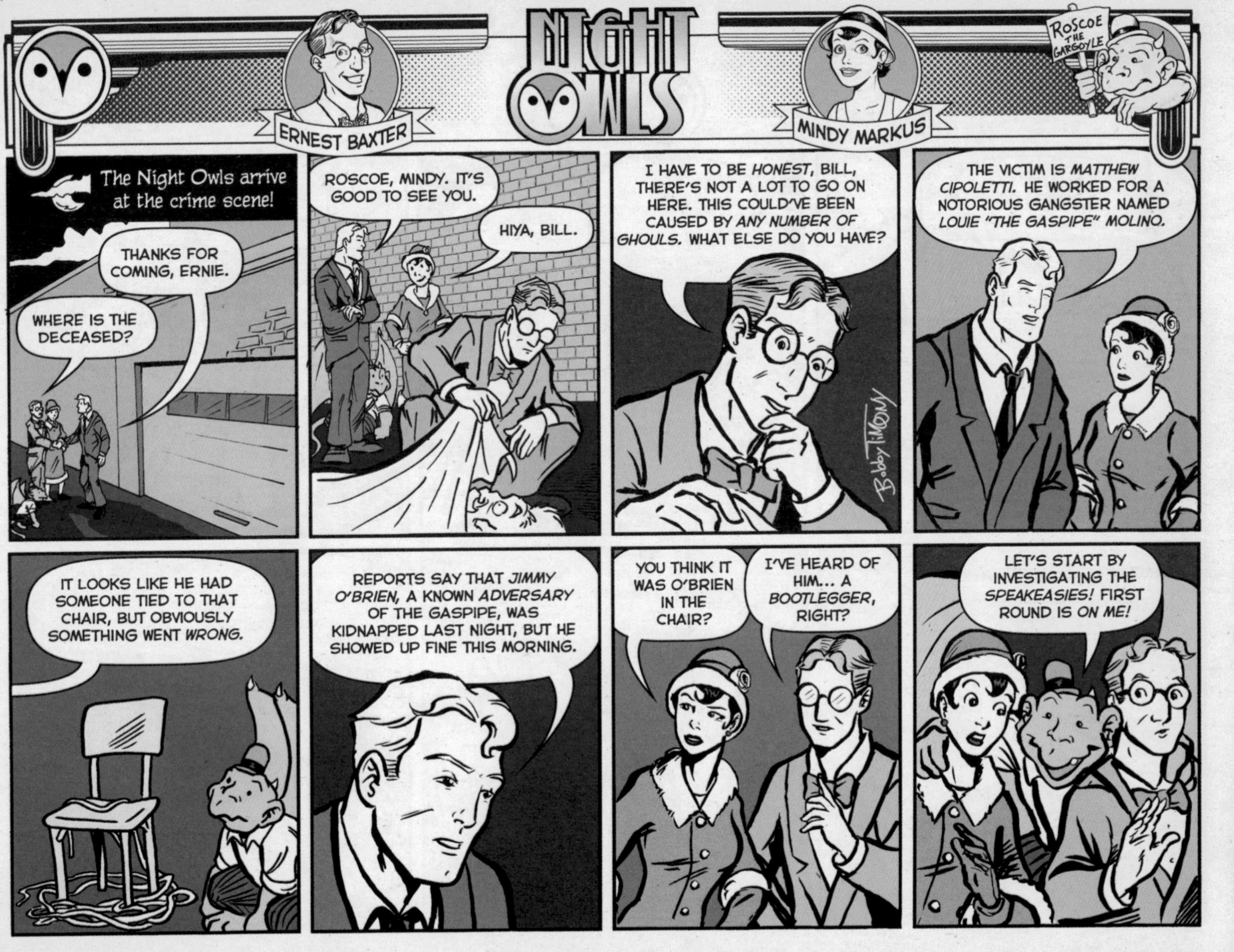
NIGHT OWLS
ERNEST BAXTER
MINDY MARKUS
ROSCOE THE GARGOYLE
The Night Owls arrive at the crime scene!
THANKS FOR COMING, ERNIE.
WHERE IS THE DECEASED?
ROSCOE, MINDY. IT'S GOOD TO SEE YOU.
HIYA, BILL.
I HAVE TO BE HONEST, BILL, THERE'S NOT A LOT TO GO ON HERE. THIS COULD'VE BEEN CAUSED BY ANY NUMBER OF GHOULS. WHAT ELSE DO YOU HAVE?
Bobby Timony
THE VICTIM IS MATTHEW CIPOLETTI. HE WORKED FOR A NOTORIOUS GANGSTER NAMED LOUIE "THE GASPIPE" MOLINO.
IT LOOKS LIKE HE HAD SOMEONE TIED TO THAT CHAIR, BUT OBVIOUSLY SOMETHING WENT WRONG.
REPORTS SAY THAT JIMMY O'BRIEN, A KNOWN ADVERSARY OF THE GASPIPE, WAS KIDNAPPED LAST NIGHT, BUT HE SHOWED UP FINE THIS MORNING.
YOU THINK IT WAS O'BRIEN IN THE CHAIR?
I'VE HEARD OF HIM... A BOOTLEGGER, RIGHT?
LET'S START BY INVESTIGATING THE SPEAKEASIES! FIRST ROUND IS ON ME!

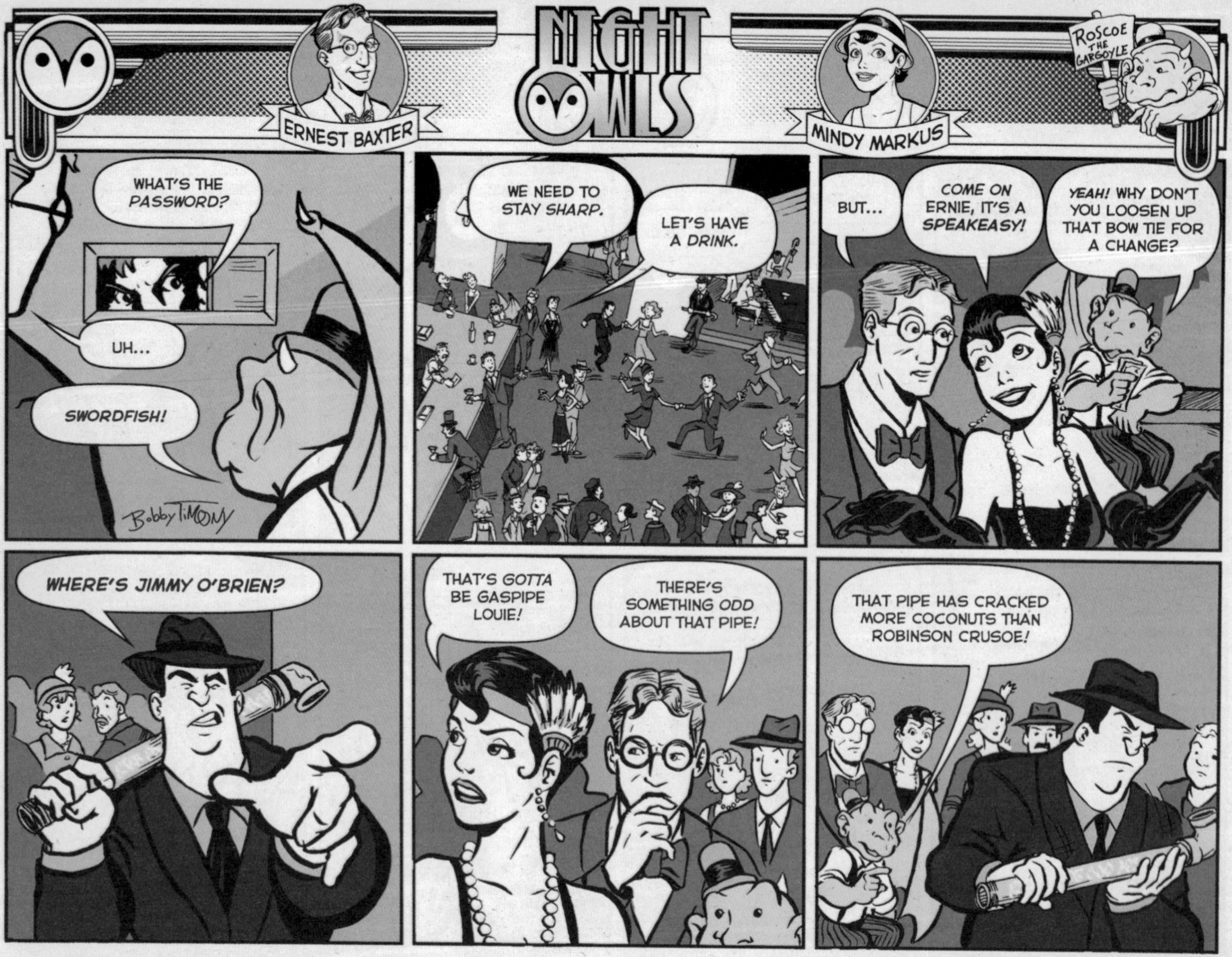
NIGHT OWLS
ERNEST BAXTER
MINDY MARKUS
ROSCOE THE GARGOYLE
WHAT'S THE *PASSWORD?*
UH...
SWORDFISH!
Bobby TiMONY
WE NEED TO STAY *SHARP.*
LET'S HAVE A *DRINK.*
BUT...
COME ON ERNIE, IT'S A *SPEAKEASY!*
YEAH! WHY DON'T YOU LOOSEN UP THAT BOW TIE FOR A CHANGE?
WHERE'S JIMMY O'BRIEN?
THAT'S *GOTTA* BE GASPIPE LOUIE!
THERE'S SOMETHING *ODD* ABOUT THAT PIPE!
THAT PIPE HAS CRACKED MORE COCONUTS THAN ROBINSON CRUSOE!

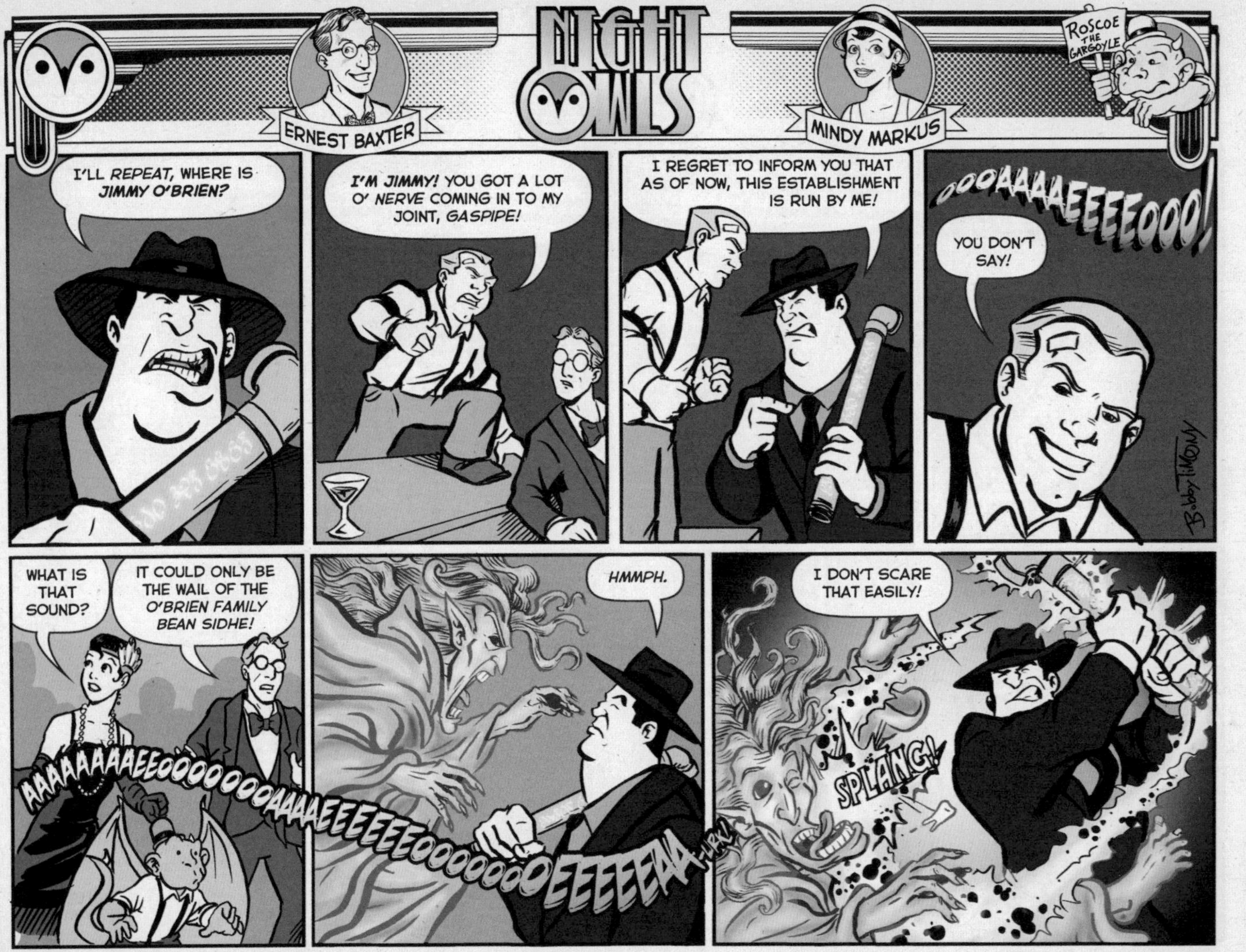
NIGHT OWLS
ERNEST BAXTER
MINDY MARKUS
ROSCOE THE GARGOYLE
I'LL *REPEAT*, WHERE IS *JIMMY O'BRIEN?*
I'M JIMMY! YOU GOT A LOT O' *NERVE* COMING IN TO MY JOINT, *GASPIPE!*
I REGRET TO INFORM YOU THAT AS OF NOW, THIS ESTABLISHMENT IS RUN BY ME!
OOOAAAAAEEEEOOO!
YOU DON'T SAY!
Bobby Timony
WHAT IS THAT SOUND?
IT COULD ONLY BE THE WAIL OF THE *O'BRIEN FAMILY BEAN SIDHE!*
AAAAAAAAEEOOOOOOOOOOAAAAEEEEEEEEOOOOOOOOEEEEEEAA
HMMPH.
I DON'T SCARE THAT EASILY!
SPLANG!

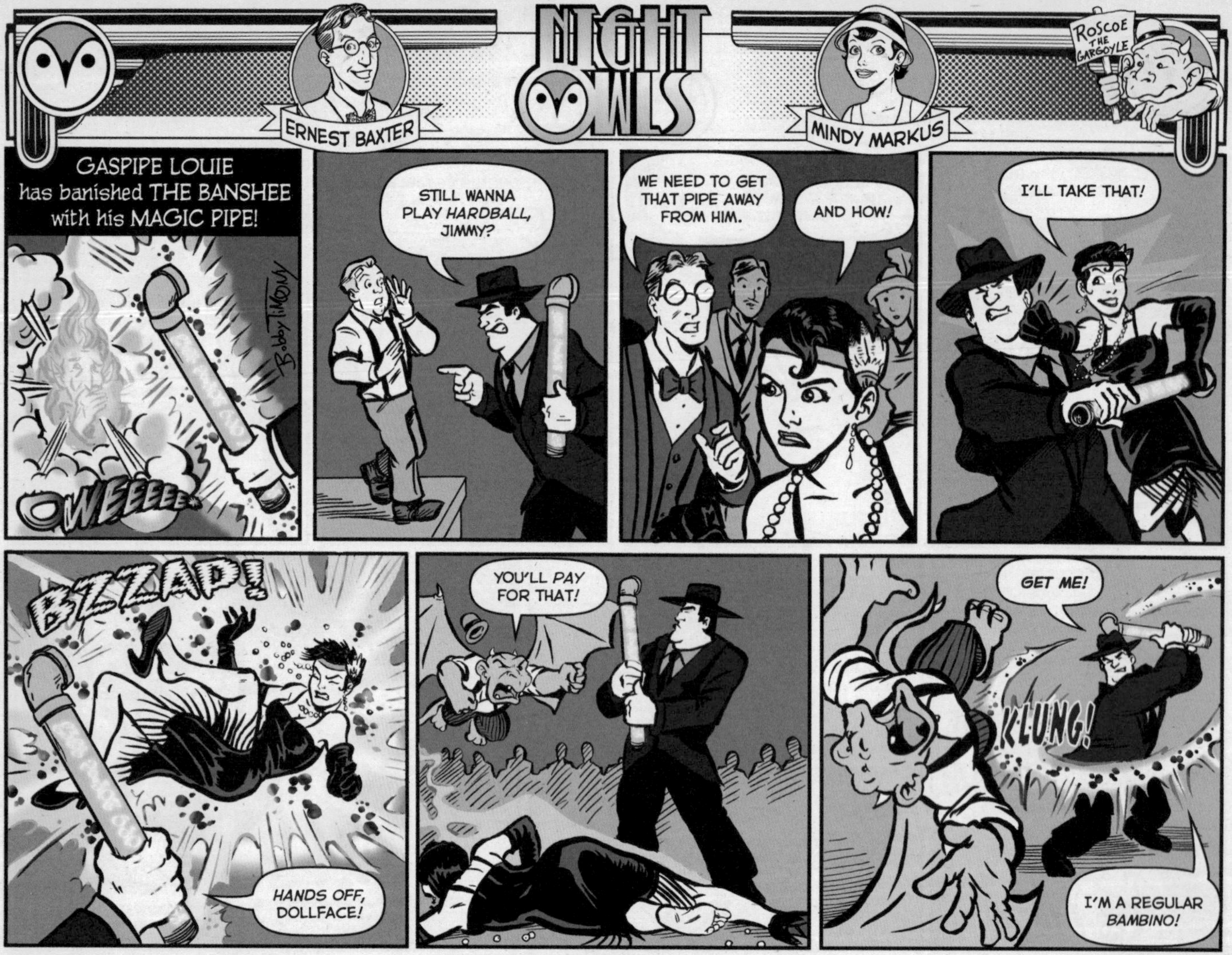
NIGHT OWLS
ERNEST BAXTER
MINDY MARKUS
ROSCOE THE GARGOYLE
GASPIPE LOUIE has banished THE BANSHEE with his MAGIC PIPE!
Bobby Timony
OWEEEEE
STILL WANNA PLAY HARDBALL, JIMMY?
WE NEED TO GET THAT PIPE AWAY FROM HIM.
AND HOW!
I'LL TAKE THAT!
BZZZAP!
HANDS OFF, DOLLFACE!
YOU'LL PAY FOR THAT!
GET ME!
KLUNG!
I'M A REGULAR BAMBINO!

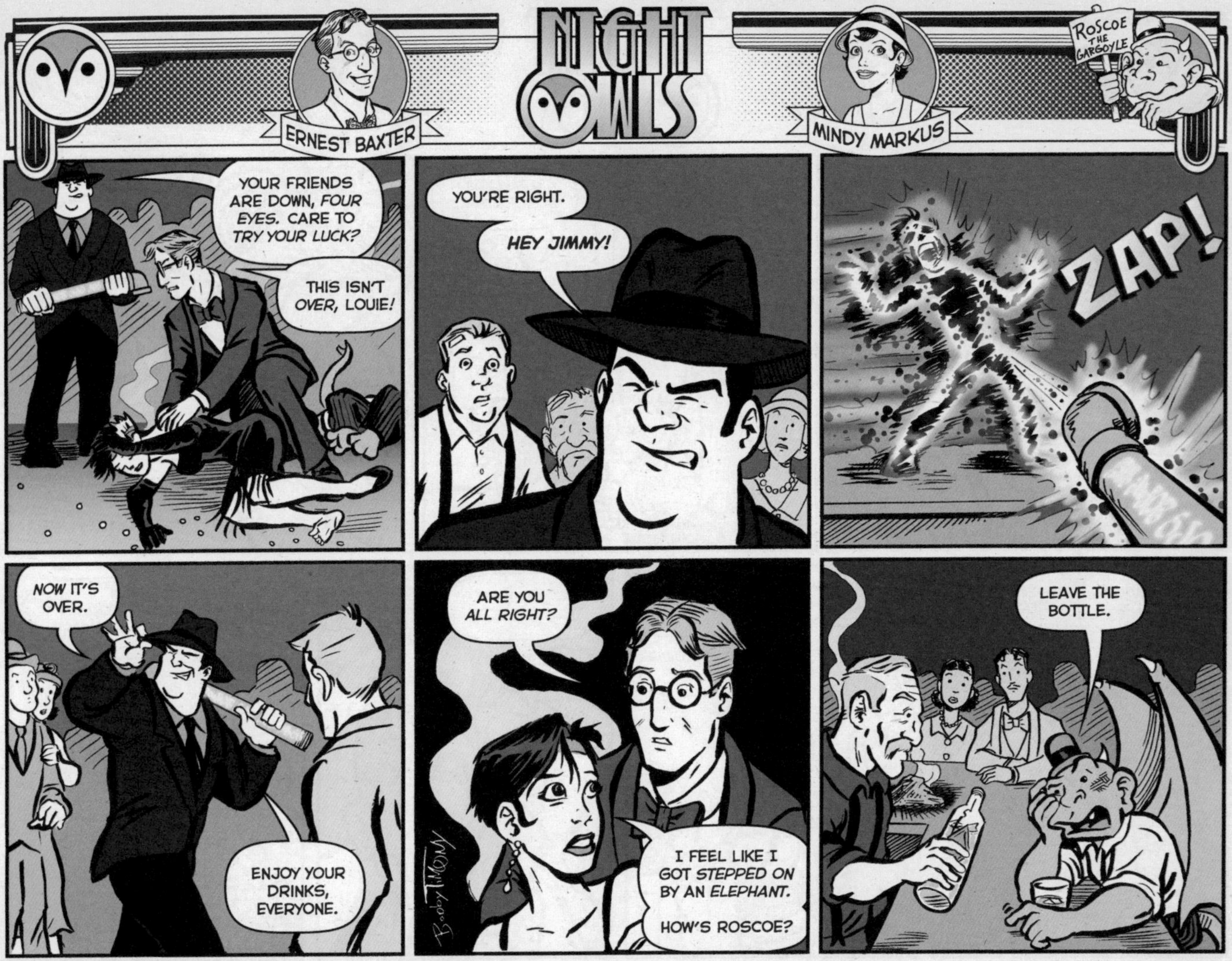
NIGHT OWLS
ERNEST BAXTER
MINDY MARKUS
ROSCOE THE GARGOYLE
YOUR FRIENDS ARE DOWN, FOUR EYES. CARE TO TRY YOUR LUCK?
THIS ISN'T OVER, LOUIE!
YOU'RE RIGHT.
HEY JIMMY!
ZAP!
NOW IT'S OVER.
ENJOY YOUR DRINKS, EVERYONE.
ARE YOU ALL RIGHT?
I FEEL LIKE I GOT STEPPED ON BY AN ELEPHANT.
HOW'S ROSCOE?
LEAVE THE BOTTLE.
Bobby Timony

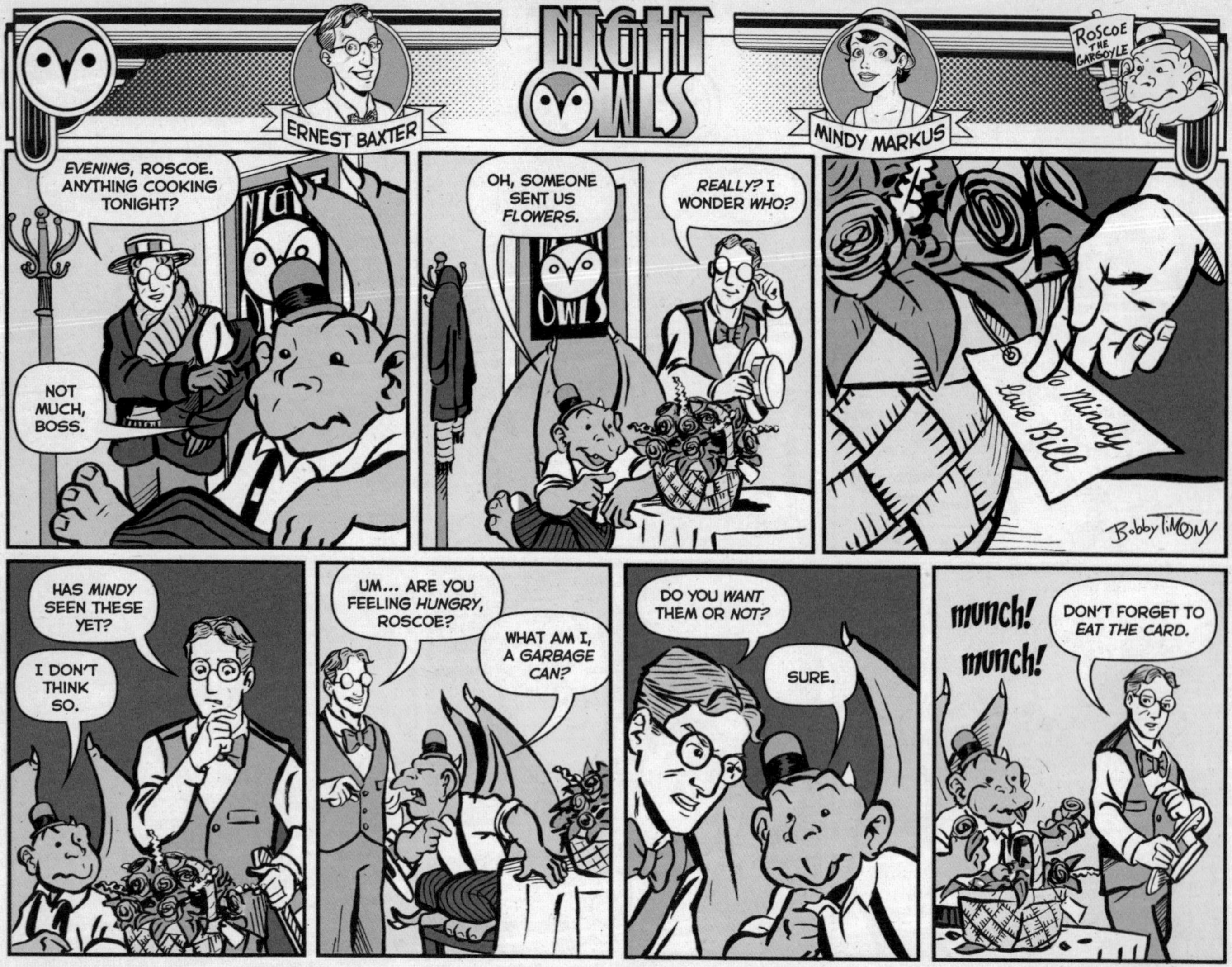
NIGHT OWLS
ERNEST BAXTER
MINDY MARKUS
ROSCOE THE GARGOYLE
EVENING, ROSCOE. ANYTHING COOKING TONIGHT?
NOT MUCH, BOSS.
OH, SOMEONE SENT US FLOWERS.
REALLY? I WONDER WHO?
To Mindy Love Bill
Bobby Timony
HAS MINDY SEEN THESE YET?
I DON'T THINK SO.
UM... ARE YOU FEELING HUNGRY, ROSCOE?
WHAT AM I, A GARBAGE CAN?
DO YOU WANT THEM OR NOT?
SURE.
munch! munch!
DON'T FORGET TO EAT THE CARD.

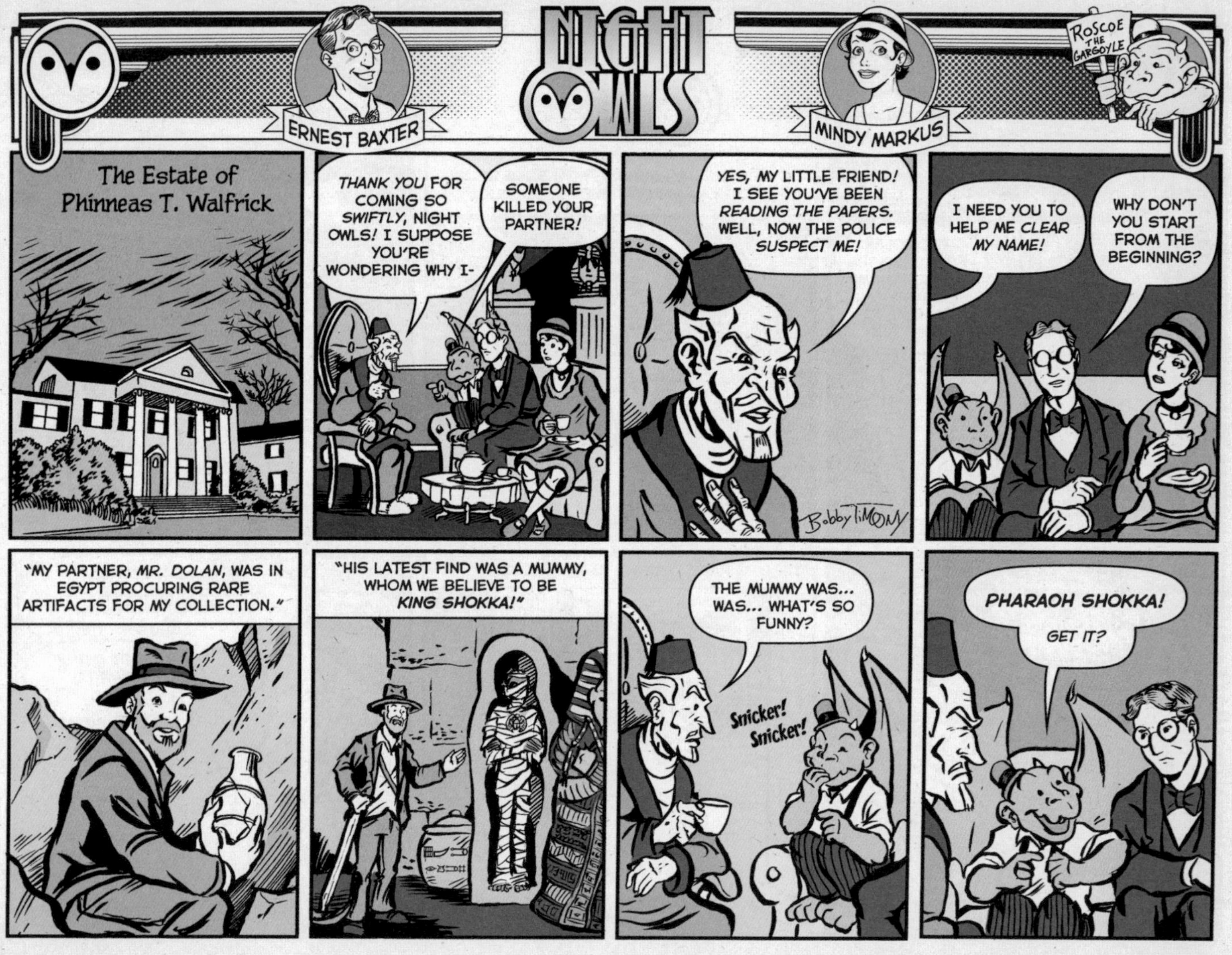
NIGHT OWLS
ERNEST BAXTER
MINDY MARKUS
ROSCOE THE GARGOYLE
The Estate of Phinneas T. Walfrick
THANK YOU FOR COMING SO SWIFTLY, NIGHT OWLS! I SUPPOSE YOU'RE WONDERING WHY I-
SOMEONE KILLED YOUR PARTNER!
YES, MY LITTLE FRIEND! I SEE YOU'VE BEEN READING THE PAPERS. WELL, NOW THE POLICE SUSPECT ME!
Bobby Timony
I NEED YOU TO HELP ME CLEAR MY NAME!
WHY DON'T YOU START FROM THE BEGINNING?
"MY PARTNER, MR. DOLAN, WAS IN EGYPT PROCURING RARE ARTIFACTS FOR MY COLLECTION."
"HIS LATEST FIND WAS A MUMMY, WHOM WE BELIEVE TO BE KING SHOKKA!"
THE MUMMY WAS... WAS... WHAT'S SO FUNNY?
Snicker! Snicker!
PHARAOH SHOKKA!
GET IT?

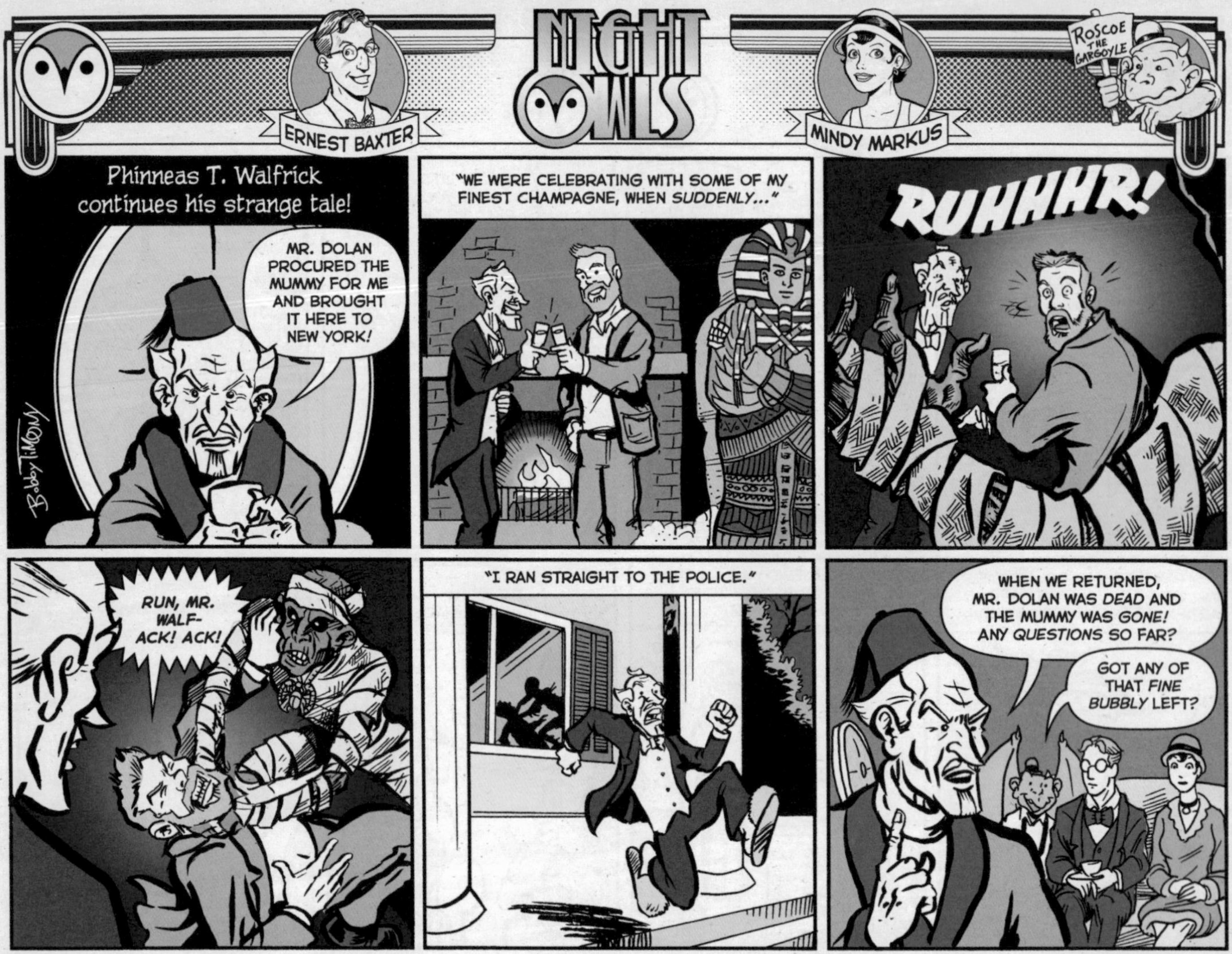

NIGHT OWLS
ERNEST BAXTER
MINDY MARKUS
ROSCOE THE GARGOYLE
Phinneas T. Walfrick continues his strange tale!
MR. DOLAN PROCURED THE MUMMY FOR ME AND BROUGHT IT HERE TO NEW YORK!
Bobby Timony
"WE WERE CELEBRATING WITH SOME OF MY FINEST CHAMPAGNE, WHEN SUDDENLY..."
RUHHHR!
RUN, MR. WALF- ACK! ACK!
"I RAN STRAIGHT TO THE POLICE."
WHEN WE RETURNED, MR. DOLAN WAS DEAD AND THE MUMMY WAS GONE! ANY QUESTIONS SO FAR?
GOT ANY OF THAT FINE BUBBLY LEFT?

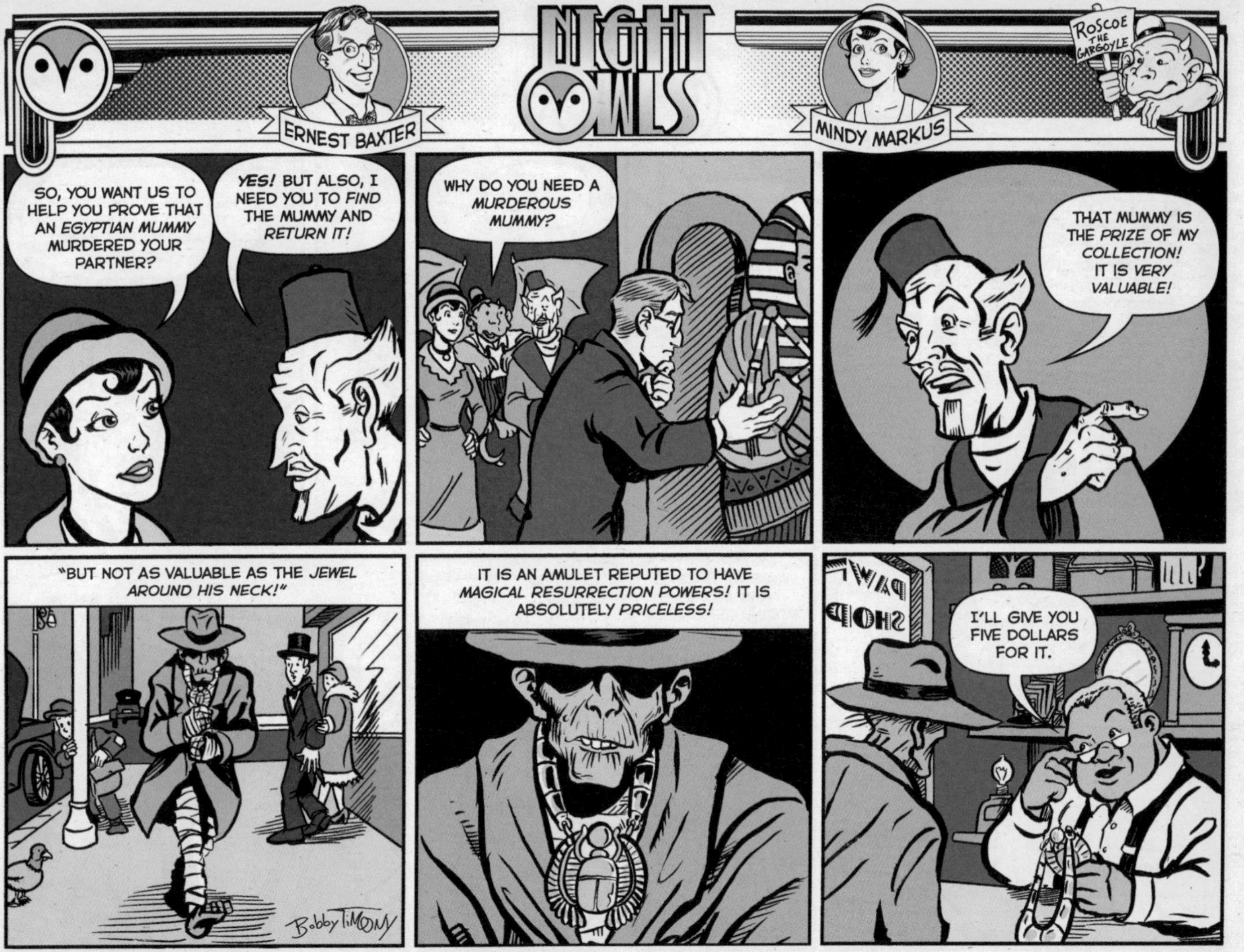
NIGHT OWLS
ERNEST BAXTER
MINDY MARKUS
ROSCOE THE GARGOYLE
SO, YOU WANT US TO HELP YOU PROVE THAT AN *EGYPTIAN MUMMY* MURDERED YOUR PARTNER?
YES! BUT ALSO, I NEED YOU TO *FIND* THE MUMMY AND *RETURN IT!*
WHY DO YOU NEED A *MURDEROUS* MUMMY?
THAT MUMMY IS THE *PRIZE OF MY COLLECTION!* IT IS *VERY* VALUABLE!
"BUT NOT AS VALUABLE AS THE *JEWEL* AROUND HIS NECK!"
Bobby Timony
IT IS AN AMULET REPUTED TO HAVE *MAGICAL RESURRECTION POWERS!* IT IS ABSOLUTELY *PRICELESS!*
PAWN SHOP
I'LL GIVE YOU FIVE DOLLARS FOR IT.

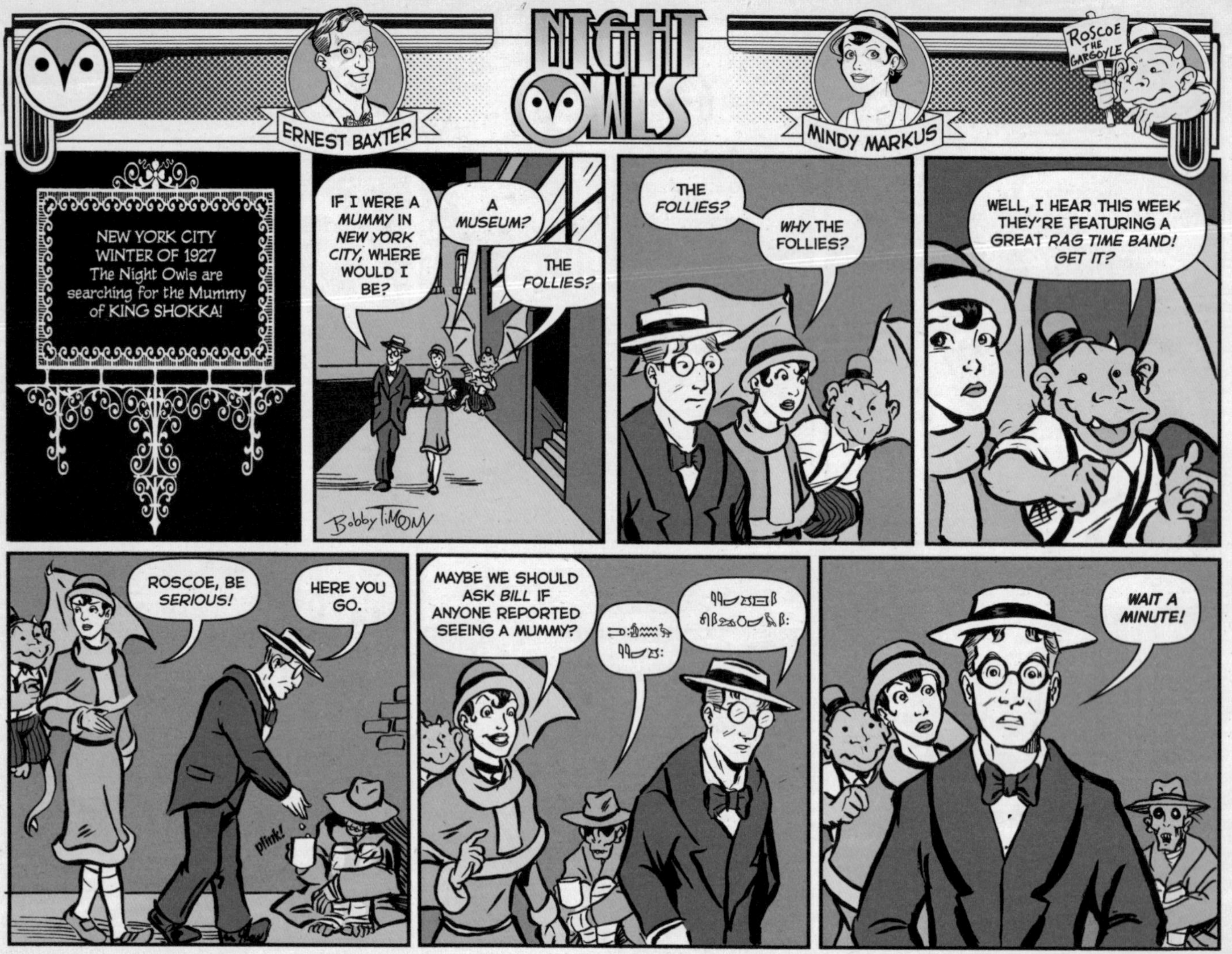
NIGHT OWLS
ERNEST BAXTER
MINDY MARKUS
ROSCOE THE GARGOYLE
NEW YORK CITY WINTER OF 1927 The Night Owls are searching for the Mummy of KING SHOKKA!
IF I WERE A MUMMY IN NEW YORK CITY, WHERE WOULD I BE?
A MUSEUM?
THE FOLLIES?
Bobby Timony
THE FOLLIES?
WHY THE FOLLIES?
WELL, I HEAR THIS WEEK THEY'RE FEATURING A GREAT RAG TIME BAND! GET IT?
ROSCOE, BE SERIOUS!
HERE YOU GO.
plink!
MAYBE WE SHOULD ASK BILL IF ANYONE REPORTED SEEING A MUMMY?
WAIT A MINUTE!

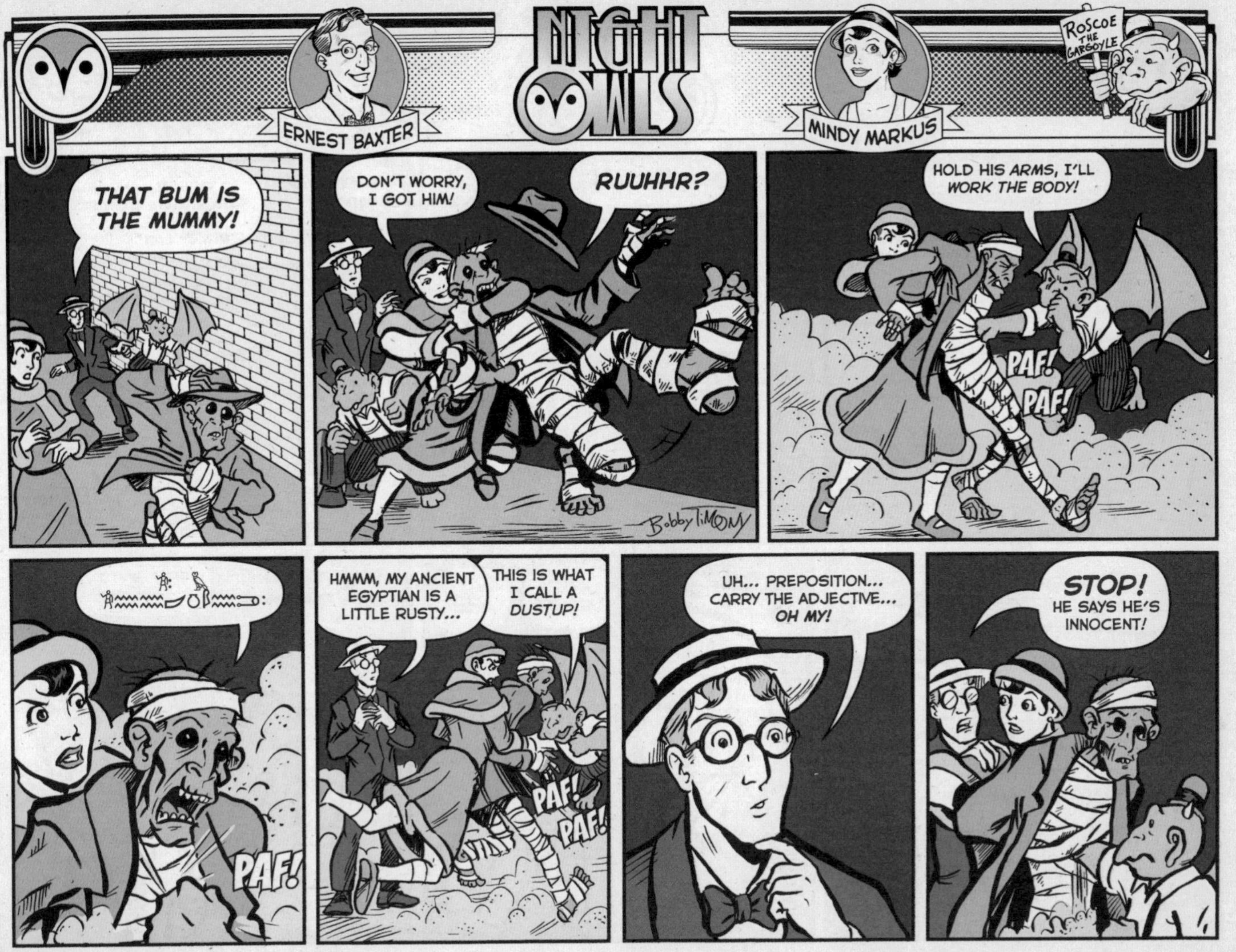

NIGHT OWLS
ERNEST BAXTER
MINDY MARKUS
ROSCOE THE GARGOYLE
THAT BUM IS THE MUMMY!
DON'T WORRY, I GOT HIM!
RUUHHR?
Bobby Timony
HOLD HIS ARMS, I'LL WORK THE BODY!
PAF!
PAF!
PAF!
HMMM, MY ANCIENT EGYPTIAN IS A LITTLE RUSTY...
THIS IS WHAT I CALL A DUSTUP!
PAF!
PAF!
UH... PREPOSITION... CARRY THE ADJECTIVE... OH MY!
STOP! HE SAYS HE'S INNOCENT!

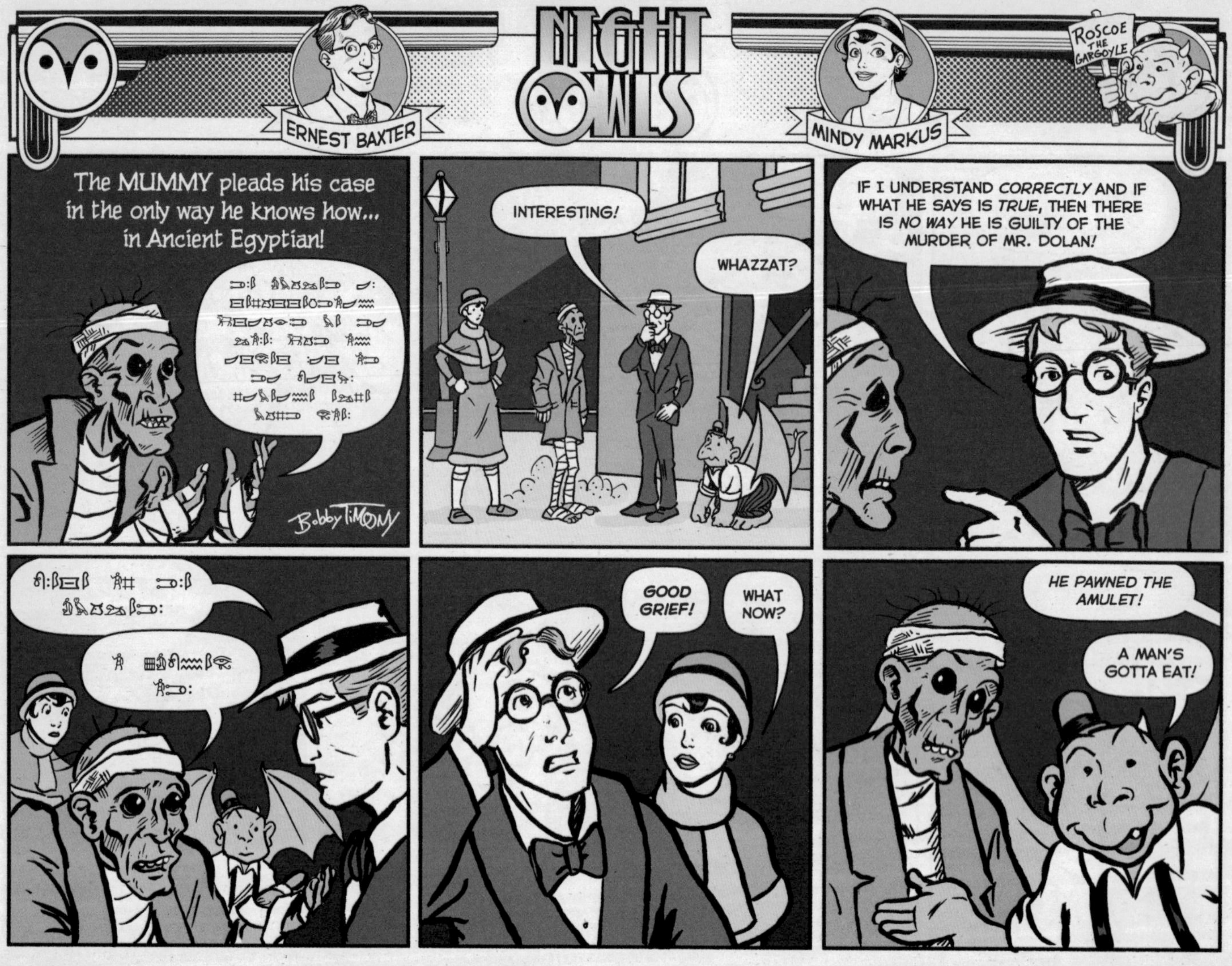
NIGHT OWLS
ERNEST BAXTER
MINDY MARKUS
ROSCOE THE GARGOYLE
The MUMMY pleads his case in the only way he knows how... in Ancient Egyptian!
Bobby Timony
INTERESTING!
WHAZZAT?
IF I UNDERSTAND CORRECTLY AND IF WHAT HE SAYS IS TRUE, THEN THERE IS NO WAY HE IS GUILTY OF THE MURDER OF MR. DOLAN!
GOOD GRIEF!
WHAT NOW?
HE PAWNED THE AMULET!
A MAN'S GOTTA EAT!

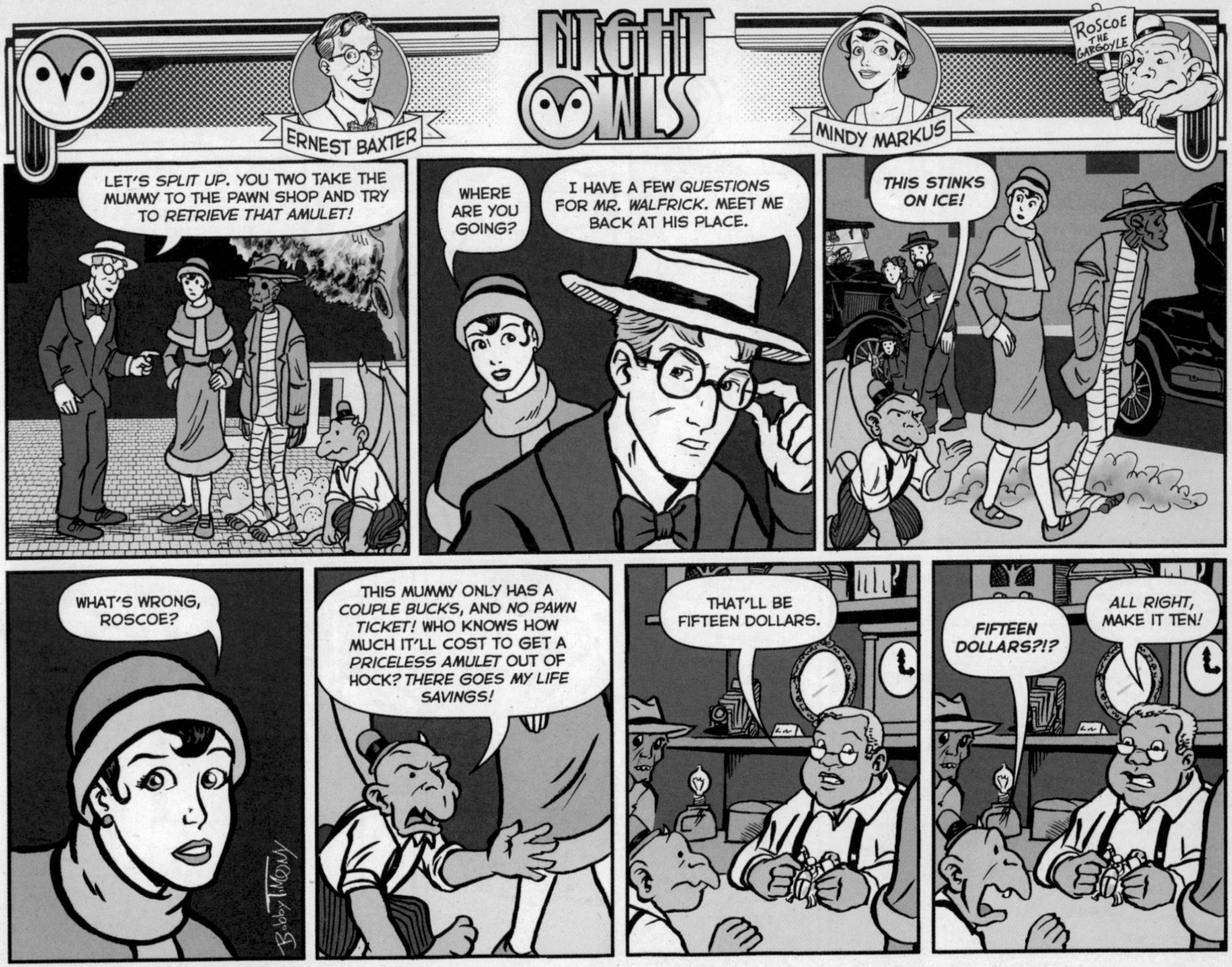
NIGHT OWLS
ERNEST BAXTER
MINDY MARKUS
ROSCOE THE GARGOYLE
LET'S SPLIT UP. YOU TWO TAKE THE MUMMY TO THE PAWN SHOP AND TRY TO RETRIEVE THAT AMULET!
WHERE ARE YOU GOING?
I HAVE A FEW QUESTIONS FOR MR. WALFRICK. MEET ME BACK AT HIS PLACE.
THIS STINKS ON ICE!
WHAT'S WRONG, ROSCOE?
THIS MUMMY ONLY HAS A COUPLE BUCKS, AND NO PAWN TICKET! WHO KNOWS HOW MUCH IT'LL COST TO GET A PRICELESS AMULET OUT OF HOCK? THERE GOES MY LIFE SAVINGS!
THAT'LL BE FIFTEEN DOLLARS.
FIFTEEN DOLLARS?!?
ALL RIGHT, MAKE IT TEN!
Bobby Timony

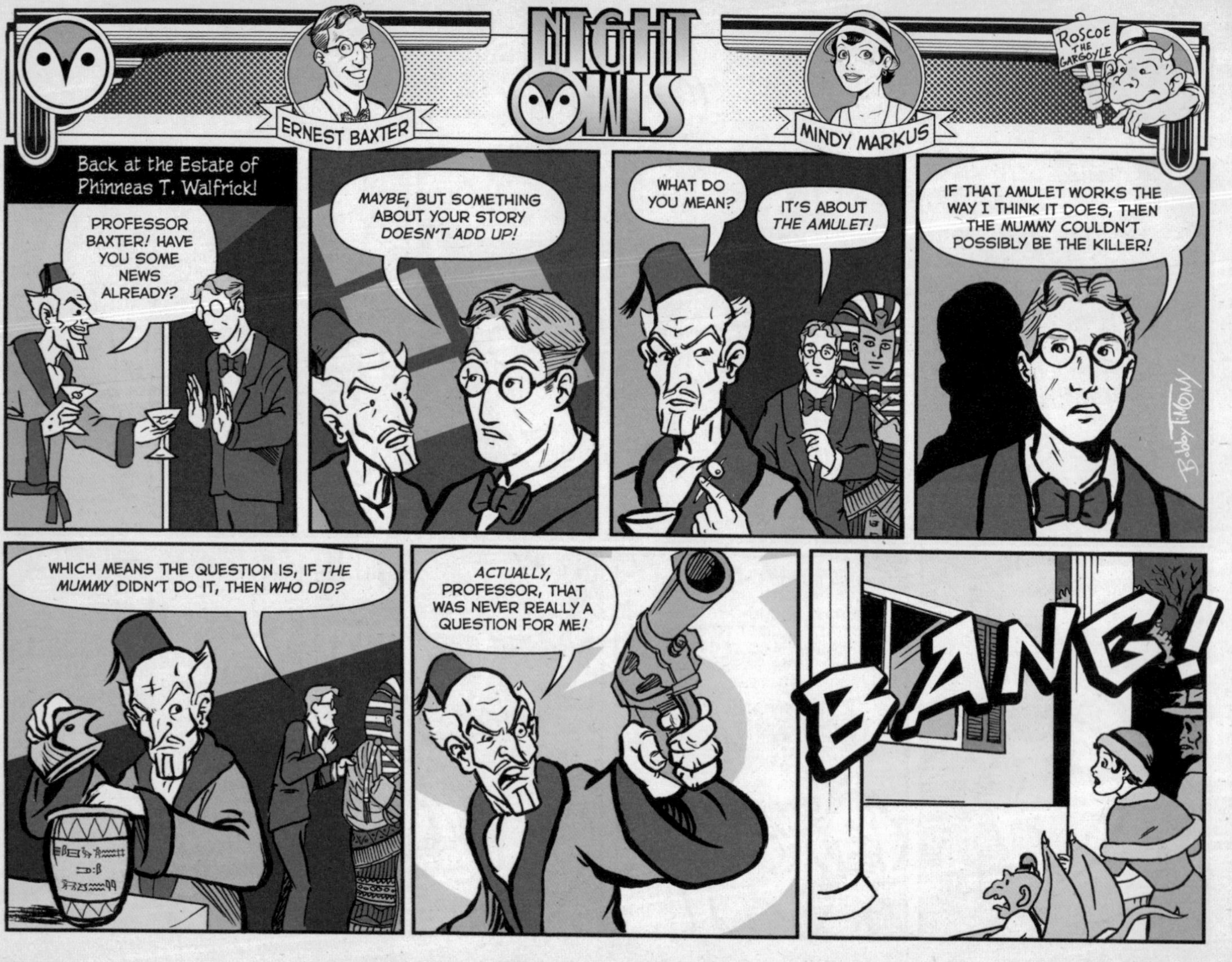

NIGHT OWLS
ERNEST BAXTER
MINDY MARKUS
ROSCOE THE GARGOYLE
Back at the Estate of Phinneas T. Walfrick!
PROFESSOR BAXTER! HAVE YOU SOME NEWS ALREADY?
MAYBE, BUT SOMETHING ABOUT YOUR STORY DOESN'T ADD UP!
WHAT DO YOU MEAN?
IT'S ABOUT THE AMULET!
IF THAT AMULET WORKS THE WAY I THINK IT DOES, THEN THE MUMMY COULDN'T POSSIBLY BE THE KILLER!
Bobby Timony
WHICH MEANS THE QUESTION IS, IF THE MUMMY DIDN'T DO IT, THEN WHO DID?
ACTUALLY, PROFESSOR, THAT WAS NEVER REALLY A QUESTION FOR ME!
BANG!

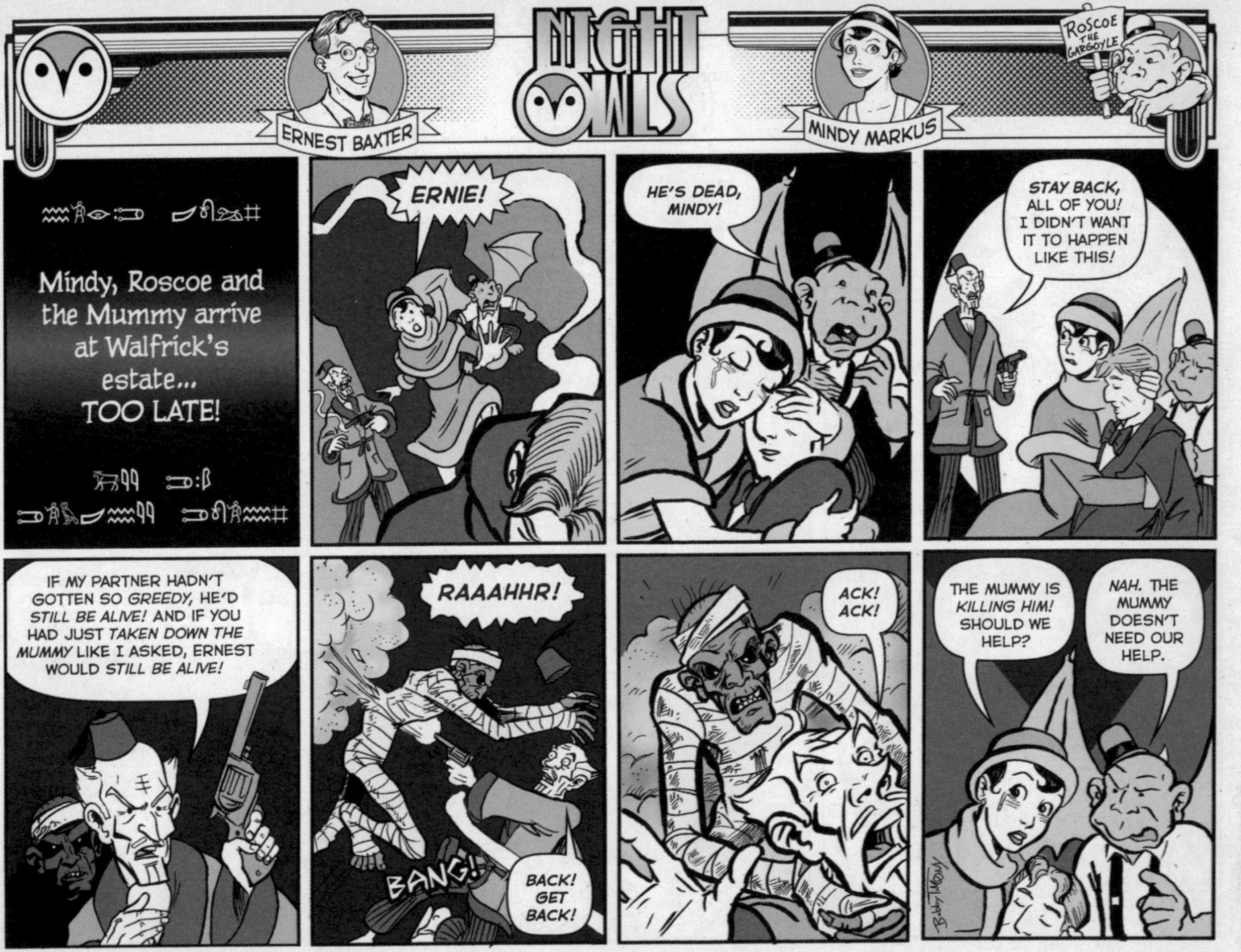
NIGHT OWLS
ERNEST BAXTER
MINDY MARKUS
ROSCOE THE GARGOYLE
Mindy, Roscoe and the Mummy arrive at Walfrick's estate... TOO LATE!
ERNIE!
HE'S DEAD, MINDY!
STAY BACK, ALL OF YOU! I DIDN'T WANT IT TO HAPPEN LIKE THIS!
IF MY PARTNER HADN'T GOTTEN SO GREEDY, HE'D STILL BE ALIVE! AND IF YOU HAD JUST TAKEN DOWN THE MUMMY LIKE I ASKED, ERNEST WOULD STILL BE ALIVE!
RAAAHHR!
BANG!
BACK! GET BACK!
ACK! ACK!
THE MUMMY IS KILLING HIM! SHOULD WE HELP?
NAH. THE MUMMY DOESN'T NEED OUR HELP.
Bobby Timony

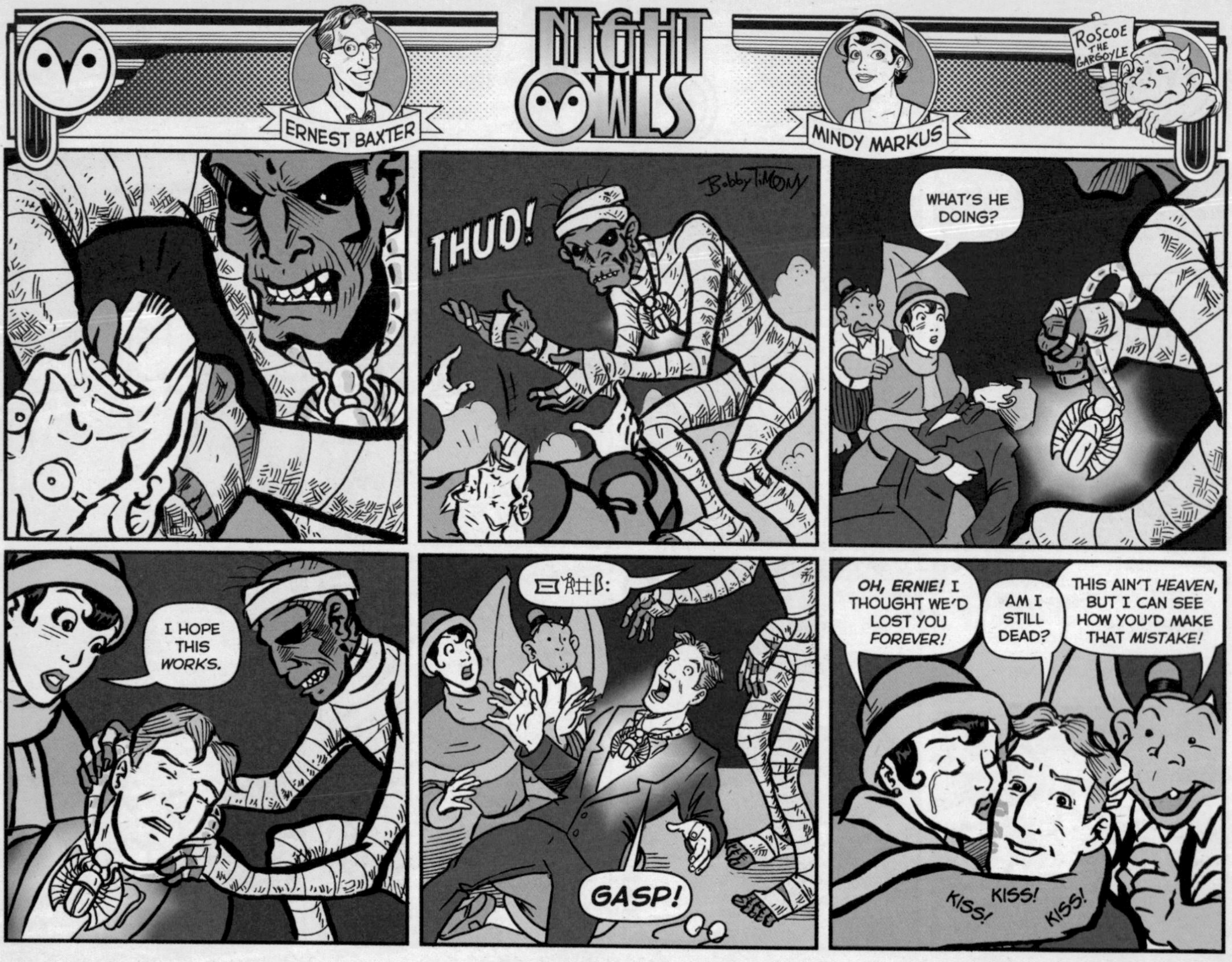
NIGHT OWLS
ERNEST BAXTER
MINDY MARKUS
ROSCOE THE GARGOYLE
Bobby TiMONY
THUD!
WHAT'S HE DOING?
I HOPE THIS *WORKS.*
GASP!
OH, ERNIE! I THOUGHT WE'D LOST YOU *FOREVER!*
AM I STILL DEAD?
THIS AIN'T *HEAVEN,* BUT I CAN SEE HOW YOU'D MAKE THAT *MISTAKE!*
KISS! KISS! KISS!

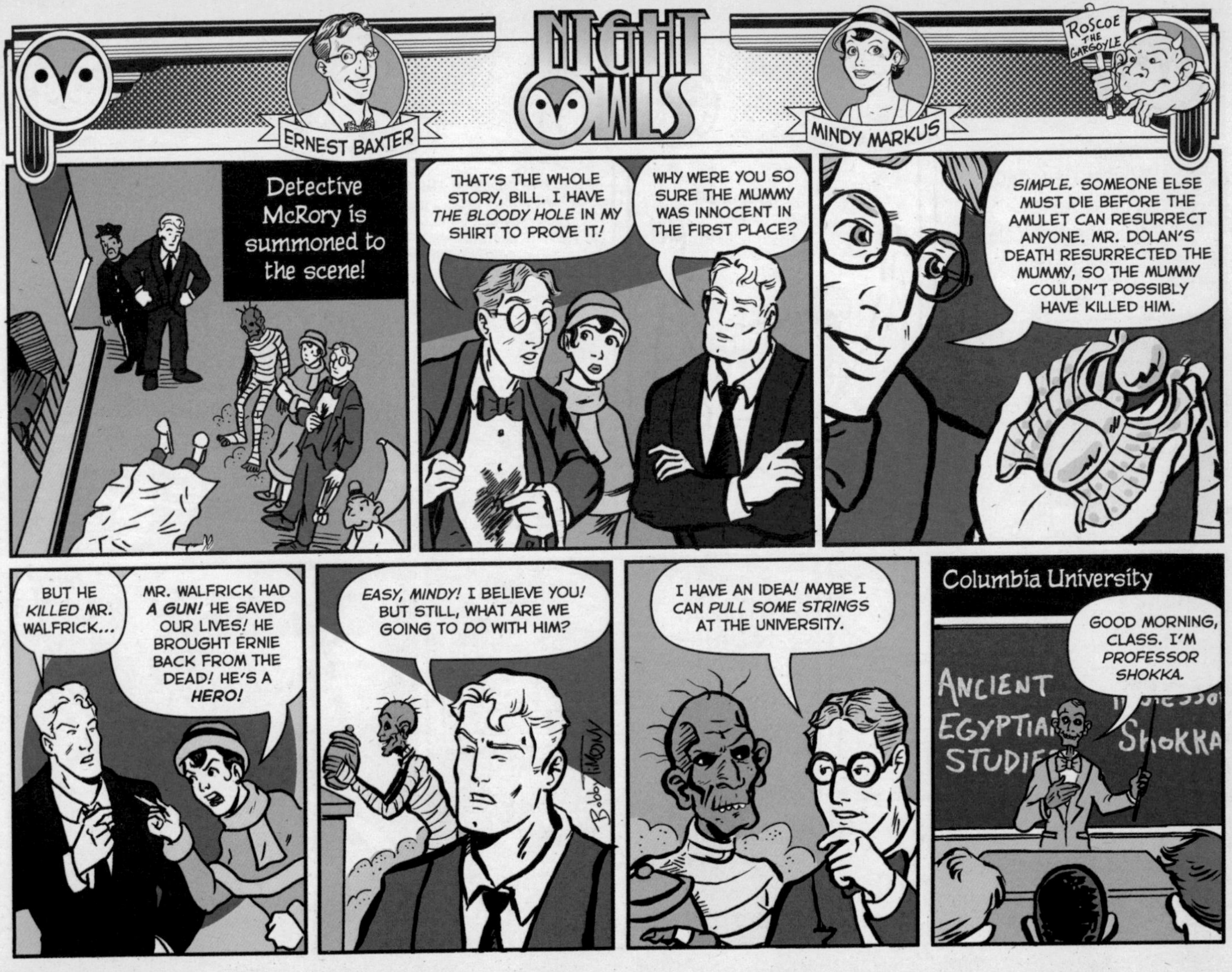
NIGHT OWLS
ERNEST BAXTER
MINDY MARKUS
ROSCOE THE GARGOYLE
Detective McRory is summoned to the scene!
THAT'S THE WHOLE STORY, BILL. I HAVE *THE BLOODY HOLE* IN MY SHIRT TO PROVE IT!
WHY WERE YOU SO SURE THE *MUMMY* WAS INNOCENT IN THE FIRST PLACE?
SIMPLE. SOMEONE ELSE MUST DIE BEFORE THE AMULET CAN RESURRECT ANYONE. MR. DOLAN'S DEATH RESURRECTED THE MUMMY, SO THE MUMMY COULDN'T POSSIBLY HAVE KILLED HIM.
BUT HE *KILLED* MR. WALFRICK...
MR. WALFRICK HAD ***A GUN!*** HE SAVED OUR LIVES! HE BROUGHT ERNIE BACK FROM THE DEAD! HE'S A ***HERO!***
EASY, MINDY! I BELIEVE YOU! BUT STILL, WHAT ARE WE GOING TO *DO* WITH HIM?
Bobby Timony
I HAVE AN IDEA! MAYBE I CAN *PULL SOME STRINGS* AT THE UNIVERSITY.
Columbia University
GOOD MORNING, CLASS. I'M *PROFESSOR SHOKKA.*
ANCIENT EGYPTIAN STUDIES
SHOKKA

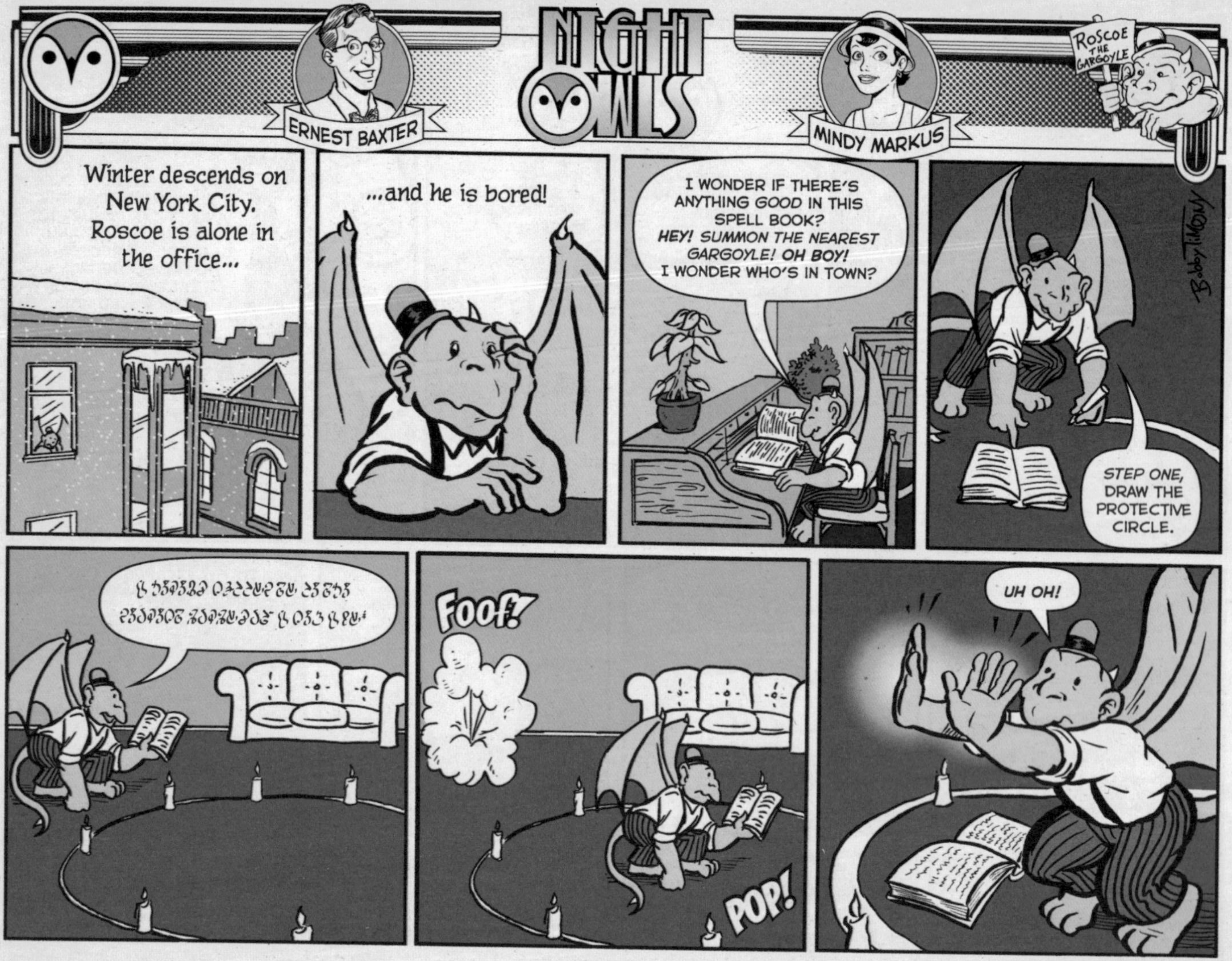
NIGHT OWLS
ERNEST BAXTER
MINDY MARKUS
ROSCOE THE GARGOYLE
Winter descends on New York City. Roscoe is alone in the office...
...and he is bored!
I WONDER IF THERE'S ANYTHING GOOD IN THIS SPELL BOOK? HEY! SUMMON THE NEAREST GARGOYLE! OH BOY! I WONDER WHO'S IN TOWN?
Bobby Timony
STEP ONE, DRAW THE PROTECTIVE CIRCLE.
Foof!
POP!
UH OH!

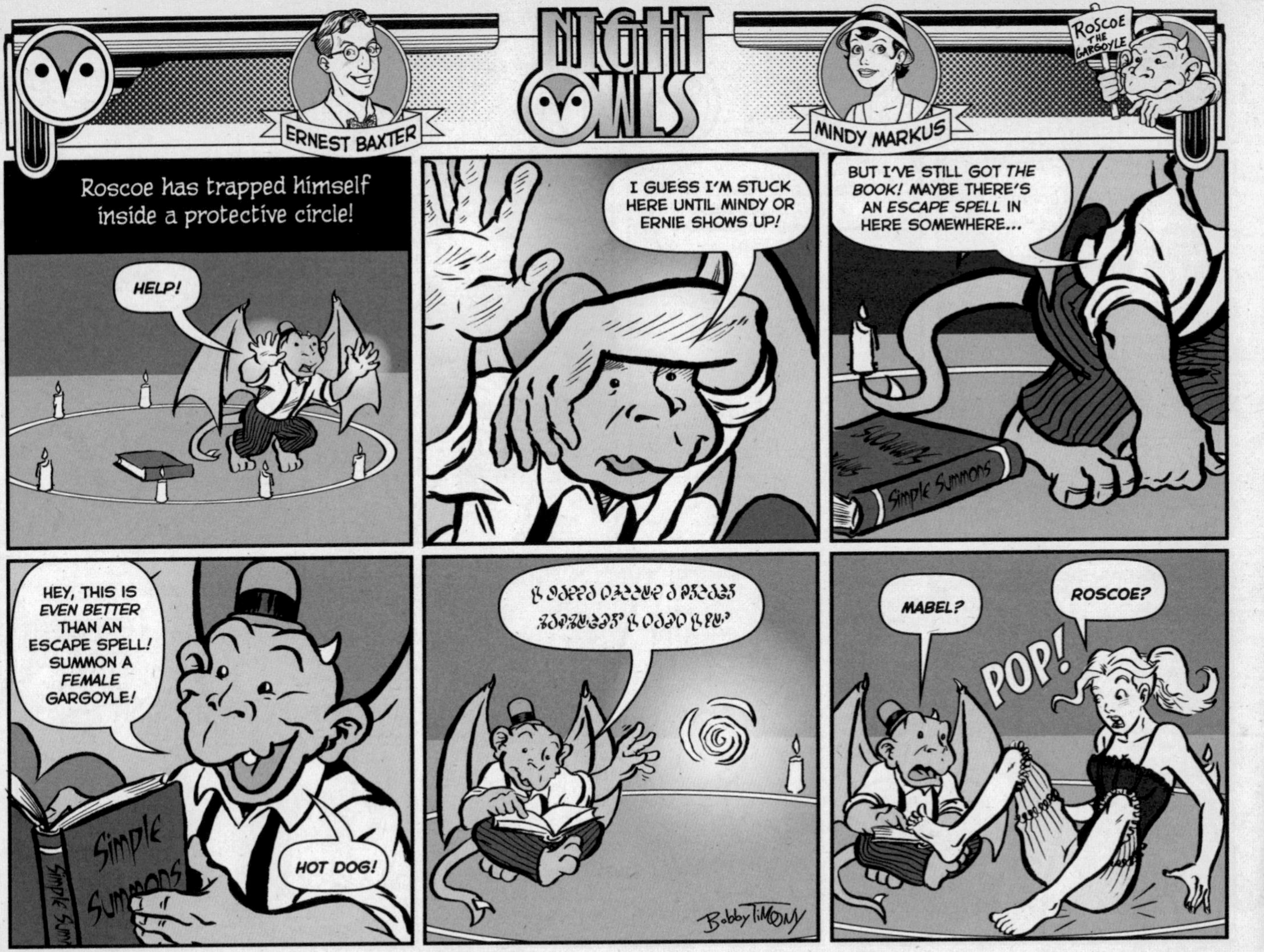
NIGHT OWLS
ERNEST BAXTER
MINDY MARKUS
ROSCOE THE GARGOYLE
Roscoe has trapped himself inside a protective circle!
HELP!
I GUESS I'M STUCK HERE UNTIL MINDY OR ERNIE SHOWS UP!
BUT I'VE STILL GOT *THE BOOK!* MAYBE THERE'S AN *ESCAPE SPELL* IN HERE SOMEWHERE...
Simple Summons
HEY, THIS IS *EVEN BETTER* THAN AN ESCAPE SPELL! SUMMON A *FEMALE* GARGOYLE!
Simple Summons
HOT DOG!
Bobby TiMONY
MABEL?
ROSCOE?
POP!

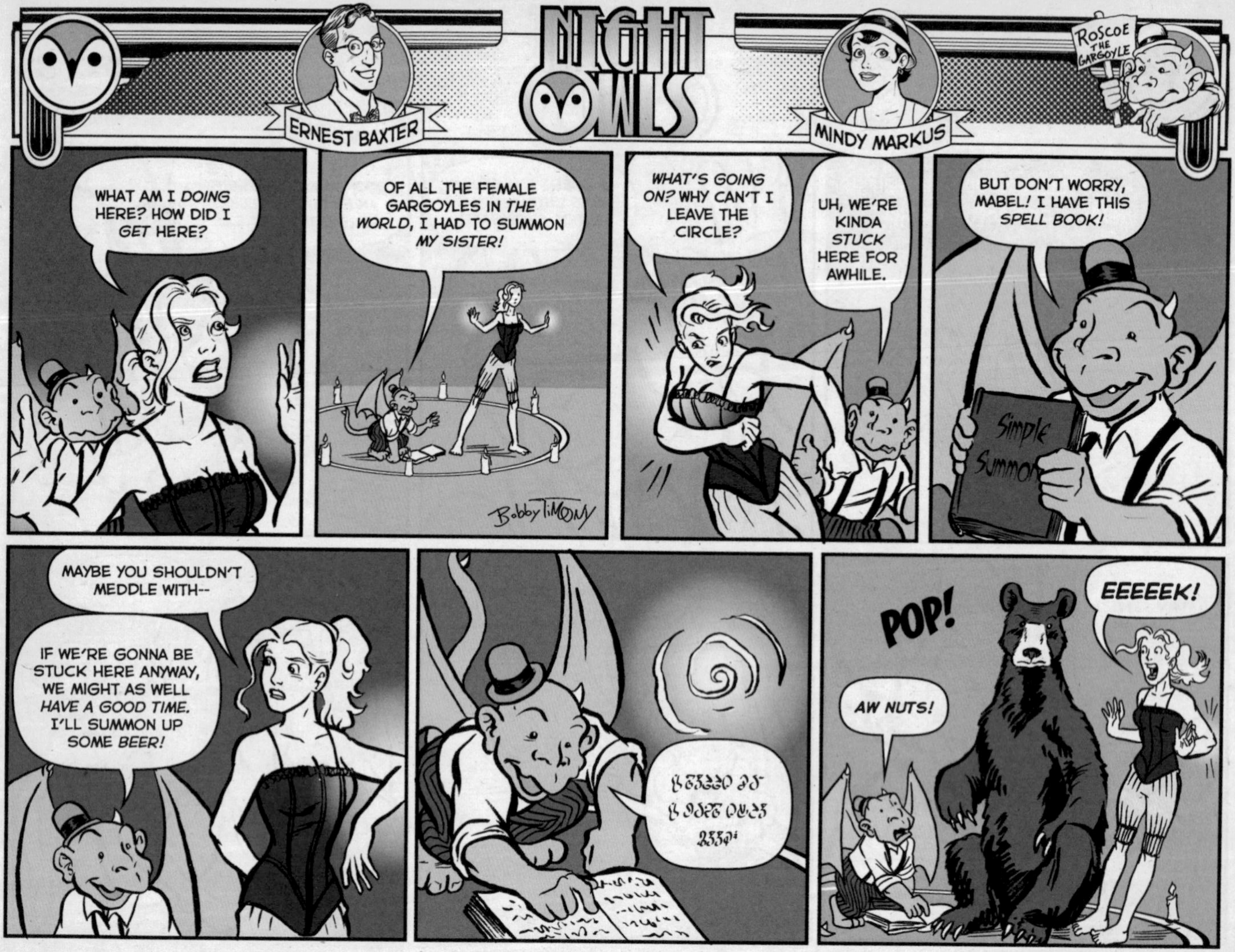
NIGHT OWLS
ERNEST BAXTER
MINDY MARKUS
ROSCOE THE GARGOYLE
WHAT AM I DOING HERE? HOW DID I GET HERE?
OF ALL THE FEMALE GARGOYLES IN THE WORLD, I HAD TO SUMMON MY SISTER!
Bobby Timony
WHAT'S GOING ON? WHY CAN'T I LEAVE THE CIRCLE?
UH, WE'RE KINDA STUCK HERE FOR AWHILE.
BUT DON'T WORRY, MABEL! I HAVE THIS SPELL BOOK!
Simple Summon
MAYBE YOU SHOULDN'T MEDDLE WITH--
IF WE'RE GONNA BE STUCK HERE ANYWAY, WE MIGHT AS WELL HAVE A GOOD TIME. I'LL SUMMON UP SOME BEER!
POP!
EEEEEK!
AW NUTS!

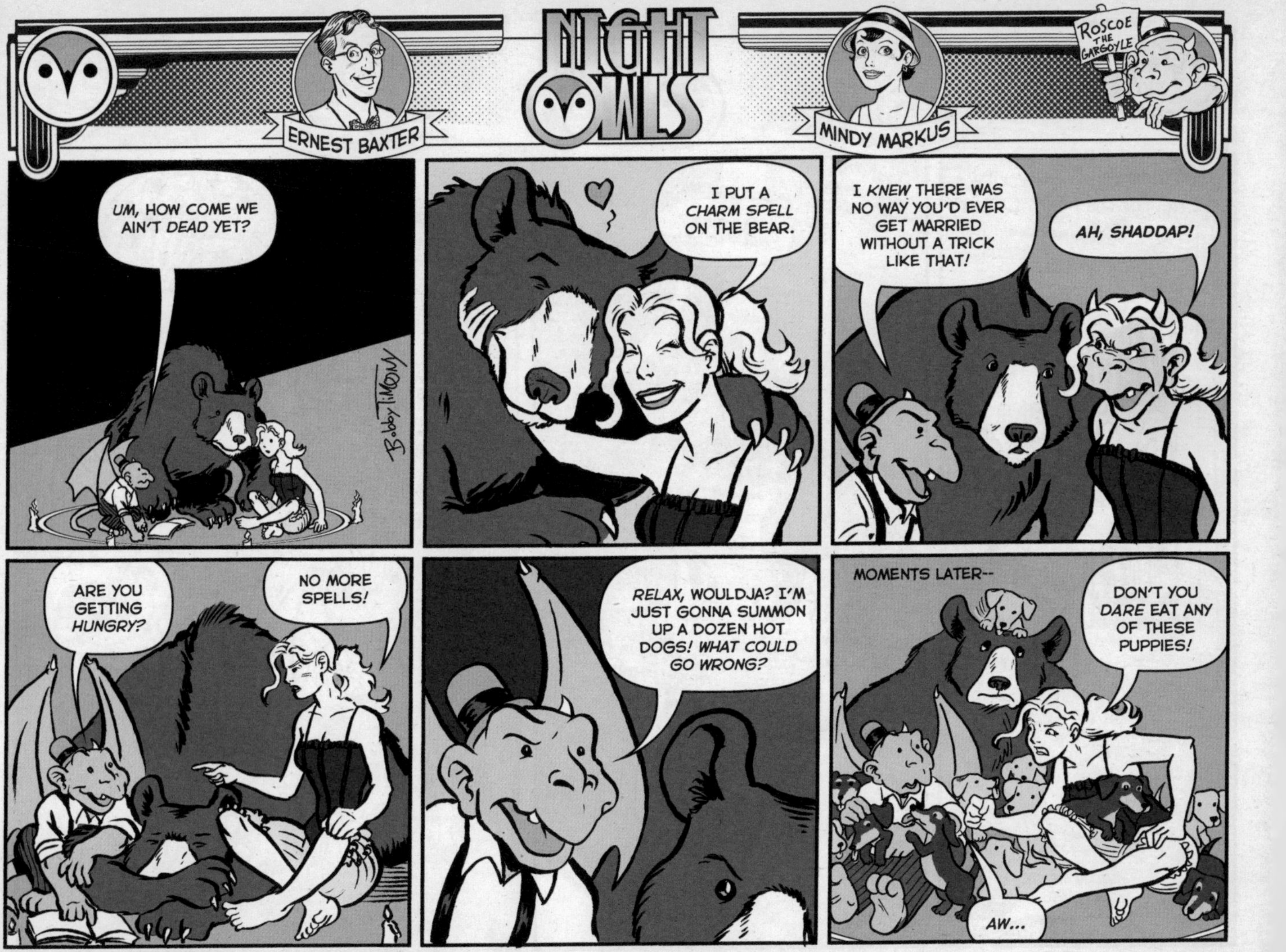
NIGHT OWLS
ERNEST BAXTER
MINDY MARKUS
ROSCOE THE GARGOYLE
UM, HOW COME WE AIN'T DEAD YET?
Bobby Timony
I PUT A CHARM SPELL ON THE BEAR.
I KNEW THERE WAS NO WAY YOU'D EVER GET MARRIED WITHOUT A TRICK LIKE THAT!
AH, SHADDAP!
ARE YOU GETTING HUNGRY?
NO MORE SPELLS!
RELAX, WOULDJA? I'M JUST GONNA SUMMON UP A DOZEN HOT DOGS! WHAT COULD GO WRONG?
MOMENTS LATER--
DON'T YOU DARE EAT ANY OF THESE PUPPIES!
AW...

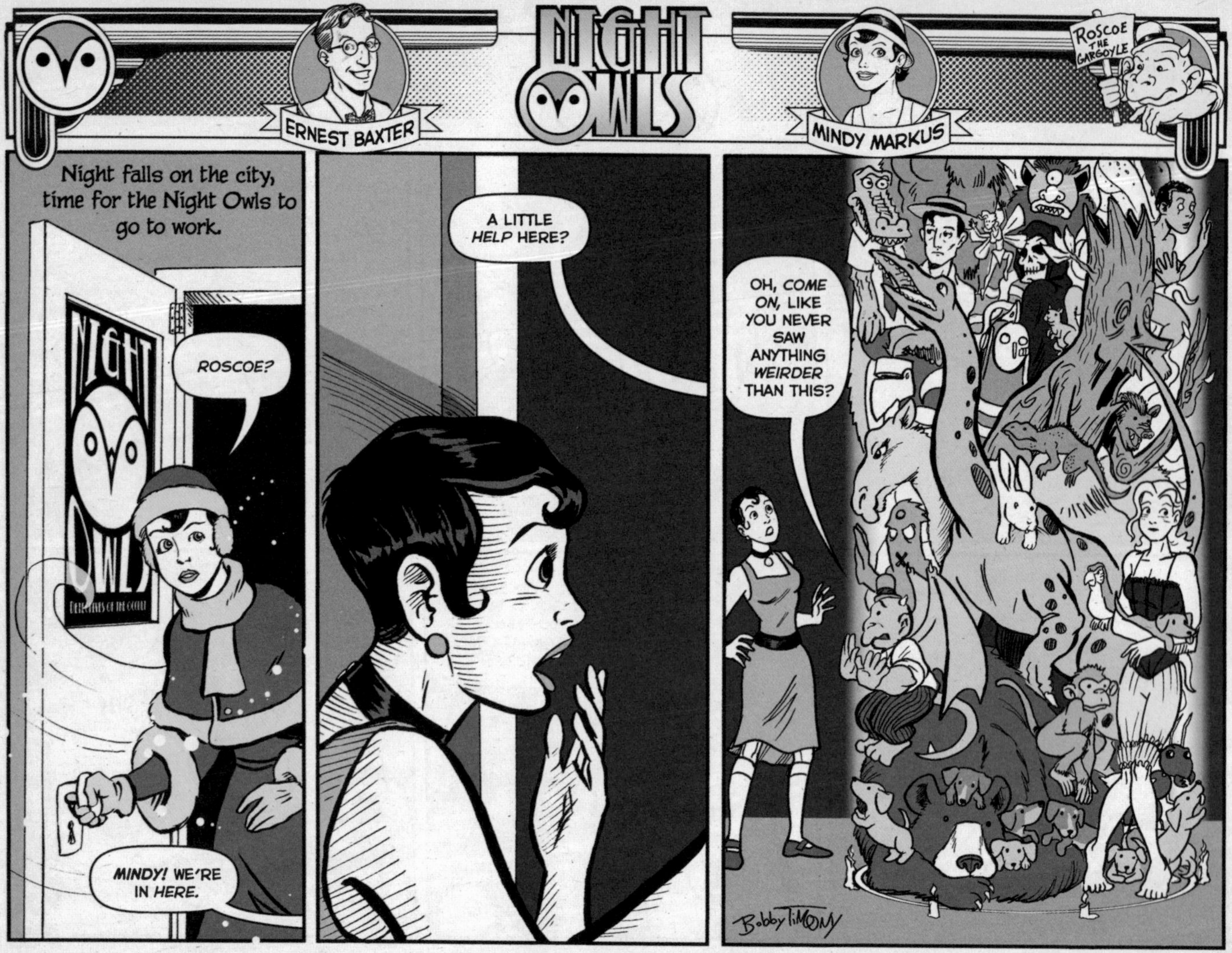
NIGHT OWLS
ERNEST BAXTER
MINDY MARKUS
ROSCOE THE GARGOYLE
Night falls on the city, time for the Night Owls to go to work.
NIGHT OWLS
DETECTIVES OF THE OCCULT
ROSCOE?
MINDY! WE'RE IN HERE.
A LITTLE HELP HERE?
OH, COME ON, LIKE YOU NEVER SAW ANYTHING WEIRDER THAN THIS?
Bobby Timony

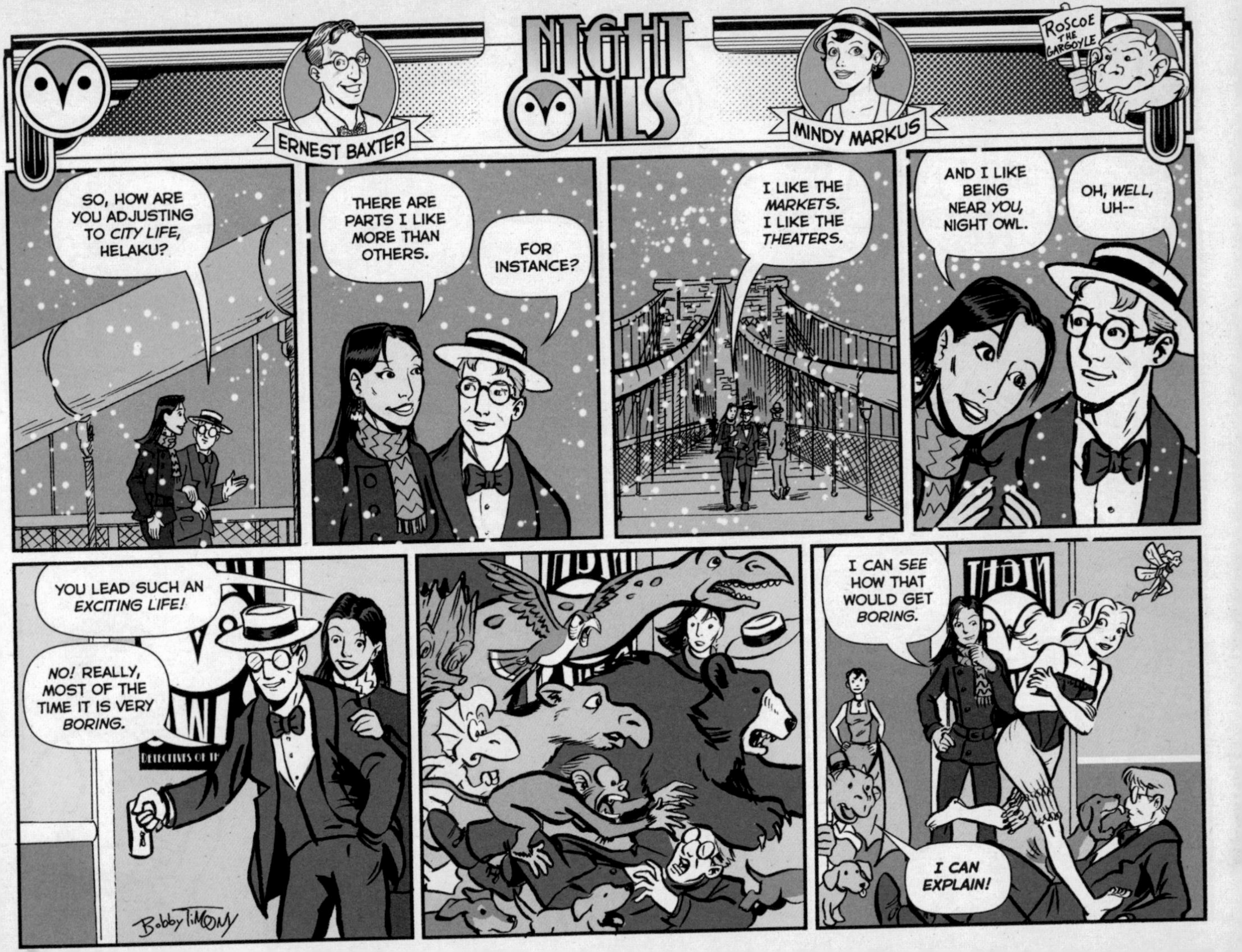
NIGHT OWLS
ERNEST BAXTER
MINDY MARKUS
ROSCOE THE GARGOYLE
SO, HOW ARE YOU ADJUSTING TO CITY LIFE, HELAKU?
THERE ARE PARTS I LIKE MORE THAN OTHERS.
FOR INSTANCE?
I LIKE THE MARKETS. I LIKE THE THEATERS.
AND I LIKE BEING NEAR YOU, NIGHT OWL.
OH, WELL, UH--
YOU LEAD SUCH AN EXCITING LIFE!
NO! REALLY, MOST OF THE TIME IT IS VERY BORING.
I CAN SEE HOW THAT WOULD GET BORING.
I CAN EXPLAIN!
Bobby Timony

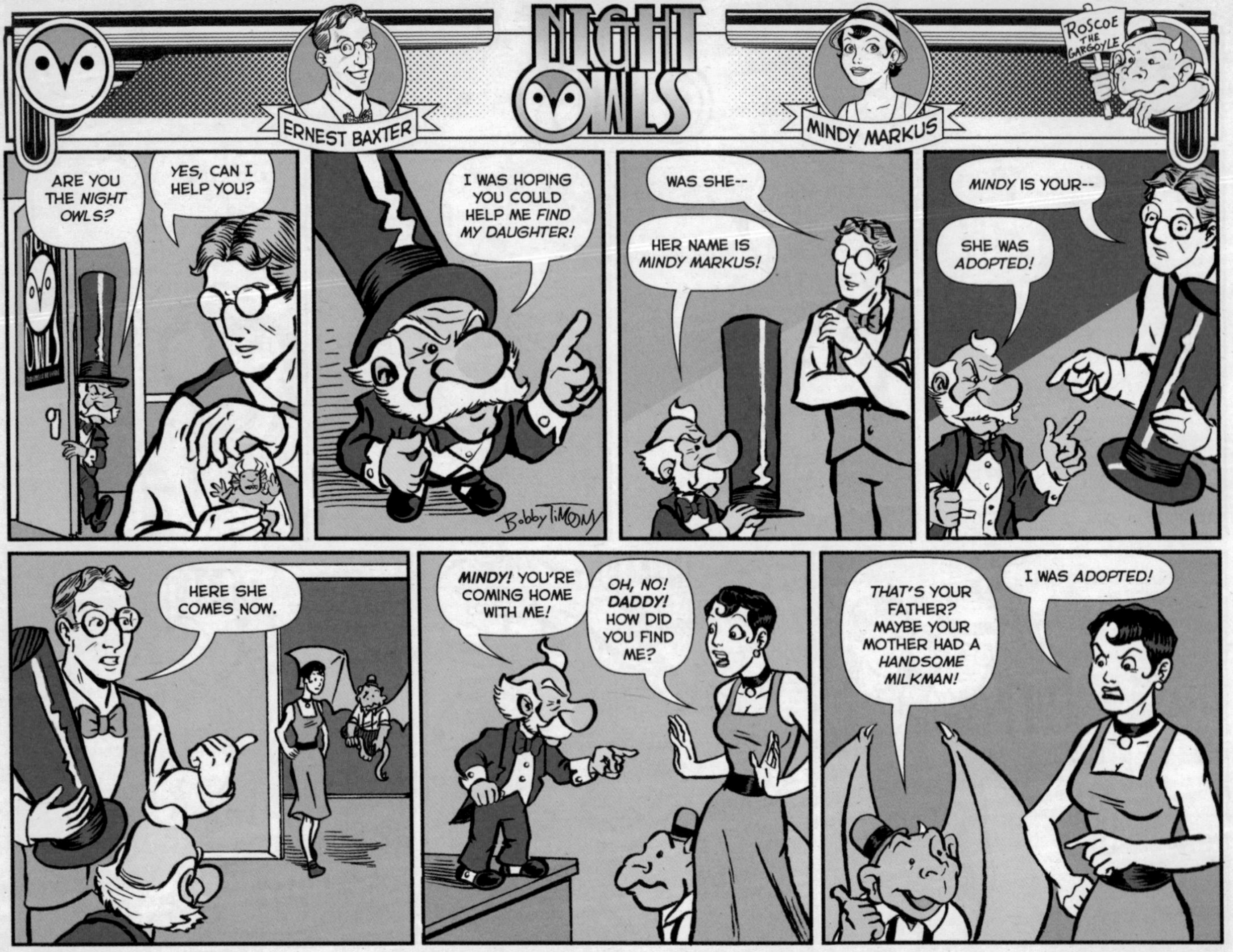
NIGHT OWLS
ERNEST BAXTER
MINDY MARKUS
ROSCOE THE GARGOYLE
ARE YOU THE *NIGHT OWLS?*
YES, CAN I HELP YOU?
I WAS HOPING YOU COULD HELP ME *FIND MY DAUGHTER!*
Bobby TiMONY
WAS SHE--
HER NAME IS *MINDY MARKUS!*
MINDY IS YOUR--
SHE WAS *ADOPTED!*
HERE SHE COMES NOW.
MINDY! YOU'RE COMING HOME WITH ME!
OH, NO! ***DADDY!*** HOW DID YOU FIND ME?
THAT'S YOUR FATHER? MAYBE YOUR MOTHER HAD A *HANDSOME MILKMAN!*
I WAS *ADOPTED!*

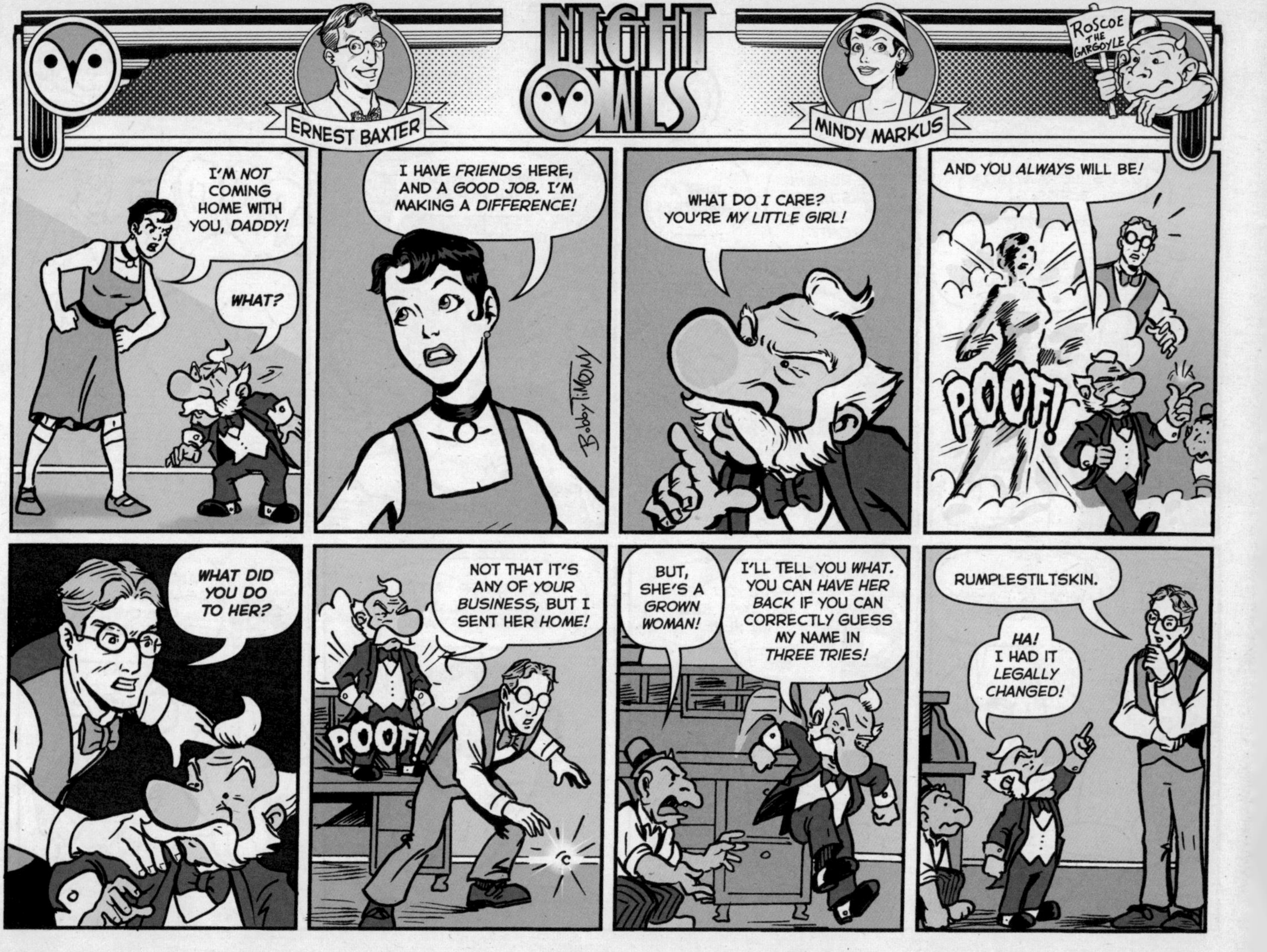
NIGHT OWLS
ERNEST BAXTER
MINDY MARKUS
ROSCOE THE GARGOYLE
I'M NOT COMING HOME WITH YOU, DADDY!
WHAT?
I HAVE FRIENDS HERE, AND A GOOD JOB. I'M MAKING A DIFFERENCE!
Bobby Timony
WHAT DO I CARE? YOU'RE MY LITTLE GIRL!
AND YOU ALWAYS WILL BE!
POOF!
WHAT DID YOU DO TO HER?
NOT THAT IT'S ANY OF YOUR BUSINESS, BUT I SENT HER HOME!
POOF!
BUT, SHE'S A GROWN WOMAN!
I'LL TELL YOU WHAT. YOU CAN HAVE HER BACK IF YOU CAN CORRECTLY GUESS MY NAME IN THREE TRIES!
RUMPLESTILTSKIN.
HA! I HAD IT LEGALLY CHANGED!

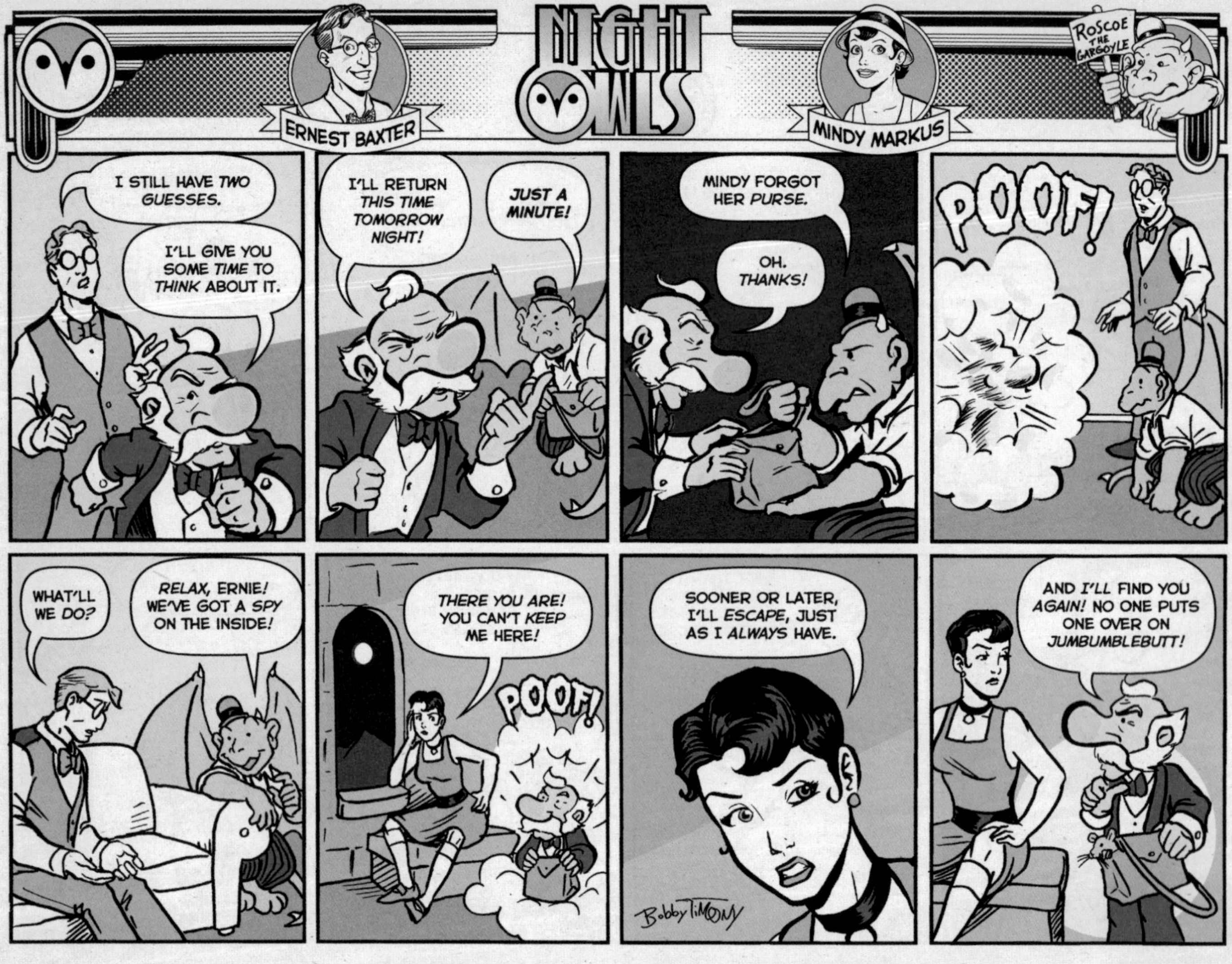
NIGHT OWLS
ERNEST BAXTER
MINDY MARKUS
ROSCOE THE GARGOYLE
I STILL HAVE TWO GUESSES.
I'LL GIVE YOU SOME TIME TO THINK ABOUT IT.
I'LL RETURN THIS TIME TOMORROW NIGHT!
JUST A MINUTE!
MINDY FORGOT HER PURSE.
OH. THANKS!
POOF!
WHAT'LL WE DO?
RELAX, ERNIE! WE'VE GOT A SPY ON THE INSIDE!
THERE YOU ARE! YOU CAN'T KEEP ME HERE!
POOF!
SOONER OR LATER, I'LL ESCAPE, JUST AS I ALWAYS HAVE.
Bobby Timony
AND I'LL FIND YOU AGAIN! NO ONE PUTS ONE OVER ON JUMBUMBLEBUTT!

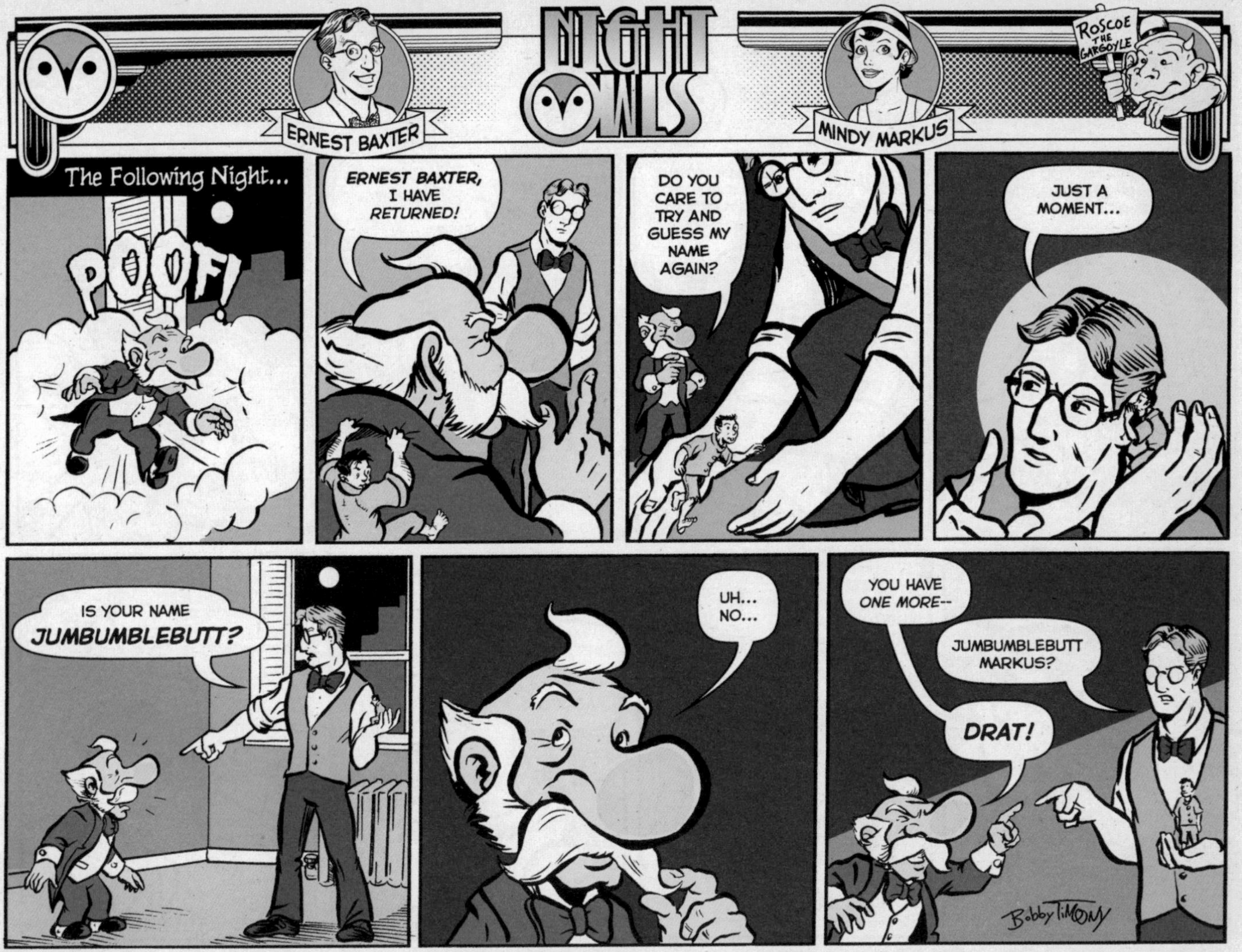
NIGHT OWLS
ERNEST BAXTER
MINDY MARKUS
ROSCOE THE GARGOYLE
The Following Night...
POOF!
ERNEST BAXTER, I HAVE RETURNED!
DO YOU CARE TO TRY AND GUESS MY NAME AGAIN?
JUST A MOMENT...
IS YOUR NAME JUMBUMBLEBUTT?
UH... NO...
YOU HAVE ONE MORE--
JUMBUMBLEBUTT MARKUS?
DRAT!
Bobby Timony

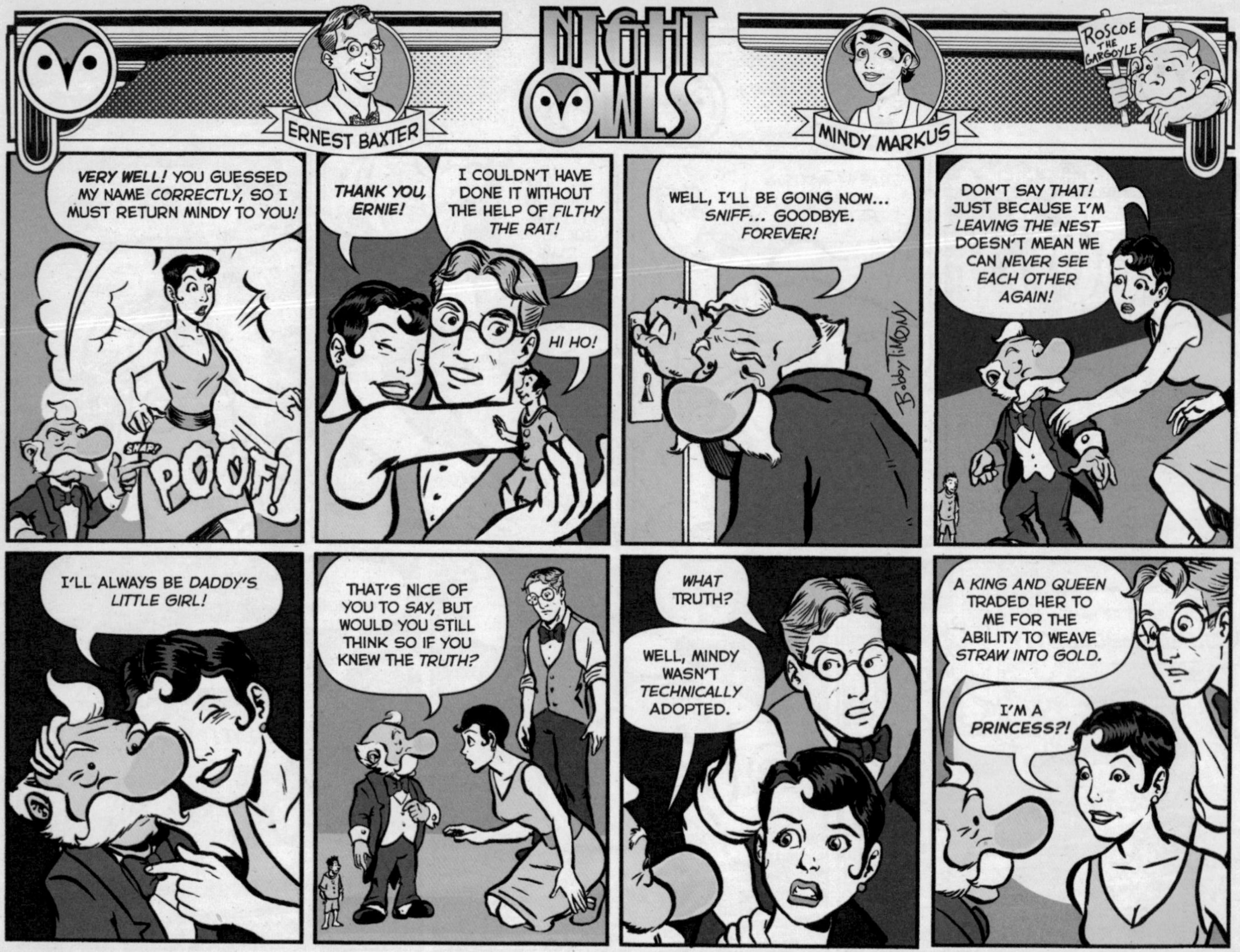
NIGHT OWLS
ERNEST BAXTER
MINDY MARKUS
ROSCOE THE GARGOYLE
VERY WELL! YOU GUESSED MY NAME CORRECTLY, SO I MUST RETURN MINDY TO YOU!
SNAP!
POOF!
THANK YOU, ERNIE!
I COULDN'T HAVE DONE IT WITHOUT THE HELP OF FILTHY THE RAT!
HI HO!
WELL, I'LL BE GOING NOW... SNIFF... GOODBYE. FOREVER!
Bobby Timony
DON'T SAY THAT! JUST BECAUSE I'M LEAVING THE NEST DOESN'T MEAN WE CAN NEVER SEE EACH OTHER AGAIN!
I'LL ALWAYS BE DADDY'S LITTLE GIRL!
THAT'S NICE OF YOU TO SAY, BUT WOULD YOU STILL THINK SO IF YOU KNEW THE TRUTH?
WHAT TRUTH?
WELL, MINDY WASN'T TECHNICALLY ADOPTED.
A KING AND QUEEN TRADED HER TO ME FOR THE ABILITY TO WEAVE STRAW INTO GOLD.
I'M A PRINCESS?!

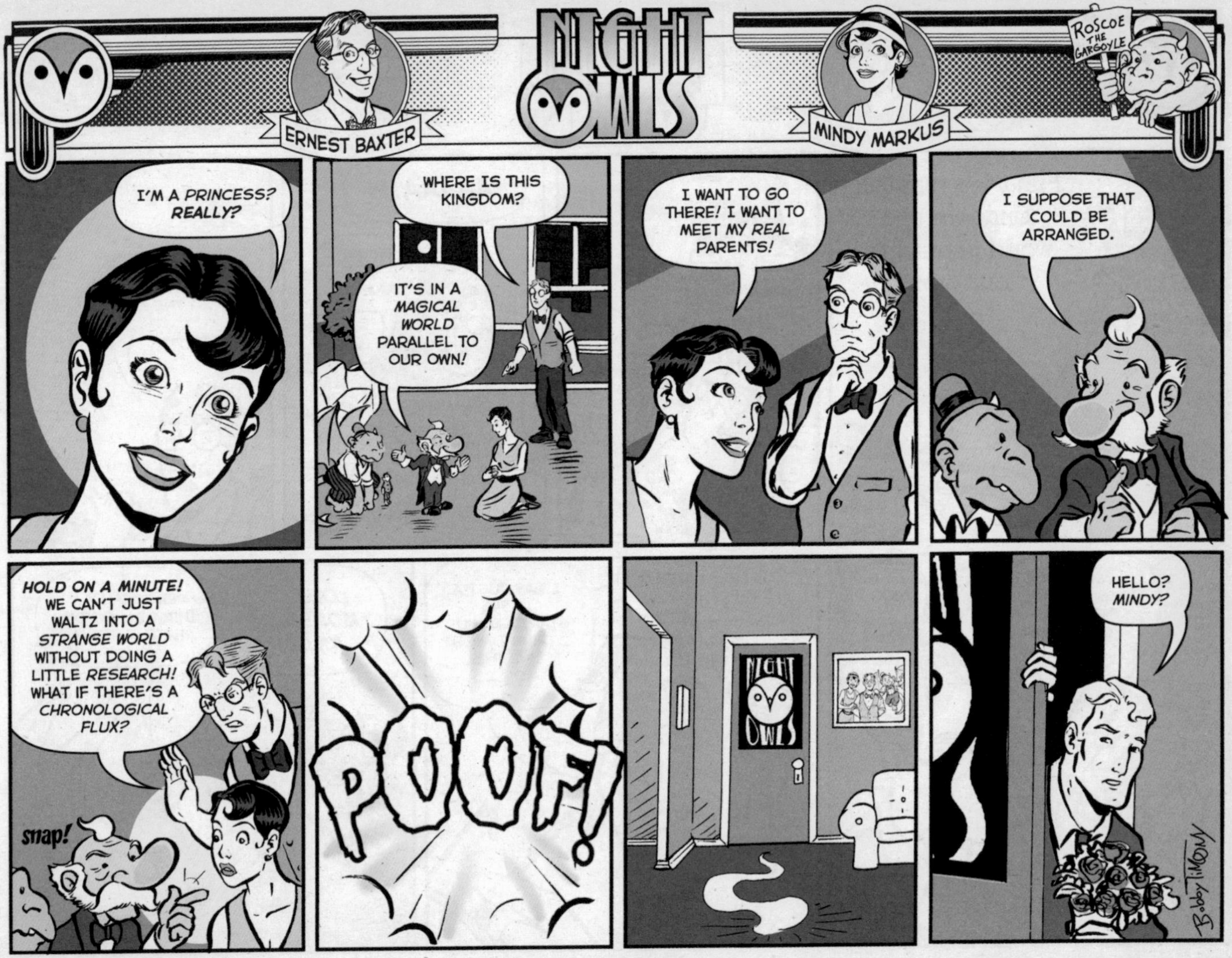

NIGHT OWLS
ERNEST BAXTER
MINDY MARKUS
ROSCOE THE GARGOYLE
I'M A *PRINCESS? REALLY?*
WHERE IS THIS KINGDOM?
IT'S IN A *MAGICAL WORLD* PARALLEL TO OUR OWN!
I WANT TO GO THERE! I WANT TO MEET MY *REAL* PARENTS!
I SUPPOSE THAT COULD BE ARRANGED.
HOLD ON A MINUTE! WE CAN'T JUST WALTZ INTO A *STRANGE WORLD* WITHOUT DOING A LITTLE *RESEARCH!* WHAT IF THERE'S A *CHRONOLOGICAL FLUX?*
snap!
POOF!
NIGHT OWLS
HELLO? *MINDY?*
Bobby Timony

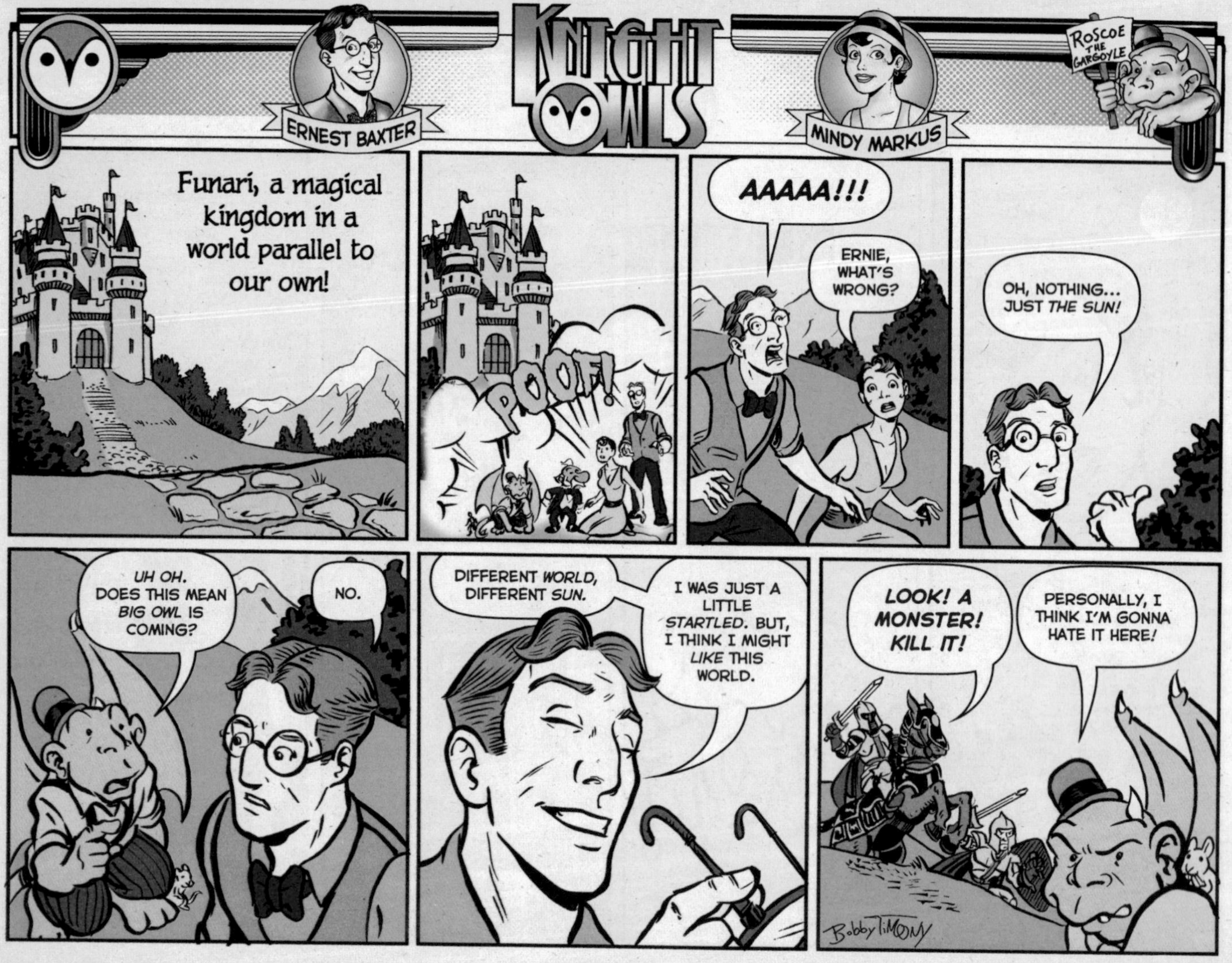
KNIGHT OWLS
ERNEST BAXTER
MINDY MARKUS
ROSCOE THE GARGOYLE
Funari, a magical kingdom in a world parallel to our own!
POOF!
AAAAA!!!
ERNIE, WHAT'S WRONG?
OH, NOTHING... JUST *THE SUN!*
UH OH. DOES THIS MEAN *BIG OWL* IS COMING?
NO.
DIFFERENT *WORLD,* DIFFERENT *SUN.*
I WAS JUST A LITTLE *STARTLED.* BUT, I THINK I MIGHT *LIKE* THIS WORLD.
LOOK! A MONSTER! KILL IT!
PERSONALLY, I THINK I'M GONNA HATE IT HERE!
Bobby Timony

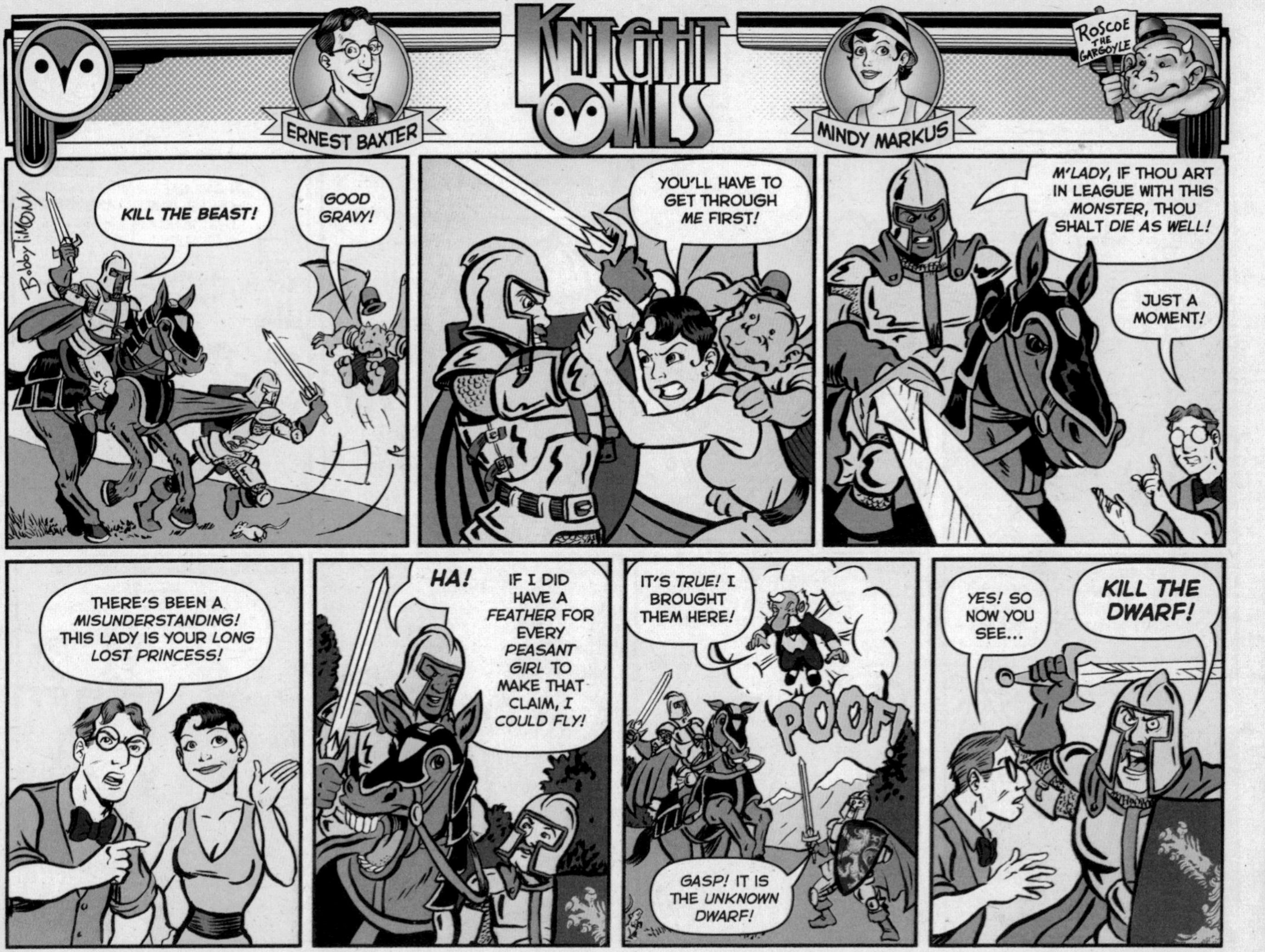
KNIGHT OWLS
ERNEST BAXTER
MINDY MARKUS
ROSCOE THE GARGOYLE
Bobby Timony
KILL THE BEAST!
GOOD GRAVY!
YOU'LL HAVE TO GET THROUGH ME FIRST!
M'LADY, IF THOU ART IN LEAGUE WITH THIS MONSTER, THOU SHALT DIE AS WELL!
JUST A MOMENT!
THERE'S BEEN A MISUNDERSTANDING! THIS LADY IS YOUR LONG LOST PRINCESS!
HA!
IF I DID HAVE A FEATHER FOR EVERY PEASANT GIRL TO MAKE THAT CLAIM, I COULD FLY!
IT'S TRUE! I BROUGHT THEM HERE!
POOF!
GASP! IT IS THE UNKNOWN DWARF!
YES! SO NOW YOU SEE...
KILL THE DWARF!

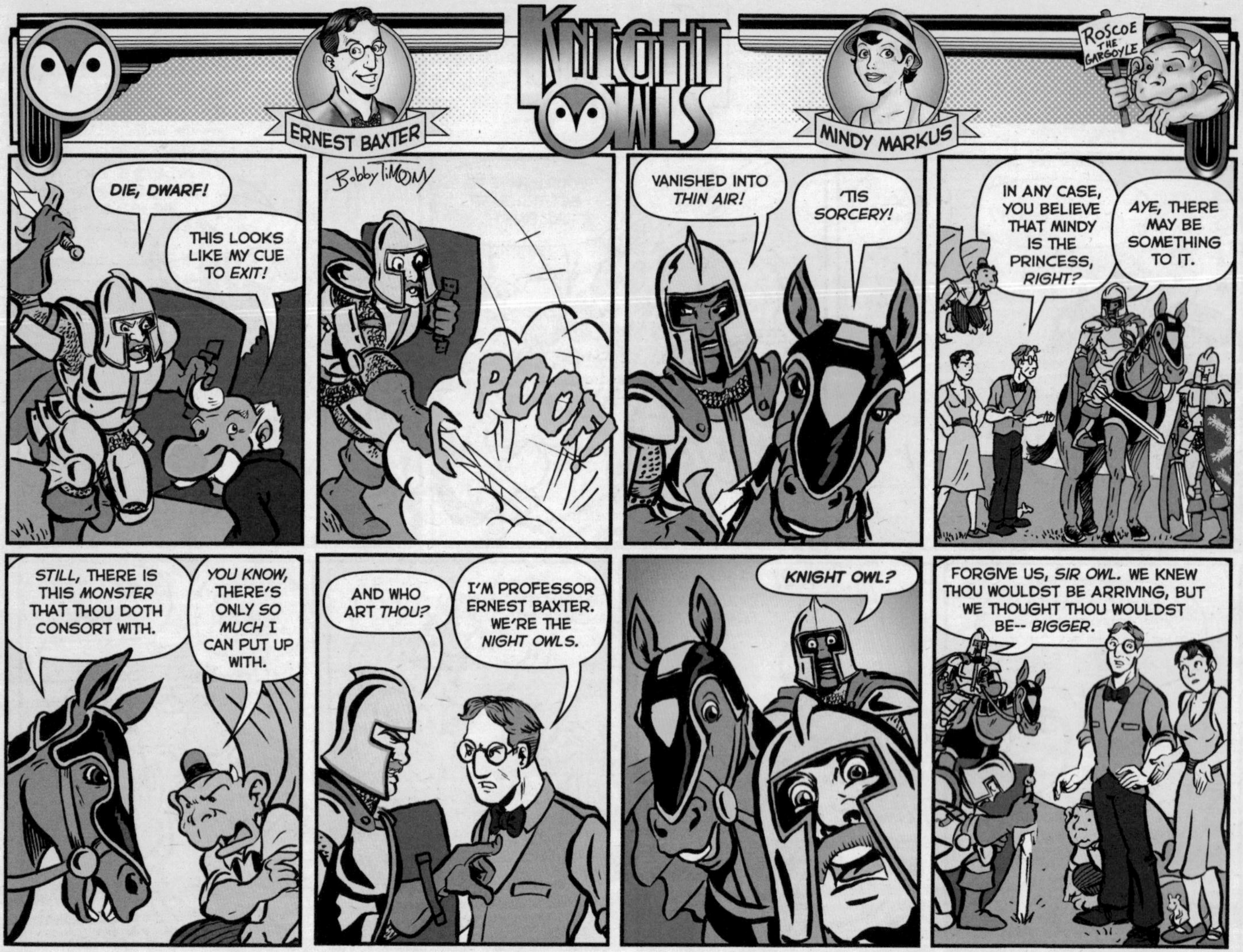
KNIGHT OWLS
ERNEST BAXTER
MINDY MARKUS
ROSCOE THE GARGOYLE
DIE, DWARF!
THIS LOOKS LIKE MY CUE TO EXIT!
Bobby Timony
POOF!
VANISHED INTO THIN AIR!
'TIS SORCERY!
IN ANY CASE, YOU BELIEVE THAT MINDY IS THE PRINCESS, RIGHT?
AYE, THERE MAY BE SOMETHING TO IT.
STILL, THERE IS THIS MONSTER THAT THOU DOTH CONSORT WITH.
YOU KNOW, THERE'S ONLY SO MUCH I CAN PUT UP WITH.
AND WHO ART THOU?
I'M PROFESSOR ERNEST BAXTER. WE'RE THE NIGHT OWLS.
KNIGHT OWL?
FORGIVE US, SIR OWL. WE KNEW THOU WOULDST BE ARRIVING, BUT WE THOUGHT THOU WOULDST BE-- BIGGER.

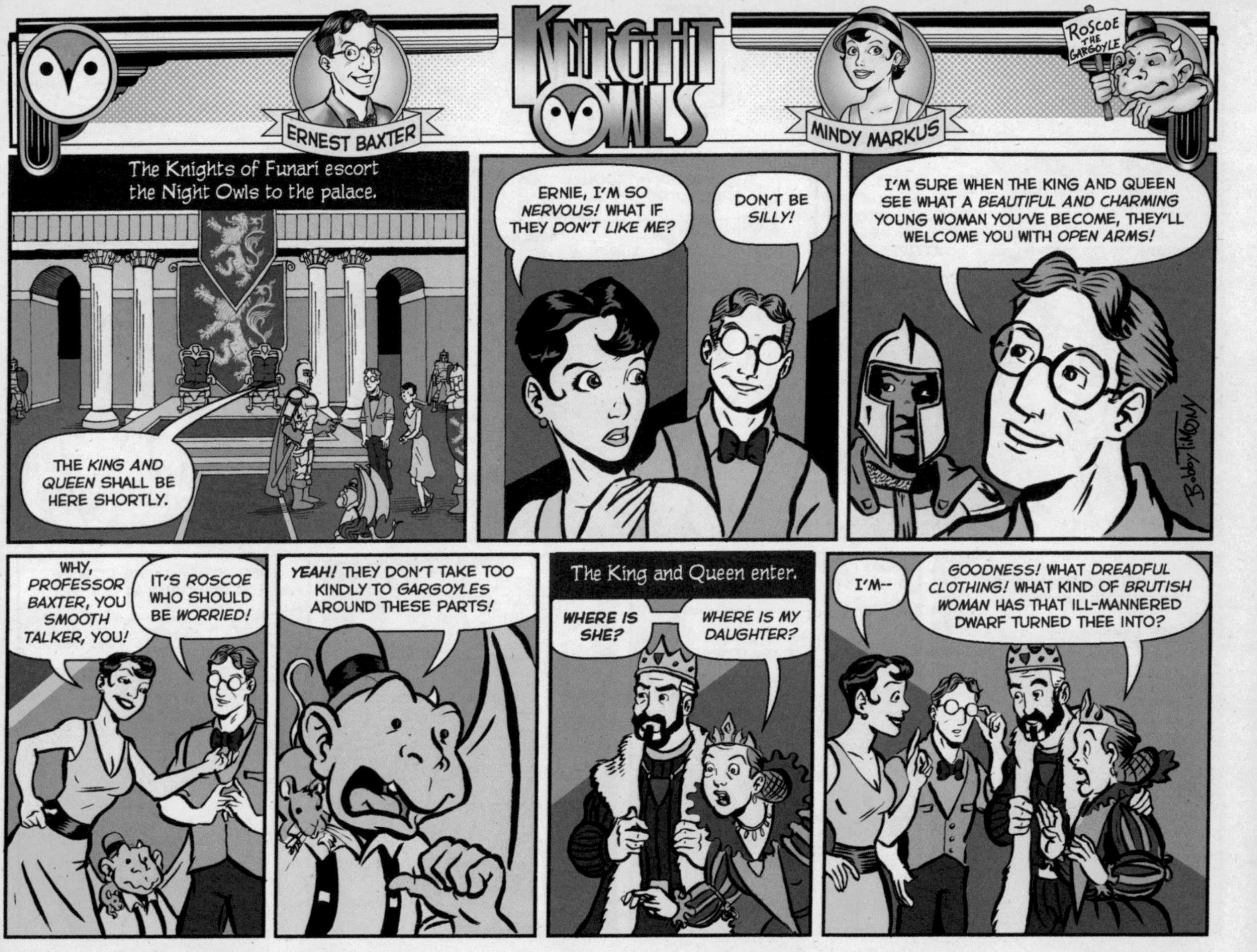
KNIGHT OWLS
ERNEST BAXTER
MINDY MARKUS
ROSCOE THE GARGOYLE
The Knights of Funari escort the Night Owls to the palace.
THE KING AND QUEEN SHALL BE HERE SHORTLY.
ERNIE, I'M SO NERVOUS! WHAT IF THEY DON'T LIKE ME?
DON'T BE SILLY!
I'M SURE WHEN THE KING AND QUEEN SEE WHAT A BEAUTIFUL AND CHARMING YOUNG WOMAN YOU'VE BECOME, THEY'LL WELCOME YOU WITH OPEN ARMS!
Bobby Timony
WHY, PROFESSOR BAXTER, YOU SMOOTH TALKER, YOU!
IT'S ROSCOE WHO SHOULD BE WORRIED!
YEAH! THEY DON'T TAKE TOO KINDLY TO GARGOYLES AROUND THESE PARTS!
The King and Queen enter.
WHERE IS SHE?
WHERE IS MY DAUGHTER?
I'M--
GOODNESS! WHAT DREADFUL CLOTHING! WHAT KIND OF BRUTISH WOMAN HAS THAT ILL-MANNERED DWARF TURNED THEE INTO?

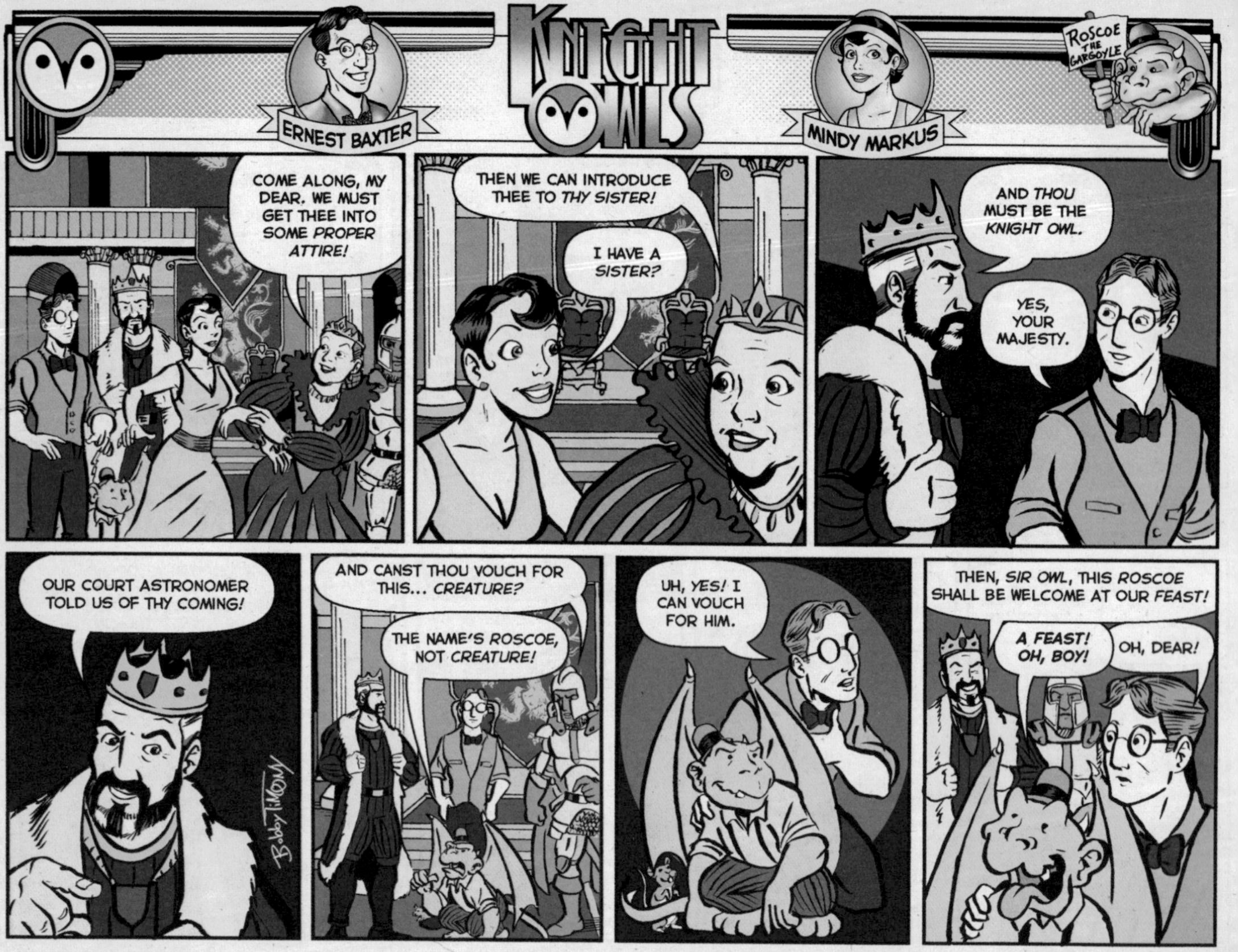

KNIGHT OWLS
ERNEST BAXTER
MINDY MARKUS
ROSCOE THE GARGOYLE
COME ALONG, MY DEAR. WE MUST GET THEE INTO SOME PROPER ATTIRE!
THEN WE CAN INTRODUCE THEE TO THY SISTER!
I HAVE A SISTER?
AND THOU MUST BE THE KNIGHT OWL.
YES, YOUR MAJESTY.
OUR COURT ASTRONOMER TOLD US OF THY COMING!
Bobby Timony
AND CANST THOU VOUCH FOR THIS... CREATURE?
THE NAME'S ROSCOE, NOT CREATURE!
UH, YES! I CAN VOUCH FOR HIM.
THEN, SIR OWL, THIS ROSCOE SHALL BE WELCOME AT OUR FEAST!
A FEAST! OH, BOY!
OH, DEAR!

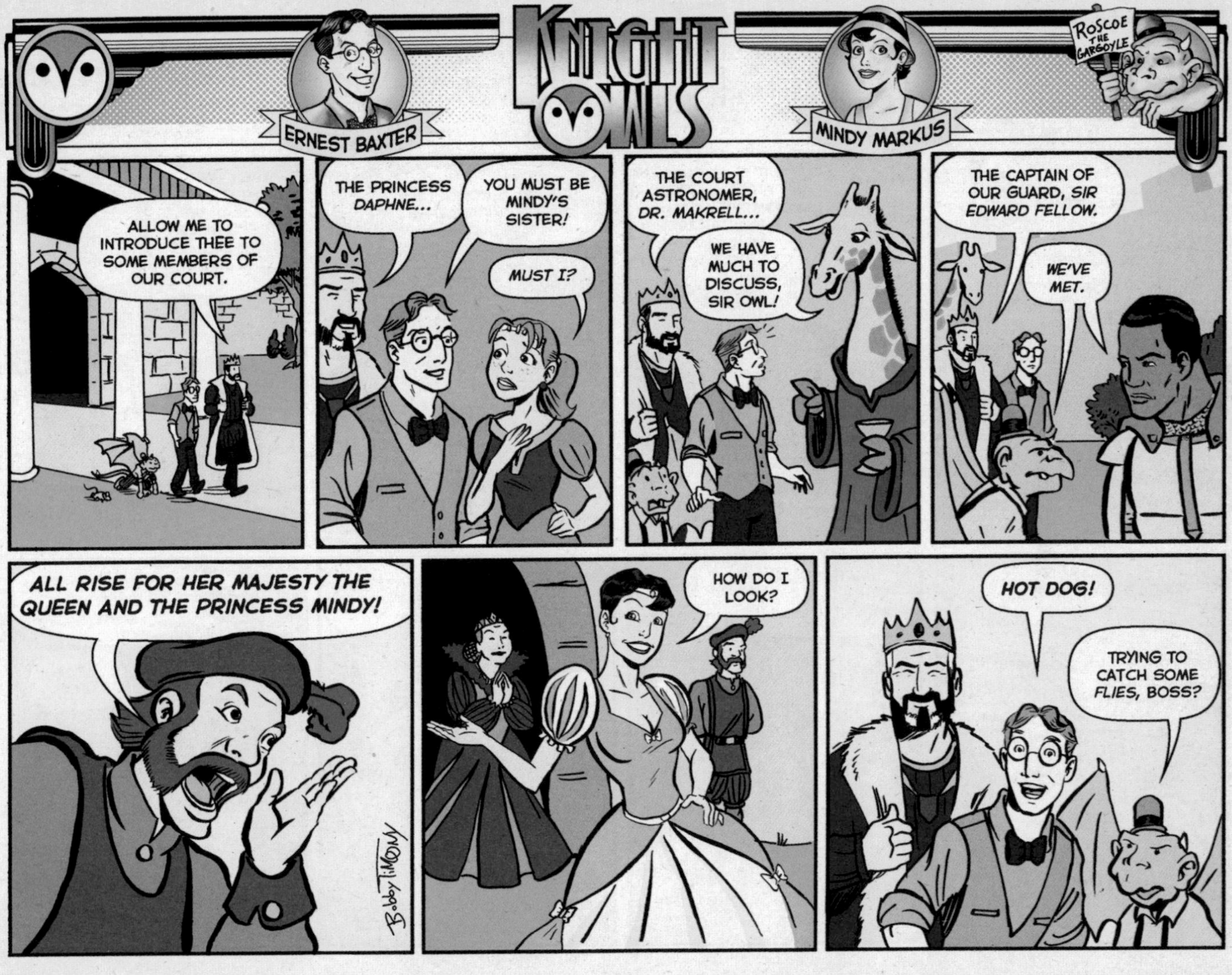

KNIGHT OWLS
ERNEST BAXTER
MINDY MARKUS
ROSCOE THE GARGOYLE
ALLOW ME TO INTRODUCE THEE TO SOME MEMBERS OF OUR COURT.
THE PRINCESS DAPHNE...
YOU MUST BE MINDY'S SISTER!
MUST I?
THE COURT ASTRONOMER, DR. MAKRELL...
WE HAVE MUCH TO DISCUSS, SIR OWL!
THE CAPTAIN OF OUR GUARD, SIR EDWARD FELLOW.
WE'VE MET.
ALL RISE FOR HER MAJESTY THE QUEEN AND THE PRINCESS MINDY!
Bobby Timony
HOW DO I LOOK?
HOT DOG!
TRYING TO CATCH SOME FLIES, BOSS?

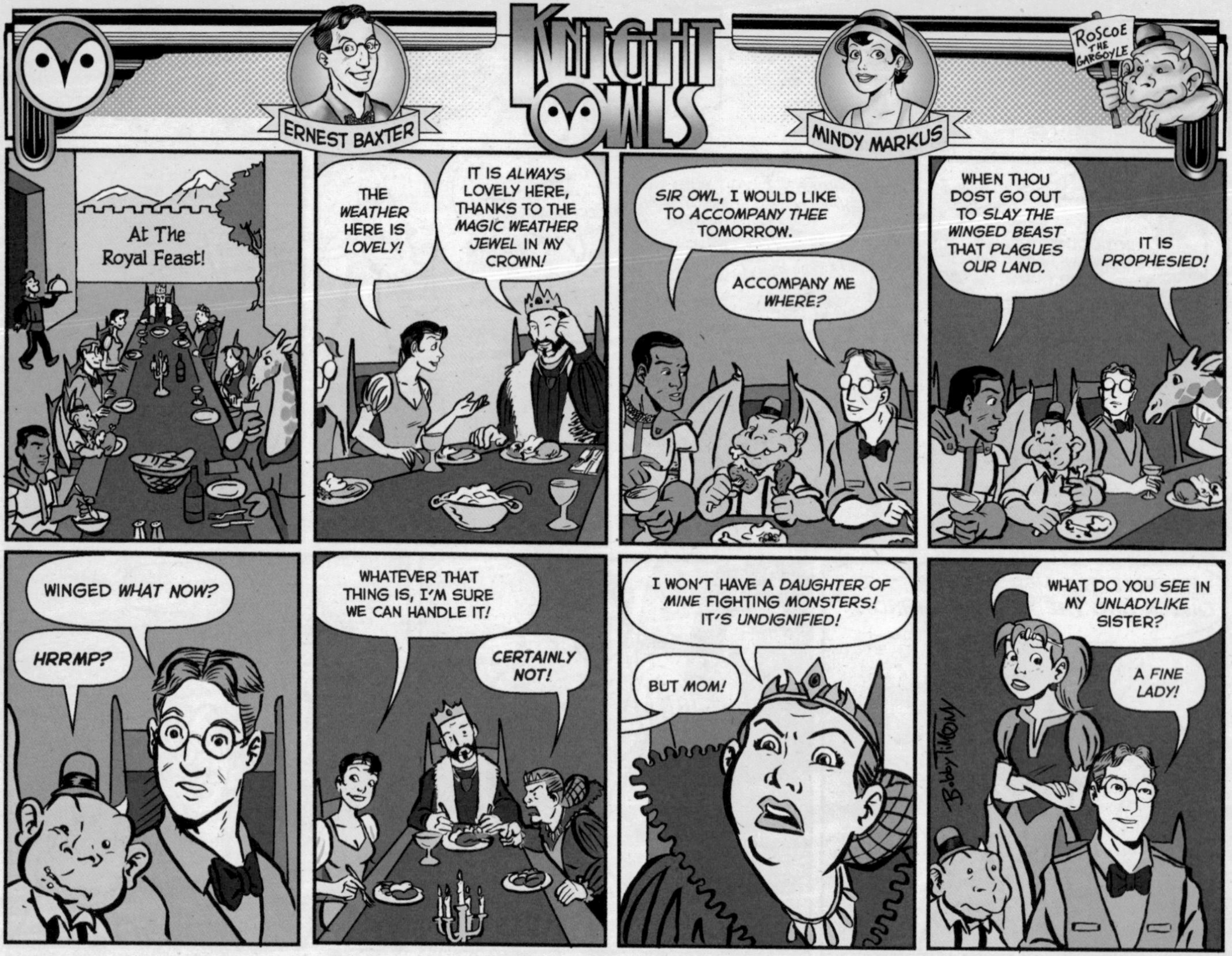
KNIGHT OWLS
ERNEST BAXTER
MINDY MARKUS
ROSCOE THE GARGOYLE
At The Royal Feast!
THE WEATHER HERE IS LOVELY!
IT IS ALWAYS LOVELY HERE, THANKS TO THE MAGIC WEATHER JEWEL IN MY CROWN!
SIR OWL, I WOULD LIKE TO ACCOMPANY THEE TOMORROW.
ACCOMPANY ME WHERE?
WHEN THOU DOST GO OUT TO SLAY THE WINGED BEAST THAT PLAGUES OUR LAND.
IT IS PROPHESIED!
WINGED WHAT NOW?
HRRMP?
WHATEVER THAT THING IS, I'M SURE WE CAN HANDLE IT!
CERTAINLY NOT!
I WON'T HAVE A DAUGHTER OF MINE FIGHTING MONSTERS! IT'S UNDIGNIFIED!
BUT MOM!
Bobby Timony
WHAT DO YOU SEE IN MY UNLADYLIKE SISTER?
A FINE LADY!

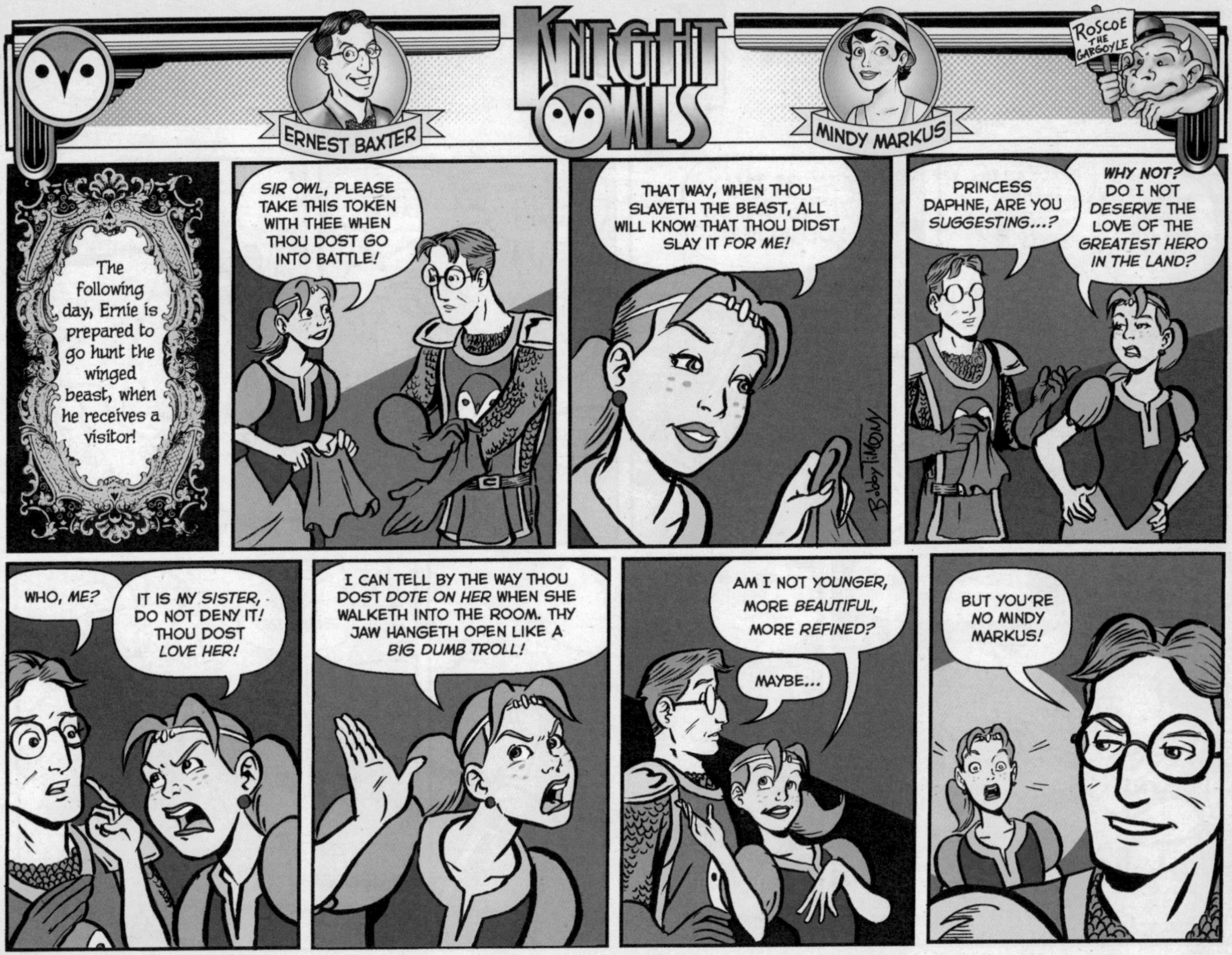
KNIGHT OWLS
ERNEST BAXTER
MINDY MARKUS
ROSCOE THE GARGOYLE
The following day, Ernie is prepared to go hunt the winged beast, when he receives a visitor!
SIR OWL, PLEASE TAKE THIS TOKEN WITH THEE WHEN THOU DOST GO INTO BATTLE!
THAT WAY, WHEN THOU SLAYETH THE BEAST, ALL WILL KNOW THAT THOU DIDST SLAY IT FOR ME!
Bobby Timony
PRINCESS DAPHNE, ARE YOU SUGGESTING...?
WHY NOT? DO I NOT DESERVE THE LOVE OF THE GREATEST HERO IN THE LAND?
WHO, ME?
IT IS MY SISTER, DO NOT DENY IT! THOU DOST LOVE HER!
I CAN TELL BY THE WAY THOU DOST DOTE ON HER WHEN SHE WALKETH INTO THE ROOM. THY JAW HANGETH OPEN LIKE A BIG DUMB TROLL!
AM I NOT YOUNGER, MORE BEAUTIFUL, MORE REFINED?
MAYBE...
BUT YOU'RE NO MINDY MARKUS!

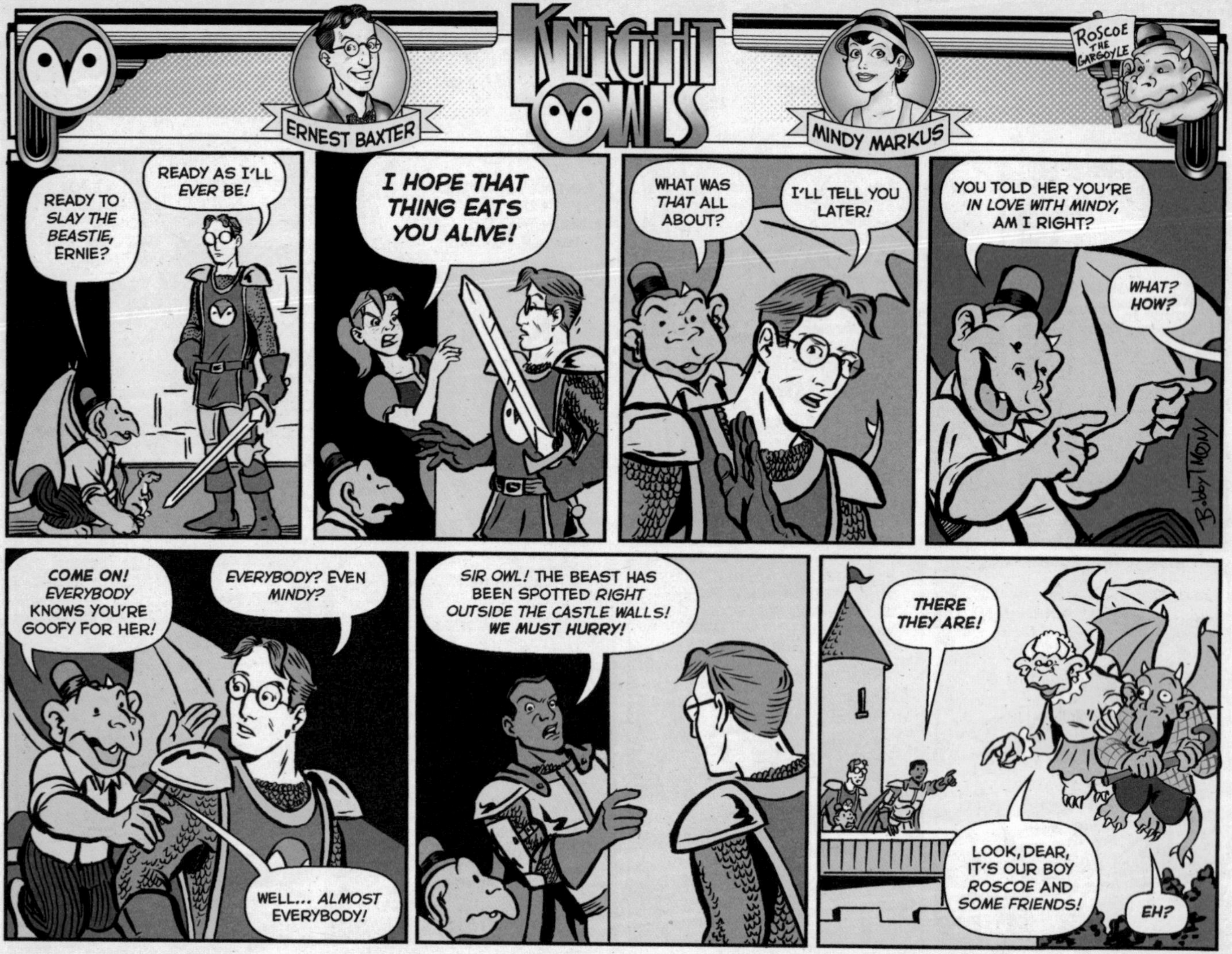
KNIGHT OWLS
ERNEST BAXTER
MINDY MARKUS
ROSCOE THE GARGOYLE
READY TO SLAY THE BEASTIE, ERNIE?
READY AS I'LL EVER BE!
I HOPE THAT THING EATS YOU ALIVE!
WHAT WAS THAT ALL ABOUT?
I'LL TELL YOU LATER!
YOU TOLD HER YOU'RE IN LOVE WITH MINDY, AM I RIGHT?
WHAT? HOW?
COME ON! EVERYBODY KNOWS YOU'RE GOOFY FOR HER!
EVERYBODY? EVEN MINDY?
WELL... ALMOST EVERYBODY!
SIR OWL! THE BEAST HAS BEEN SPOTTED RIGHT OUTSIDE THE CASTLE WALLS! WE MUST HURRY!
THERE THEY ARE!
LOOK, DEAR, IT'S OUR BOY ROSCOE AND SOME FRIENDS!
EH?

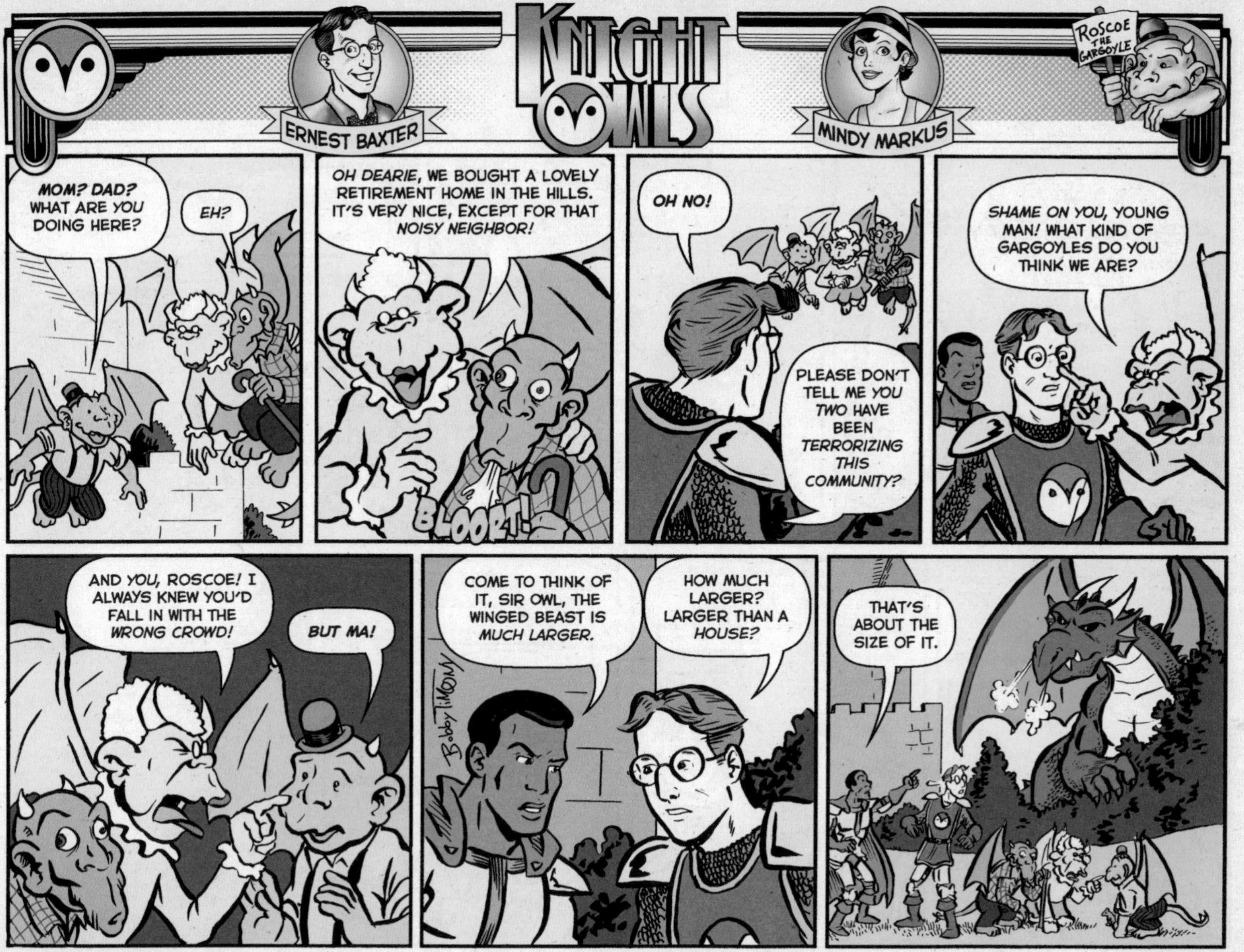
KNIGHT OWLS
ERNEST BAXTER
MINDY MARKUS
ROSCOE THE GARGOYLE
MOM? DAD? WHAT ARE YOU DOING HERE?
EH?
OH DEARIE, WE BOUGHT A LOVELY RETIREMENT HOME IN THE HILLS. IT'S VERY NICE, EXCEPT FOR THAT NOISY NEIGHBOR!
BLOORT!
OH NO!
PLEASE DON'T TELL ME YOU TWO HAVE BEEN TERRORIZING THIS COMMUNITY?
SHAME ON YOU, YOUNG MAN! WHAT KIND OF GARGOYLES DO YOU THINK WE ARE?
AND YOU, ROSCOE! I ALWAYS KNEW YOU'D FALL IN WITH THE WRONG CROWD!
BUT MA!
Bobby Timony
COME TO THINK OF IT, SIR OWL, THE WINGED BEAST IS MUCH LARGER.
HOW MUCH LARGER? LARGER THAN A HOUSE?
THAT'S ABOUT THE SIZE OF IT.

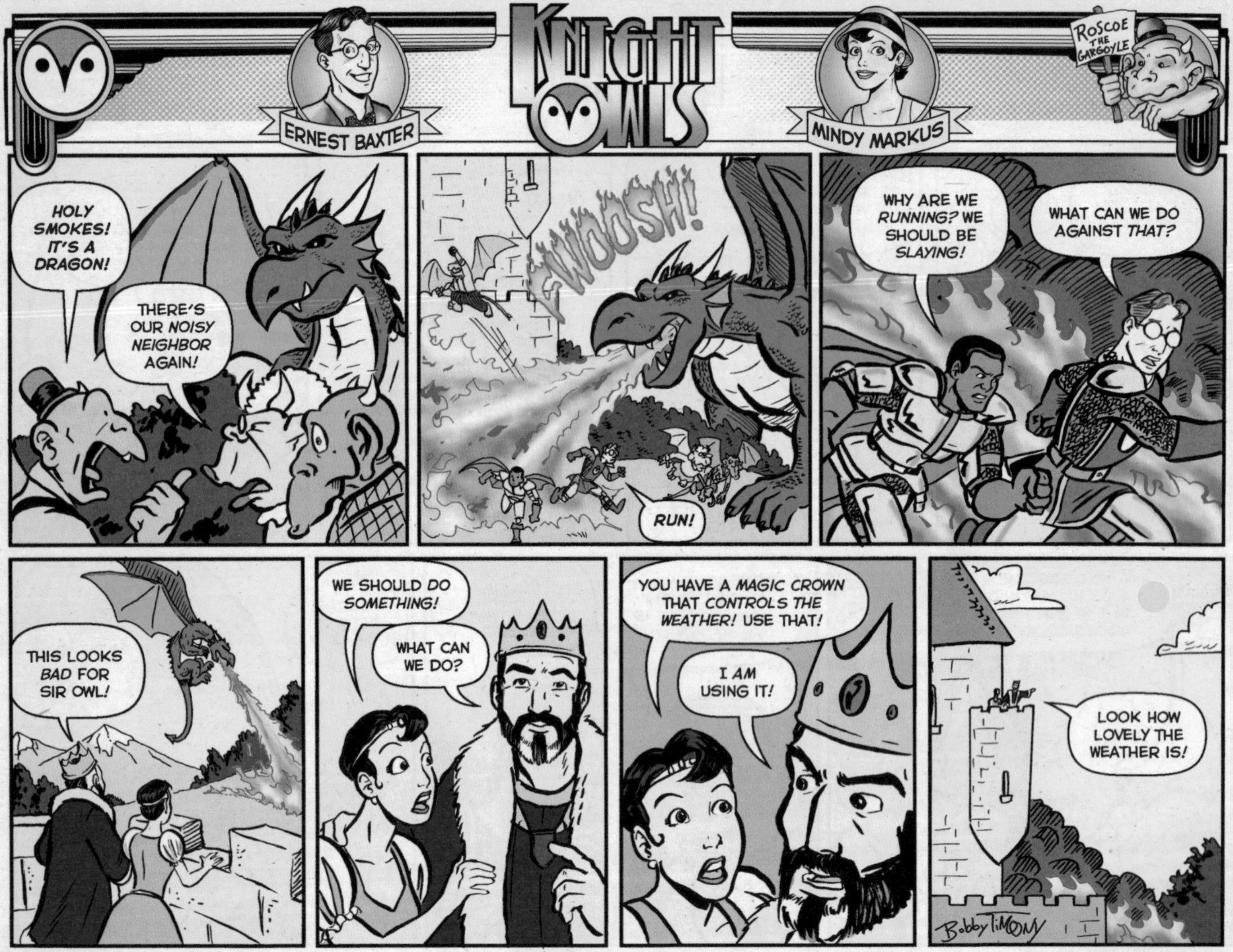
KNIGHT OWLS
ERNEST BAXTER
MINDY MARKUS
ROSCOE THE GARGOYLE
HOLY SMOKES! IT'S A DRAGON!
THERE'S OUR NOISY NEIGHBOR AGAIN!
FWOOSH!
RUN!
WHY ARE WE RUNNING? WE SHOULD BE SLAYING!
WHAT CAN WE DO AGAINST THAT?
THIS LOOKS BAD FOR SIR OWL!
WE SHOULD DO SOMETHING!
WHAT CAN WE DO?
YOU HAVE A MAGIC CROWN THAT CONTROLS THE WEATHER! USE THAT!
I AM USING IT!
LOOK HOW LOVELY THE WEATHER IS!
Bobby Timony

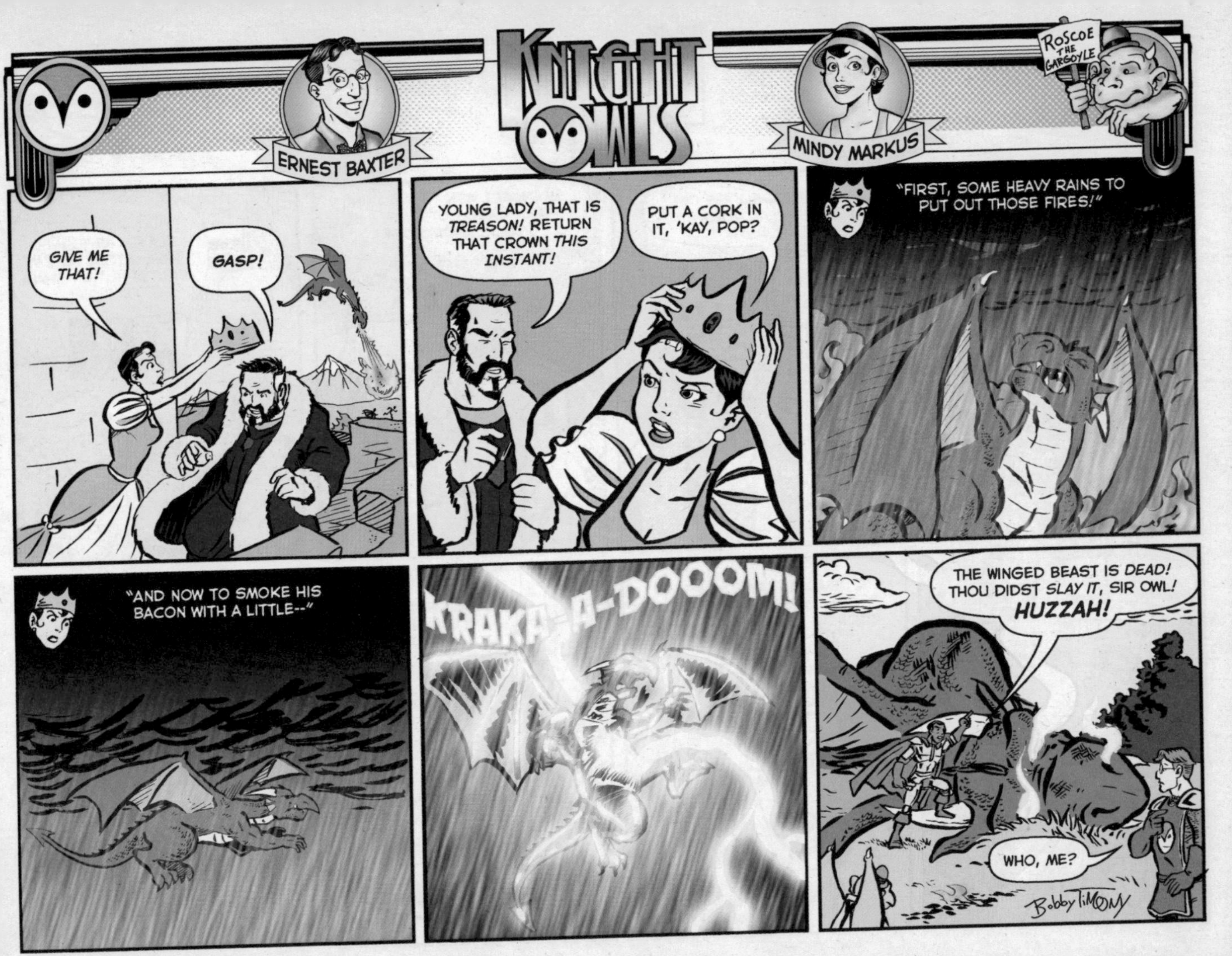
KNIGHT OWLS
ERNEST BAXTER
MINDY MARKUS
ROSCOE THE GARGOYLE
GIVE ME THAT!
GASP!
YOUNG LADY, THAT IS *TREASON!* RETURN THAT CROWN *THIS INSTANT!*
PUT A CORK IN IT, 'KAY, POP?
"FIRST, SOME HEAVY RAINS TO PUT OUT THOSE FIRES!"
"AND NOW TO SMOKE HIS BACON WITH A LITTLE--"
KRAKA-A-DOOOM!
THE WINGED BEAST IS *DEAD!* THOU DIDST *SLAY IT,* SIR OWL! **HUZZAH!**
WHO, ME?
Bobby TiMONY

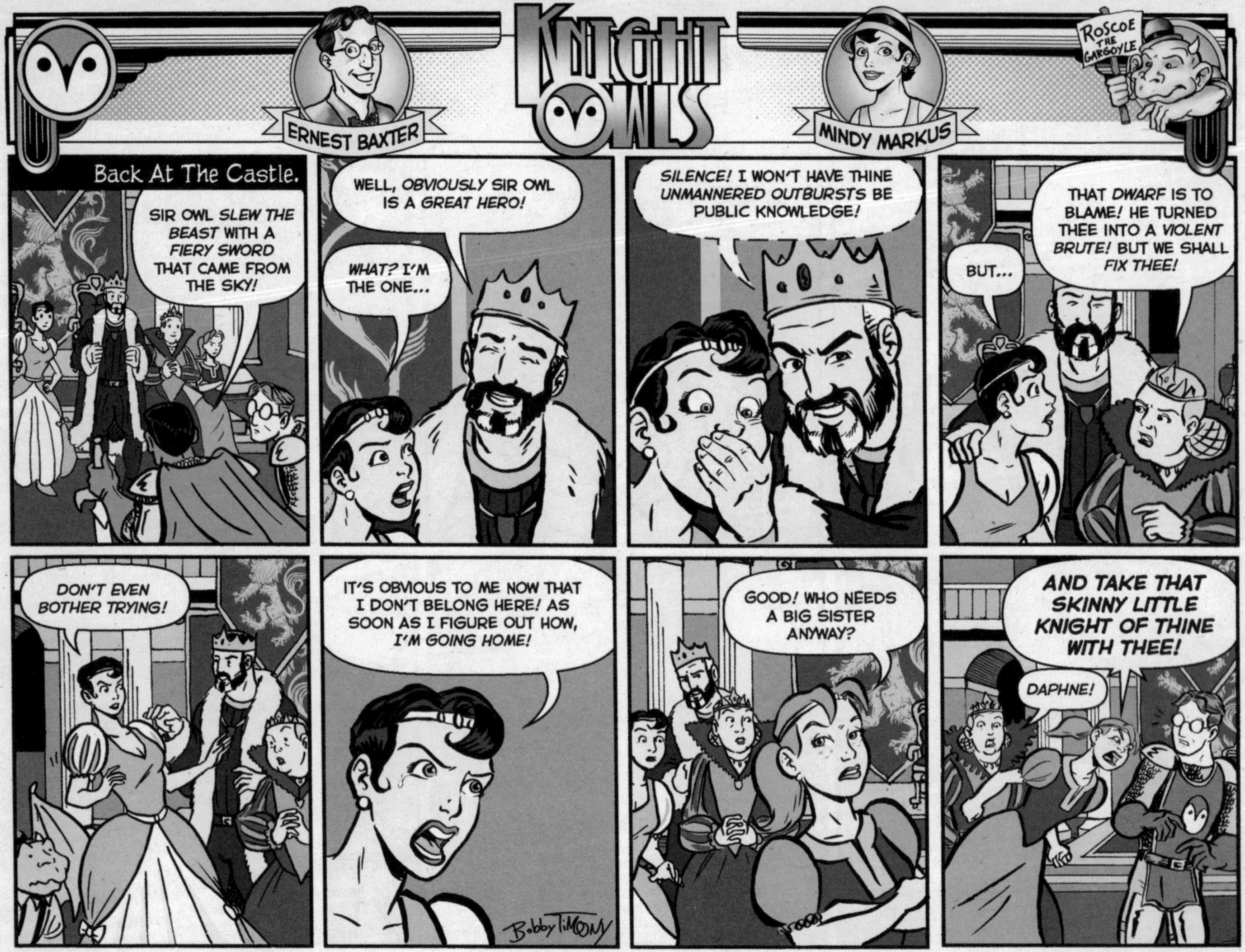
KNIGHT OWLS
ERNEST BAXTER
MINDY MARKUS
ROSCOE THE GARGOYLE
Back At The Castle.
SIR OWL SLEW THE BEAST WITH A FIERY SWORD THAT CAME FROM THE SKY!
WELL, OBVIOUSLY SIR OWL IS A GREAT HERO!
WHAT? I'M THE ONE...
SILENCE! I WON'T HAVE THINE UNMANNERED OUTBURSTS BE PUBLIC KNOWLEDGE!
BUT...
THAT DWARF IS TO BLAME! HE TURNED THEE INTO A VIOLENT BRUTE! BUT WE SHALL FIX THEE!
DON'T EVEN BOTHER TRYING!
IT'S OBVIOUS TO ME NOW THAT I DON'T BELONG HERE! AS SOON AS I FIGURE OUT HOW, I'M GOING HOME!
Bobby Timony
GOOD! WHO NEEDS A BIG SISTER ANYWAY?
AND TAKE THAT SKINNY LITTLE KNIGHT OF THINE WITH THEE!
DAPHNE!

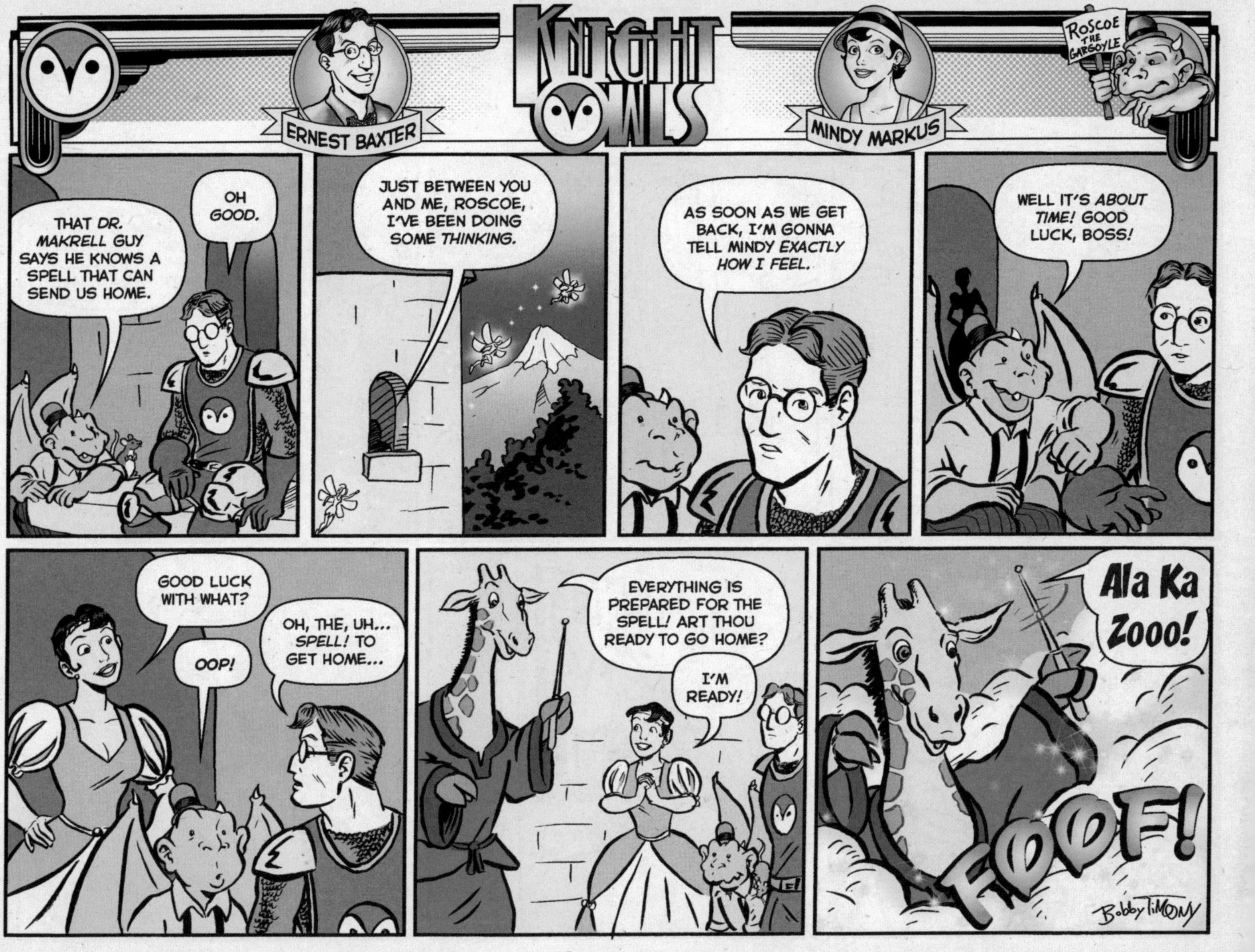
KNIGHT OWLS
ERNEST BAXTER
MINDY MARKUS
ROSCOE THE GARGOYLE
THAT DR. MAKRELL GUY SAYS HE KNOWS A SPELL THAT CAN SEND US HOME.
OH GOOD.
JUST BETWEEN YOU AND ME, ROSCOE, I'VE BEEN DOING SOME THINKING.
AS SOON AS WE GET BACK, I'M GONNA TELL MINDY EXACTLY HOW I FEEL.
WELL IT'S ABOUT TIME! GOOD LUCK, BOSS!
GOOD LUCK WITH WHAT?
OOP!
OH, THE, UH... SPELL! TO GET HOME...
EVERYTHING IS PREPARED FOR THE SPELL! ART THOU READY TO GO HOME?
I'M READY!
Ala Ka Zooo!
FOOF!
Bobby Timony

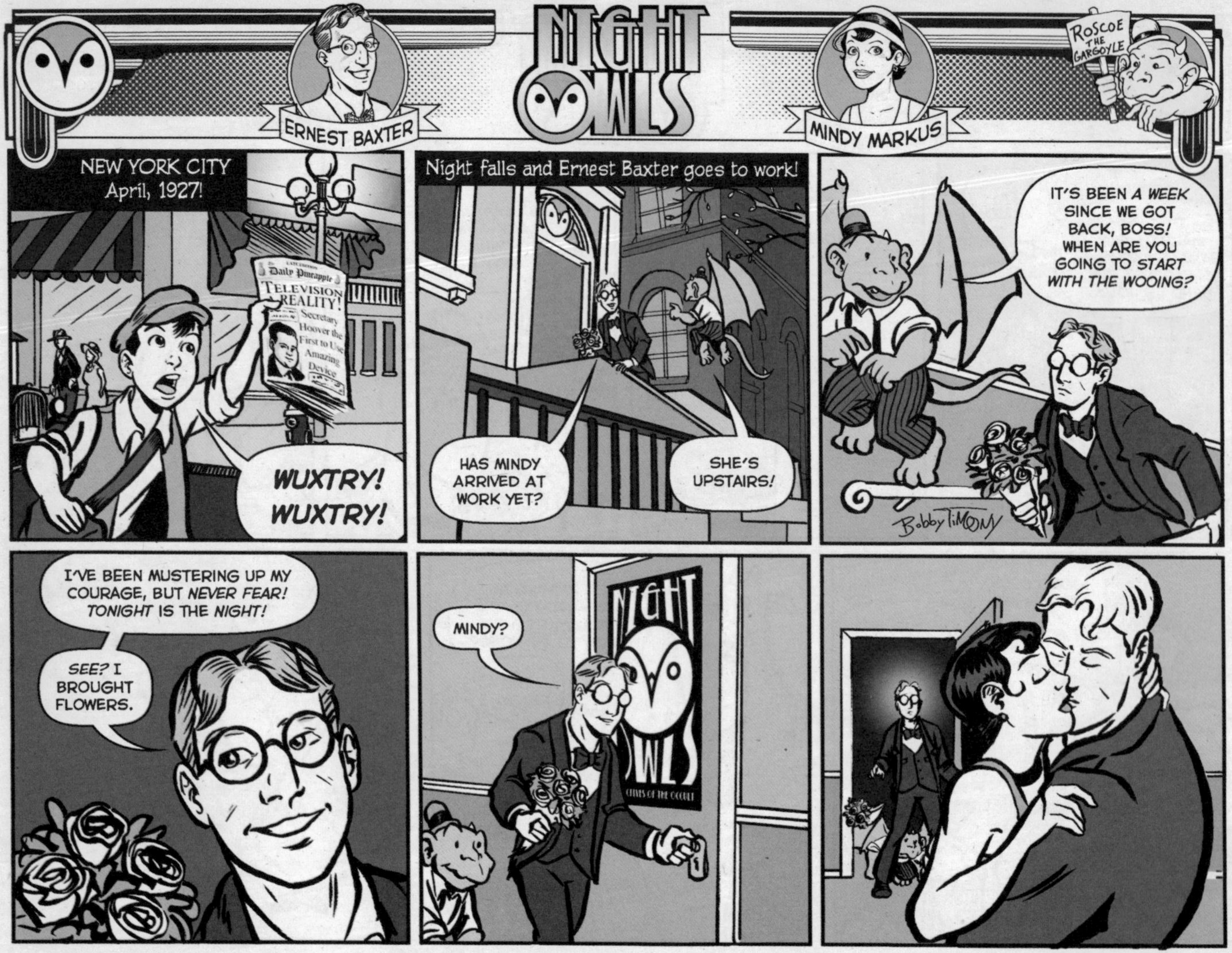

NIGHT OWLS
ERNEST BAXTER
MINDY MARKUS
ROSCOE THE GARGOYLE
NEW YORK CITY
April, 1927!
Daily Pineapple
TELEVISION A REALITY!
Secretary Hoover the First to Use Amazing Device
WUXTRY! WUXTRY!
Night falls and Ernest Baxter goes to work!
HAS MINDY ARRIVED AT WORK YET?
SHE'S UPSTAIRS!
IT'S BEEN A WEEK SINCE WE GOT BACK, BOSS! WHEN ARE YOU GOING TO START WITH THE WOOING?
Bobby Timony
I'VE BEEN MUSTERING UP MY COURAGE, BUT NEVER FEAR! TONIGHT IS THE NIGHT!
SEE? I BROUGHT FLOWERS.
MINDY?
NIGHT OWLS

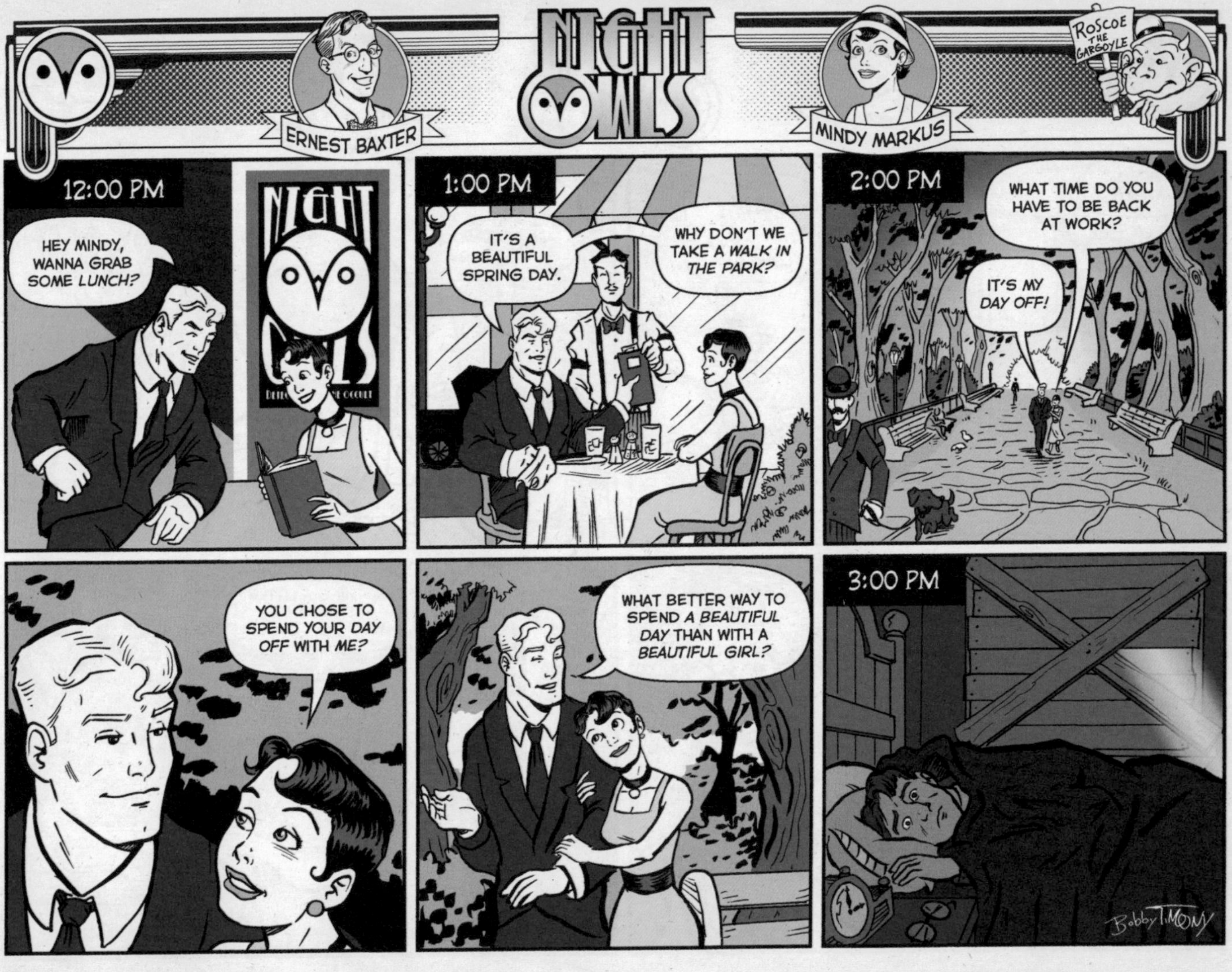
NIGHT OWLS
ERNEST BAXTER
MINDY MARKUS
ROSCOE THE GARGOYLE
12:00 PM
HEY MINDY, WANNA GRAB SOME LUNCH?
1:00 PM
IT'S A BEAUTIFUL SPRING DAY.
WHY DON'T WE TAKE A WALK IN THE PARK?
2:00 PM
WHAT TIME DO YOU HAVE TO BE BACK AT WORK?
IT'S MY DAY OFF!
YOU CHOSE TO SPEND YOUR DAY OFF WITH ME?
WHAT BETTER WAY TO SPEND A BEAUTIFUL DAY THAN WITH A BEAUTIFUL GIRL?
3:00 PM
Bobby Timony

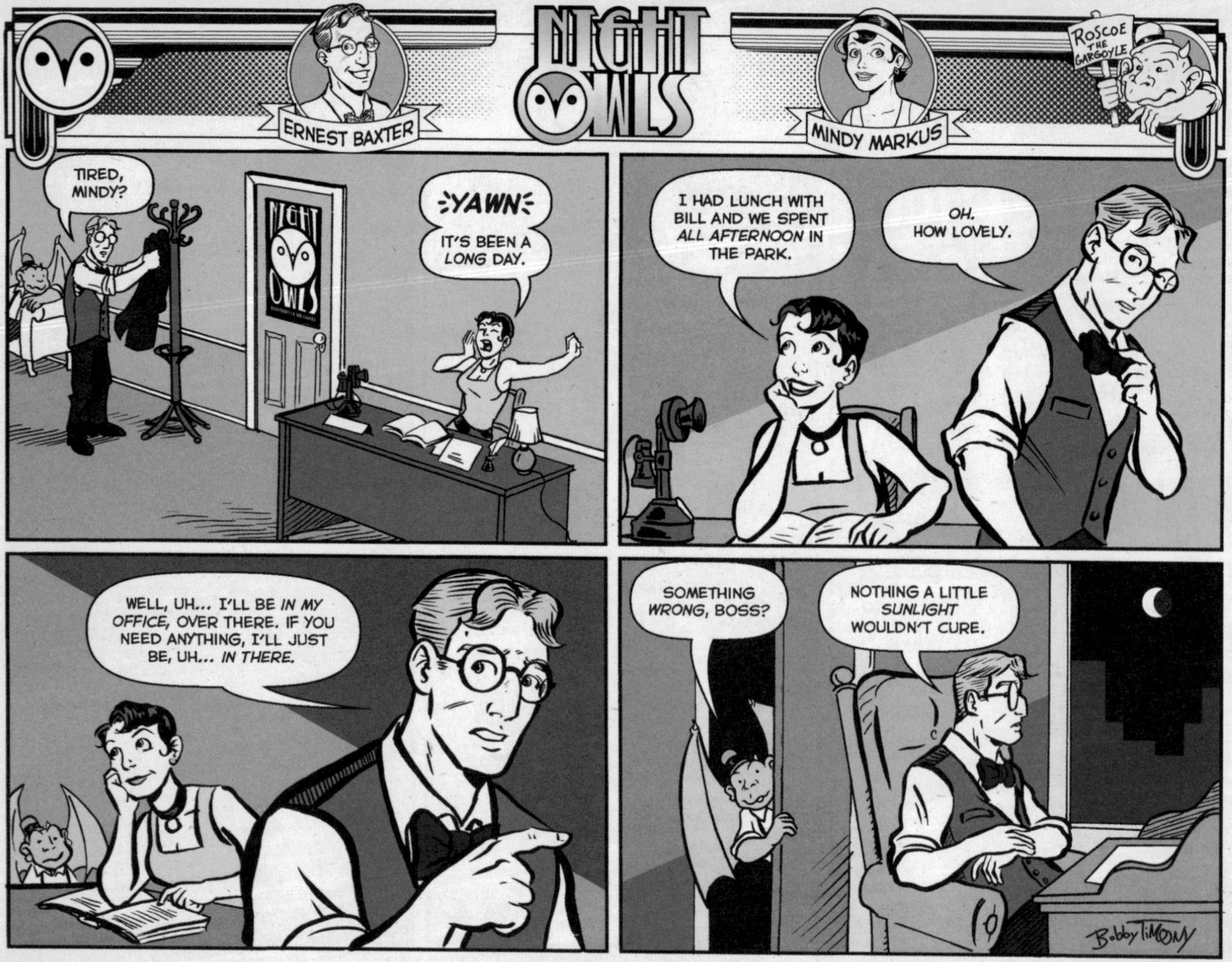

NIGHT OWLS
ERNEST BAXTER
MINDY MARKUS
ROSCOE THE GARGOYLE
TIRED, MINDY?
YAWN
IT'S BEEN A LONG DAY.
I HAD LUNCH WITH BILL AND WE SPENT ALL AFTERNOON IN THE PARK.
OH. HOW LOVELY.
WELL, UH... I'LL BE IN MY OFFICE, OVER THERE. IF YOU NEED ANYTHING, I'LL JUST BE, UH... IN THERE.
SOMETHING WRONG, BOSS?
NOTHING A LITTLE SUNLIGHT WOULDN'T CURE.
Bobby Timony

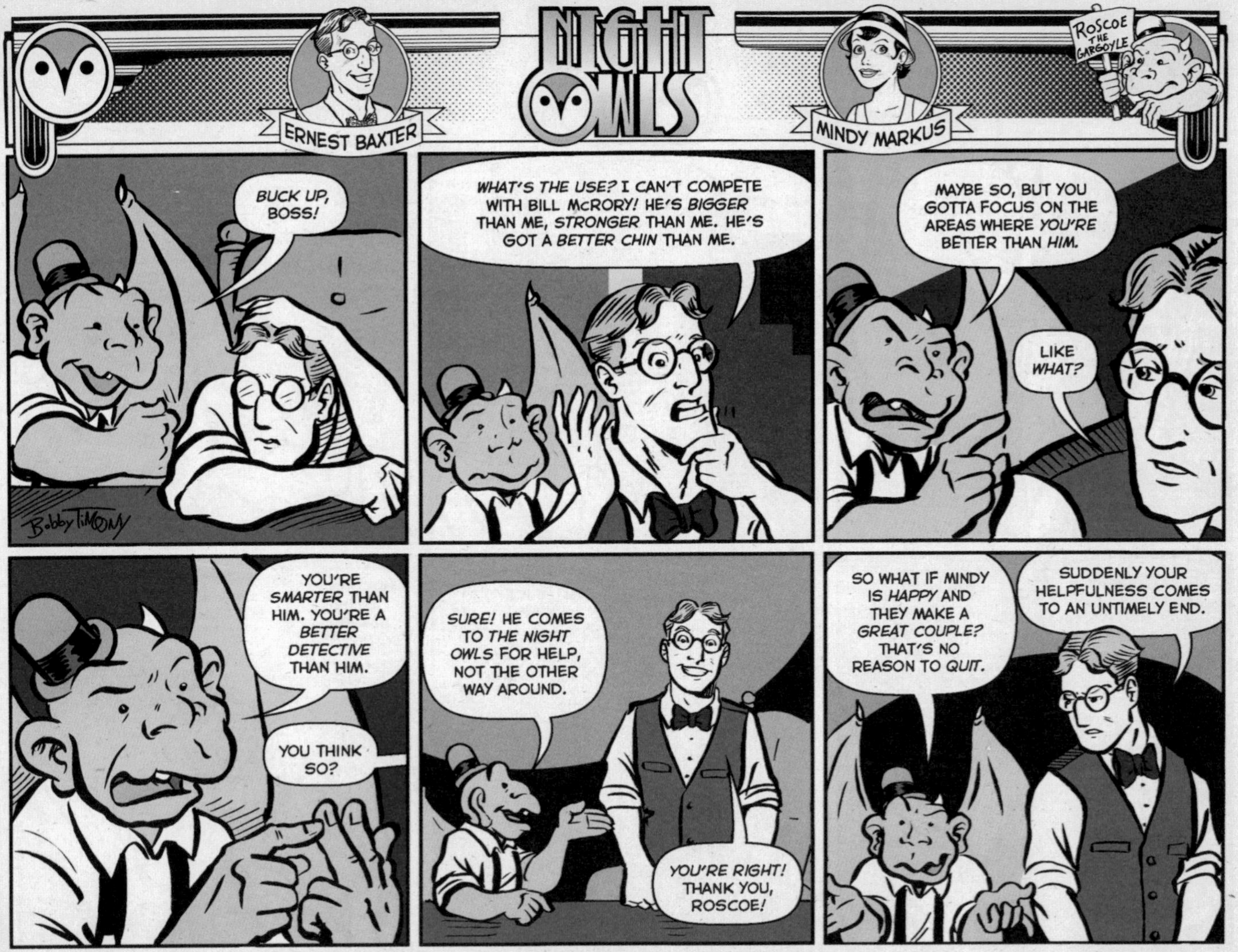
NIGHT OWLS
ERNEST BAXTER
MINDY MARKUS
ROSCOE THE GARGOYLE
BUCK UP, BOSS!
Bobby Timony
WHAT'S THE USE? I CAN'T COMPETE WITH BILL McRORY! HE'S BIGGER THAN ME, STRONGER THAN ME. HE'S GOT A BETTER CHIN THAN ME.
MAYBE SO, BUT YOU GOTTA FOCUS ON THE AREAS WHERE YOU'RE BETTER THAN HIM.
LIKE WHAT?
YOU'RE SMARTER THAN HIM. YOU'RE A BETTER DETECTIVE THAN HIM.
YOU THINK SO?
SURE! HE COMES TO THE NIGHT OWLS FOR HELP, NOT THE OTHER WAY AROUND.
YOU'RE RIGHT! THANK YOU, ROSCOE!
SO WHAT IF MINDY IS HAPPY AND THEY MAKE A GREAT COUPLE? THAT'S NO REASON TO QUIT.
SUDDENLY YOUR HELPFULNESS COMES TO AN UNTIMELY END.

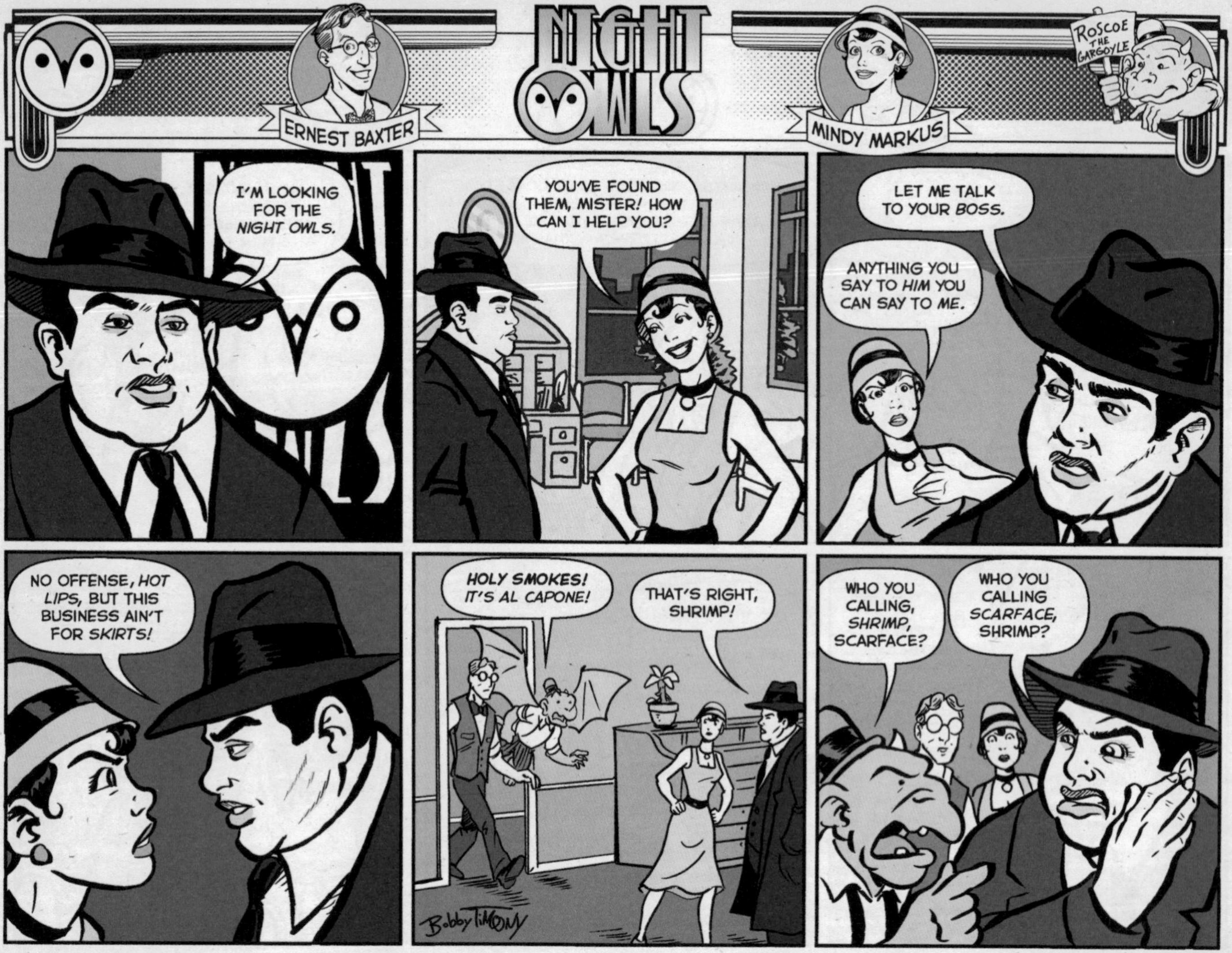
NIGHT OWLS
ERNEST BAXTER
MINDY MARKUS
ROSCOE THE GARGOYLE
I'M LOOKING FOR THE *NIGHT OWLS.*
YOU'VE FOUND THEM, *MISTER!* HOW CAN I HELP *YOU?*
LET ME TALK TO YOUR *BOSS.*
ANYTHING YOU SAY TO *HIM* YOU CAN SAY TO *ME.*
NO OFFENSE, *HOT LIPS*, BUT THIS BUSINESS AIN'T FOR *SKIRTS!*
HOLY SMOKES! IT'S AL CAPONE!
THAT'S RIGHT, SHRIMP!
WHO YOU CALLING, *SHRIMP*, SCARFACE?
WHO YOU CALLING *SCARFACE*, SHRIMP?
Bobby Timony

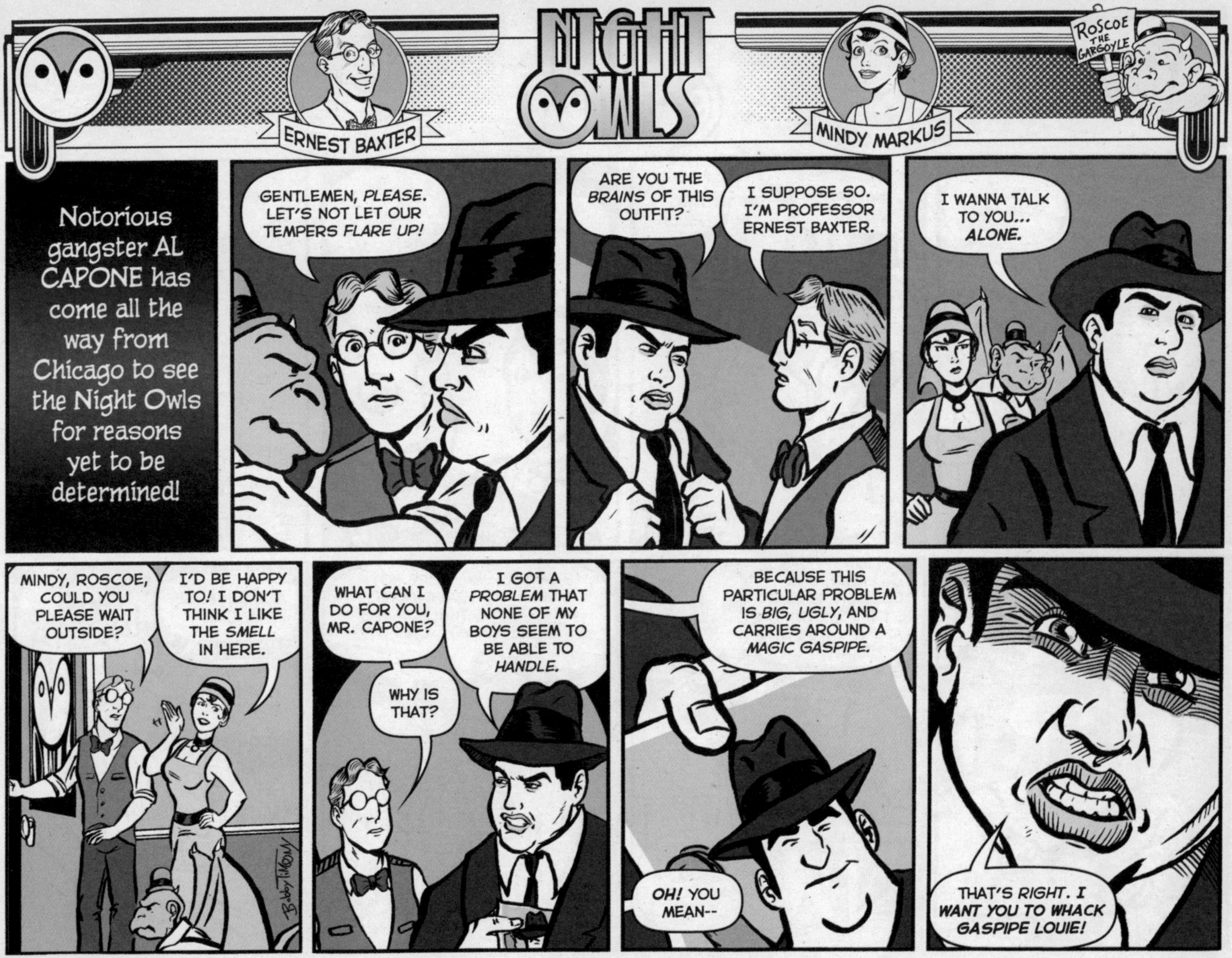
NIGHT OWLS
ERNEST BAXTER
MINDY MARKUS
ROSCOE THE GARGOYLE
Notorious gangster AL CAPONE has come all the way from Chicago to see the Night Owls for reasons yet to be determined!
GENTLEMEN, PLEASE. LET'S NOT LET OUR TEMPERS FLARE UP!
ARE YOU THE BRAINS OF THIS OUTFIT?
I SUPPOSE SO. I'M PROFESSOR ERNEST BAXTER.
I WANNA TALK TO YOU... ALONE.
MINDY, ROSCOE, COULD YOU PLEASE WAIT OUTSIDE?
I'D BE HAPPY TO! I DON'T THINK I LIKE THE SMELL IN HERE.
WHAT CAN I DO FOR YOU, MR. CAPONE?
I GOT A PROBLEM THAT NONE OF MY BOYS SEEM TO BE ABLE TO HANDLE.
WHY IS THAT?
BECAUSE THIS PARTICULAR PROBLEM IS BIG, UGLY, AND CARRIES AROUND A MAGIC GASPIPE.
OH! YOU MEAN--
THAT'S RIGHT. I WANT YOU TO WHACK GASPIPE LOUIE!

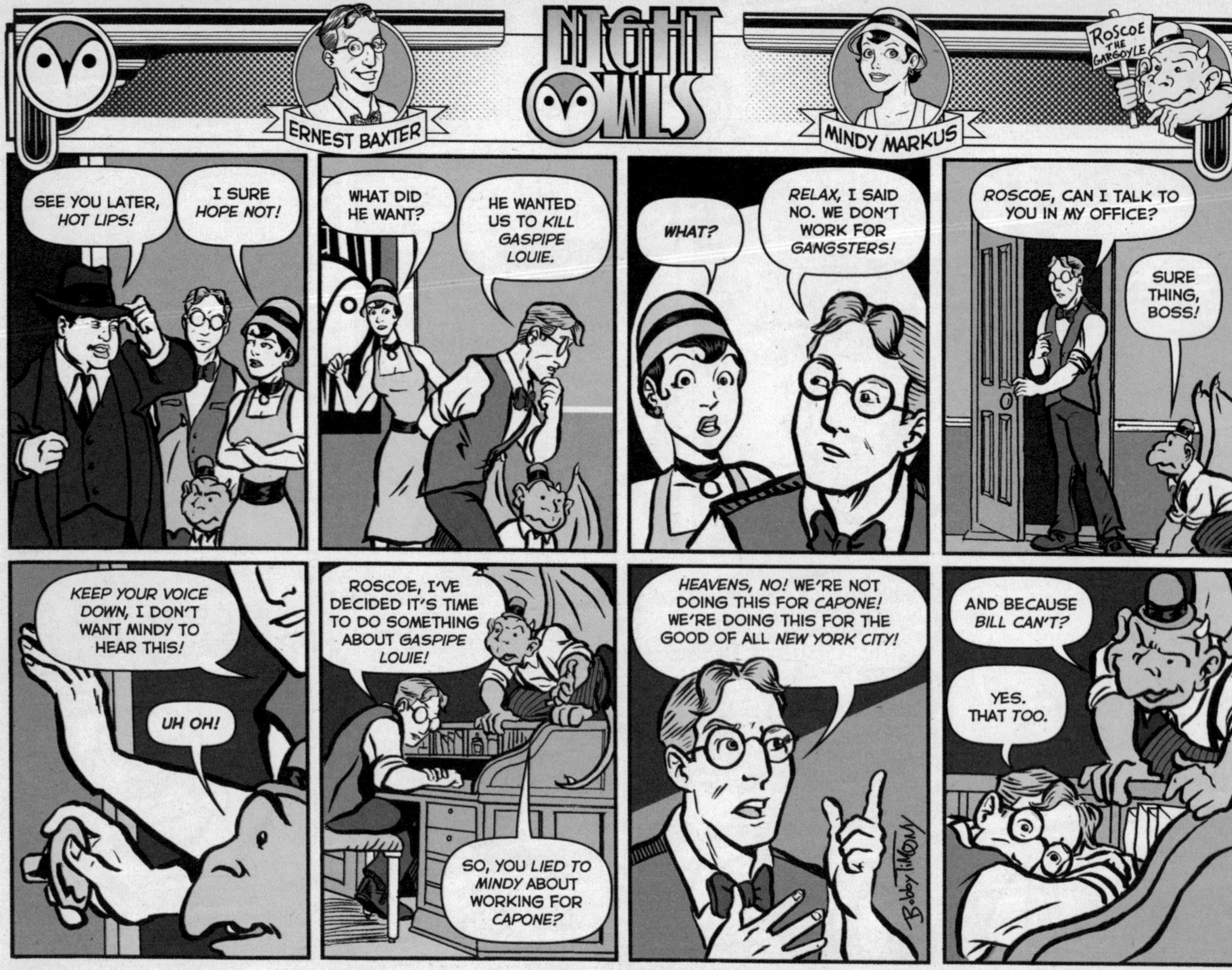
NIGHT OWLS
ERNEST BAXTER
MINDY MARKUS
ROSCOE THE GARGOYLE
SEE YOU LATER, HOT LIPS!
I SURE HOPE NOT!
WHAT DID HE WANT?
HE WANTED US TO KILL GASPIPE LOUIE.
WHAT?
RELAX, I SAID NO. WE DON'T WORK FOR GANGSTERS!
ROSCOE, CAN I TALK TO YOU IN MY OFFICE?
SURE THING, BOSS!
KEEP YOUR VOICE DOWN, I DON'T WANT MINDY TO HEAR THIS!
UH OH!
ROSCOE, I'VE DECIDED IT'S TIME TO DO SOMETHING ABOUT GASPIPE LOUIE!
SO, YOU LIED TO MINDY ABOUT WORKING FOR CAPONE?
HEAVENS, NO! WE'RE NOT DOING THIS FOR CAPONE! WE'RE DOING THIS FOR THE GOOD OF ALL NEW YORK CITY!
Bobby Timony
AND BECAUSE BILL CAN'T?
YES. THAT TOO.

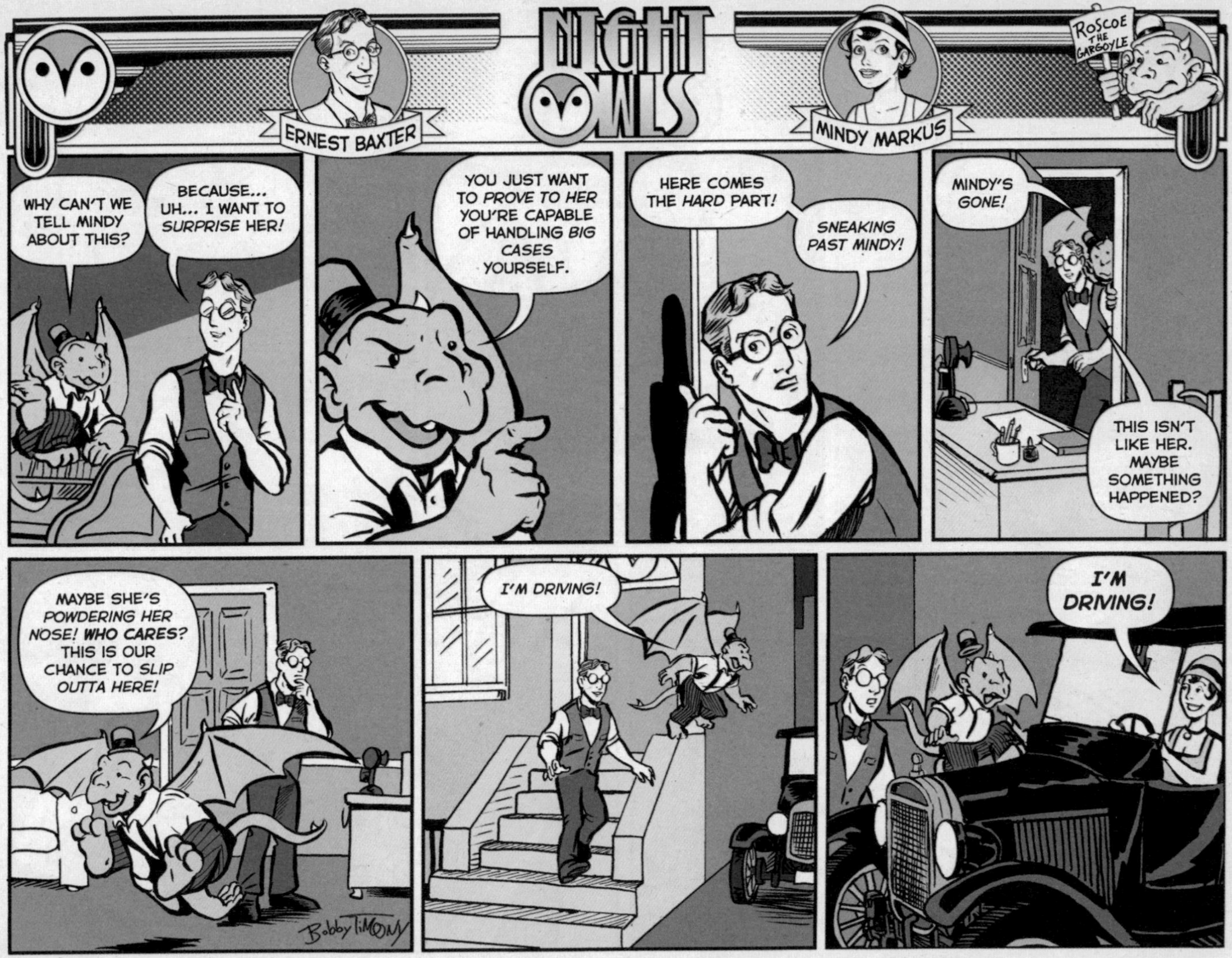
NIGHT OWLS
ERNEST BAXTER
MINDY MARKUS
ROSCOE THE GARGOYLE
WHY CAN'T WE TELL MINDY ABOUT THIS?
BECAUSE... UH... I WANT TO SURPRISE HER!
YOU JUST WANT TO PROVE TO HER YOU'RE CAPABLE OF HANDLING BIG CASES YOURSELF.
HERE COMES THE HARD PART!
SNEAKING PAST MINDY!
MINDY'S GONE!
THIS ISN'T LIKE HER. MAYBE SOMETHING HAPPENED?
MAYBE SHE'S POWDERING HER NOSE! WHO CARES? THIS IS OUR CHANCE TO SLIP OUTTA HERE!
I'M DRIVING!
I'M DRIVING!
Bobby Timony

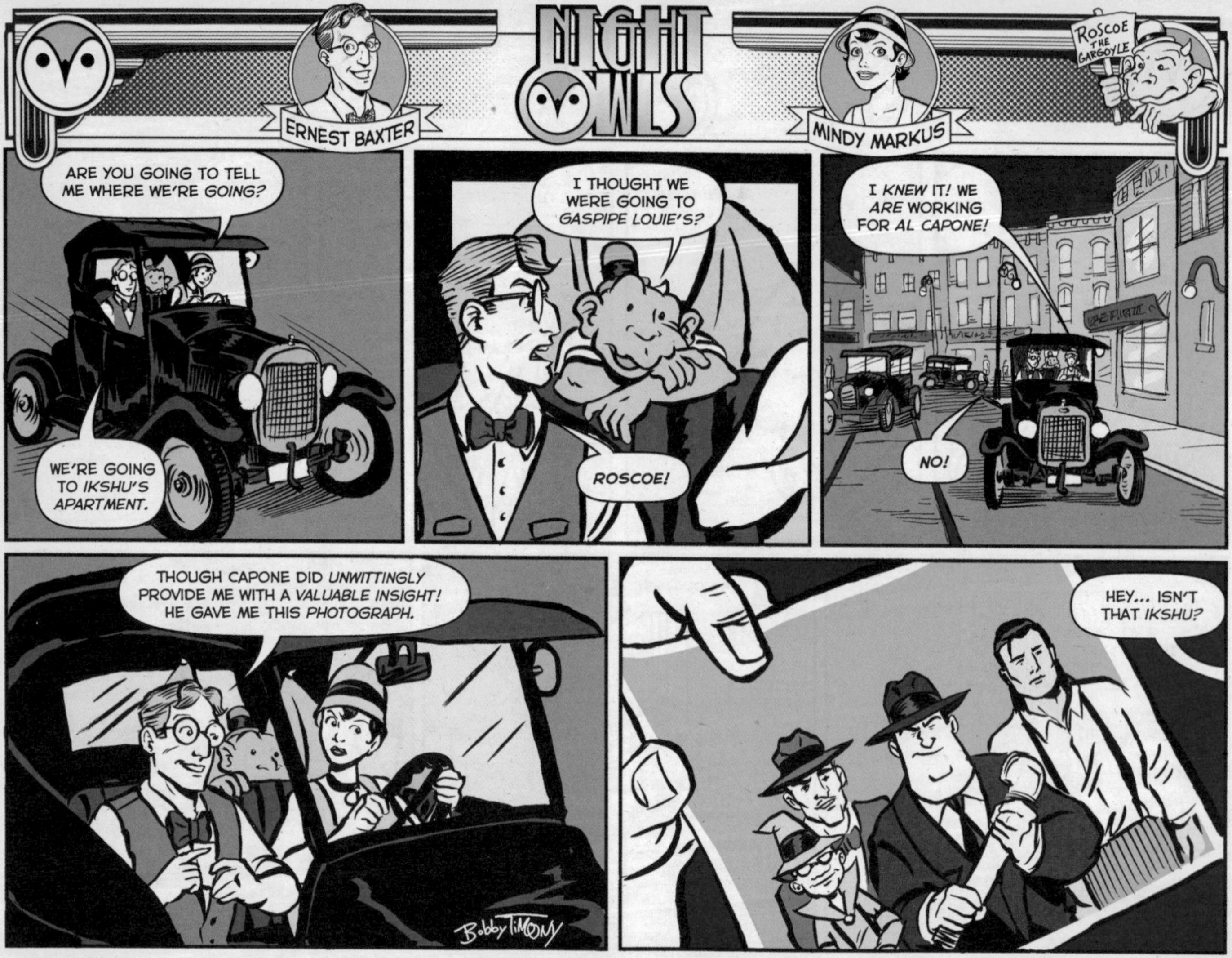
NIGHT OWLS
ERNEST BAXTER
MINDY MARKUS
ROSCOE THE GARGOYLE
ARE YOU GOING TO TELL ME WHERE WE'RE GOING?
WE'RE GOING TO IKSHU'S APARTMENT.
I THOUGHT WE WERE GOING TO GASPIPE LOUIE'S?
ROSCOE!
I KNEW IT! WE ARE WORKING FOR AL CAPONE!
NO!
THOUGH CAPONE DID UNWITTINGLY PROVIDE ME WITH A VALUABLE INSIGHT! HE GAVE ME THIS PHOTOGRAPH.
HEY... ISN'T THAT IKSHU?
Bobby Timony

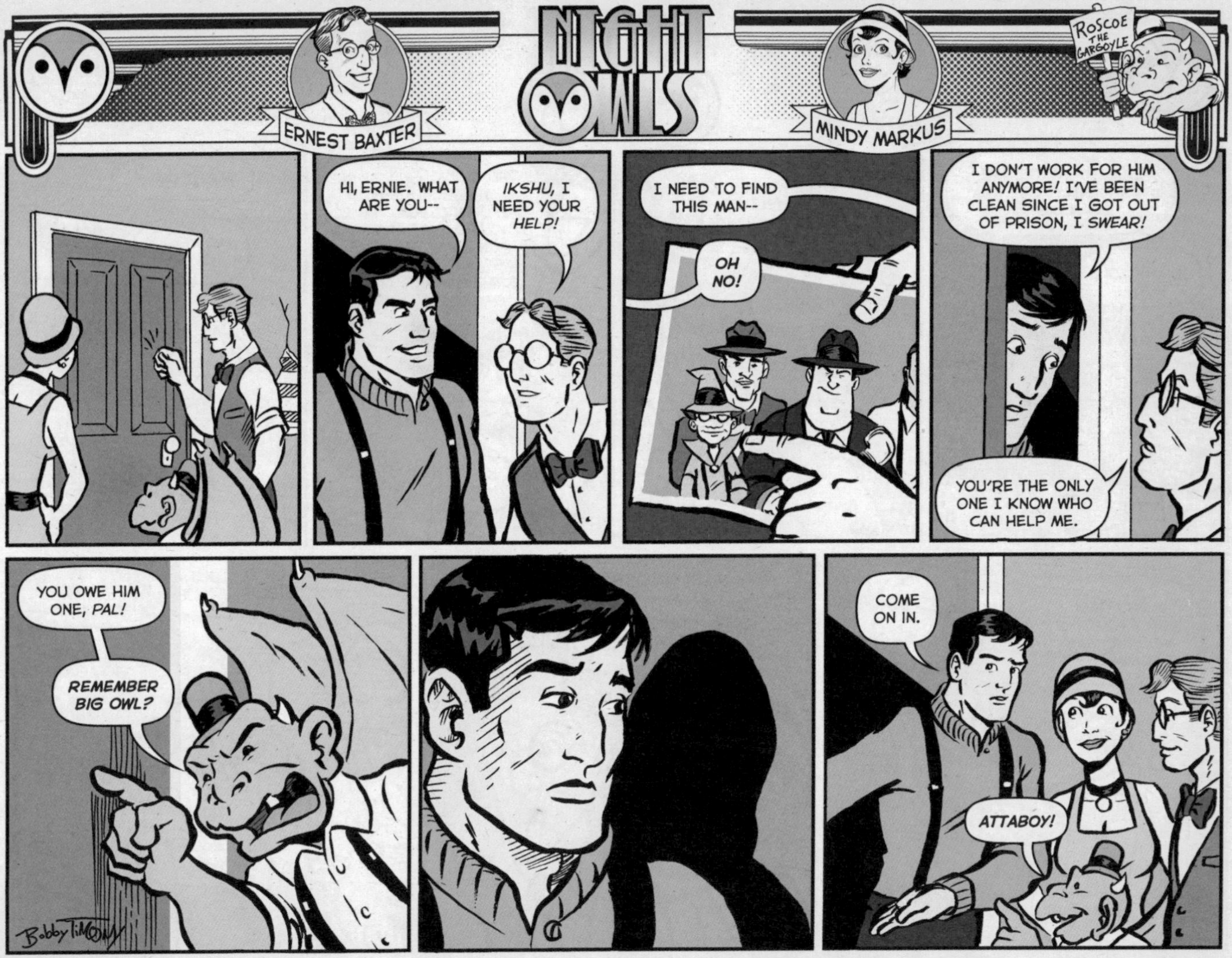
NIGHT OWLS
ERNEST BAXTER
MINDY MARKUS
ROSCOE THE GARGOYLE
HI, ERNIE. WHAT ARE YOU--
IKSHU, I NEED YOUR HELP!
I NEED TO FIND THIS MAN--
OH NO!
I DON'T WORK FOR HIM ANYMORE! I'VE BEEN CLEAN SINCE I GOT OUT OF PRISON, I SWEAR!
YOU'RE THE ONLY ONE I KNOW WHO CAN HELP ME.
YOU OWE HIM ONE, PAL!
REMEMBER BIG OWL?
COME ON IN.
ATTABOY!
Bobby Timony

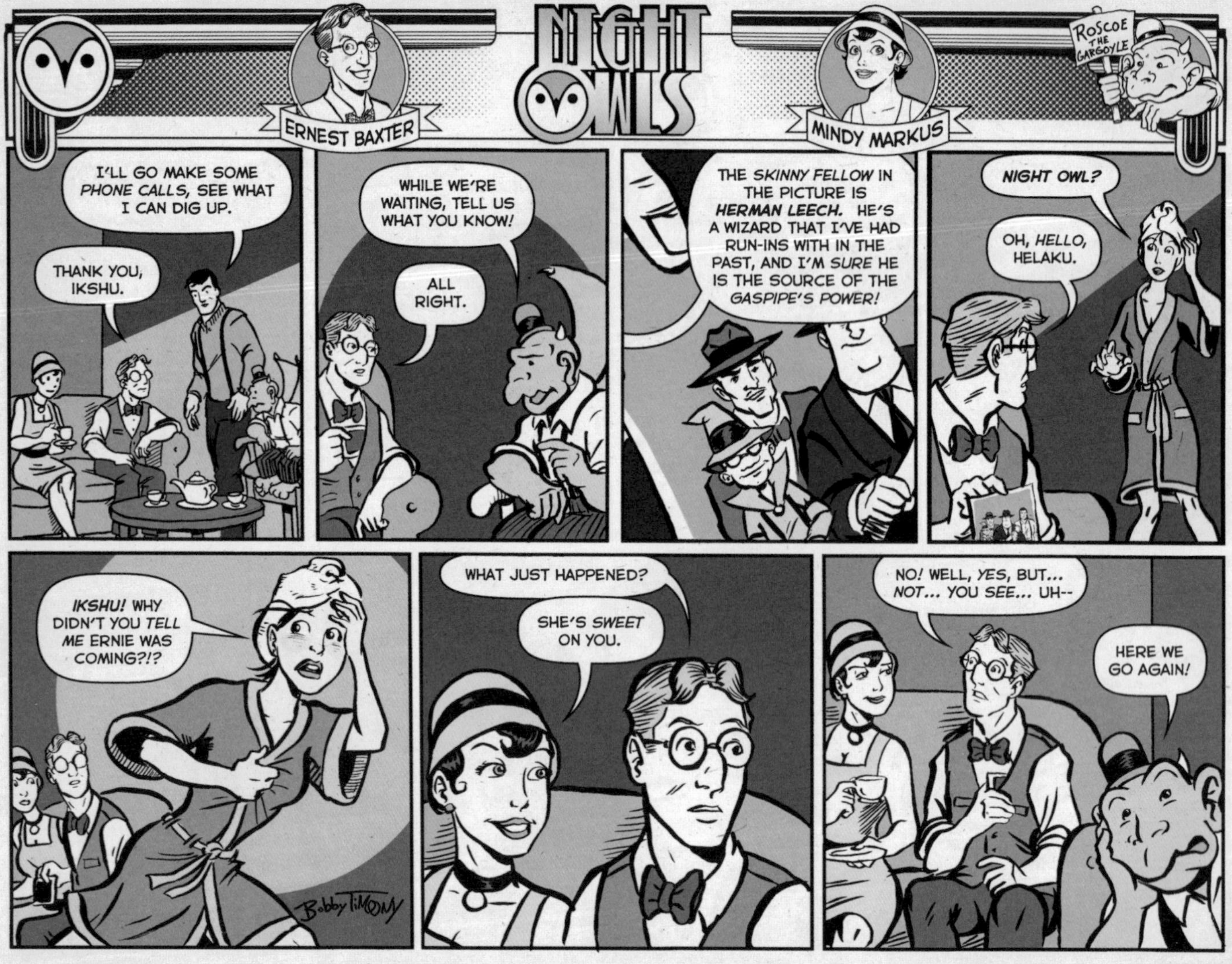
NIGHT OWLS
ERNEST BAXTER
MINDY MARKUS
ROSCOE THE GARGOYLE
I'LL GO MAKE SOME PHONE CALLS, SEE WHAT I CAN DIG UP.
THANK YOU, IKSHU.
WHILE WE'RE WAITING, TELL US WHAT YOU KNOW!
ALL RIGHT.
THE SKINNY FELLOW IN THE PICTURE IS HERMAN LEECH. HE'S A WIZARD THAT I'VE HAD RUN-INS WITH IN THE PAST, AND I'M SURE HE IS THE SOURCE OF THE GASPIPE'S POWER!
NIGHT OWL?
OH, HELLO, HELAKU.
IKSHU! WHY DIDN'T YOU TELL ME ERNIE WAS COMING?!?
Bobby Timony
WHAT JUST HAPPENED?
SHE'S SWEET ON YOU.
NO! WELL, YES, BUT... NOT... YOU SEE... UH--
HERE WE GO AGAIN!

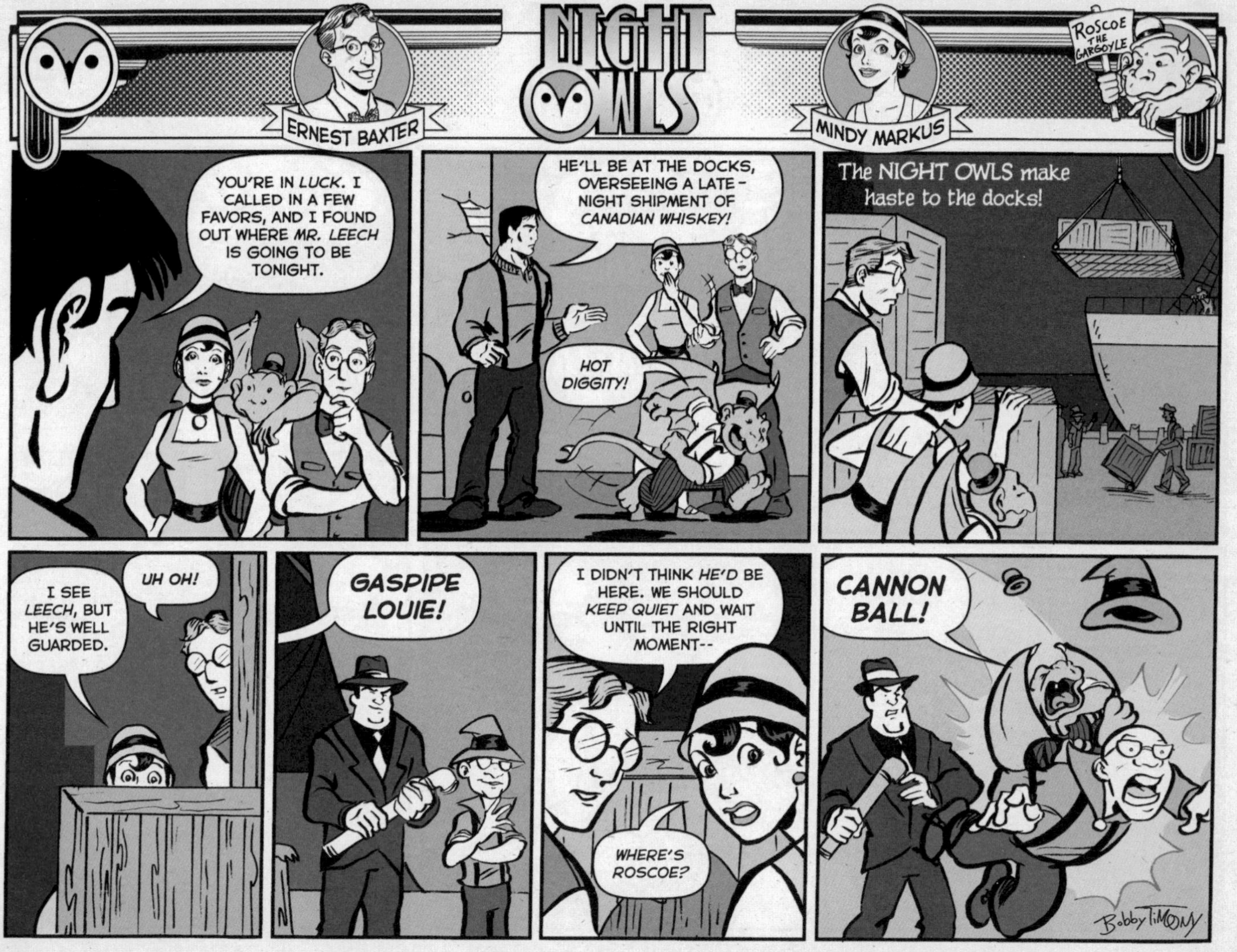
NIGHT OWLS
ERNEST BAXTER
MINDY MARKUS
ROSCOE THE GARGOYLE
YOU'RE IN LUCK. I CALLED IN A FEW FAVORS, AND I FOUND OUT WHERE MR. LEECH IS GOING TO BE TONIGHT.
HE'LL BE AT THE DOCKS, OVERSEEING A LATE-NIGHT SHIPMENT OF CANADIAN WHISKEY!
HOT DIGGITY!
The NIGHT OWLS make haste to the docks!
I SEE LEECH, BUT HE'S WELL GUARDED.
UH OH!
GASPIPE LOUIE!
I DIDN'T THINK HE'D BE HERE. WE SHOULD KEEP QUIET AND WAIT UNTIL THE RIGHT MOMENT--
WHERE'S ROSCOE?
CANNON BALL!
Bobby Timony

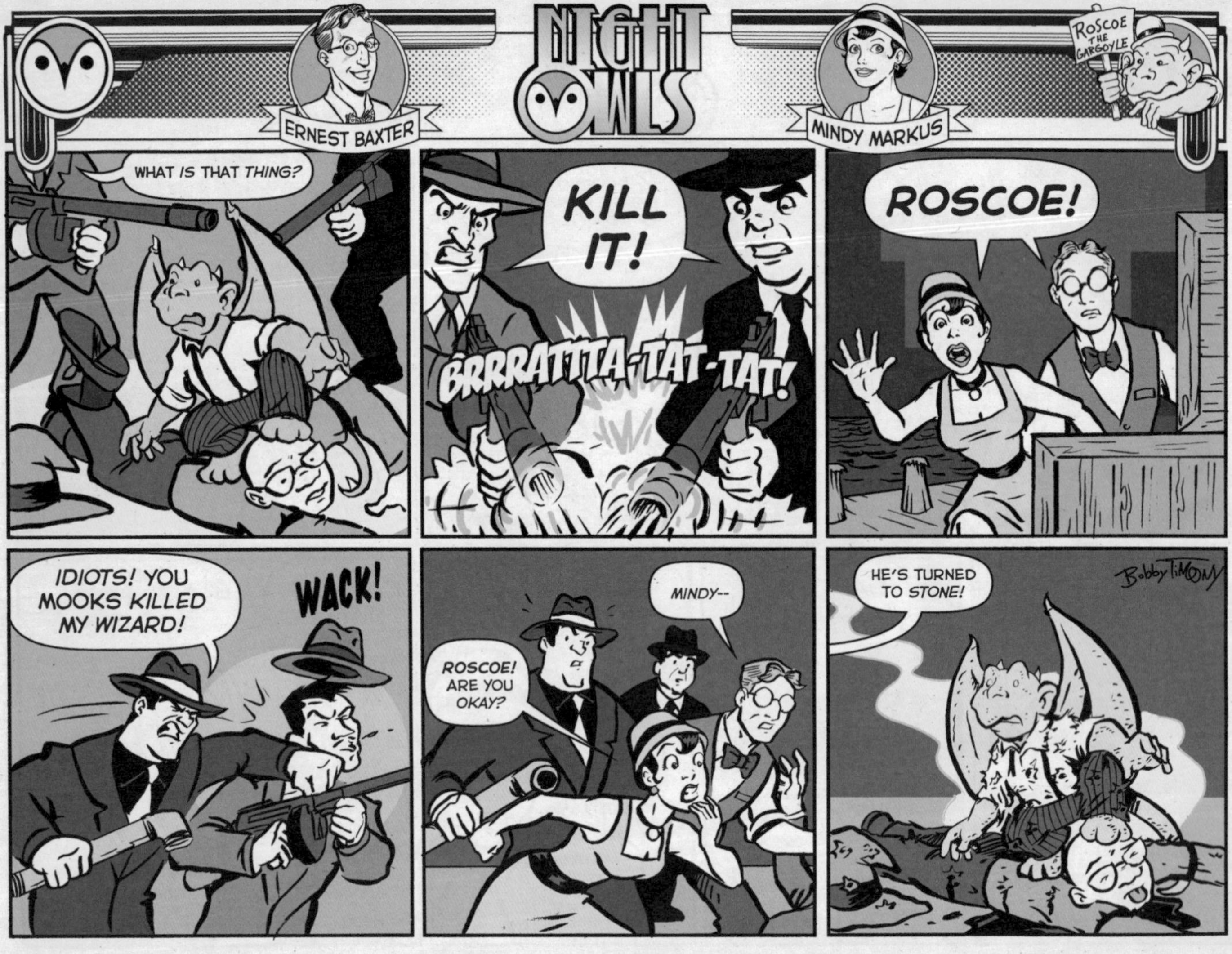
NIGHT OWLS
ERNEST BAXTER
MINDY MARKUS
ROSCOE THE GARGOYLE
WHAT IS THAT THING?
KILL IT!
BRRRATTTA-TAT-TAT!
ROSCOE!
IDIOTS! YOU MOOKS KILLED MY WIZARD!
WACK!
MINDY--
ROSCOE! ARE YOU OKAY?
HE'S TURNED TO STONE!
Bobby Timony

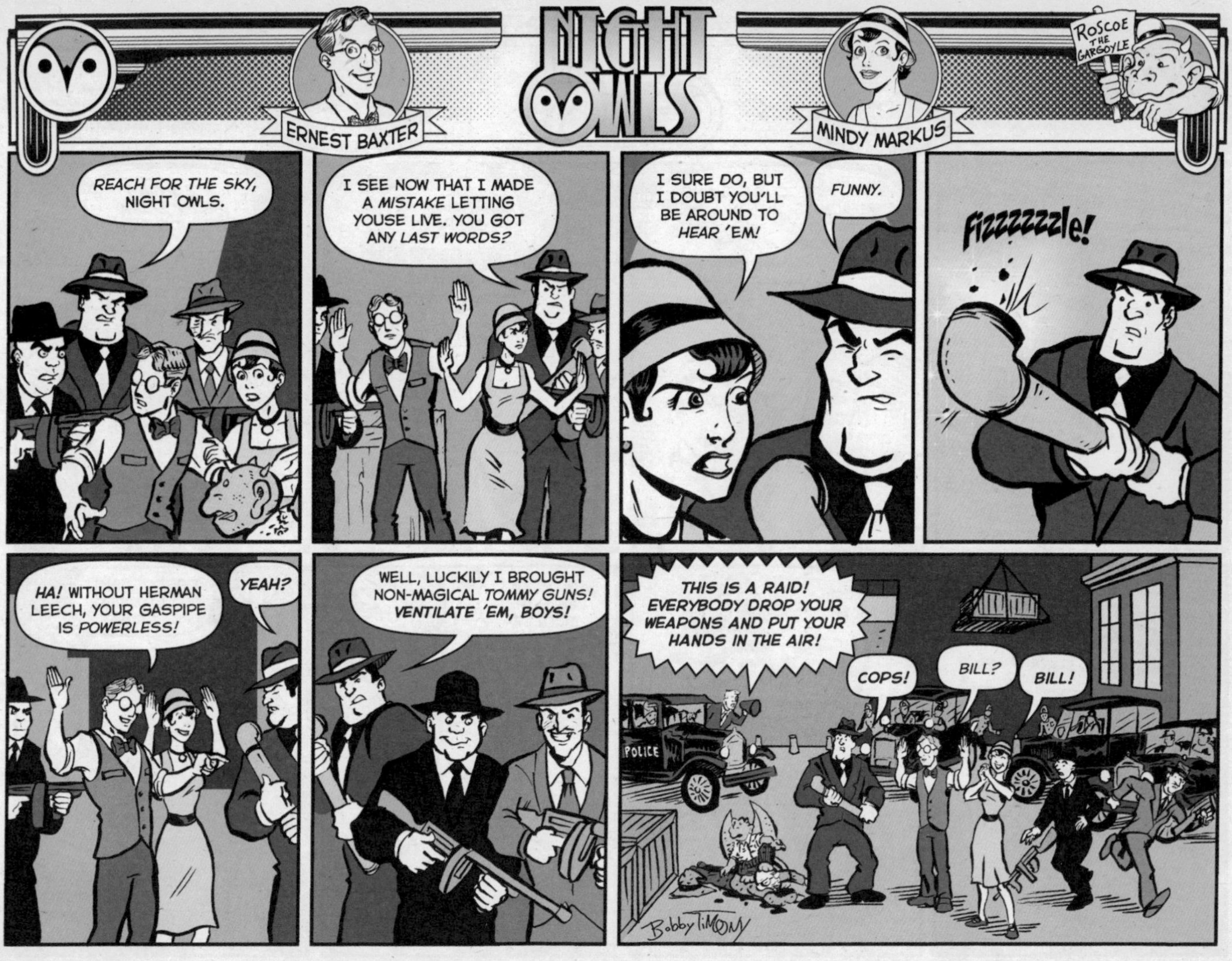
NIGHT OWLS
ERNEST BAXTER
MINDY MARKUS
ROSCOE THE GARGOYLE
REACH FOR THE SKY, NIGHT OWLS.
I SEE NOW THAT I MADE A MISTAKE LETTING YOUSE LIVE. YOU GOT ANY LAST WORDS?
I SURE DO, BUT I DOUBT YOU'LL BE AROUND TO HEAR 'EM!
FUNNY.
Fizzzzzzle!
HA! WITHOUT HERMAN LEECH, YOUR GASPIPE IS POWERLESS!
YEAH?
WELL, LUCKILY I BROUGHT NON-MAGICAL TOMMY GUNS! VENTILATE 'EM, BOYS!
THIS IS A RAID! EVERYBODY DROP YOUR WEAPONS AND PUT YOUR HANDS IN THE AIR!
COPS!
BILL?
BILL!
POLICE
Bobby TiMONY

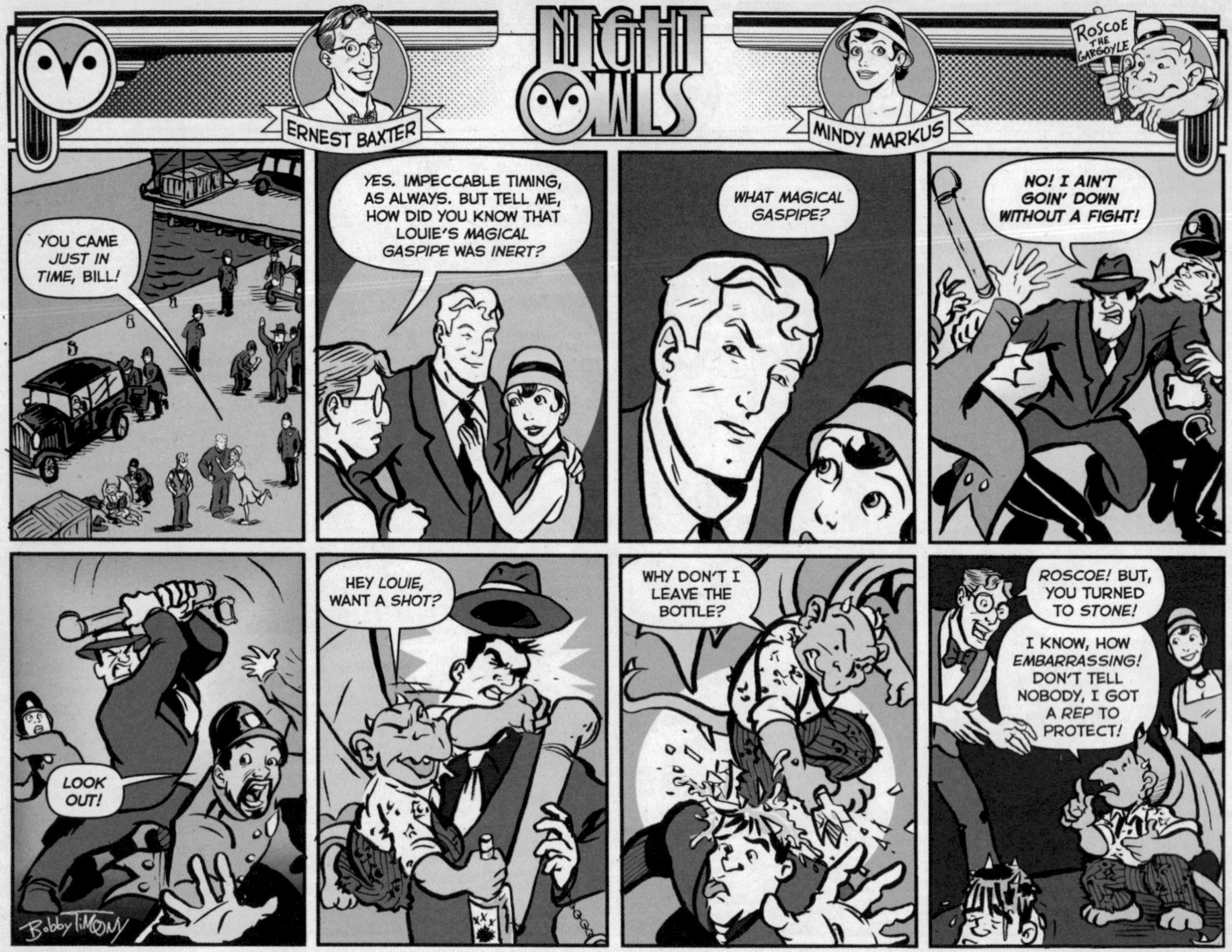
NIGHT OWLS
ERNEST BAXTER
MINDY MARKUS
ROSCOE THE GARGOYLE
YOU CAME JUST IN TIME, BILL!
YES. IMPECCABLE TIMING, AS ALWAYS. BUT TELL ME, HOW DID YOU KNOW THAT LOUIE'S MAGICAL GASPIPE WAS INERT?
WHAT MAGICAL GASPIPE?
NO! I AIN'T GOIN' DOWN WITHOUT A FIGHT!
LOOK OUT!
HEY LOUIE, WANT A SHOT?
WHY DON'T I LEAVE THE BOTTLE?
ROSCOE! BUT, YOU TURNED TO STONE!
I KNOW, HOW EMBARRASSING! DON'T TELL NOBODY, I GOT A REP TO PROTECT!
Bobby Timony

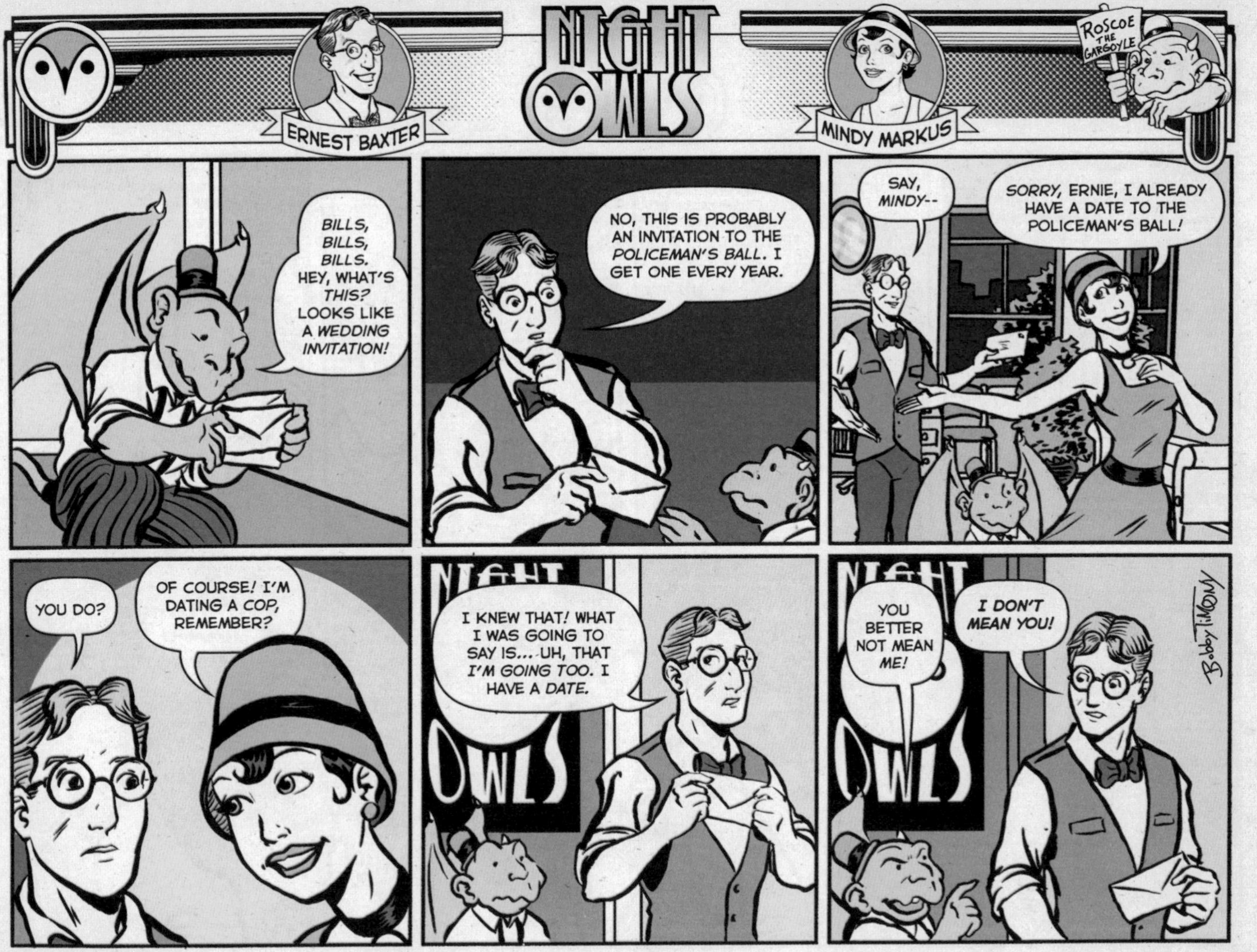
NIGHT OWLS
ERNEST BAXTER
MINDY MARKUS
ROSCOE THE GARGOYLE
BILLS, BILLS, BILLS. HEY, WHAT'S THIS? LOOKS LIKE A WEDDING INVITATION!
NO, THIS IS PROBABLY AN INVITATION TO THE POLICEMAN'S BALL. I GET ONE EVERY YEAR.
SAY, MINDY--
SORRY, ERNIE, I ALREADY HAVE A DATE TO THE POLICEMAN'S BALL!
YOU DO?
OF COURSE! I'M DATING A COP, REMEMBER?
I KNEW THAT! WHAT I WAS GOING TO SAY IS... UH, THAT I'M GOING TOO. I HAVE A DATE.
YOU BETTER NOT MEAN ME!
I DON'T MEAN YOU!
Bobby Timony

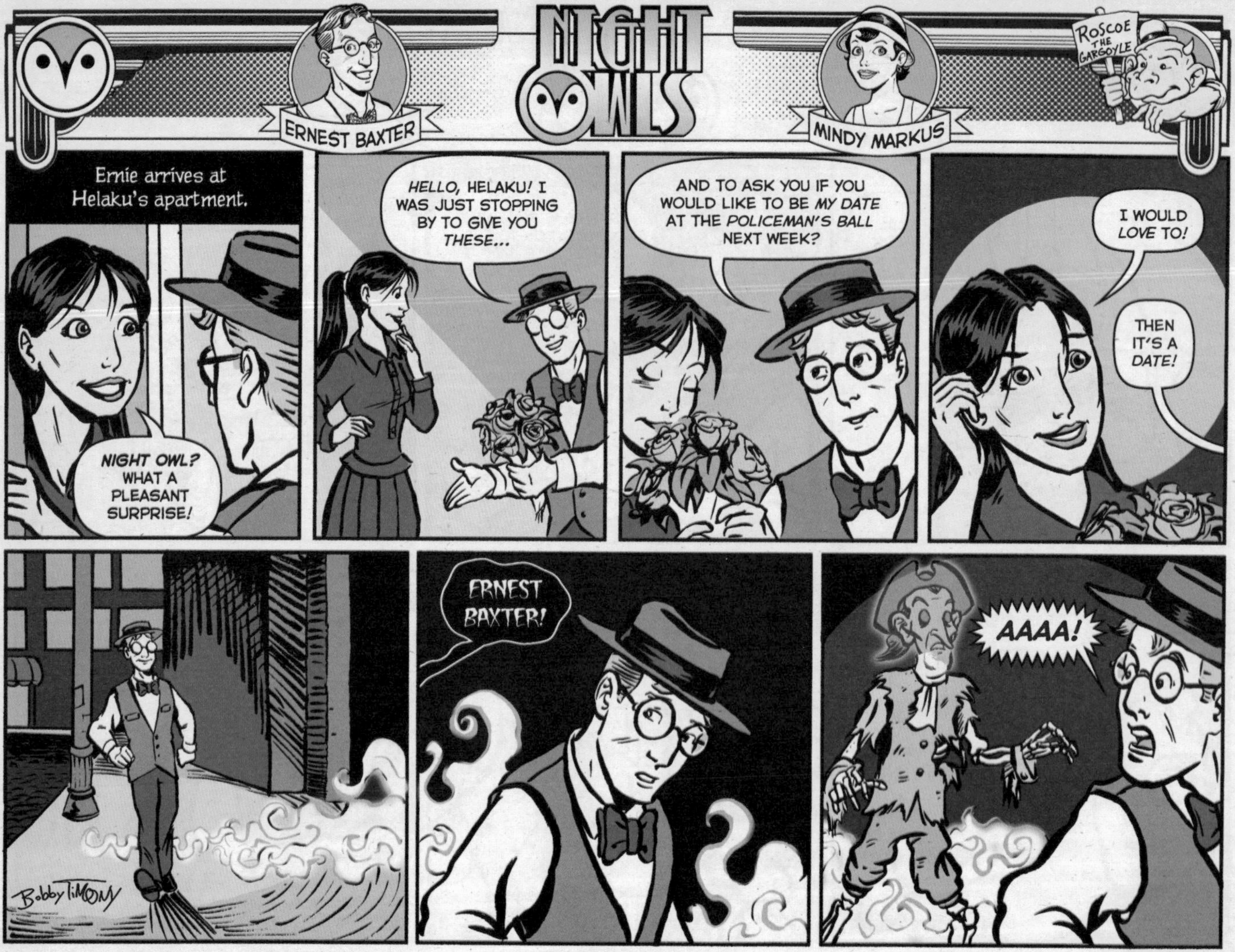
NIGHT OWLS
ERNEST BAXTER
MINDY MARKUS
ROSCOE THE GARGOYLE
Ernie arrives at Helaku's apartment.
NIGHT OWL? WHAT A PLEASANT SURPRISE!
HELLO, HELAKU! I WAS JUST STOPPING BY TO GIVE YOU THESE...
AND TO ASK YOU IF YOU WOULD LIKE TO BE MY DATE AT THE POLICEMAN'S BALL NEXT WEEK?
I WOULD LOVE TO!
THEN IT'S A DATE!
Bobby Timony
ERNEST BAXTER!
AAAA!

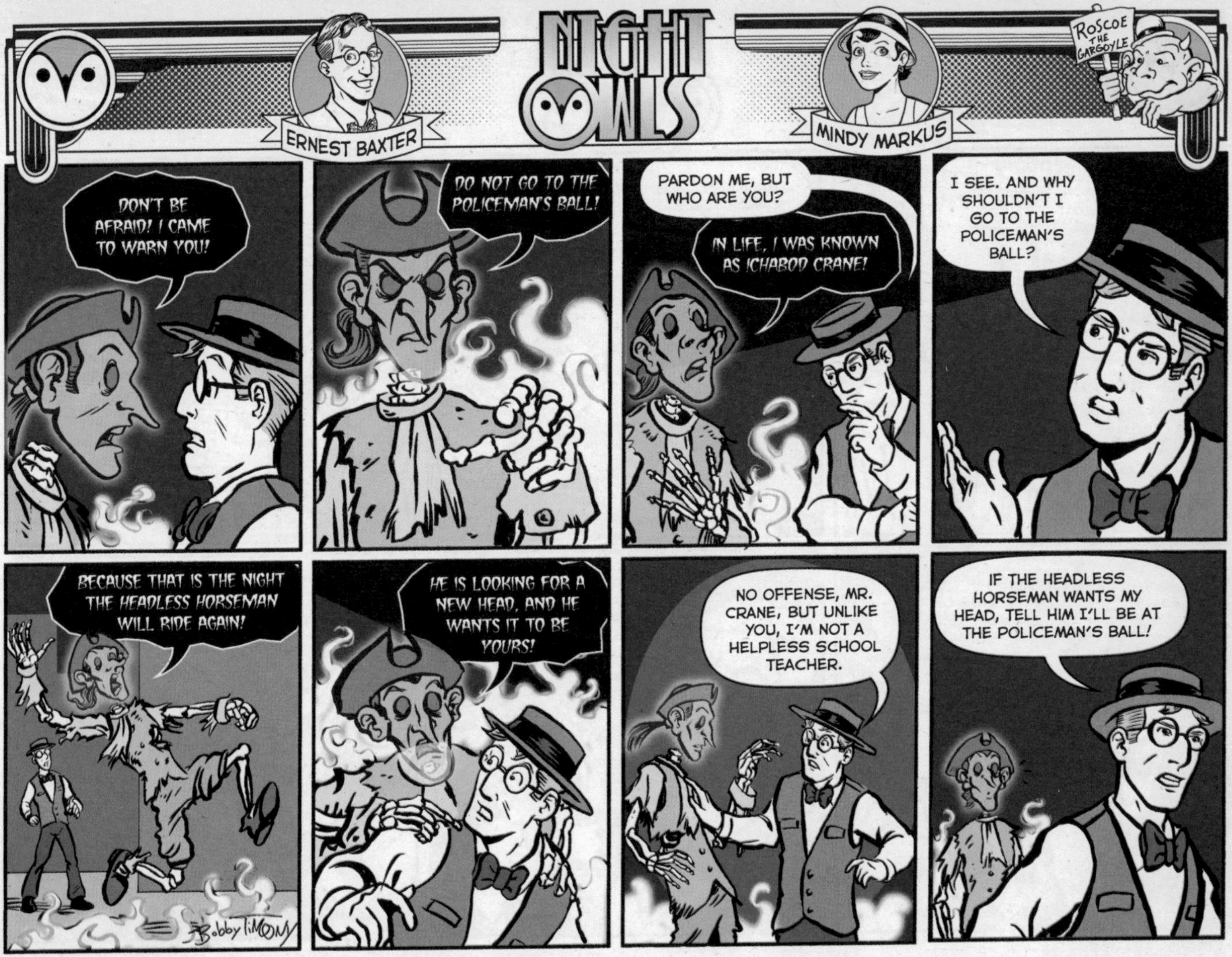
NIGHT OWLS
ERNEST BAXTER
MINDY MARKUS
ROSCOE THE GARGOYLE
DON'T BE AFRAID! I CAME TO WARN YOU!
DO NOT GO TO THE POLICEMAN'S BALL!
PARDON ME, BUT WHO ARE YOU?
IN LIFE, I WAS KNOWN AS ICHABOD CRANE!
I SEE. AND WHY SHOULDN'T I GO TO THE POLICEMAN'S BALL?
BECAUSE THAT IS THE NIGHT THE HEADLESS HORSEMAN WILL RIDE AGAIN!
HE IS LOOKING FOR A NEW HEAD, AND HE WANTS IT TO BE YOURS!
NO OFFENSE, MR. CRANE, BUT UNLIKE YOU, I'M NOT A HELPLESS SCHOOL TEACHER.
IF THE HEADLESS HORSEMAN WANTS MY HEAD, TELL HIM I'LL BE AT THE POLICEMAN'S BALL!
Bobby Timony

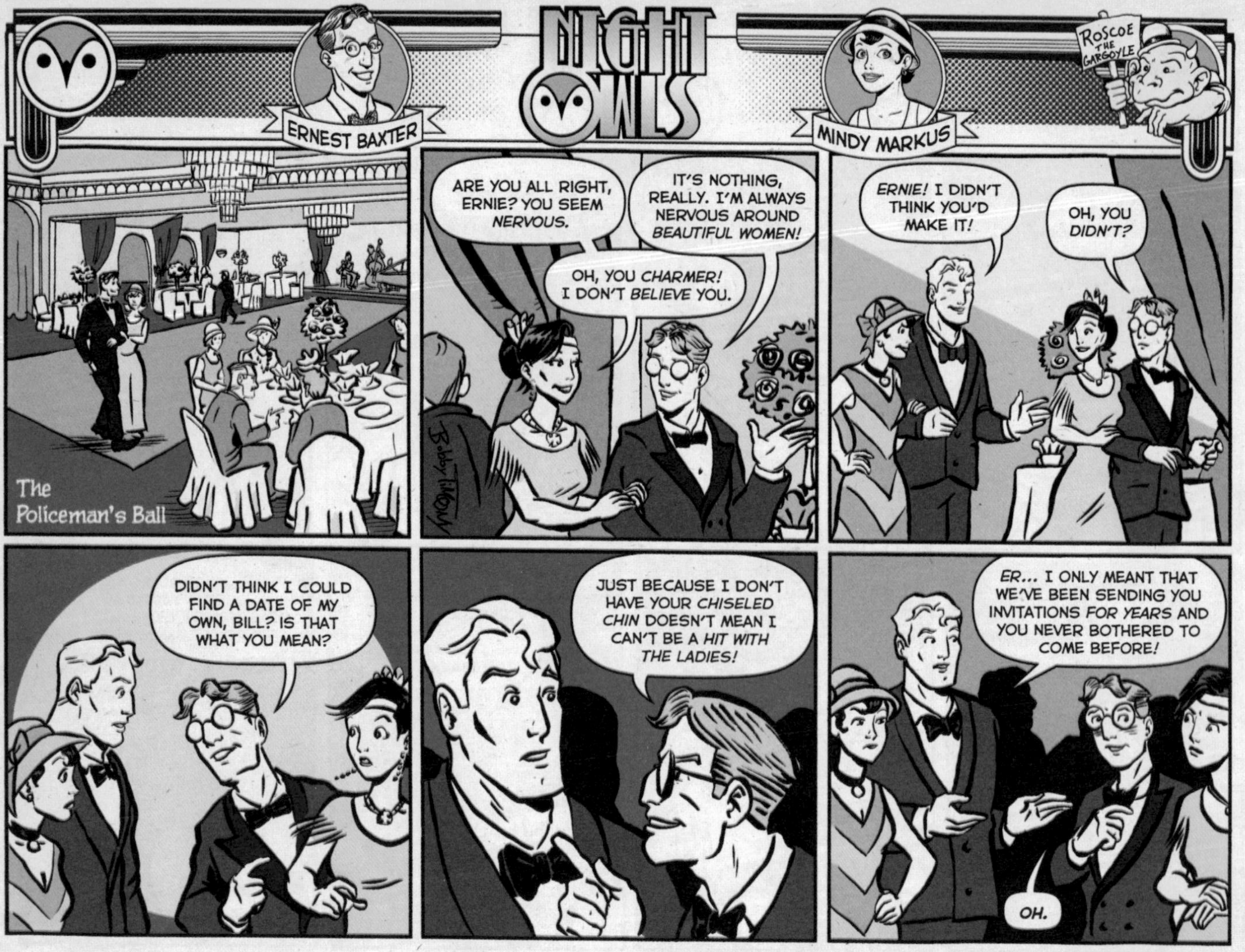
NIGHT OWLS
ERNEST BAXTER
MINDY MARKUS
ROSCOE THE GARGOYLE
The Policeman's Ball
ARE YOU ALL RIGHT, ERNIE? YOU SEEM NERVOUS.
IT'S NOTHING, REALLY. I'M ALWAYS NERVOUS AROUND BEAUTIFUL WOMEN!
OH, YOU CHARMER! I DON'T BELIEVE YOU.
ERNIE! I DIDN'T THINK YOU'D MAKE IT!
OH, YOU DIDN'T?
DIDN'T THINK I COULD FIND A DATE OF MY OWN, BILL? IS THAT WHAT YOU MEAN?
JUST BECAUSE I DON'T HAVE YOUR CHISELED CHIN DOESN'T MEAN I CAN'T BE A HIT WITH THE LADIES!
ER... I ONLY MEANT THAT WE'VE BEEN SENDING YOU INVITATIONS FOR YEARS AND YOU NEVER BOTHERED TO COME BEFORE!
OH.

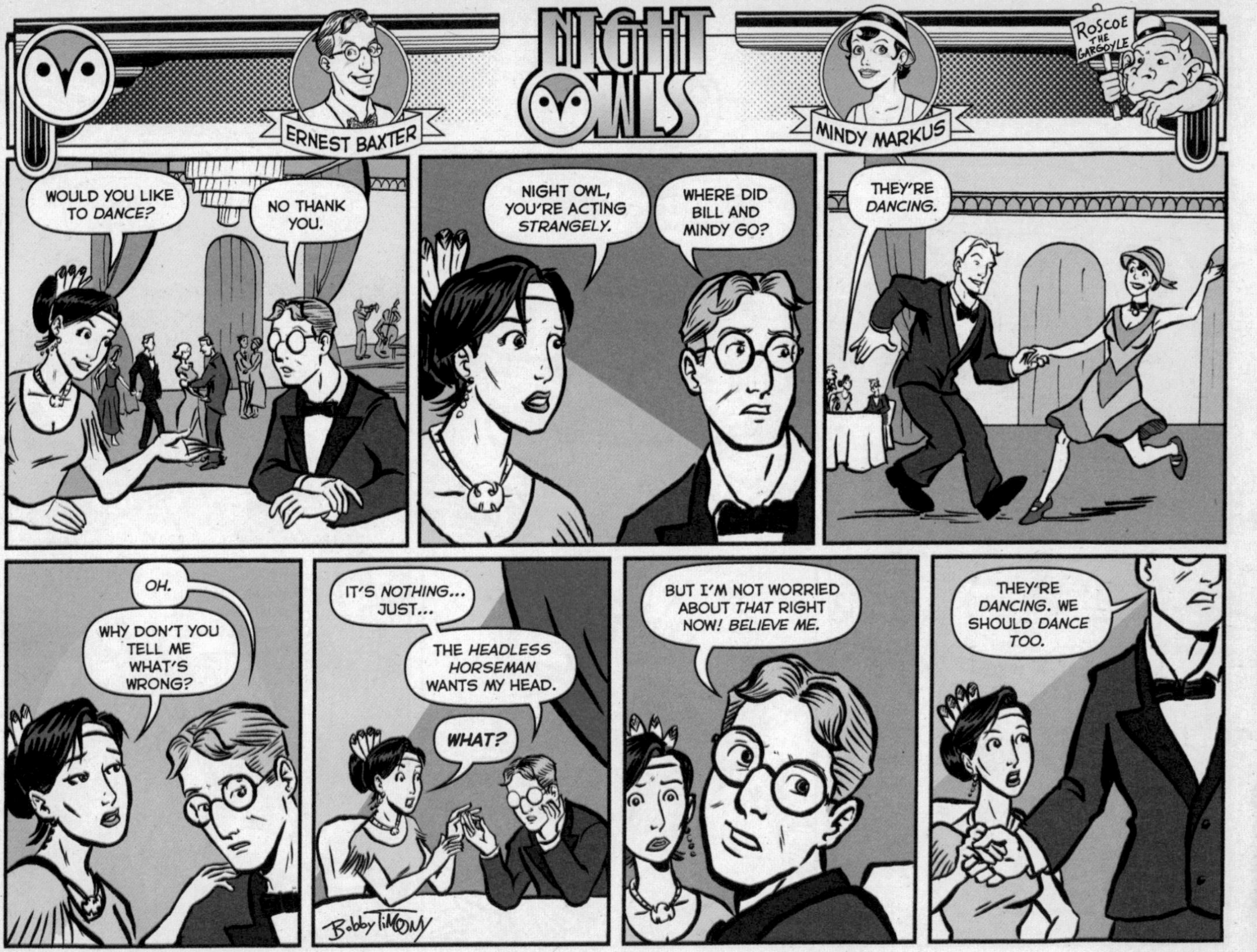
NIGHT OWLS
ERNEST BAXTER
MINDY MARKUS
ROSCOE THE GARGOYLE
WOULD YOU LIKE TO DANCE?
NO THANK YOU.
NIGHT OWL, YOU'RE ACTING STRANGELY.
WHERE DID BILL AND MINDY GO?
THEY'RE DANCING.
OH.
WHY DON'T YOU TELL ME WHAT'S WRONG?
IT'S NOTHING... JUST...
THE HEADLESS HORSEMAN WANTS MY HEAD.
WHAT?
BUT I'M NOT WORRIED ABOUT THAT RIGHT NOW! BELIEVE ME.
THEY'RE DANCING. WE SHOULD DANCE TOO.
Bobby Timony

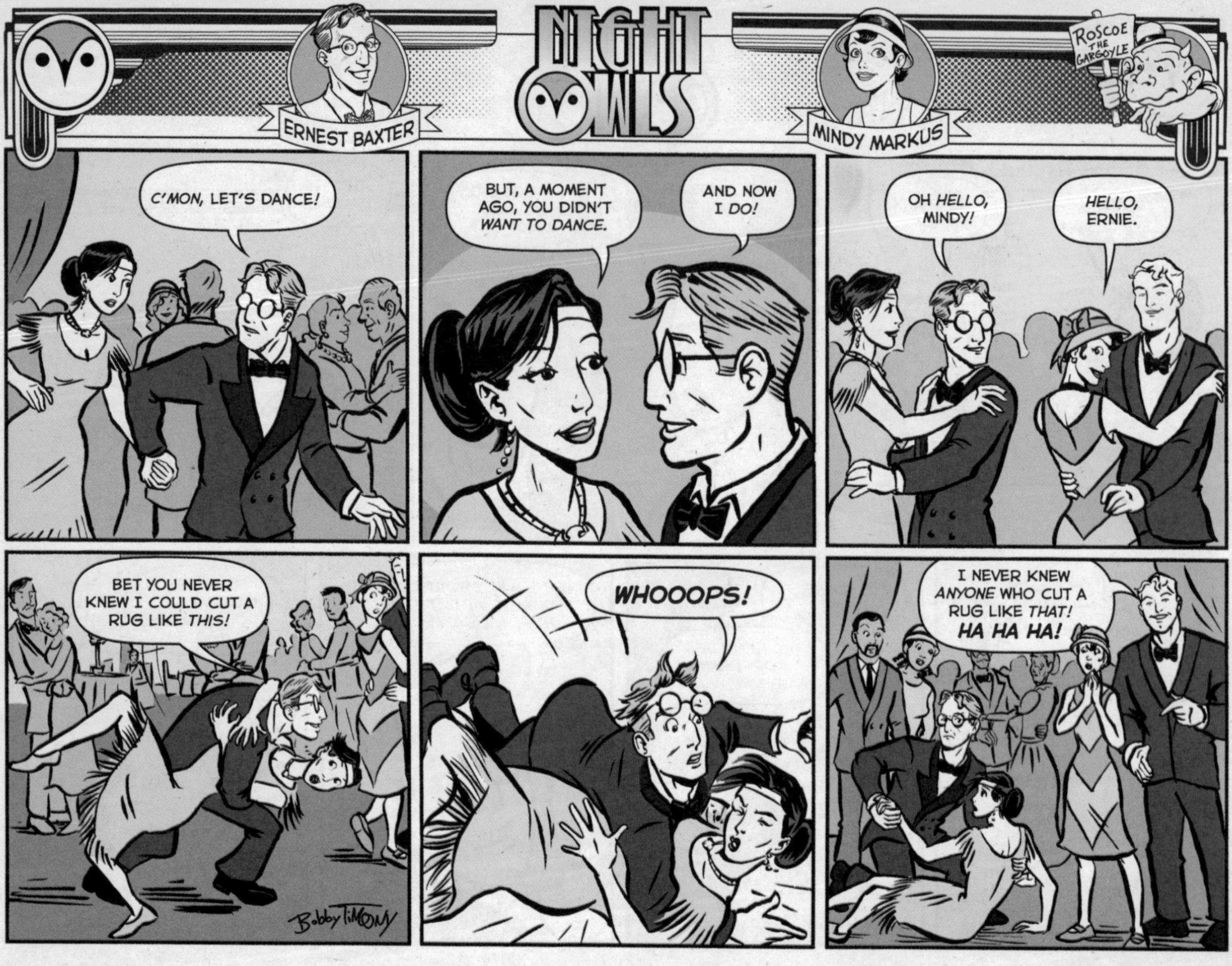
NIGHT OWLS
ERNEST BAXTER
MINDY MARKUS
ROSCOE THE GARGOYLE
C'MON, LET'S DANCE!
BUT, A MOMENT AGO, YOU DIDN'T *WANT TO DANCE.*
AND NOW I *DO!*
OH *HELLO,* MINDY!
HELLO, ERNIE.
BET YOU NEVER KNEW I COULD CUT A RUG LIKE *THIS!*
WHOOOPS!
I NEVER KNEW *ANYONE* WHO CUT A RUG LIKE *THAT!* **HA HA HA!**
Bobby TiMONY

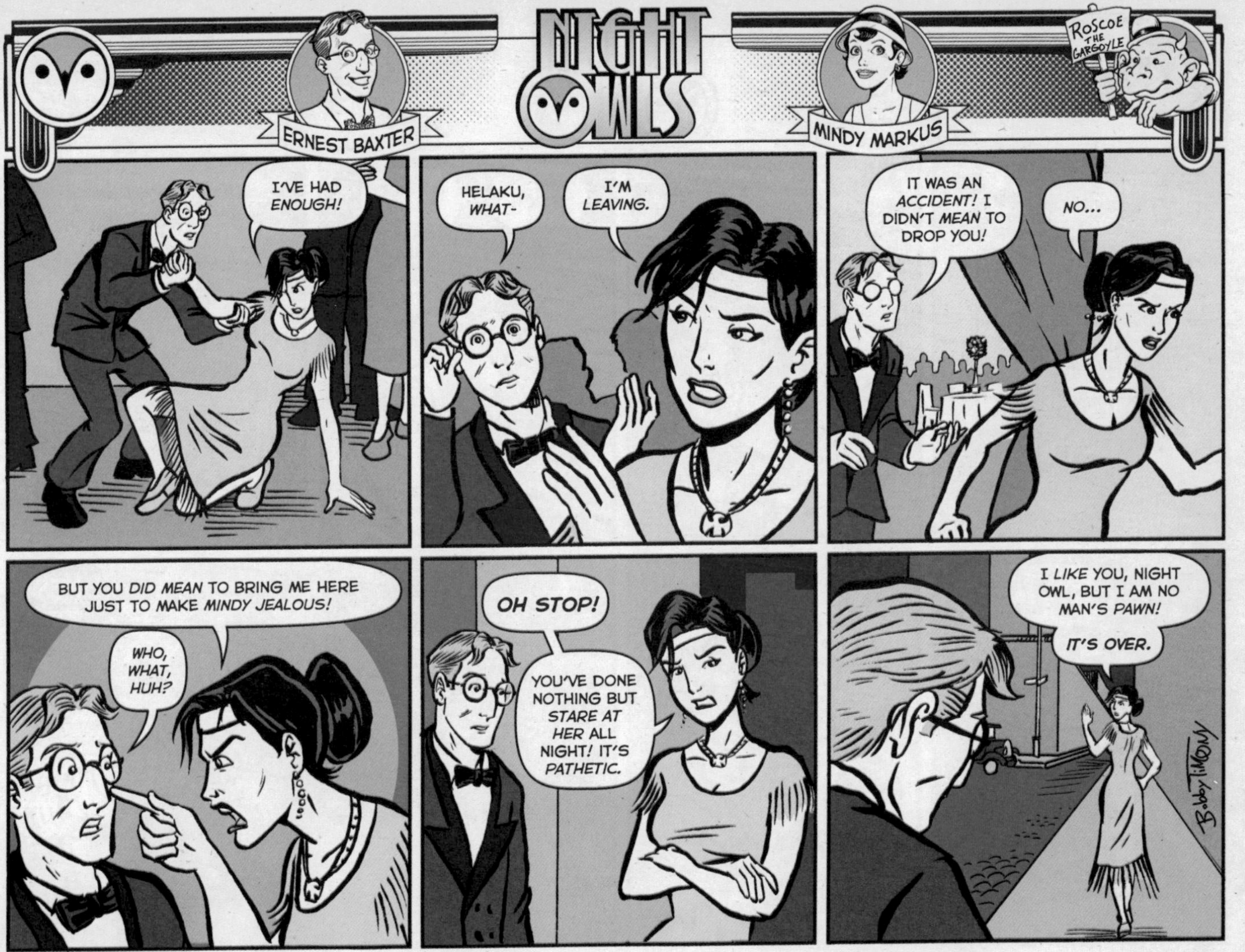
NIGHT OWLS
ERNEST BAXTER
MINDY MARKUS
ROSCOE THE GARGOYLE
I'VE HAD ENOUGH!
HELAKU, WHAT-
I'M LEAVING.
IT WAS AN ACCIDENT! I DIDN'T MEAN TO DROP YOU!
NO...
BUT YOU DID MEAN TO BRING ME HERE JUST TO MAKE MINDY JEALOUS!
WHO, WHAT, HUH?
OH STOP!
YOU'VE DONE NOTHING BUT STARE AT HER ALL NIGHT! IT'S PATHETIC.
I LIKE YOU, NIGHT OWL, BUT I AM NO MAN'S PAWN!
IT'S OVER.
Bobby Timony

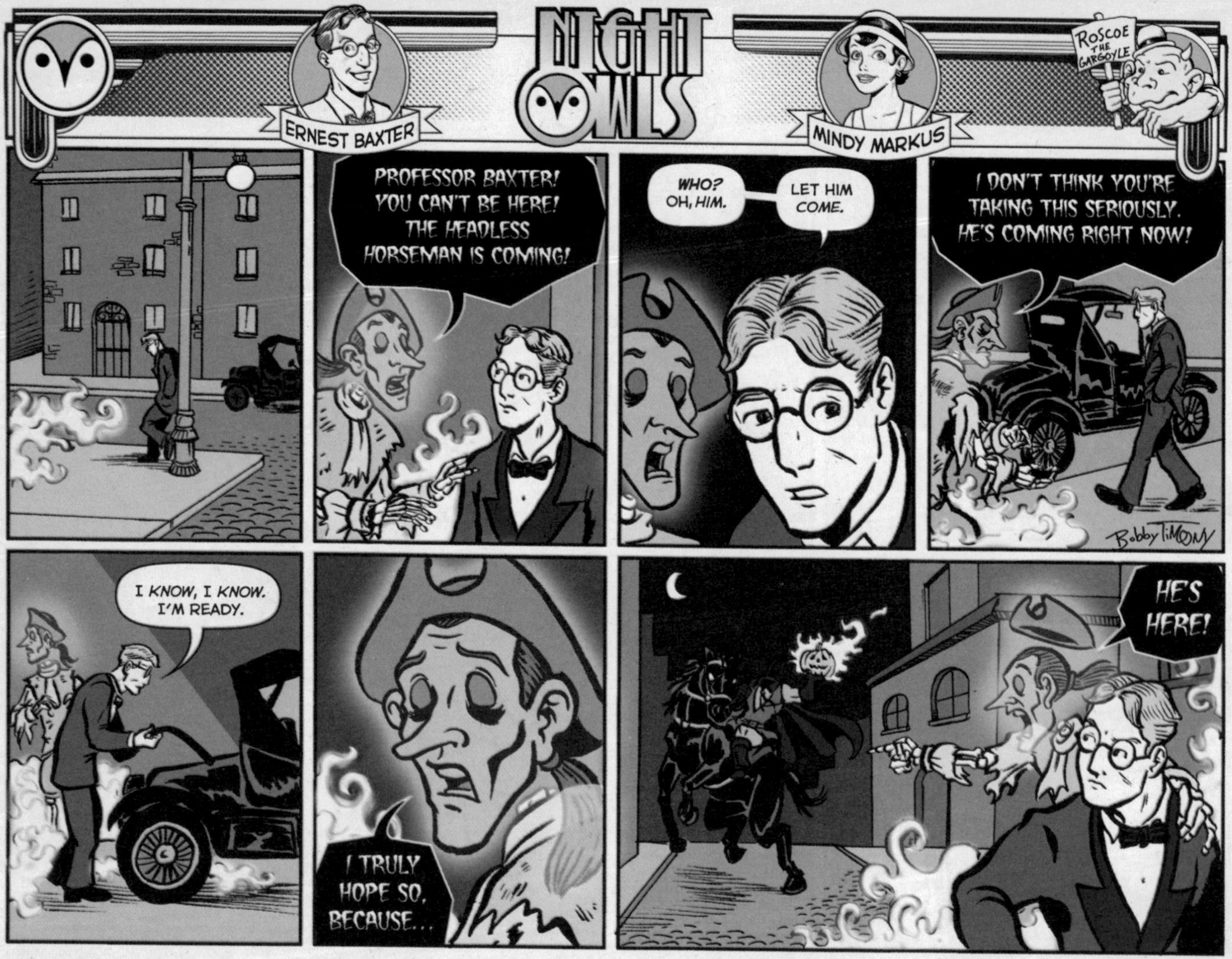
NIGHT OWLS
ERNEST BAXTER
MINDY MARKUS
ROSCOE THE GARGOYLE
PROFESSOR BAXTER! YOU CAN'T BE HERE! THE HEADLESS HORSEMAN IS COMING!
WHO? OH, HIM.
LET HIM COME.
I DON'T THINK YOU'RE TAKING THIS SERIOUSLY. HE'S COMING RIGHT NOW!
Bobby Timony
I KNOW, I KNOW. I'M READY.
I TRULY HOPE SO, BECAUSE...
HE'S HERE!

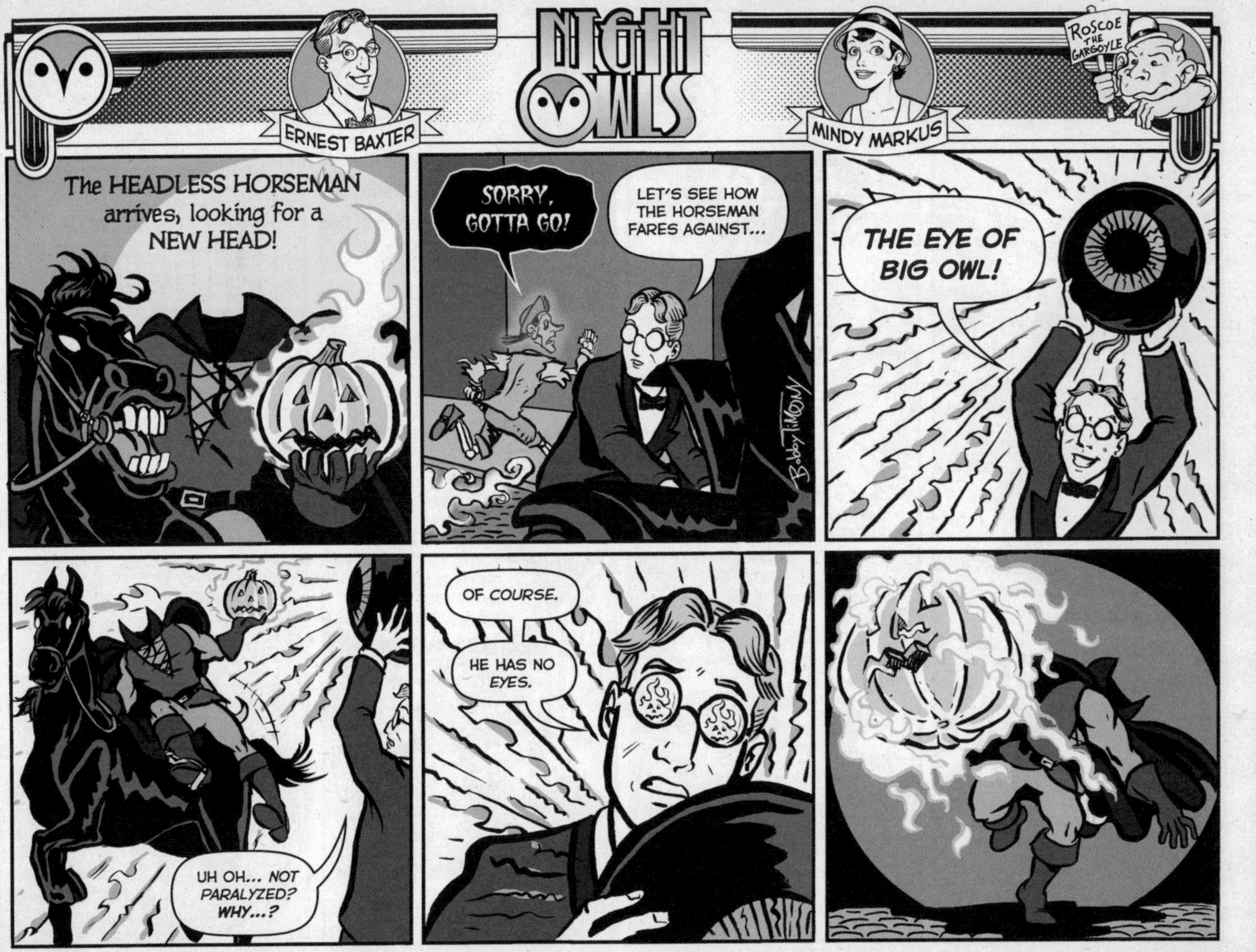
NIGHT OWLS
ERNEST BAXTER
MINDY MARKUS
ROSCOE THE GARGOYLE
The HEADLESS HORSEMAN arrives, looking for a NEW HEAD!
SORRY, GOTTA GO!
LET'S SEE HOW THE HORSEMAN FARES AGAINST...
Bobby Timony
THE EYE OF BIG OWL!
UH OH... NOT PARALYZED? WHY...?
OF COURSE.
HE HAS NO EYES.

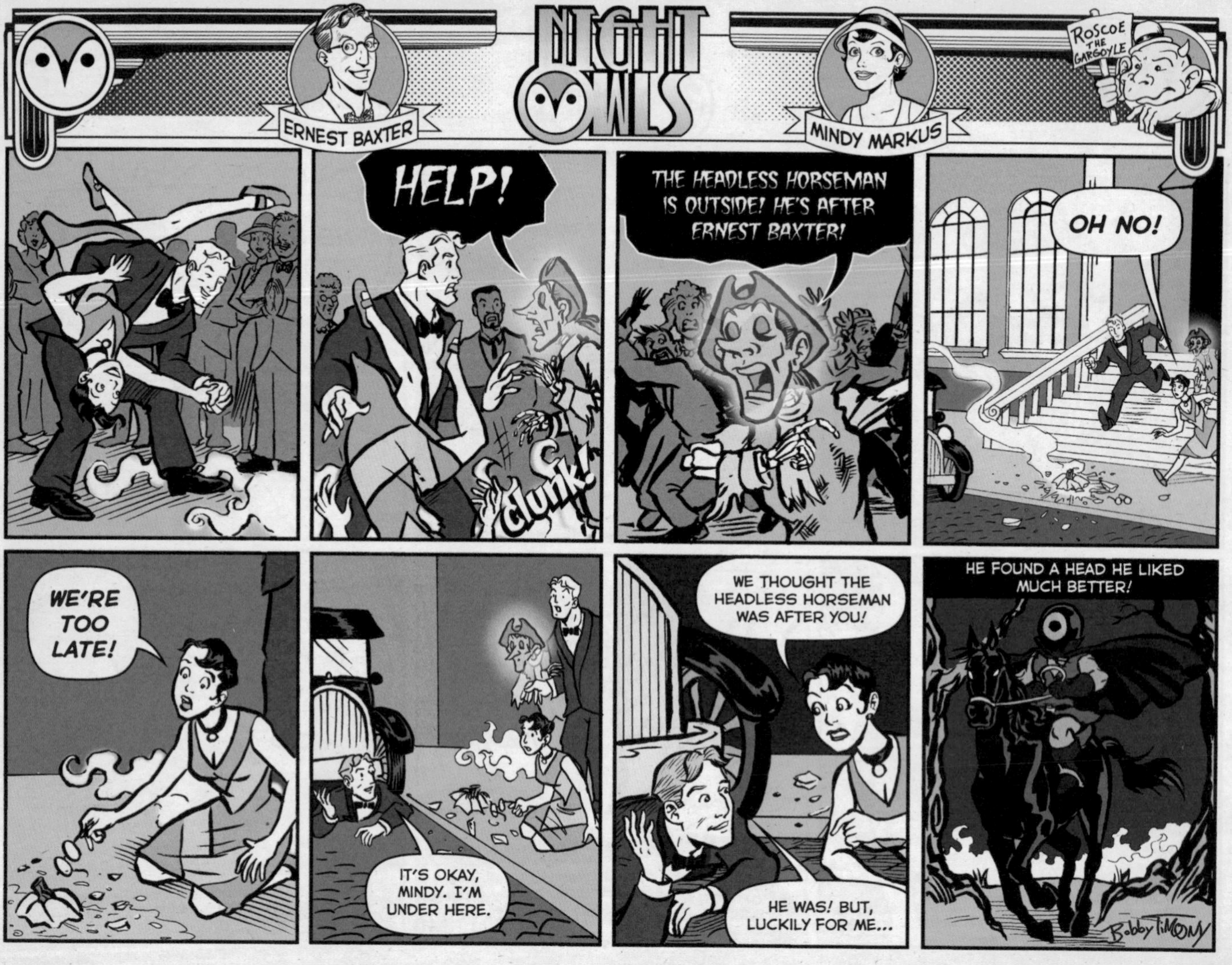

NIGHT OWLS
ERNEST BAXTER
MINDY MARKUS
ROSCOE THE GARGOYLE
HELP!
CLUNK!
THE HEADLESS HORSEMAN IS OUTSIDE! HE'S AFTER ERNEST BAXTER!
OH NO!
WE'RE TOO LATE!
IT'S OKAY, MINDY. I'M UNDER HERE.
WE THOUGHT THE HEADLESS HORSEMAN WAS AFTER YOU!
HE WAS! BUT, LUCKILY FOR ME...
HE FOUND A HEAD HE LIKED MUCH BETTER!
Bobby Timony

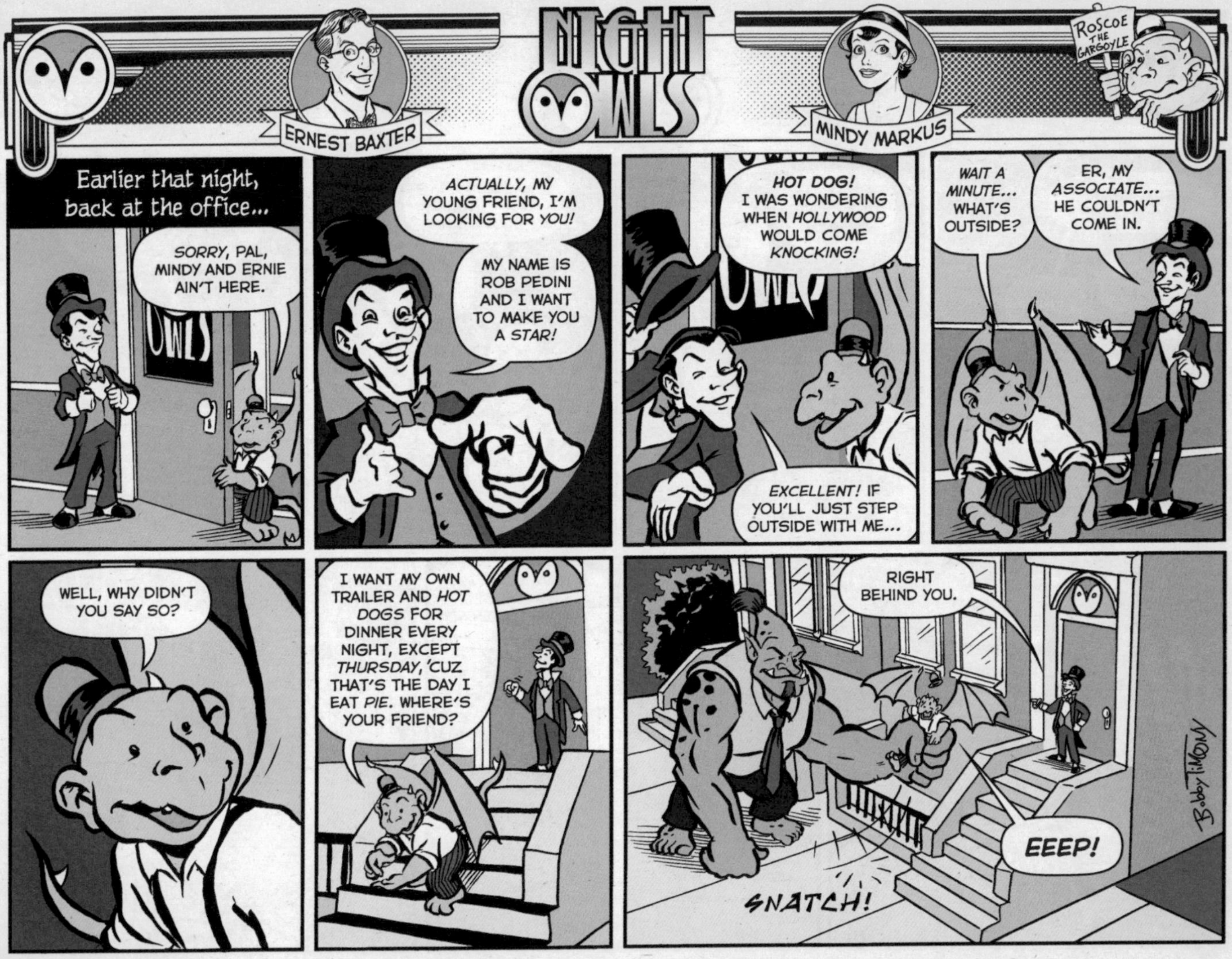
NIGHT OWLS
ERNEST BAXTER
MINDY MARKUS
ROSCOE THE GARGOYLE
Earlier that night, back at the office...
SORRY, PAL, MINDY AND ERNIE AIN'T HERE.
ACTUALLY, MY YOUNG FRIEND, I'M LOOKING FOR YOU!
MY NAME IS ROB PEDINI AND I WANT TO MAKE YOU A STAR!
HOT DOG! I WAS WONDERING WHEN HOLLYWOOD WOULD COME KNOCKING!
EXCELLENT! IF YOU'LL JUST STEP OUTSIDE WITH ME...
WAIT A MINUTE... WHAT'S OUTSIDE?
ER, MY ASSOCIATE... HE COULDN'T COME IN.
WELL, WHY DIDN'T YOU SAY SO?
I WANT MY OWN TRAILER AND HOT DOGS FOR DINNER EVERY NIGHT, EXCEPT THURSDAY, 'CUZ THAT'S THE DAY I EAT PIE. WHERE'S YOUR FRIEND?
RIGHT BEHIND YOU.
EEEP!
SNATCH!
Bobby Timony

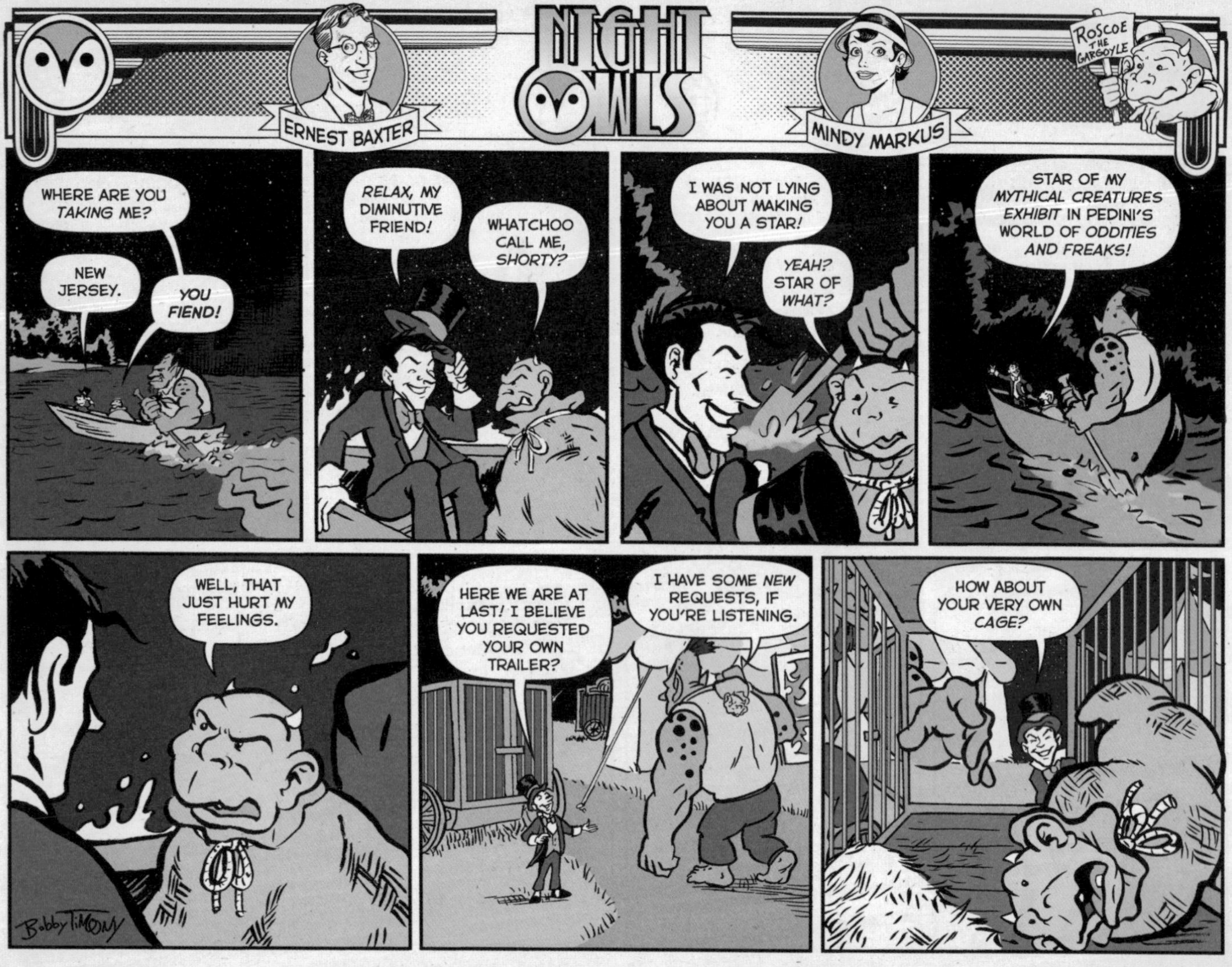
NIGHT OWLS
ERNEST BAXTER
MINDY MARKUS
ROSCOE THE GARGOYLE
WHERE ARE YOU TAKING ME?
NEW JERSEY.
YOU FIEND!
RELAX, MY DIMINUTIVE FRIEND!
WHATCHOO CALL ME, SHORTY?
I WAS NOT LYING ABOUT MAKING YOU A STAR!
YEAH? STAR OF WHAT?
STAR OF MY MYTHICAL CREATURES EXHIBIT IN PEDINI'S WORLD OF ODDITIES AND FREAKS!
WELL, THAT JUST HURT MY FEELINGS.
Bobby TiMONY
HERE WE ARE AT LAST! I BELIEVE YOU REQUESTED YOUR OWN TRAILER?
I HAVE SOME NEW REQUESTS, IF YOU'RE LISTENING.
HOW ABOUT YOUR VERY OWN CAGE?

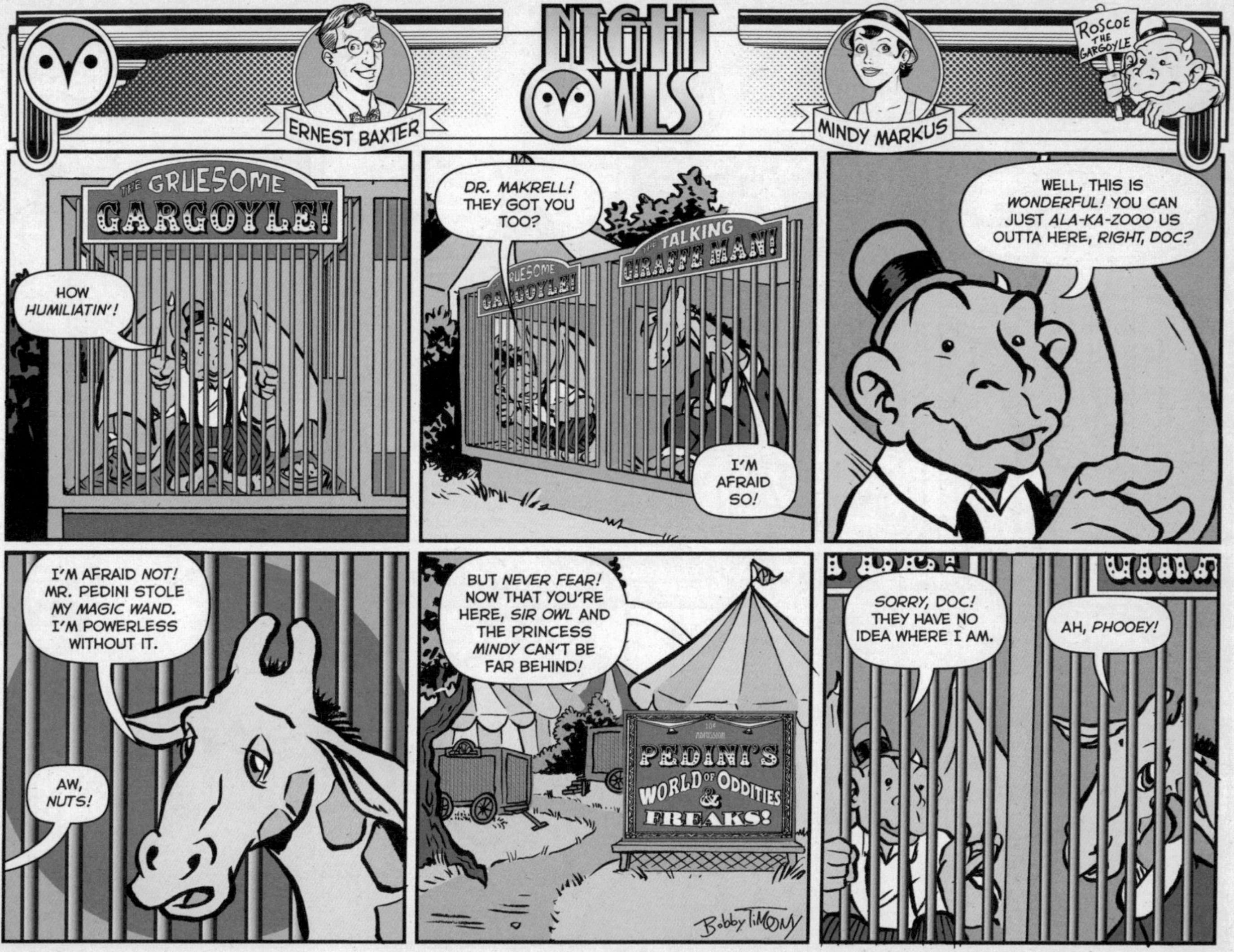
NIGHT OWLS
ERNEST BAXTER
MINDY MARKUS
ROSCOE THE GARGOYLE
THE GRUESOME GARGOYLE!
HOW HUMILIATIN'!
DR. MAKRELL! THEY GOT YOU TOO?
THE TALKING GIRAFFE MAN!
I'M AFRAID SO!
WELL, THIS IS WONDERFUL! YOU CAN JUST ALA-KA-ZOOO US OUTTA HERE, RIGHT, DOC?
I'M AFRAID NOT! MR. PEDINI STOLE MY MAGIC WAND. I'M POWERLESS WITHOUT IT.
AW, NUTS!
BUT NEVER FEAR! NOW THAT YOU'RE HERE, SIR OWL AND THE PRINCESS MINDY CAN'T BE FAR BEHIND!
PEDINI'S WORLD OF ODDITIES & FREAKS!
SORRY, DOC! THEY HAVE NO IDEA WHERE I AM.
AH, PHOOEY!
Bobby Timony

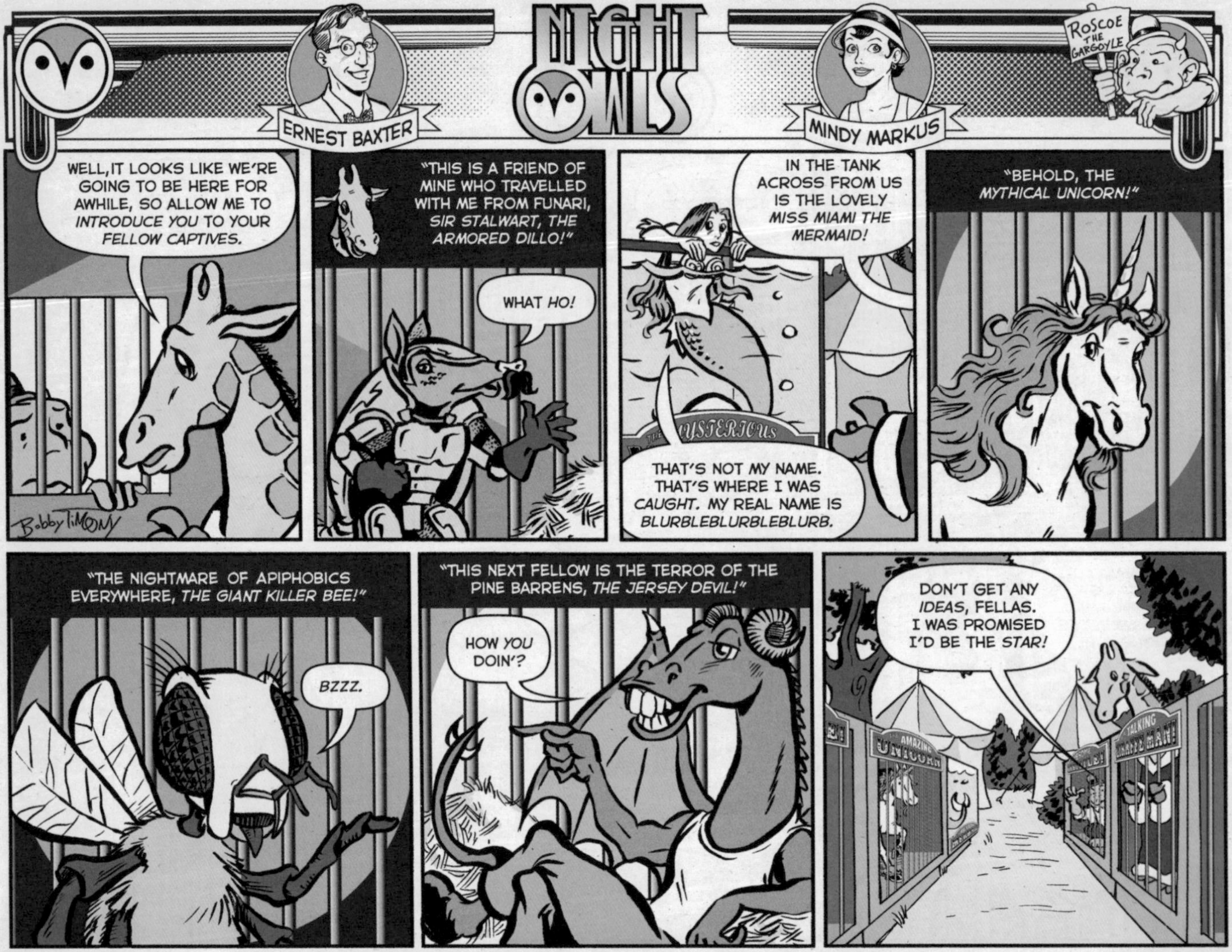

NIGHT OWLS
ERNEST BAXTER
MINDY MARKUS
ROSCOE THE GARGOYLE
WELL, IT LOOKS LIKE WE'RE GOING TO BE HERE FOR AWHILE, SO ALLOW ME TO INTRODUCE YOU TO YOUR FELLOW CAPTIVES.
Bobby Timony
"THIS IS A FRIEND OF MINE WHO TRAVELLED WITH ME FROM FUNARI, SIR STALWART, THE ARMORED DILLO!"
WHAT HO!
IN THE TANK ACROSS FROM US IS THE LOVELY MISS MIAMI THE MERMAID!
THE MYSTERIOUS
THAT'S NOT MY NAME. THAT'S WHERE I WAS CAUGHT. MY REAL NAME IS BLURBLEBLURBLEBLURB.
"BEHOLD, THE MYTHICAL UNICORN!"
"THE NIGHTMARE OF APIPHOBICS EVERYWHERE, THE GIANT KILLER BEE!"
BZZZ.
"THIS NEXT FELLOW IS THE TERROR OF THE PINE BARRENS, THE JERSEY DEVIL!"
HOW YOU DOIN'?
DON'T GET ANY IDEAS, FELLAS. I WAS PROMISED I'D BE THE STAR!
THE AMAZING UNICORN
TALKING GIRAFFE MAN!

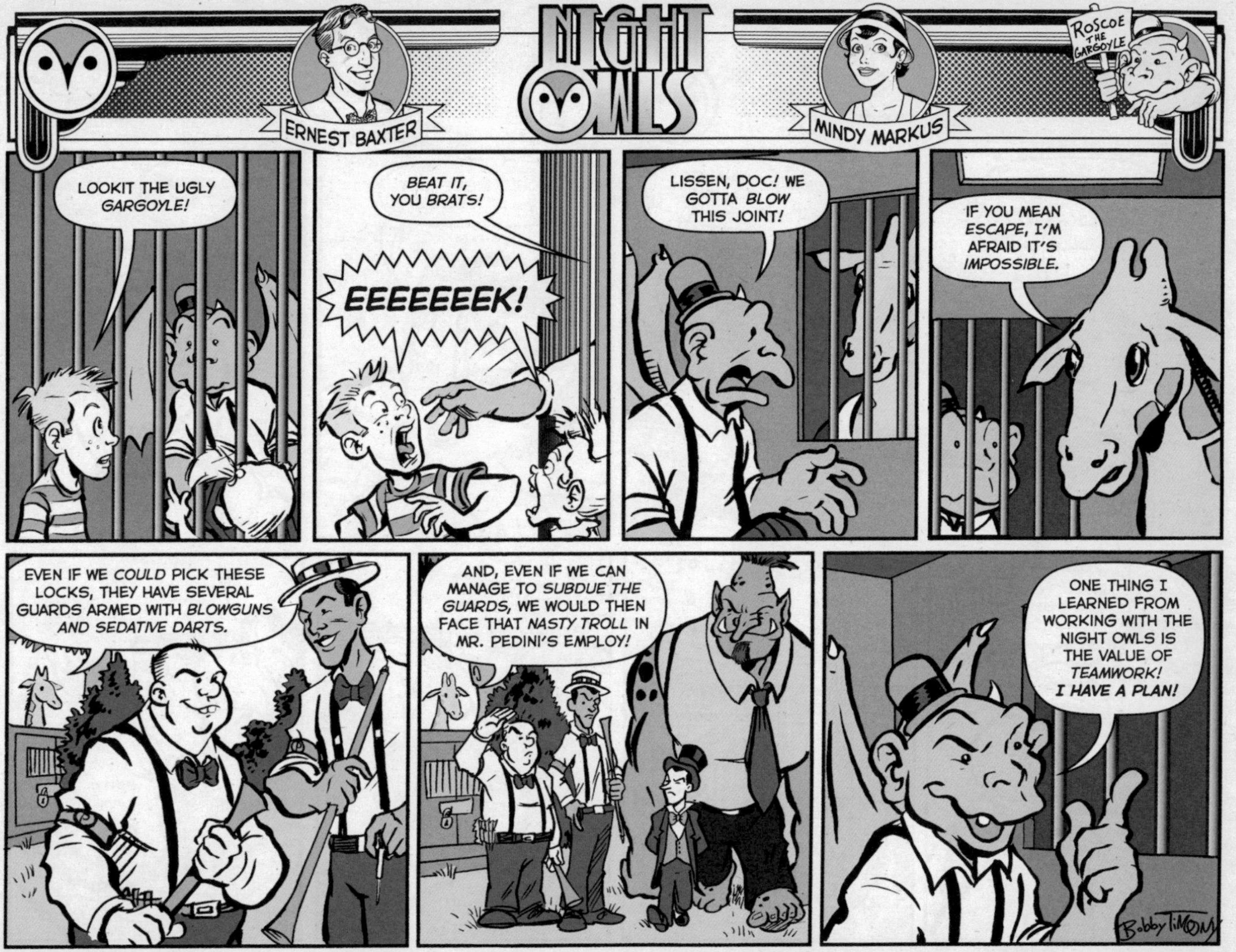
NIGHT OWLS
ERNEST BAXTER
MINDY MARKUS
ROSCOE THE GARGOYLE
LOOKIT THE UGLY *GARGOYLE!*
BEAT IT, YOU BRATS!
EEEEEEEEK!
LISSEN, DOC! WE GOTTA *BLOW* THIS JOINT!
IF YOU MEAN *ESCAPE*, I'M AFRAID IT'S *IMPOSSIBLE.*
EVEN IF WE *COULD* PICK THESE LOCKS, THEY HAVE SEVERAL GUARDS ARMED WITH *BLOWGUNS AND SEDATIVE DARTS.*
AND, EVEN IF WE CAN MANAGE TO *SUBDUE THE GUARDS*, WE WOULD THEN FACE THAT *NASTY TROLL* IN MR. PEDINI'S EMPLOY!
ONE THING I LEARNED FROM WORKING WITH THE NIGHT OWLS IS THE VALUE OF *TEAMWORK!* ***I HAVE A PLAN!***
Bobby TiMONY

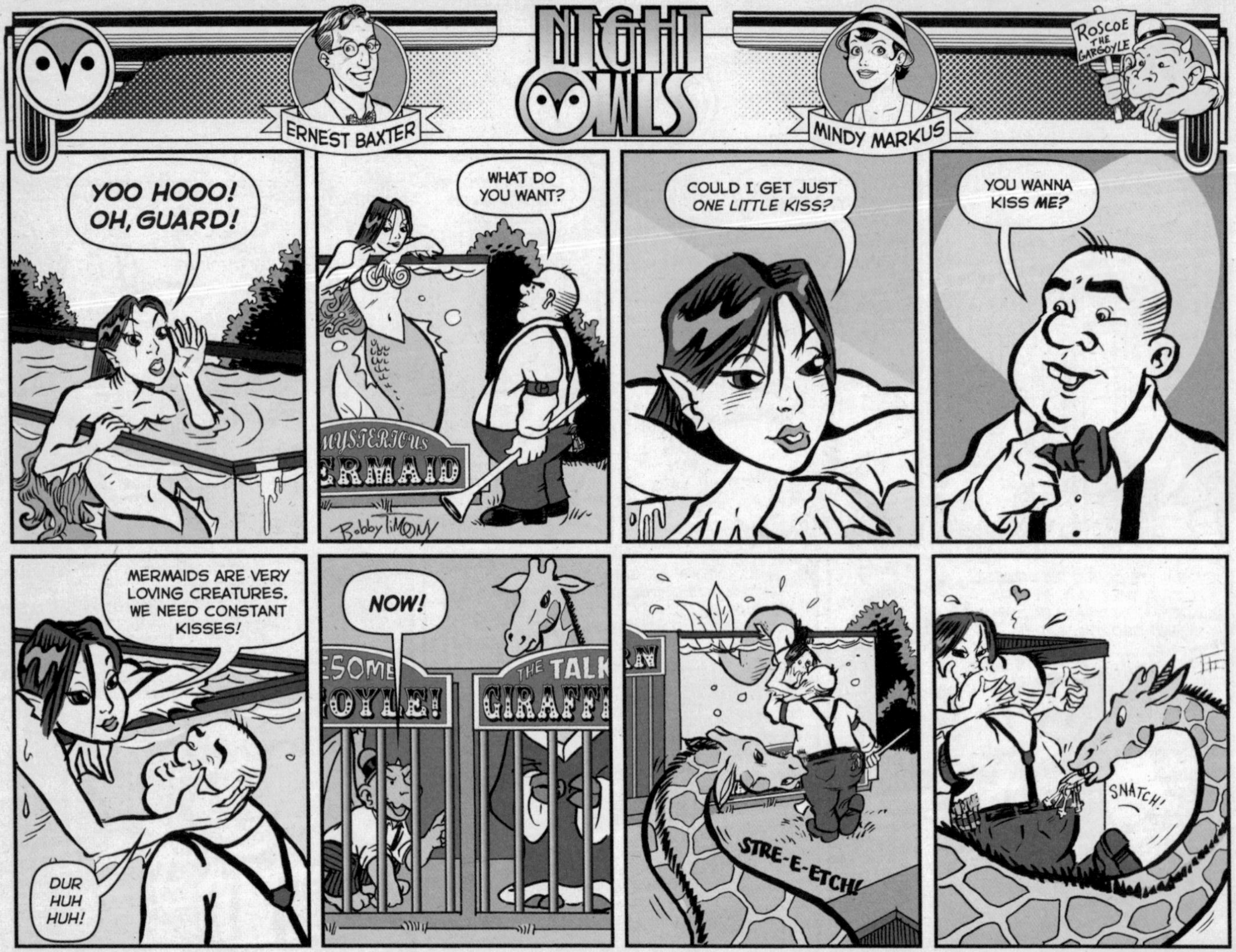
NIGHT OWLS
ERNEST BAXTER
MINDY MARKUS
ROSCOE THE GARGOYLE
YOO HOOO! OH, GUARD!
WHAT DO YOU WANT?
MYSTERIOUS ERMAID
Bobby Timony
COULD I GET JUST ONE LITTLE KISS?
YOU WANNA KISS ME?
MERMAIDS ARE VERY LOVING CREATURES. WE NEED CONSTANT KISSES!
DUR HUH HUH!
NOW!
ESOME OYLE!
THE TALK GIRAFF
STRE-E-ETCH!
SNATCH!

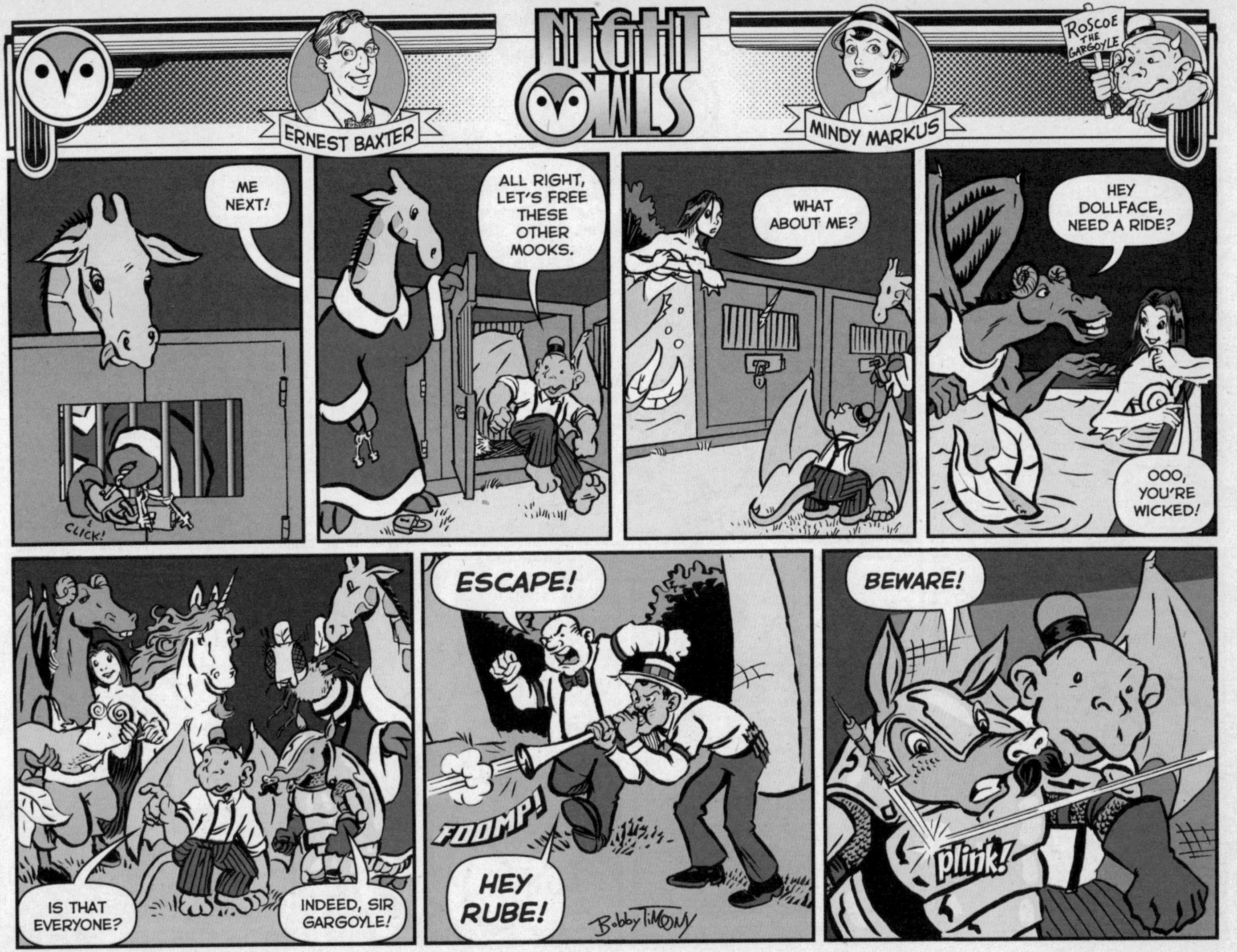
NIGHT OWLS
ERNEST BAXTER
MINDY MARKUS
ROSCOE THE GARGOYLE
ME NEXT!
CLICK!
ALL RIGHT, LET'S FREE THESE OTHER MOOKS.
WHAT ABOUT ME?
HEY DOLLFACE, NEED A RIDE?
OOO, YOU'RE WICKED!
IS THAT EVERYONE?
INDEED, SIR GARGOYLE!
ESCAPE!
FOOMP!
HEY RUBE!
Bobby TIMONY
BEWARE!
plink!

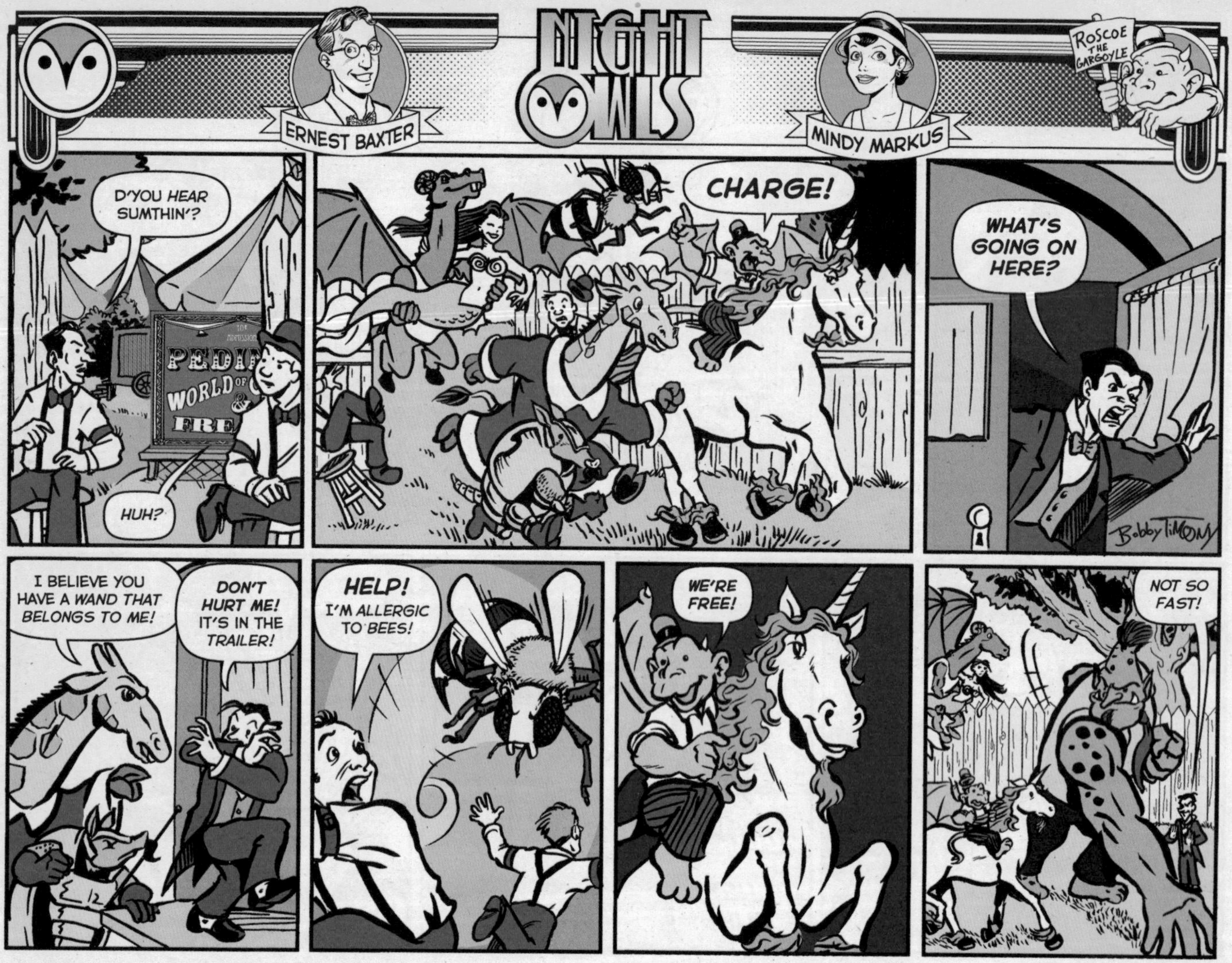
NIGHT OWLS
ERNEST BAXTER
MINDY MARKUS
ROSCOE THE GARGOYLE
D'YOU HEAR SUMTHIN'?
HUH?
CHARGE!
WHAT'S GOING ON HERE?
Bobby Timony
I BELIEVE YOU HAVE A WAND THAT BELONGS TO ME!
DON'T HURT ME! IT'S IN THE TRAILER!
HELP! I'M ALLERGIC TO BEES!
WE'RE FREE!
NOT SO FAST!

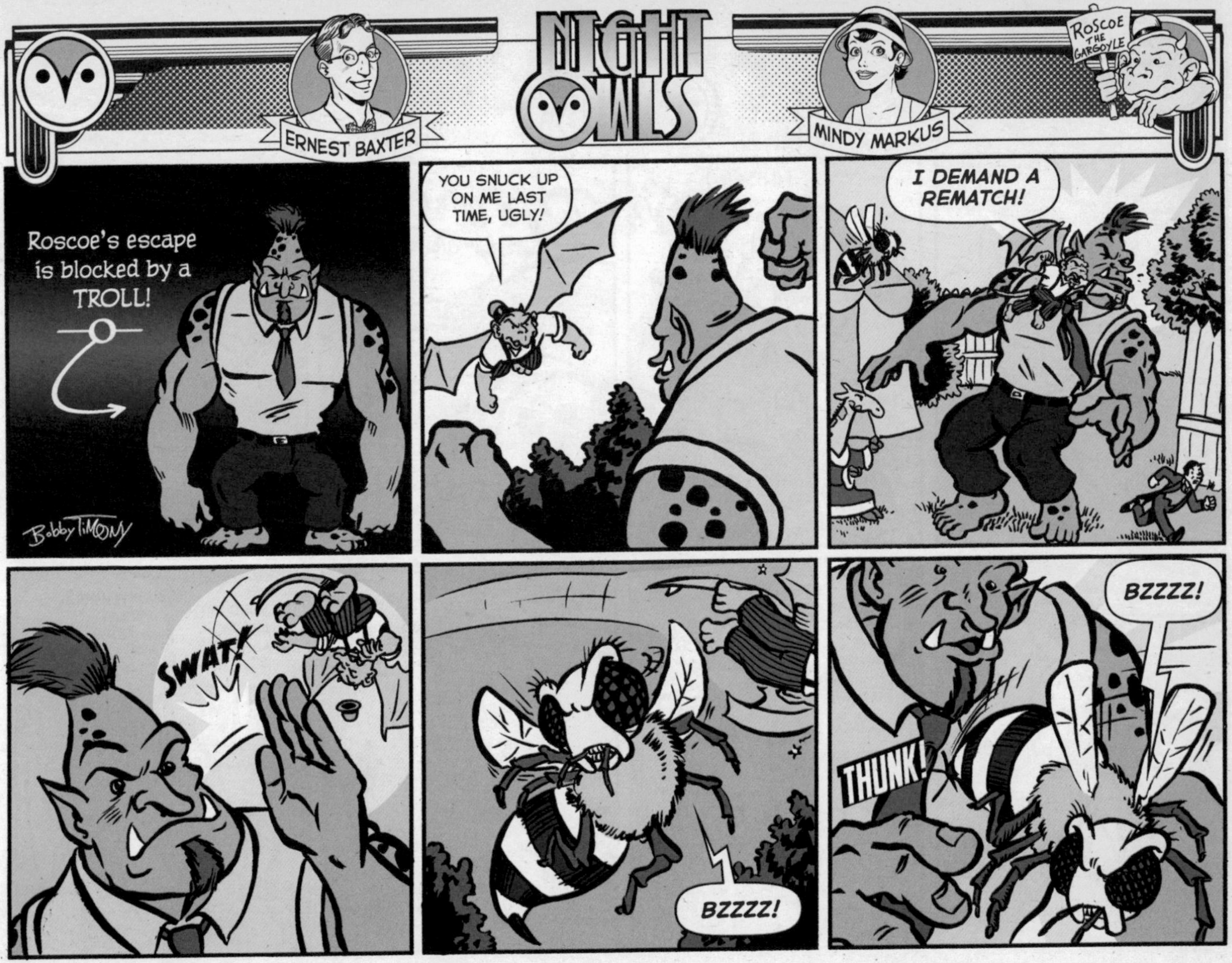
NIGHT OWLS
ERNEST BAXTER
MINDY MARKUS
ROSCOE THE GARGOYLE
Roscoe's escape is blocked by a TROLL!
Bobby Timony
YOU SNUCK UP ON ME LAST TIME, UGLY!
I DEMAND A REMATCH!
SWAT!
BZZZZ!
BZZZZ!
THUNK!

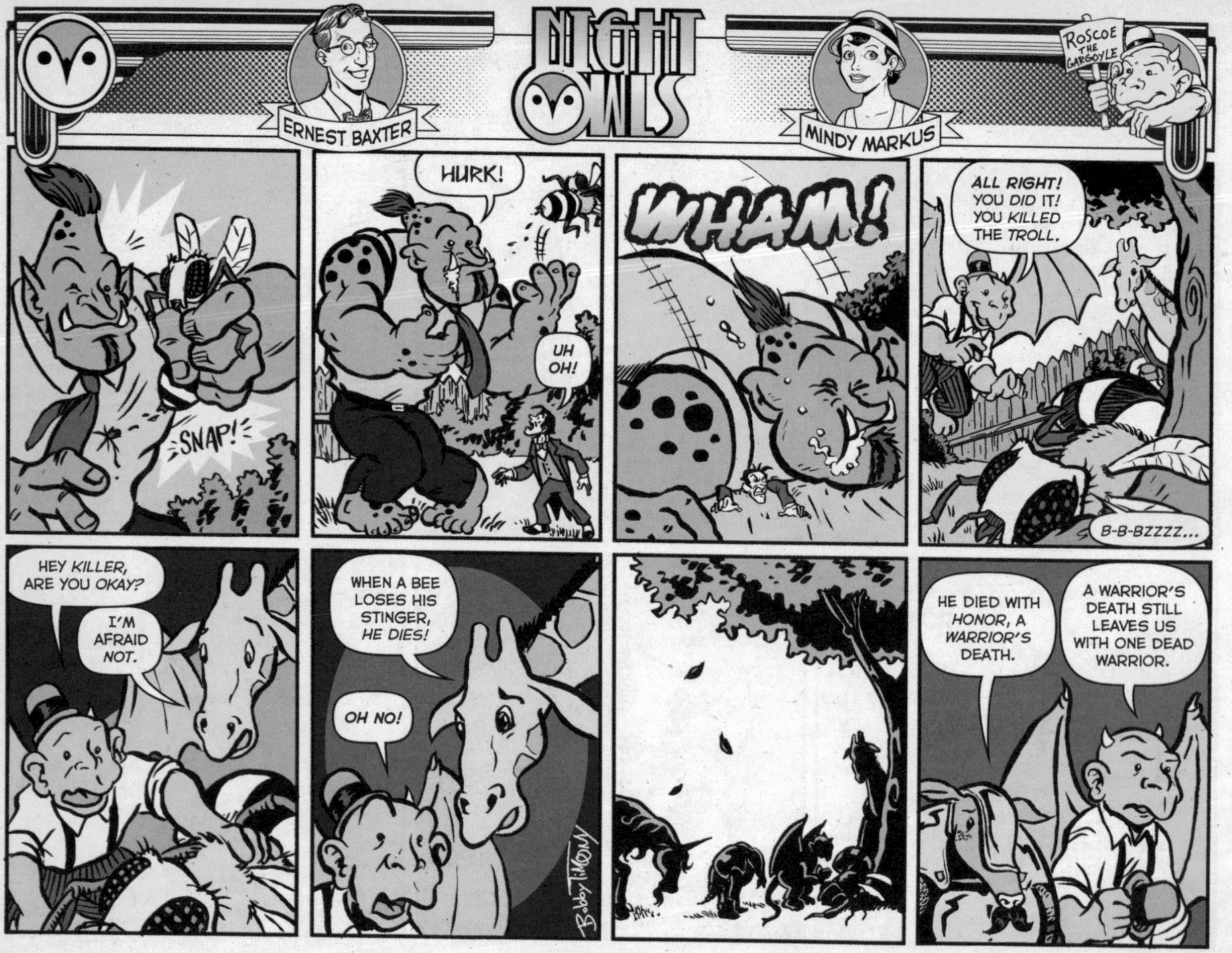
NIGHT OWLS
ERNEST BAXTER
MINDY MARKUS
ROSCOE THE GARGOYLE
SNAP!
HURK!
UH OH!
WHAM!
ALL RIGHT! YOU DID IT! YOU KILLED THE TROLL.
B-B-BZZZZ...
HEY KILLER, ARE YOU OKAY?
I'M AFRAID NOT.
WHEN A BEE LOSES HIS STINGER, HE DIES!
OH NO!
HE DIED WITH HONOR, A WARRIOR'S DEATH.
A WARRIOR'S DEATH STILL LEAVES US WITH ONE DEAD WARRIOR.
Bobby Timony

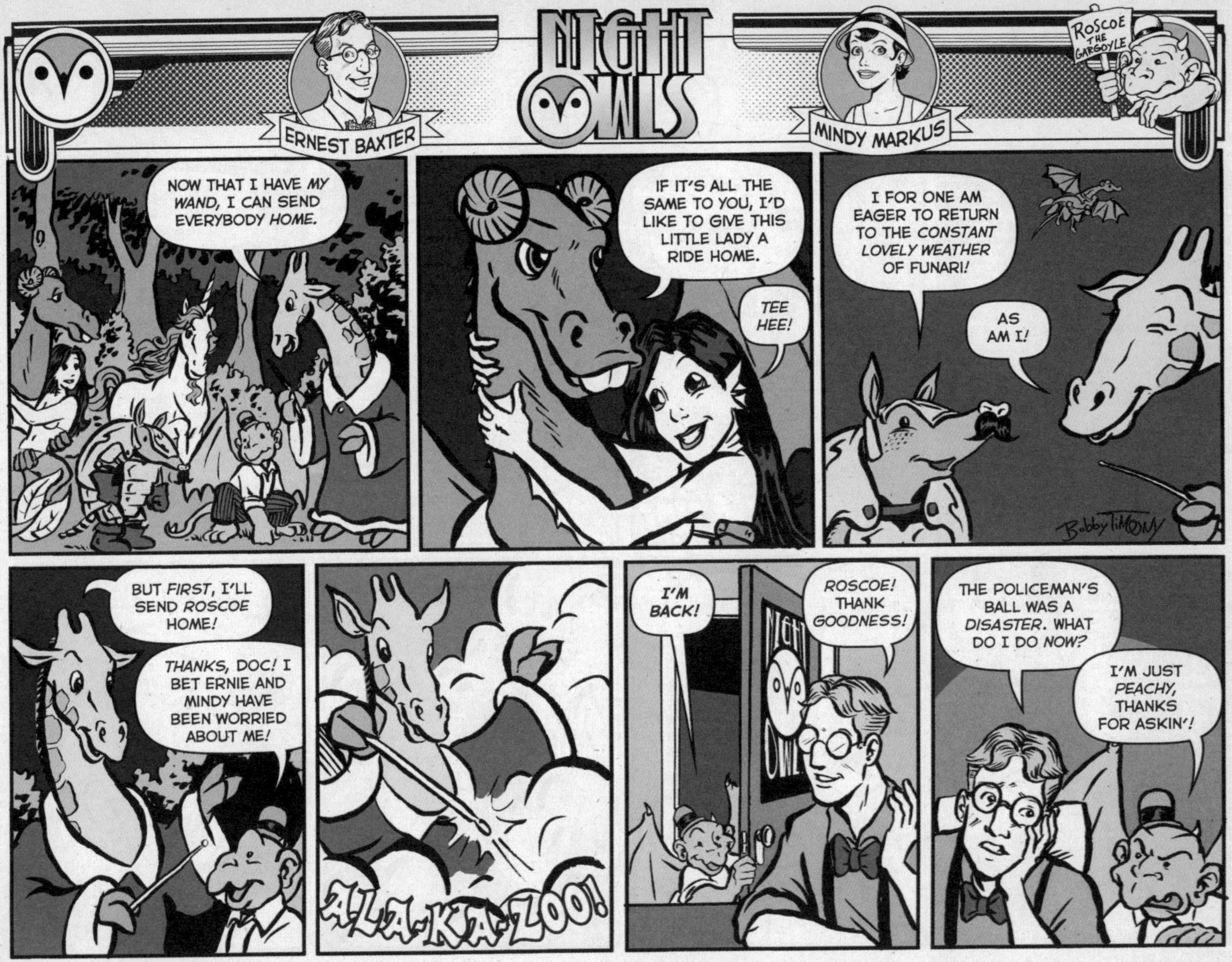
NIGHT OWLS
ERNEST BAXTER
MINDY MARKUS
ROSCOE THE GARGOYLE
NOW THAT I HAVE MY WAND, I CAN SEND EVERYBODY HOME.
IF IT'S ALL THE SAME TO YOU, I'D LIKE TO GIVE THIS LITTLE LADY A RIDE HOME.
TEE HEE!
I FOR ONE AM EAGER TO RETURN TO THE CONSTANT LOVELY WEATHER OF FUNARI!
AS AM I!
Bobby Timony
BUT FIRST, I'LL SEND ROSCOE HOME!
THANKS, DOC! I BET ERNIE AND MINDY HAVE BEEN WORRIED ABOUT ME!
ALA-KA-ZOO!
I'M BACK!
ROSCOE! THANK GOODNESS!
THE POLICEMAN'S BALL WAS A DISASTER. WHAT DO I DO NOW?
I'M JUST PEACHY, THANKS FOR ASKIN'!

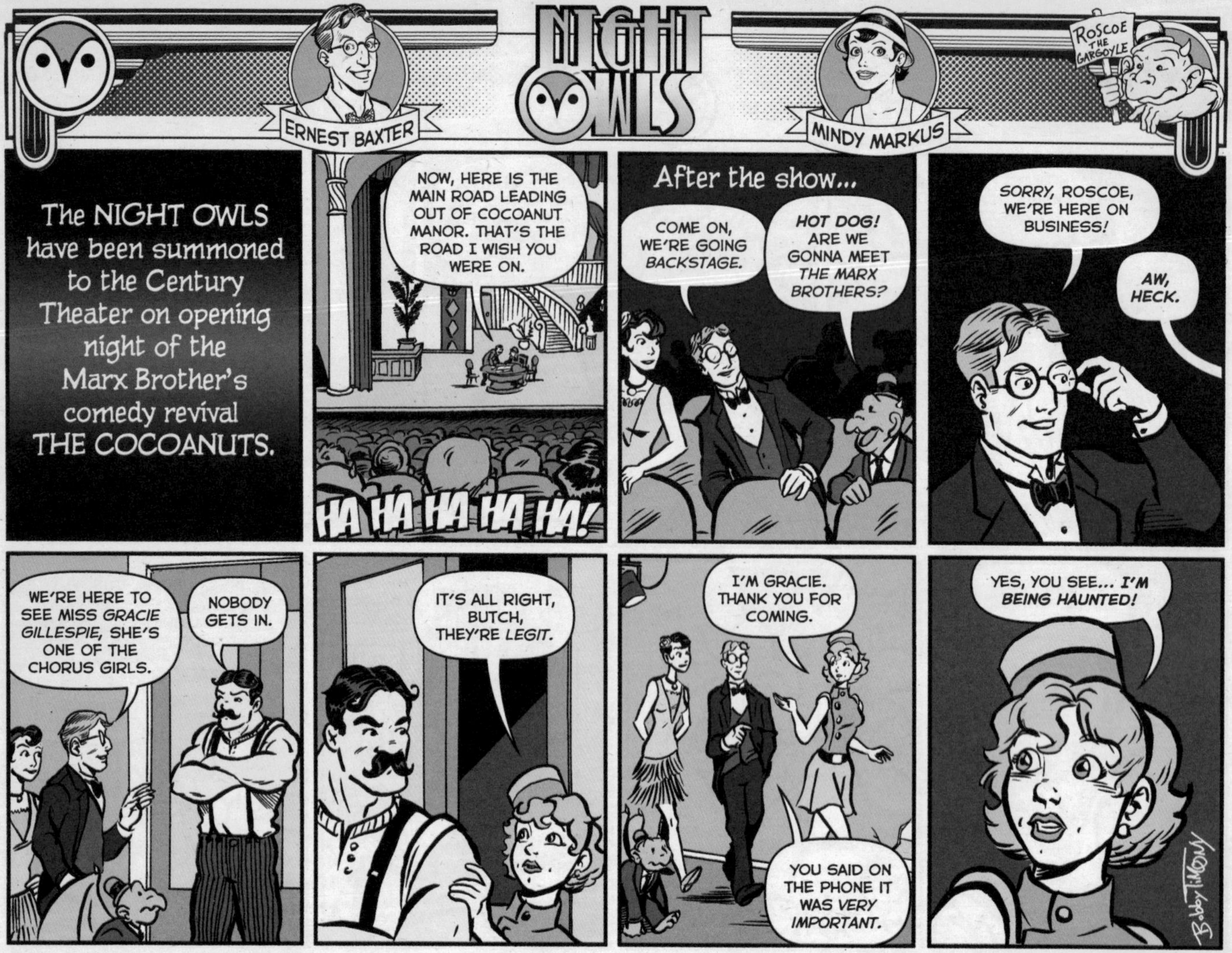
NIGHT OWLS
ERNEST BAXTER
MINDY MARKUS
ROSCOE THE GARGOYLE
The NIGHT OWLS have been summoned to the Century Theater on opening night of the Marx Brother's comedy revival THE COCOANUTS.
NOW, HERE IS THE MAIN ROAD LEADING OUT OF COCOANUT MANOR. THAT'S THE ROAD I WISH YOU WERE ON.
HA HA HA HA HA!
After the show...
COME ON, WE'RE GOING BACKSTAGE.
HOT DOG! ARE WE GONNA MEET THE MARX BROTHERS?
SORRY, ROSCOE, WE'RE HERE ON BUSINESS!
AW, HECK.
WE'RE HERE TO SEE MISS GRACIE GILLESPIE, SHE'S ONE OF THE CHORUS GIRLS.
NOBODY GETS IN.
IT'S ALL RIGHT, BUTCH, THEY'RE LEGIT.
I'M GRACIE. THANK YOU FOR COMING.
YOU SAID ON THE PHONE IT WAS VERY IMPORTANT.
YES, YOU SEE... I'M BEING HAUNTED!
Bobby Timony

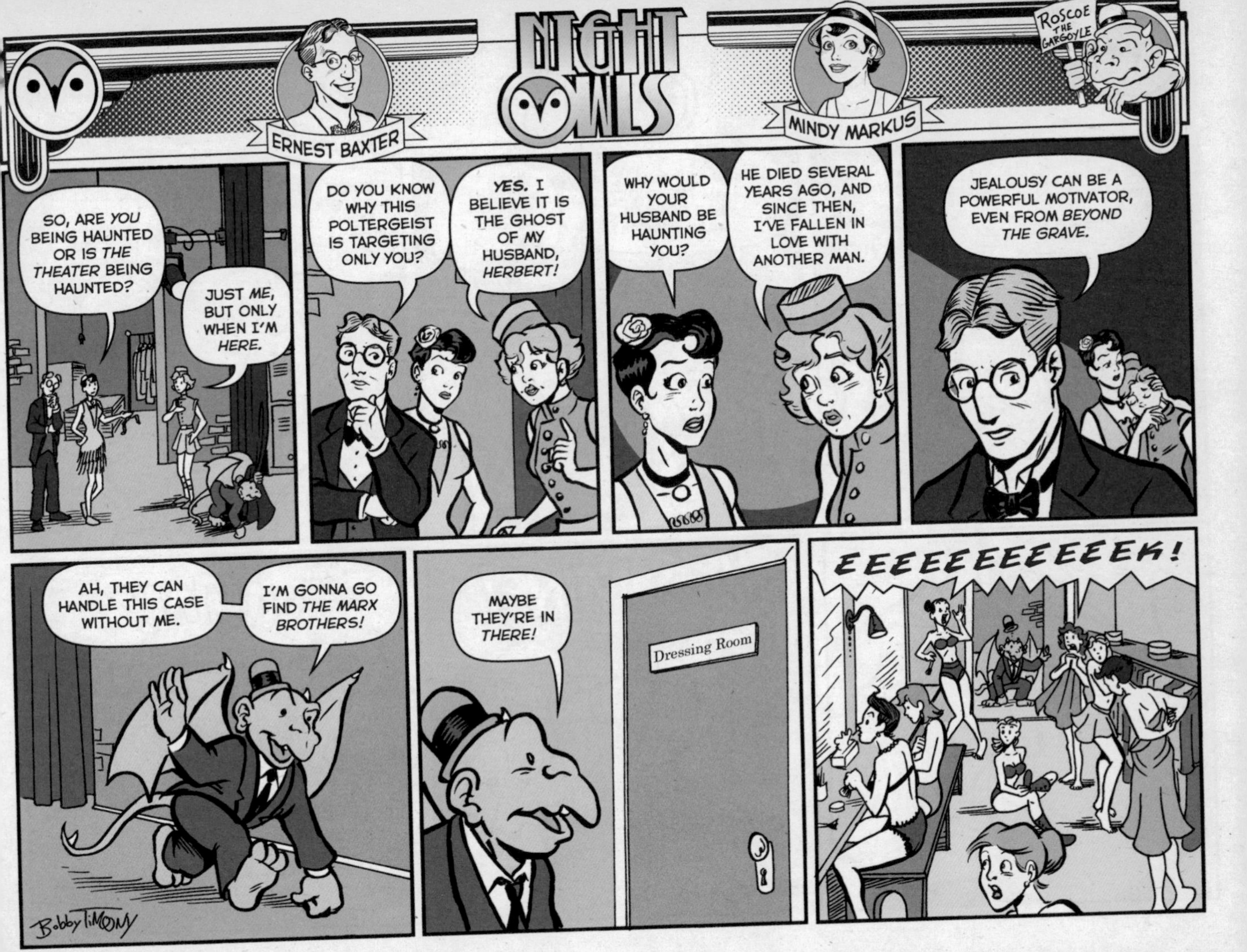
NIGHT OWLS
ERNEST BAXTER
MINDY MARKUS
ROSCOE THE GARGOYLE
SO, ARE YOU BEING HAUNTED OR IS THE THEATER BEING HAUNTED?
JUST ME, BUT ONLY WHEN I'M HERE.
DO YOU KNOW WHY THIS POLTERGEIST IS TARGETING ONLY YOU?
YES. I BELIEVE IT IS THE GHOST OF MY HUSBAND, HERBERT!
WHY WOULD YOUR HUSBAND BE HAUNTING YOU?
HE DIED SEVERAL YEARS AGO, AND SINCE THEN, I'VE FALLEN IN LOVE WITH ANOTHER MAN.
JEALOUSY CAN BE A POWERFUL MOTIVATOR, EVEN FROM BEYOND THE GRAVE.
AH, THEY CAN HANDLE THIS CASE WITHOUT ME.
I'M GONNA GO FIND THE MARX BROTHERS!
MAYBE THEY'RE IN THERE!
Dressing Room
EEEEEEEEEEEEK!
Bobby Timony

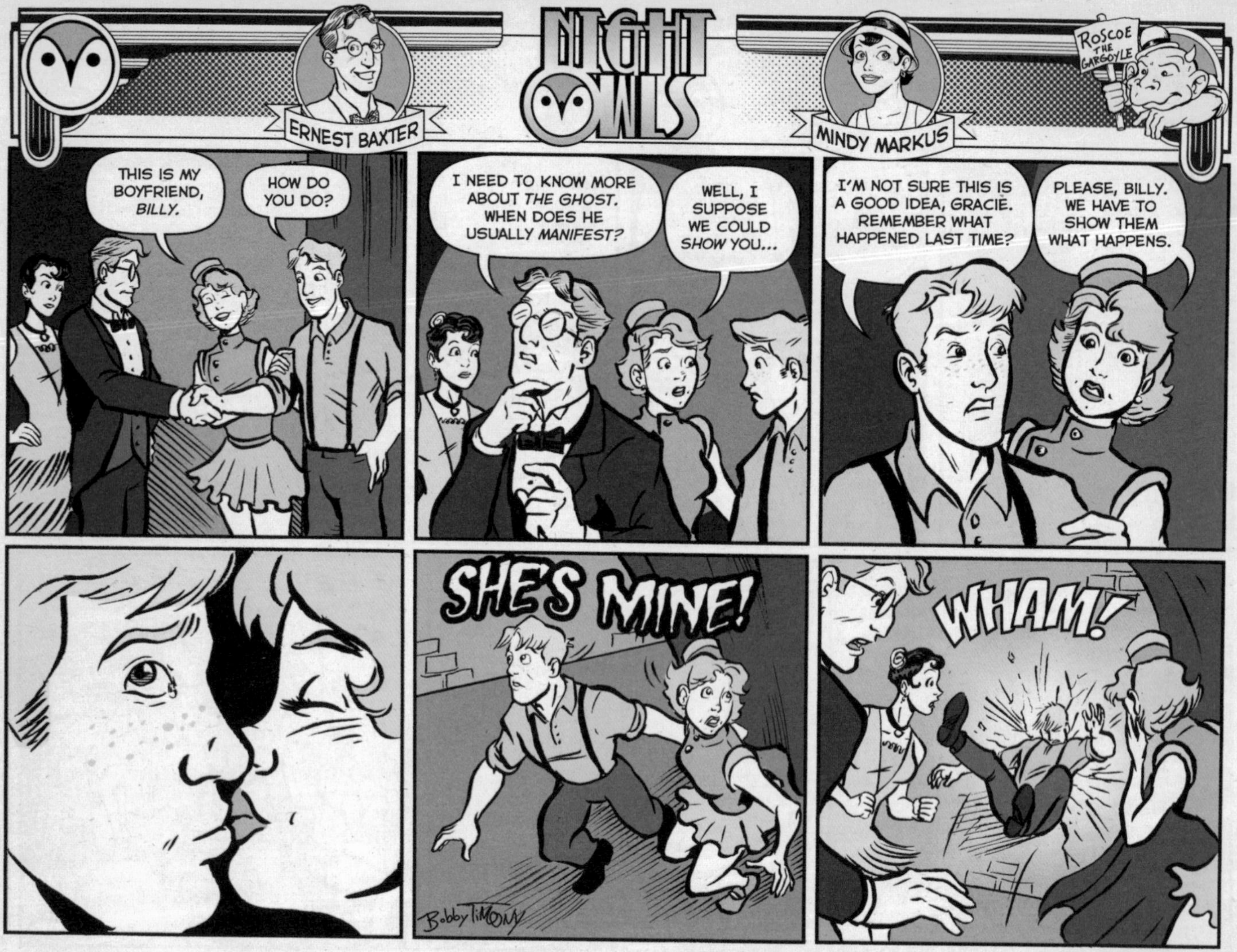
NIGHT OWLS
ERNEST BAXTER
MINDY MARKUS
ROSCOE THE GARGOYLE
THIS IS MY BOYFRIEND, BILLY.
HOW DO YOU DO?
I NEED TO KNOW MORE ABOUT THE GHOST. WHEN DOES HE USUALLY MANIFEST?
WELL, I SUPPOSE WE COULD SHOW YOU...
I'M NOT SURE THIS IS A GOOD IDEA, GRACIE. REMEMBER WHAT HAPPENED LAST TIME?
PLEASE, BILLY. WE HAVE TO SHOW THEM WHAT HAPPENS.
SHE'S MINE!
Bobby Timony
WHAM!

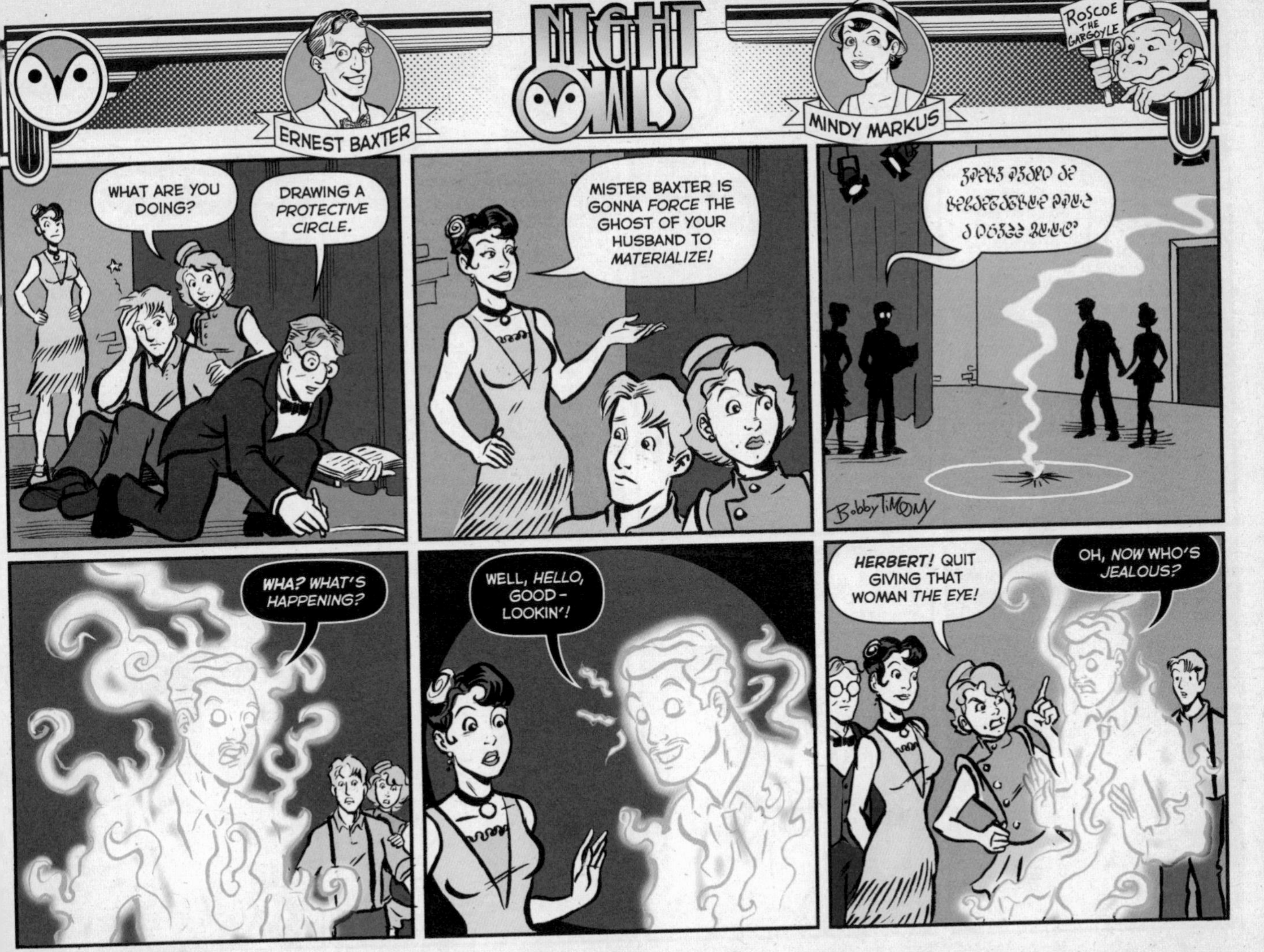

NIGHT OWLS
ERNEST BAXTER
MINDY MARKUS
ROSCOE THE GARGOYLE
WHAT ARE YOU DOING?
DRAWING A PROTECTIVE CIRCLE.
MISTER BAXTER IS GONNA FORCE THE GHOST OF YOUR HUSBAND TO MATERIALIZE!
Bobby Timony
WHA? WHAT'S HAPPENING?
WELL, HELLO, GOOD-LOOKIN'!
HERBERT! QUIT GIVING THAT WOMAN THE EYE!
OH, NOW WHO'S JEALOUS?

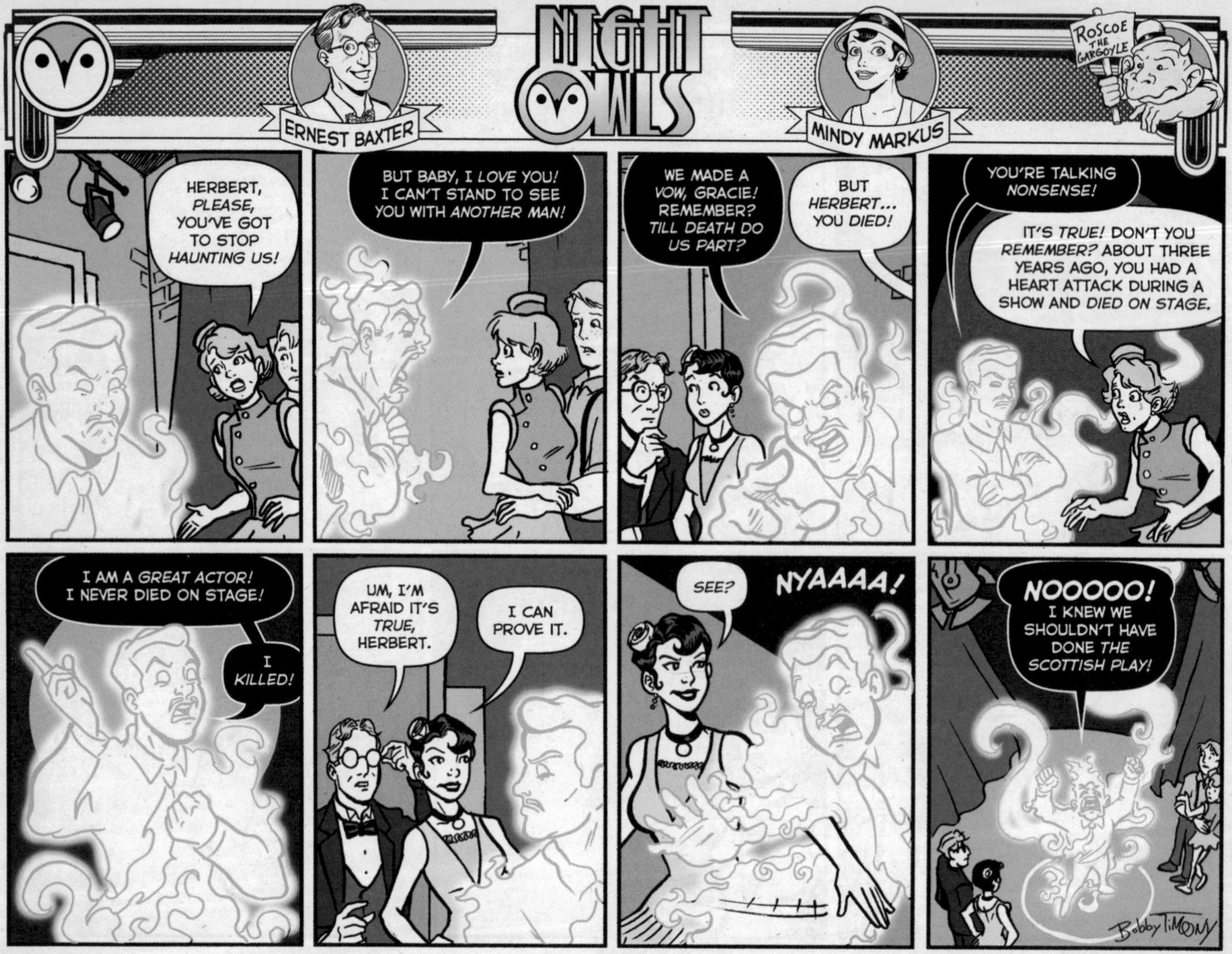
NIGHT OWLS
ERNEST BAXTER
MINDY MARKUS
ROSCOE THE GARGOYLE
HERBERT, PLEASE, YOU'VE GOT TO STOP HAUNTING US!
BUT BABY, I LOVE YOU! I CAN'T STAND TO SEE YOU WITH ANOTHER MAN!
WE MADE A VOW, GRACIE! REMEMBER? TILL DEATH DO US PART?
BUT HERBERT... YOU DIED!
YOU'RE TALKING NONSENSE!
IT'S TRUE! DON'T YOU REMEMBER? ABOUT THREE YEARS AGO, YOU HAD A HEART ATTACK DURING A SHOW AND DIED ON STAGE.
I AM A GREAT ACTOR! I NEVER DIED ON STAGE!
I KILLED!
UM, I'M AFRAID IT'S TRUE, HERBERT.
I CAN PROVE IT.
SEE?
NYAAAA!
NOOOOO! I KNEW WE SHOULDN'T HAVE DONE THE SCOTTISH PLAY!
Bobby TiMONY

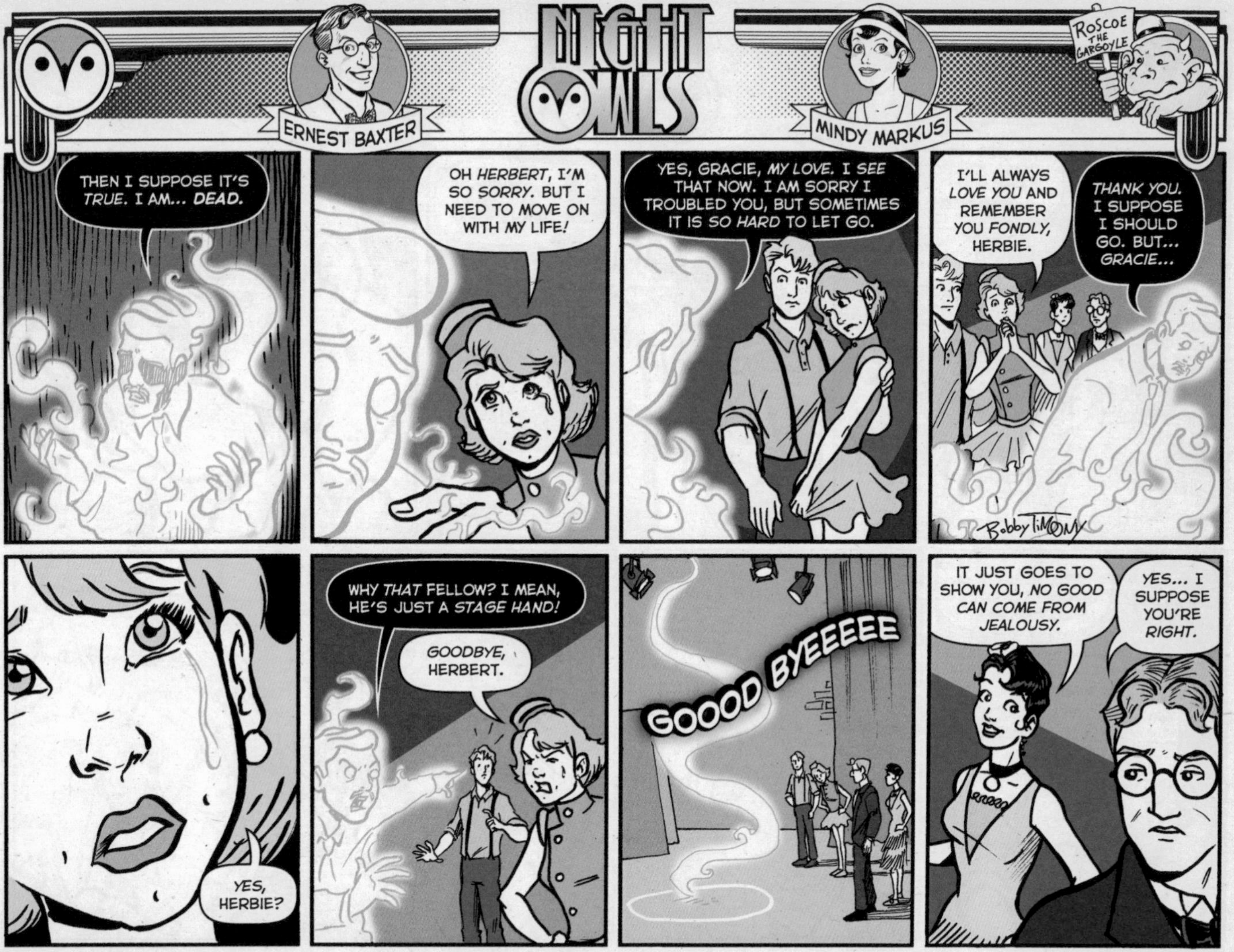
NIGHT OWLS
ERNEST BAXTER
MINDY MARKUS
ROSCOE THE GARGOYLE
THEN I SUPPOSE IT'S TRUE. I AM... DEAD.
OH HERBERT, I'M SO SORRY. BUT I NEED TO MOVE ON WITH MY LIFE!
YES, GRACIE, MY LOVE. I SEE THAT NOW. I AM SORRY I TROUBLED YOU, BUT SOMETIMES IT IS SO HARD TO LET GO.
I'LL ALWAYS LOVE YOU AND REMEMBER YOU FONDLY, HERBIE.
THANK YOU. I SUPPOSE I SHOULD GO. BUT... GRACIE...
Bobby TIMONY
YES, HERBIE?
WHY THAT FELLOW? I MEAN, HE'S JUST A STAGE HAND!
GOODBYE, HERBERT.
GOOOD BYEEEEE
IT JUST GOES TO SHOW YOU, NO GOOD CAN COME FROM JEALOUSY.
YES... I SUPPOSE YOU'RE RIGHT.

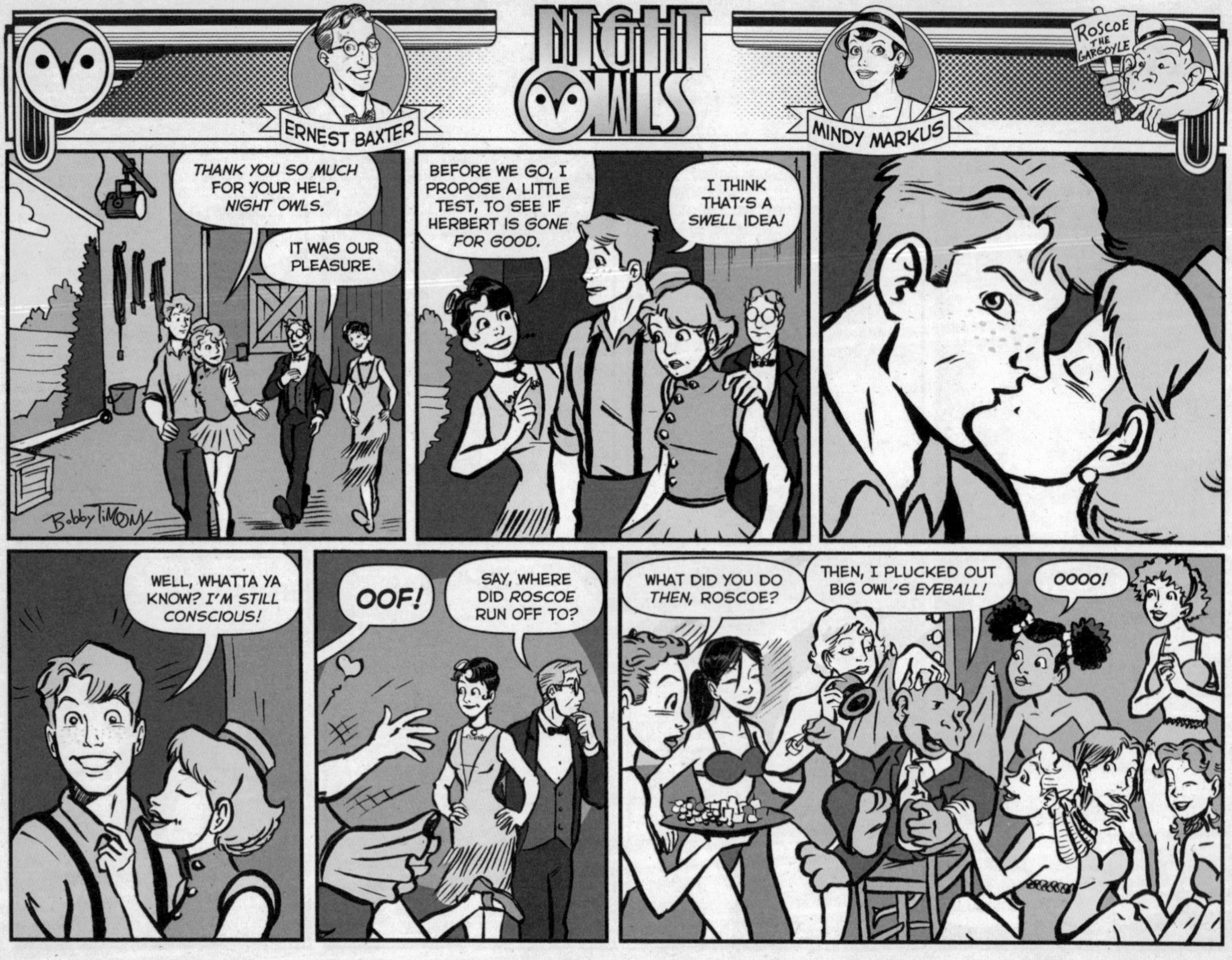
NIGHT OWLS
ERNEST BAXTER
MINDY MARKUS
ROSCOE THE GARGOYLE
THANK YOU SO MUCH FOR YOUR HELP, NIGHT OWLS.
IT WAS OUR PLEASURE.
Bobby Timony
BEFORE WE GO, I PROPOSE A LITTLE TEST, TO SEE IF HERBERT IS GONE FOR GOOD.
I THINK THAT'S A SWELL IDEA!
WELL, WHATTA YA KNOW? I'M STILL CONSCIOUS!
OOF!
SAY, WHERE DID ROSCOE RUN OFF TO?
WHAT DID YOU DO THEN, ROSCOE?
THEN, I PLUCKED OUT BIG OWL'S EYEBALL!
OOOO!

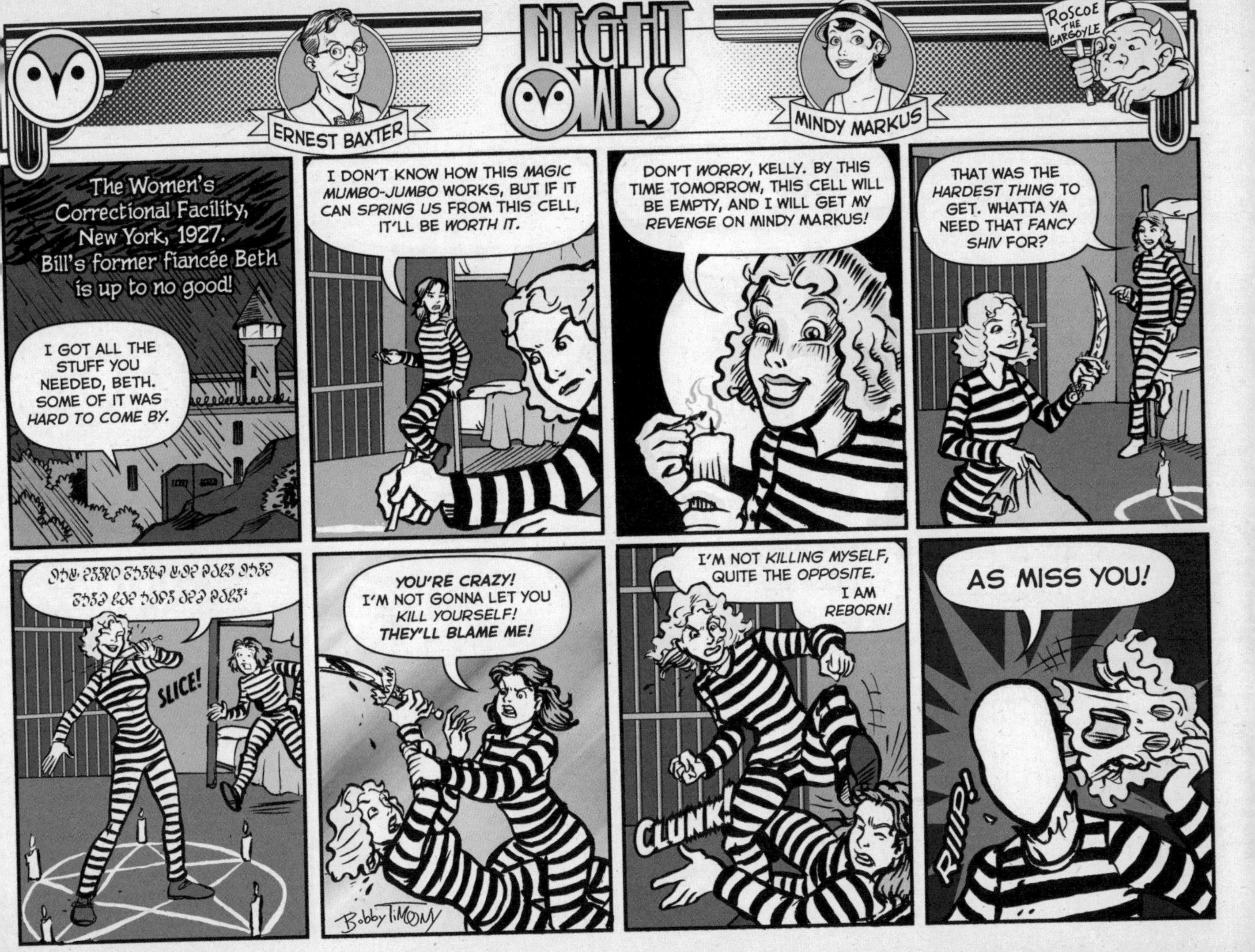
NIGHT OWLS
ERNEST BAXTER
MINDY MARKUS
ROSCOE THE GARGOYLE
The Women's Correctional Facility, New York, 1927. Bill's former fiancée Beth is up to no good!
I GOT ALL THE STUFF YOU NEEDED, BETH. SOME OF IT WAS HARD TO COME BY.
I DON'T KNOW HOW THIS MAGIC MUMBO-JUMBO WORKS, BUT IF IT CAN SPRING US FROM THIS CELL, IT'LL BE WORTH IT.
DON'T WORRY, KELLY. BY THIS TIME TOMORROW, THIS CELL WILL BE EMPTY, AND I WILL GET MY REVENGE ON MINDY MARKUS!
THAT WAS THE HARDEST THING TO GET. WHATTA YA NEED THAT FANCY SHIV FOR?
SLICE!
YOU'RE CRAZY! I'M NOT GONNA LET YOU KILL YOURSELF! THEY'LL BLAME ME!
I'M NOT KILLING MYSELF, QUITE THE OPPOSITE.
I AM REBORN!
CLUNK!
AS MISS YOU!
RIIIP!
Bobby Timony

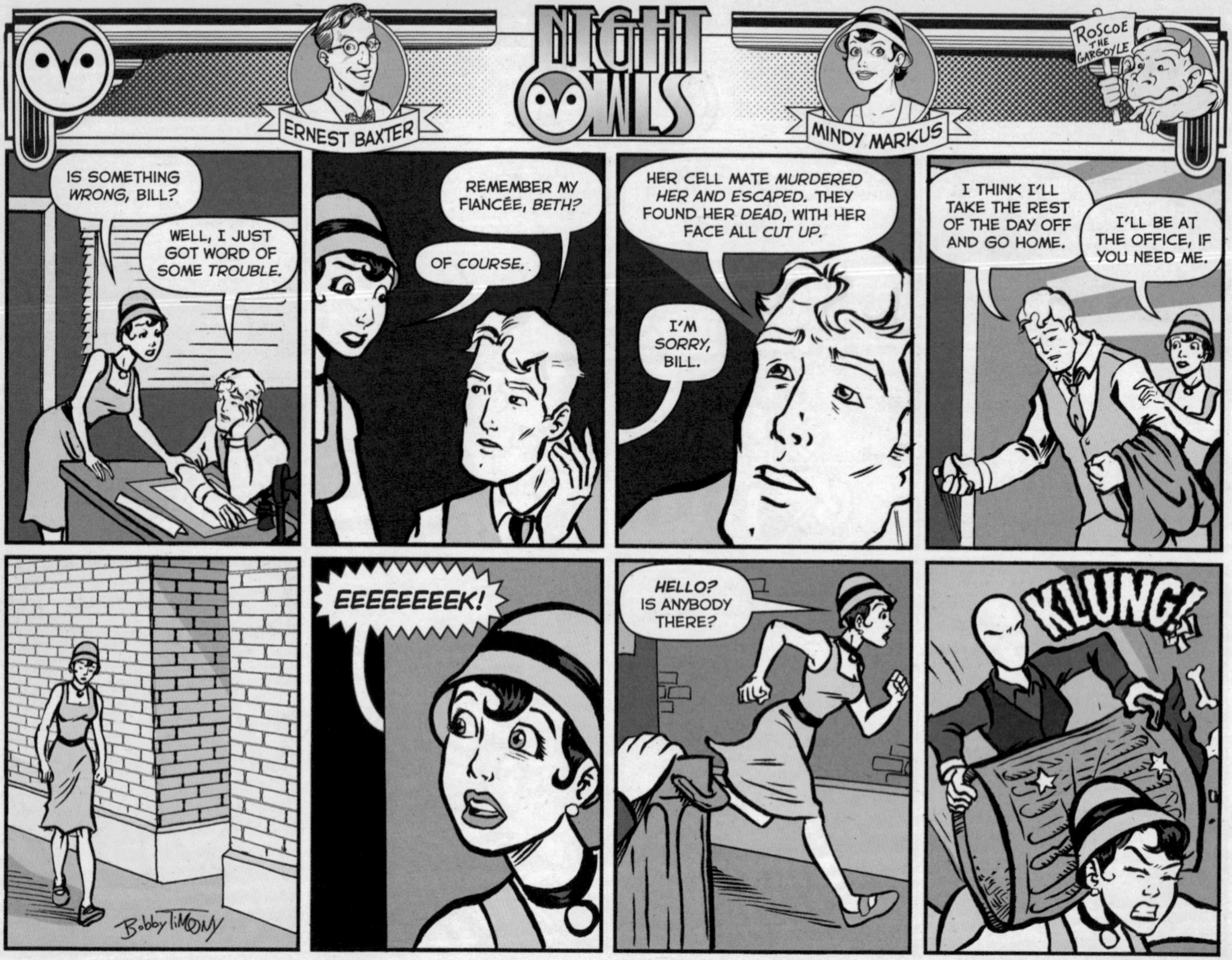
NIGHT OWLS
ERNEST BAXTER
MINDY MARKUS
ROSCOE THE GARGOYLE
IS SOMETHING WRONG, BILL?
WELL, I JUST GOT WORD OF SOME TROUBLE.
REMEMBER MY FIANCÉE, BETH?
OF COURSE.
HER CELL MATE MURDERED HER AND ESCAPED. THEY FOUND HER DEAD, WITH HER FACE ALL CUT UP.
I'M SORRY, BILL.
I THINK I'LL TAKE THE REST OF THE DAY OFF AND GO HOME.
I'LL BE AT THE OFFICE, IF YOU NEED ME.
Bobby TiMONY
EEEEEEEEK!
HELLO? IS ANYBODY THERE?
KLUNG!

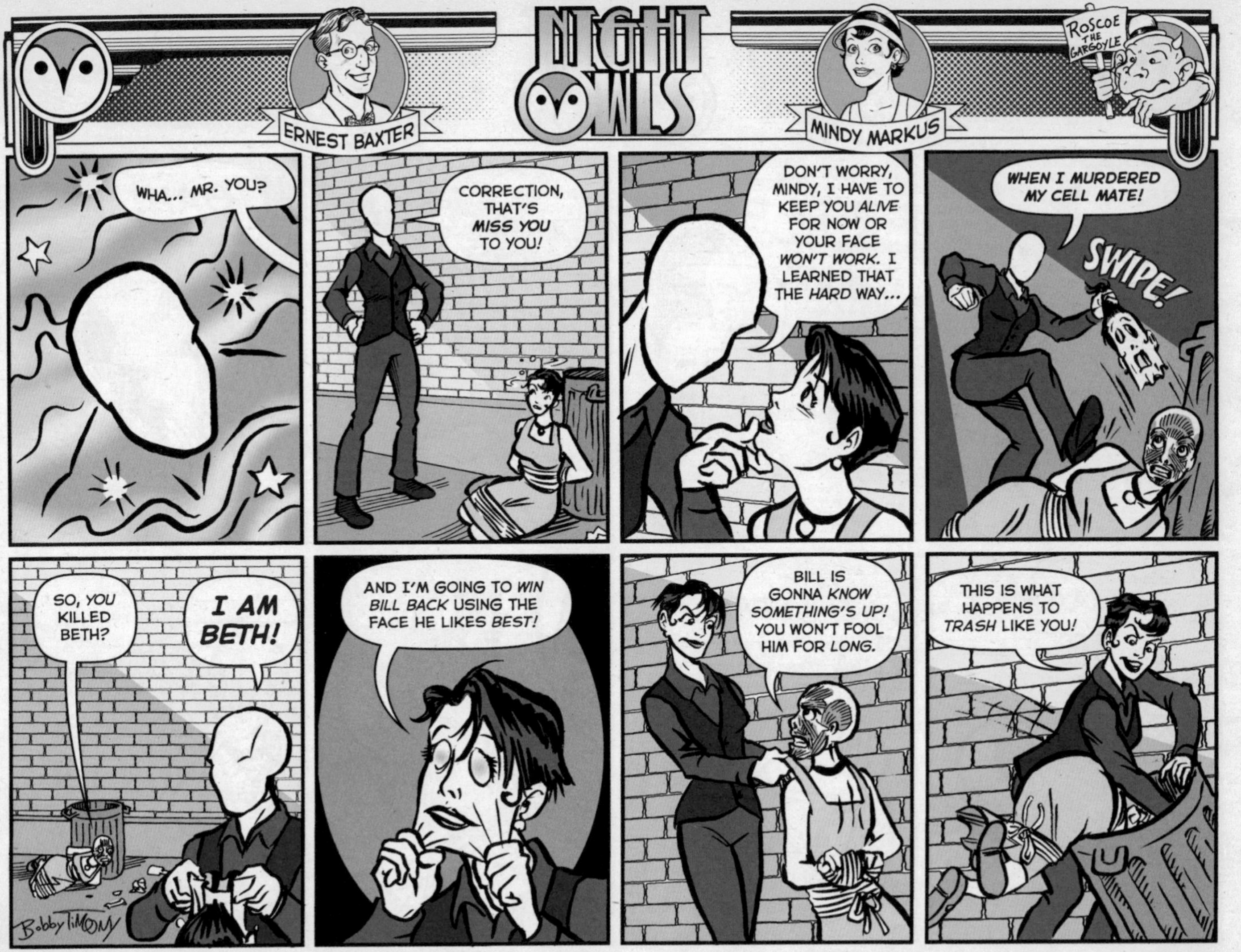

NIGHT OWLS
ERNEST BAXTER
MINDY MARKUS
ROSCOE THE GARGOYLE
WHA... MR. YOU?
CORRECTION, THAT'S MISS YOU TO YOU!
DON'T WORRY, MINDY, I HAVE TO KEEP YOU ALIVE FOR NOW OR YOUR FACE WON'T WORK. I LEARNED THAT THE HARD WAY...
WHEN I MURDERED MY CELL MATE!
SWIPE!
SO, YOU KILLED BETH?
I AM BETH!
AND I'M GOING TO WIN BILL BACK USING THE FACE HE LIKES BEST!
BILL IS GONNA KNOW SOMETHING'S UP! YOU WON'T FOOL HIM FOR LONG.
THIS IS WHAT HAPPENS TO TRASH LIKE YOU!
Bobby Timony

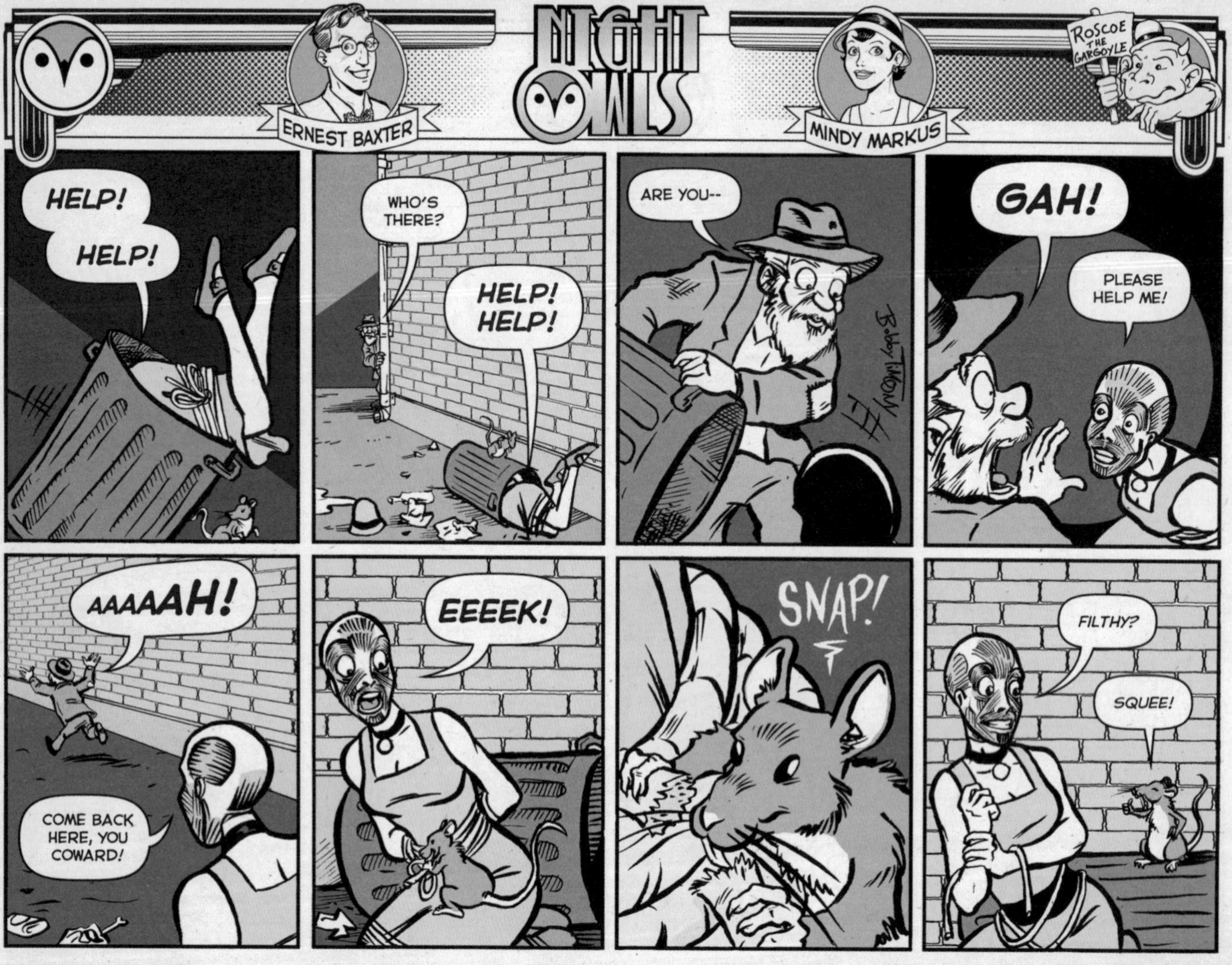
NIGHT OWLS
ERNEST BAXTER
MINDY MARKUS
ROSCOE THE GARGOYLE
HELP!
HELP!
WHO'S THERE?
HELP! HELP!
ARE YOU--
GAH!
PLEASE HELP ME!
AAAAAH!
COME BACK HERE, YOU COWARD!
EEEEK!
SNAP!
FILTHY?
SQUEE!

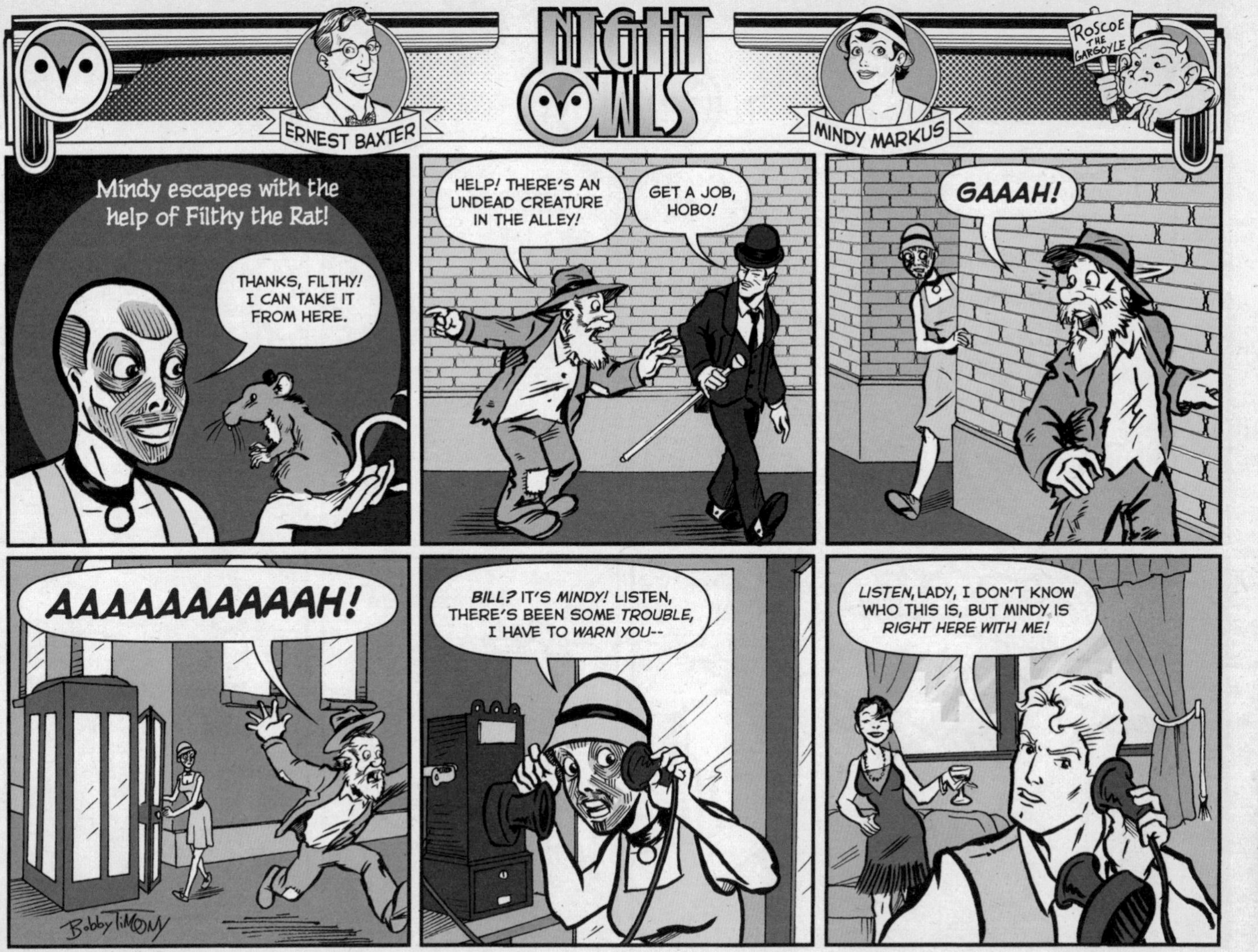
NIGHT OWLS
ERNEST BAXTER
MINDY MARKUS
ROSCOE THE GARGOYLE
Mindy escapes with the help of Filthy the Rat!
THANKS, FILTHY! I CAN TAKE IT FROM HERE.
HELP! THERE'S AN UNDEAD CREATURE IN THE ALLEY!
GET A JOB, HOBO!
GAAAH!
AAAAAAAAAAH!
BILL? IT'S MINDY! LISTEN, THERE'S BEEN SOME TROUBLE, I HAVE TO WARN YOU--
LISTEN, LADY, I DON'T KNOW WHO THIS IS, BUT MINDY IS RIGHT HERE WITH ME!
Bobby Timony

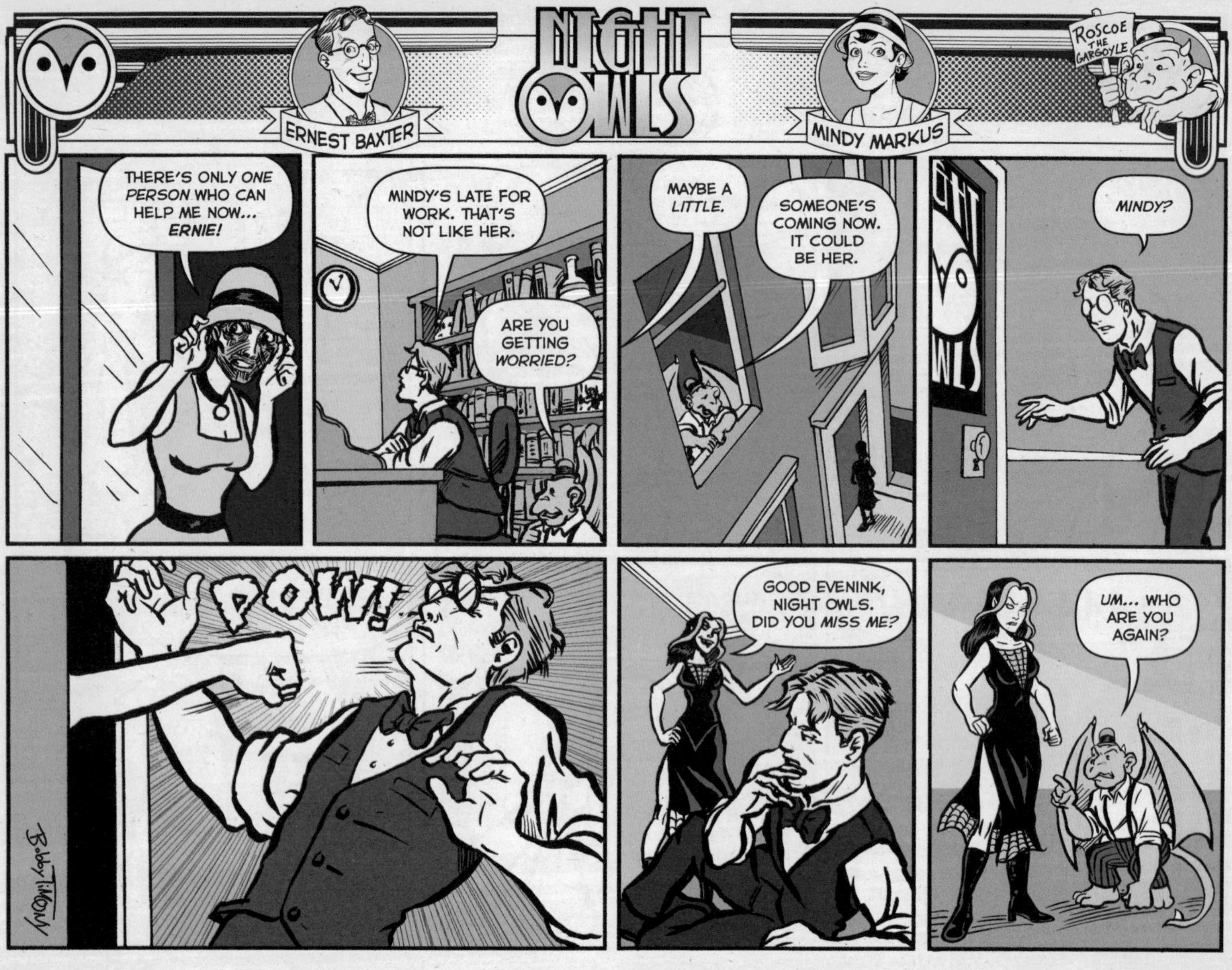
NIGHT OWLS
ERNEST BAXTER
MINDY MARKUS
ROSCOE THE GARGOYLE
THERE'S ONLY ONE PERSON WHO CAN HELP ME NOW... ERNIE!
MINDY'S LATE FOR WORK. THAT'S NOT LIKE HER.
ARE YOU GETTING WORRIED?
MAYBE A LITTLE.
SOMEONE'S COMING NOW. IT COULD BE HER.
MINDY?
POW!
GOOD EVENINK, NIGHT OWLS. DID YOU MISS ME?
UM... WHO ARE YOU AGAIN?
Bobby Timony

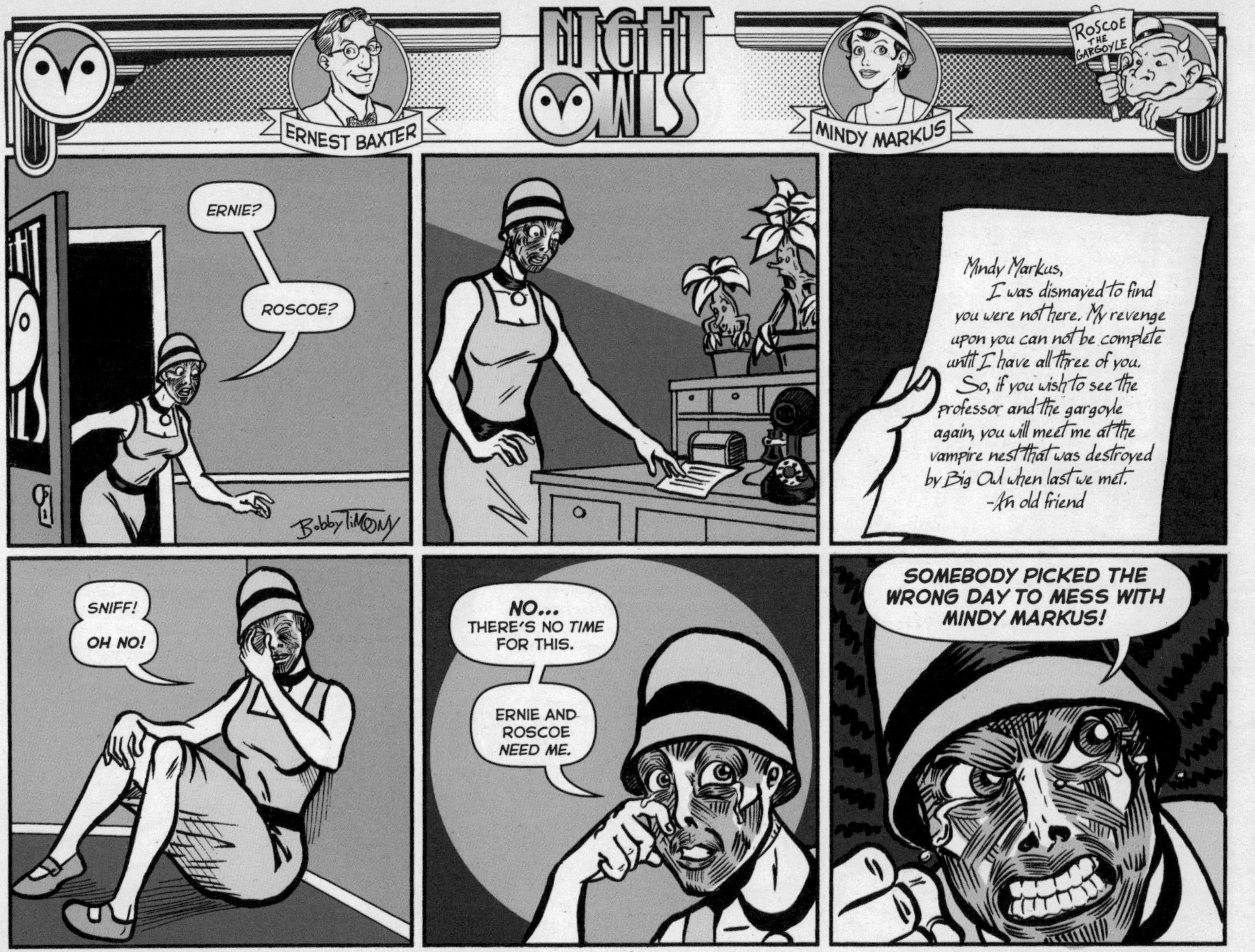
NIGHT OWLS
ERNEST BAXTER
MINDY MARKUS
ROSCOE THE GARGOYLE
ERNIE?
ROSCOE?
Bobby Timony
Mindy Markus,
I was dismayed to find you were not here. My revenge upon you can not be complete until I have all three of you.
So, if you wish to see the professor and the gargoyle again, you will meet me at the vampire nest that was destroyed by Big Owl when last we met.
-An old friend
SNIFF!
OH NO!
NO... THERE'S NO TIME FOR THIS.
ERNIE AND ROSCOE NEED ME.
SOMEBODY PICKED THE WRONG DAY TO MESS WITH MINDY MARKUS!

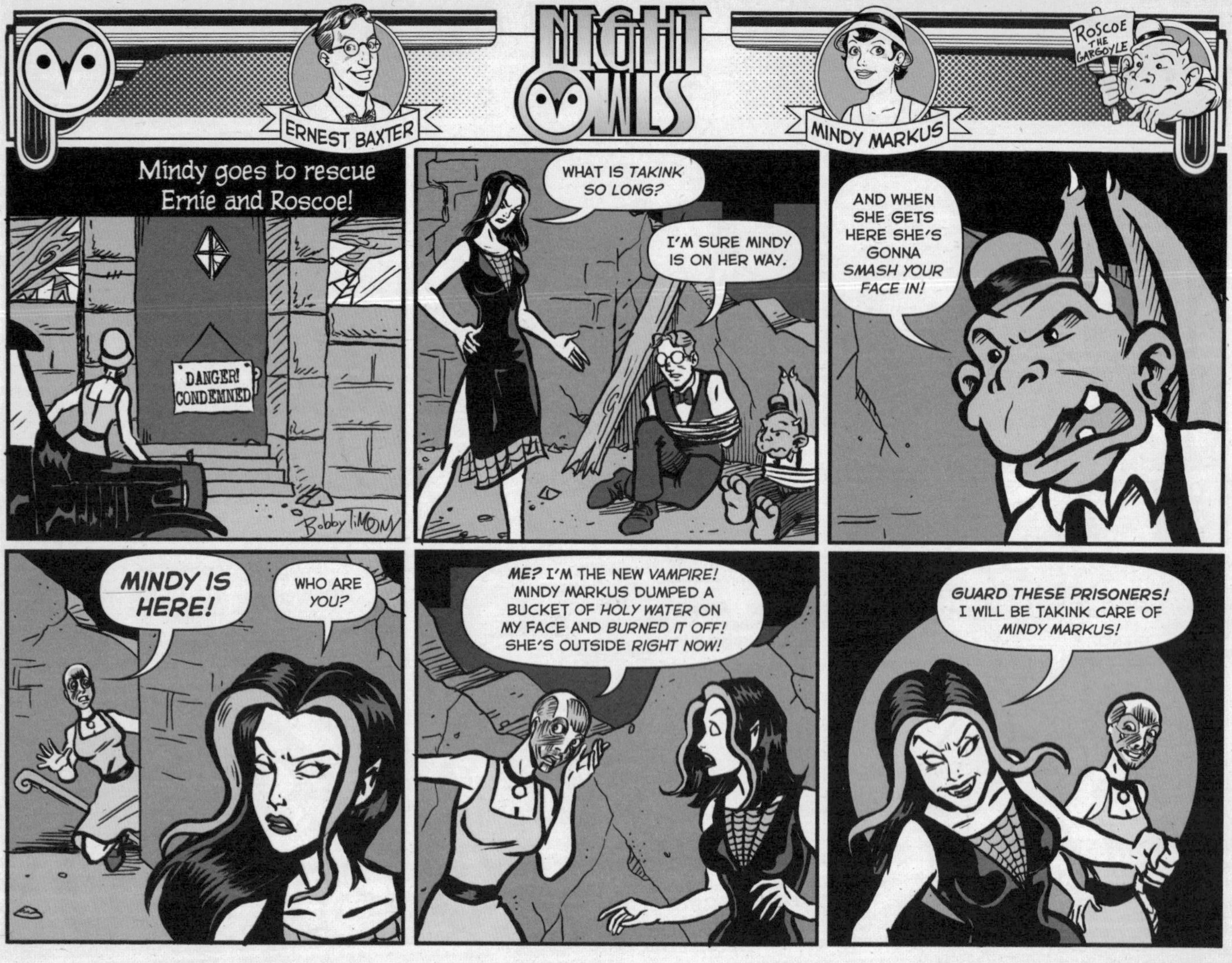
NIGHT OWLS
ERNEST BAXTER
MINDY MARKUS
ROSCOE THE GARGOYLE
Mindy goes to rescue Ernie and Roscoe!
DANGER! CONDEMNED
Bobby Timony
WHAT IS *TAKINK* SO LONG?
I'M SURE MINDY IS ON HER WAY.
AND WHEN SHE GETS HERE SHE'S GONNA *SMASH YOUR FACE IN!*
MINDY IS HERE!
WHO ARE *YOU?*
ME? I'M THE NEW *VAMPIRE!* MINDY MARKUS DUMPED A BUCKET OF *HOLY WATER* ON MY FACE AND *BURNED IT OFF!* SHE'S OUTSIDE *RIGHT NOW!*
GUARD THESE PRISONERS! I WILL BE TAKINK CARE OF *MINDY MARKUS!*

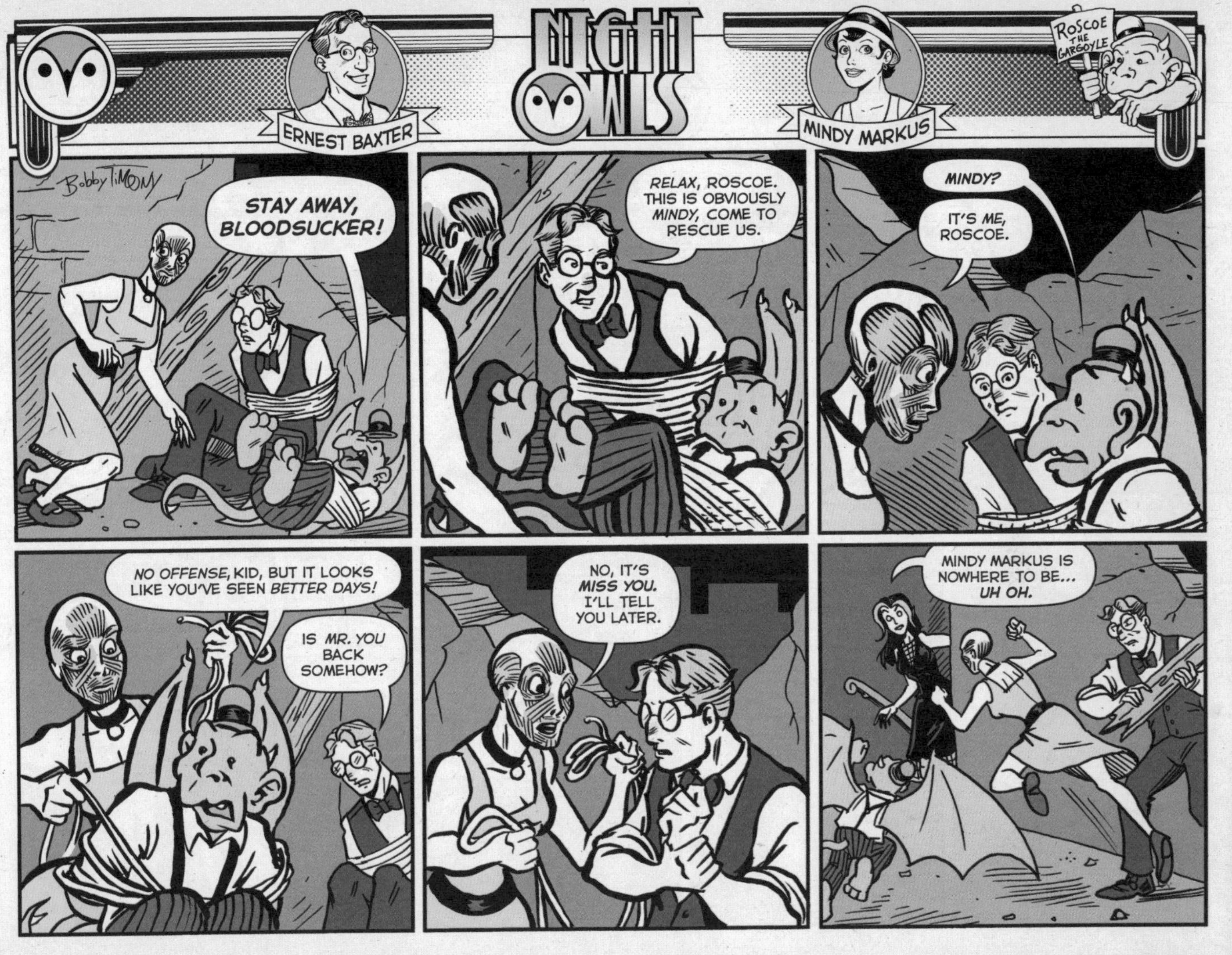
NIGHT OWLS
ERNEST BAXTER
MINDY MARKUS
ROSCOE THE GARGOYLE
Bobby Timony
STAY AWAY, BLOODSUCKER!
RELAX, ROSCOE. THIS IS OBVIOUSLY MINDY, COME TO RESCUE US.
MINDY?
IT'S ME, ROSCOE.
NO OFFENSE, KID, BUT IT LOOKS LIKE YOU'VE SEEN BETTER DAYS!
IS MR. YOU BACK SOMEHOW?
NO, IT'S MISS YOU. I'LL TELL YOU LATER.
MINDY MARKUS IS NOWHERE TO BE... UH OH.

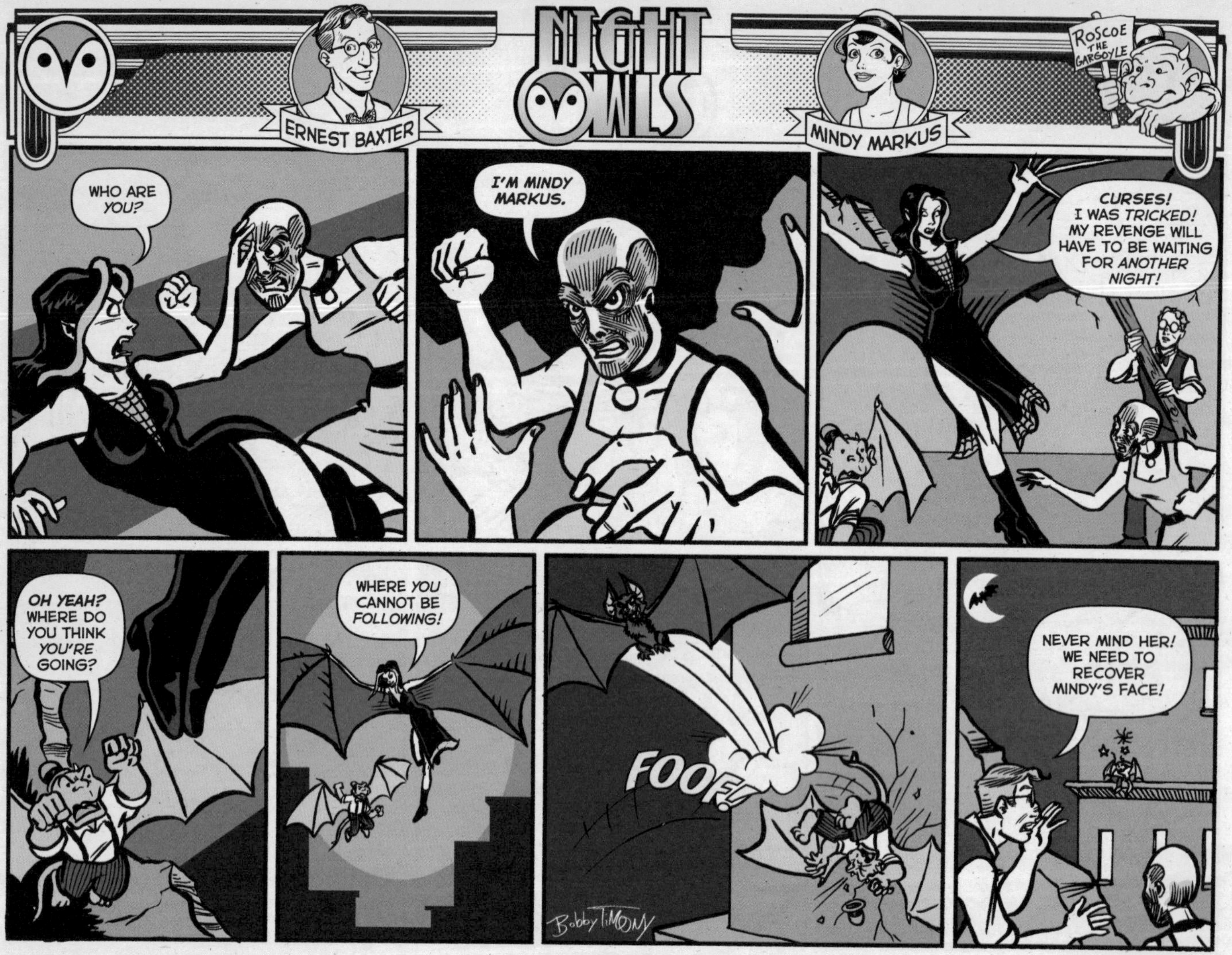

NIGHT OWLS
ERNEST BAXTER
MINDY MARKUS
ROSCOE THE GARGOYLE
WHO ARE *YOU?*
I'M MINDY MARKUS.
CURSES! I WAS *TRICKED!* MY REVENGE WILL HAVE TO BE WAITING FOR *ANOTHER NIGHT!*
OH YEAH? WHERE DO YOU THINK *YOU'RE* GOING?
WHERE *YOU* CANNOT BE *FOLLOWING!*
FOOF!
NEVER MIND HER! WE NEED TO RECOVER MINDY'S FACE!
Bobby TiMONY

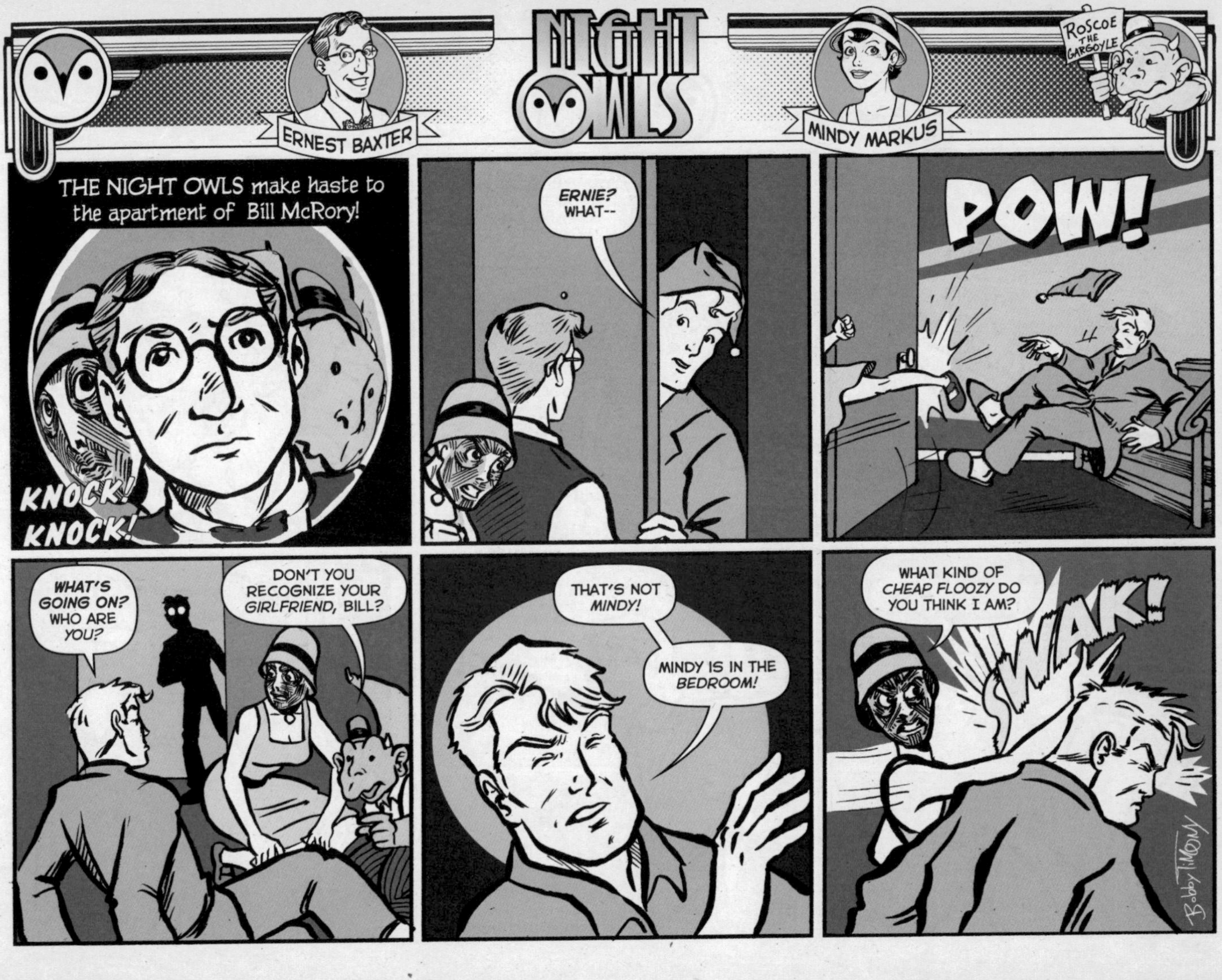
NIGHT OWLS
ERNEST BAXTER
MINDY MARKUS
ROSCOE THE GARGOYLE
THE NIGHT OWLS make haste to the apartment of Bill McRory!
KNOCK! KNOCK!
ERNIE? WHAT--
POW!
WHAT'S GOING ON? WHO ARE YOU?
DON'T YOU RECOGNIZE YOUR GIRLFRIEND, BILL?
THAT'S NOT MINDY!
MINDY IS IN THE BEDROOM!
WHAT KIND OF CHEAP FLOOZY DO YOU THINK I AM?
WAK!
Bobby Timony

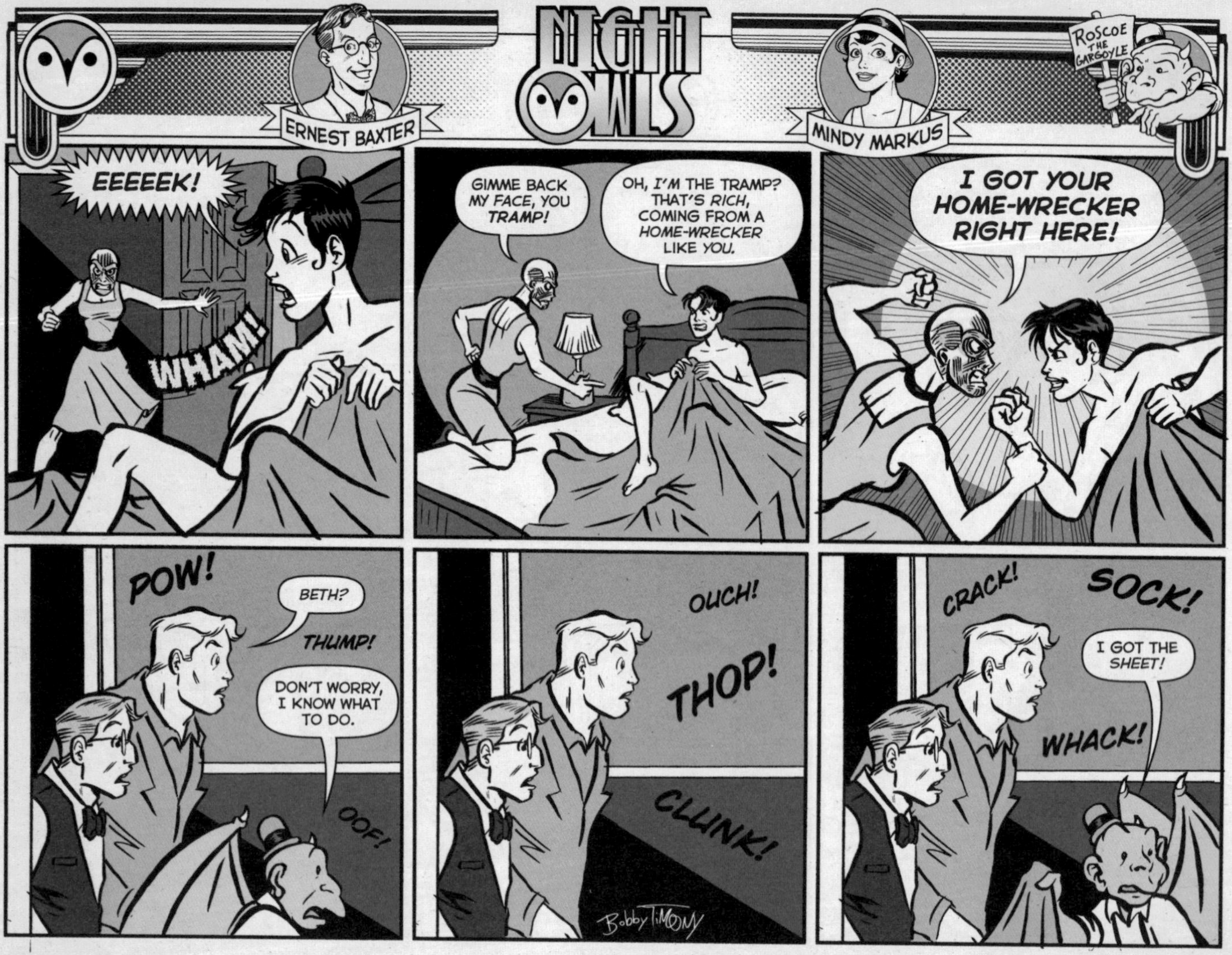
NIGHT OWLS
ERNEST BAXTER
MINDY MARKUS
ROSCOE THE GARGOYLE
EEEEEK!
WHAM!
GIMME BACK MY FACE, YOU TRAMP!
OH, I'M THE TRAMP? THAT'S RICH, COMING FROM A HOME-WRECKER LIKE YOU.
I GOT YOUR HOME-WRECKER RIGHT HERE!
POW!
BETH?
THUMP!
DON'T WORRY, I KNOW WHAT TO DO.
OOF!
OUCH!
THOP!
CLUNK!
CRACK!
SOCK!
I GOT THE SHEET!
WHACK!
Bobby Timony

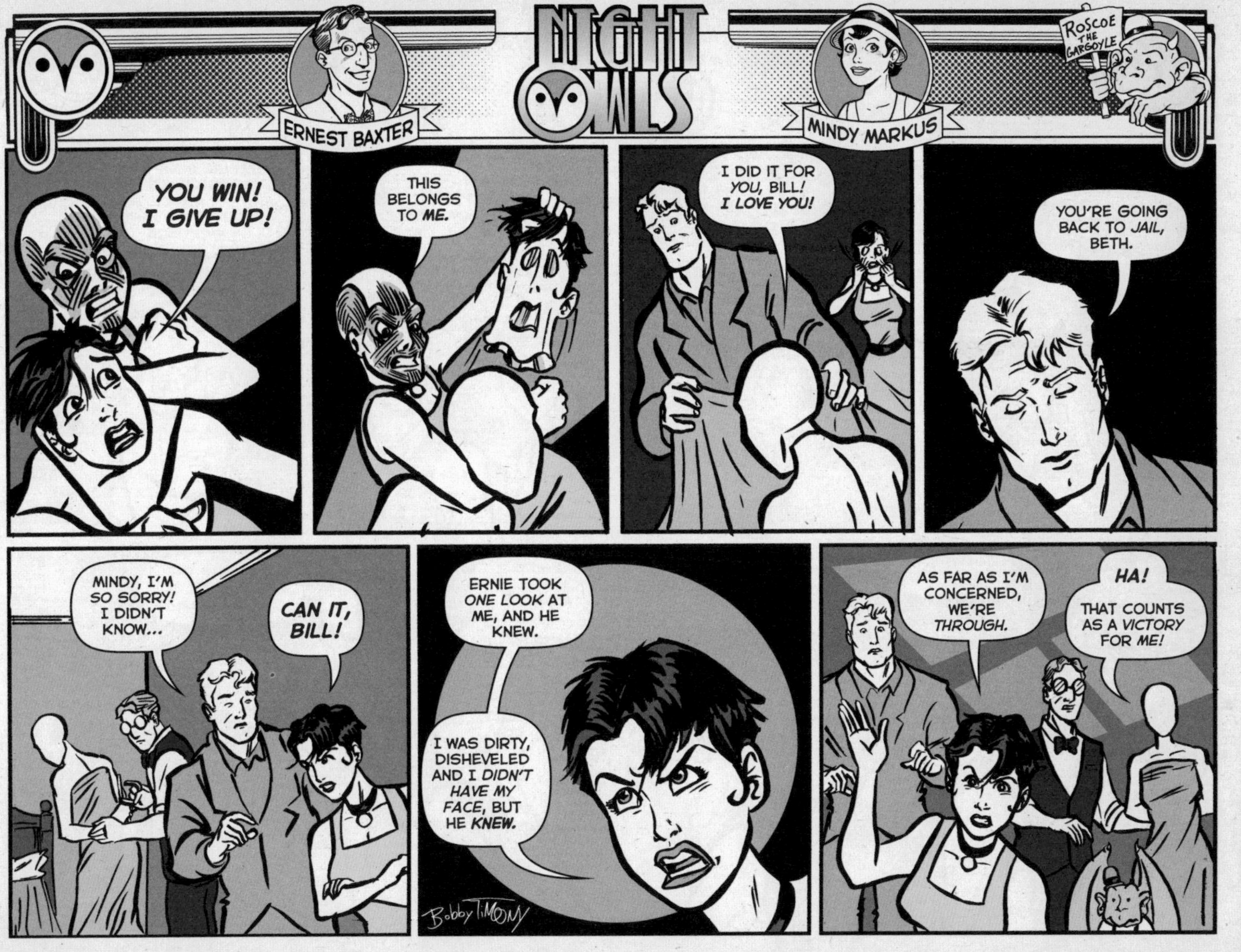
NIGHT OWLS
ERNEST BAXTER
MINDY MARKUS
ROSCOE THE GARGOYLE
YOU WIN! I GIVE UP!
THIS BELONGS TO ME.
I DID IT FOR YOU, BILL! I LOVE YOU!
YOU'RE GOING BACK TO JAIL, BETH.
MINDY, I'M SO SORRY! I DIDN'T KNOW...
CAN IT, BILL!
ERNIE TOOK ONE LOOK AT ME, AND HE KNEW.
I WAS DIRTY, DISHEVELED AND I DIDN'T HAVE MY FACE, BUT HE KNEW.
AS FAR AS I'M CONCERNED, WE'RE THROUGH.
HA!
THAT COUNTS AS A VICTORY FOR ME!
Bobby TiMOONY

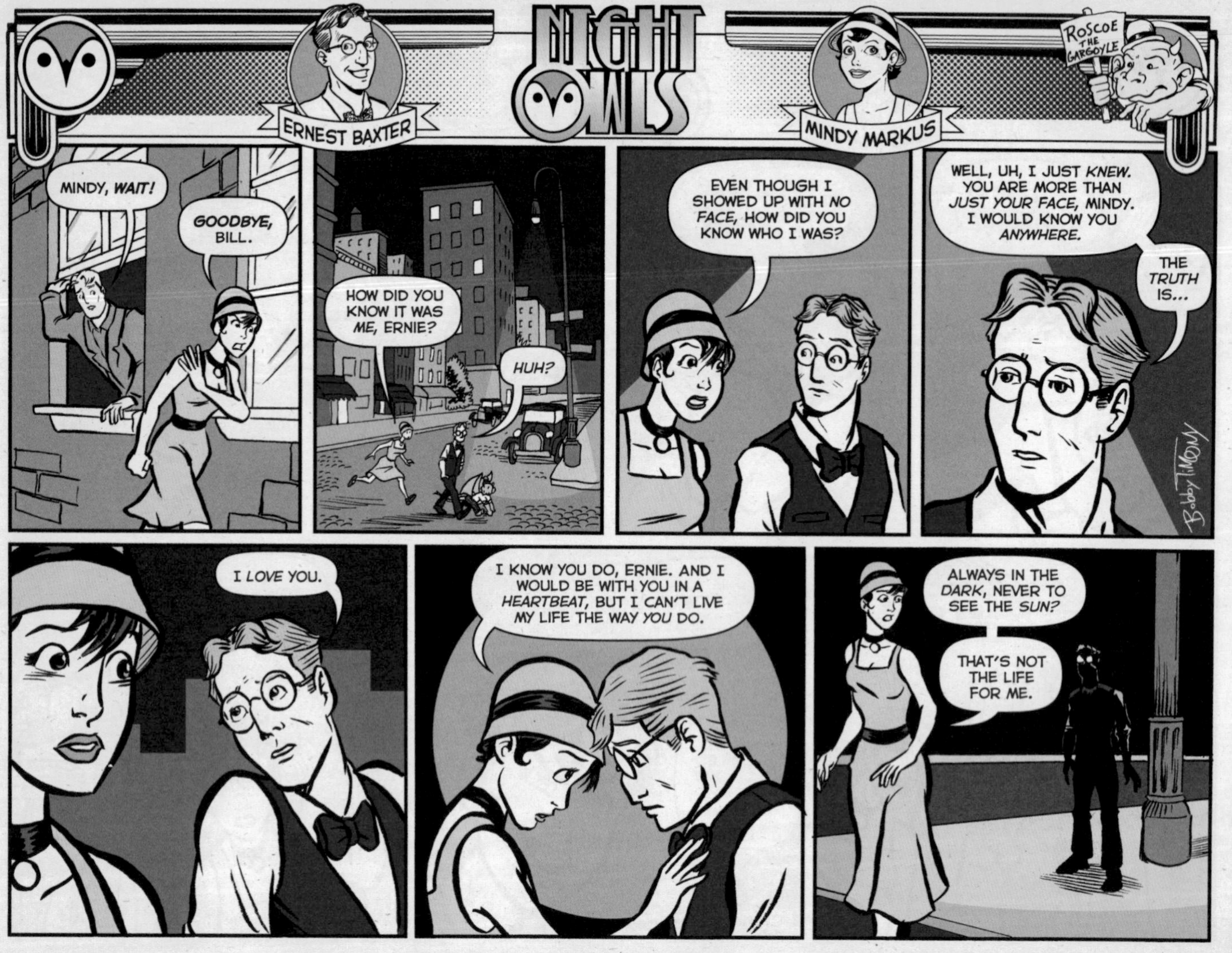
NIGHT OWLS
ERNEST BAXTER
MINDY MARKUS
ROSCOE THE GARGOYLE
MINDY, WAIT!
GOODBYE, BILL.
HOW DID YOU KNOW IT WAS ME, ERNIE?
HUH?
EVEN THOUGH I SHOWED UP WITH NO FACE, HOW DID YOU KNOW WHO I WAS?
WELL, UH, I JUST KNEW. YOU ARE MORE THAN JUST YOUR FACE, MINDY. I WOULD KNOW YOU ANYWHERE.
THE TRUTH IS...
Bobby Timony
I LOVE YOU.
I KNOW YOU DO, ERNIE. AND I WOULD BE WITH YOU IN A HEARTBEAT, BUT I CAN'T LIVE MY LIFE THE WAY YOU DO.
ALWAYS IN THE DARK, NEVER TO SEE THE SUN?
THAT'S NOT THE LIFE FOR ME.

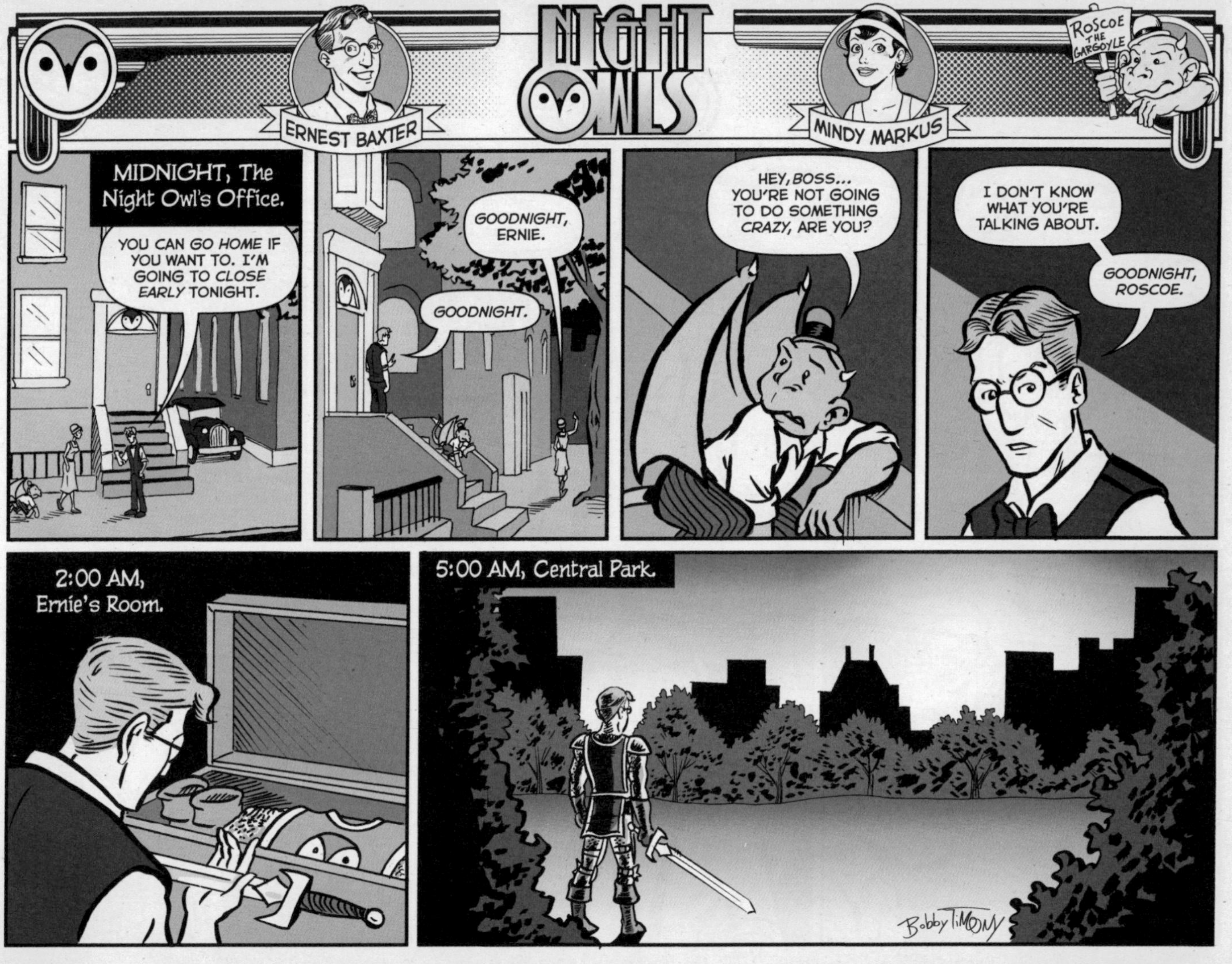
NIGHT OWLS
ERNEST BAXTER
MINDY MARKUS
ROSCOE THE GARGOYLE
MIDNIGHT, The Night Owl's Office.
YOU CAN GO HOME IF YOU WANT TO. I'M GOING TO CLOSE EARLY TONIGHT.
GOODNIGHT, ERNIE.
GOODNIGHT.
HEY, BOSS... YOU'RE NOT GOING TO DO SOMETHING CRAZY, ARE YOU?
I DON'T KNOW WHAT YOU'RE TALKING ABOUT.
GOODNIGHT, ROSCOE.
2:00 AM, Ernie's Room.
5:00 AM, Central Park.
Bobby Timony

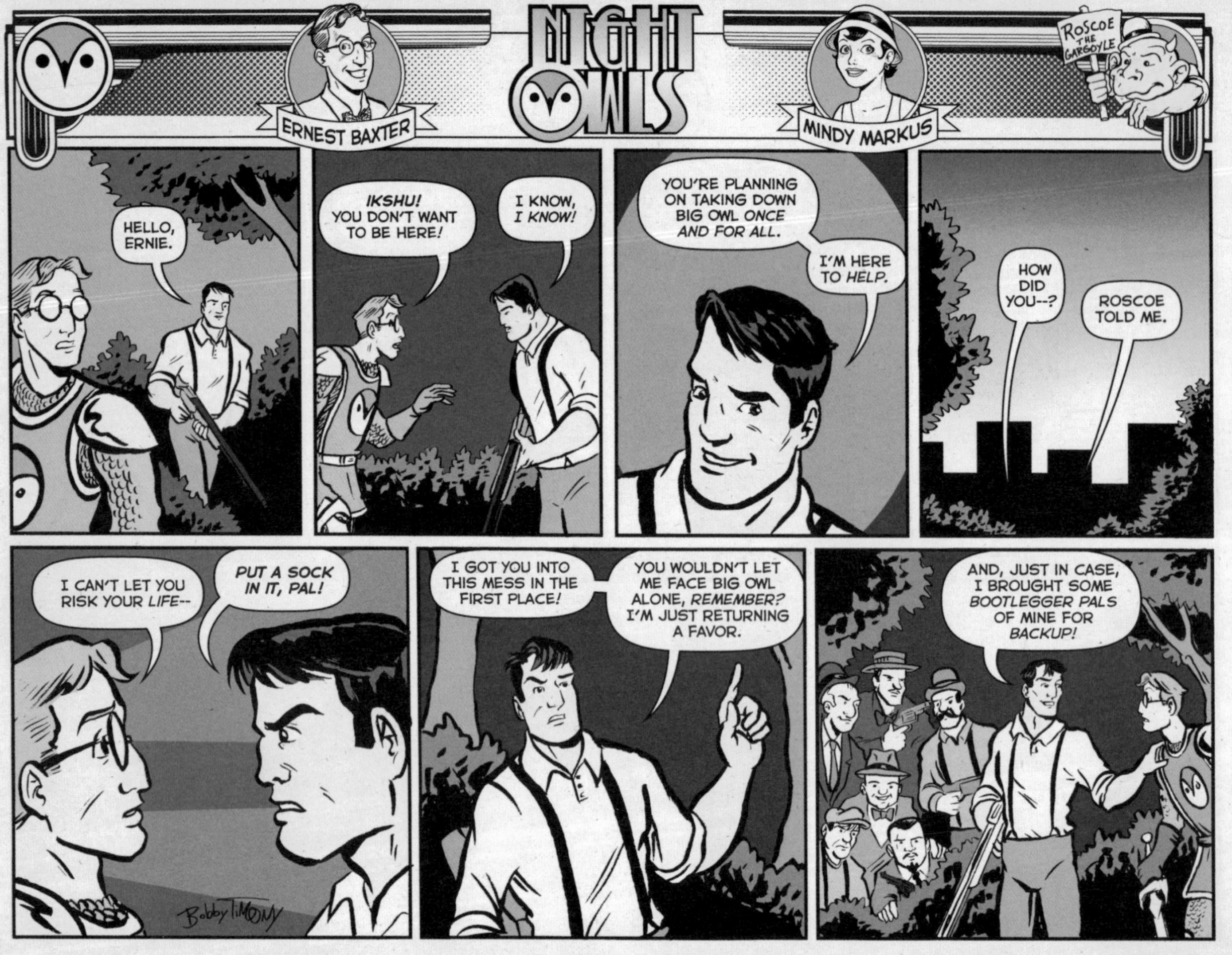
NIGHT OWLS
ERNEST BAXTER
MINDY MARKUS
ROSCOE THE GARGOYLE
HELLO, ERNIE.
IKSHU! YOU DON'T WANT TO BE HERE!
I KNOW, I KNOW!
YOU'RE PLANNING ON TAKING DOWN BIG OWL ONCE AND FOR ALL.
I'M HERE TO HELP.
HOW DID YOU--?
ROSCOE TOLD ME.
I CAN'T LET YOU RISK YOUR LIFE--
PUT A SOCK IN IT, PAL!
I GOT YOU INTO THIS MESS IN THE FIRST PLACE!
YOU WOULDN'T LET ME FACE BIG OWL ALONE, REMEMBER? I'M JUST RETURNING A FAVOR.
AND, JUST IN CASE, I BROUGHT SOME BOOTLEGGER PALS OF MINE FOR BACKUP!
Bobby TiMONY

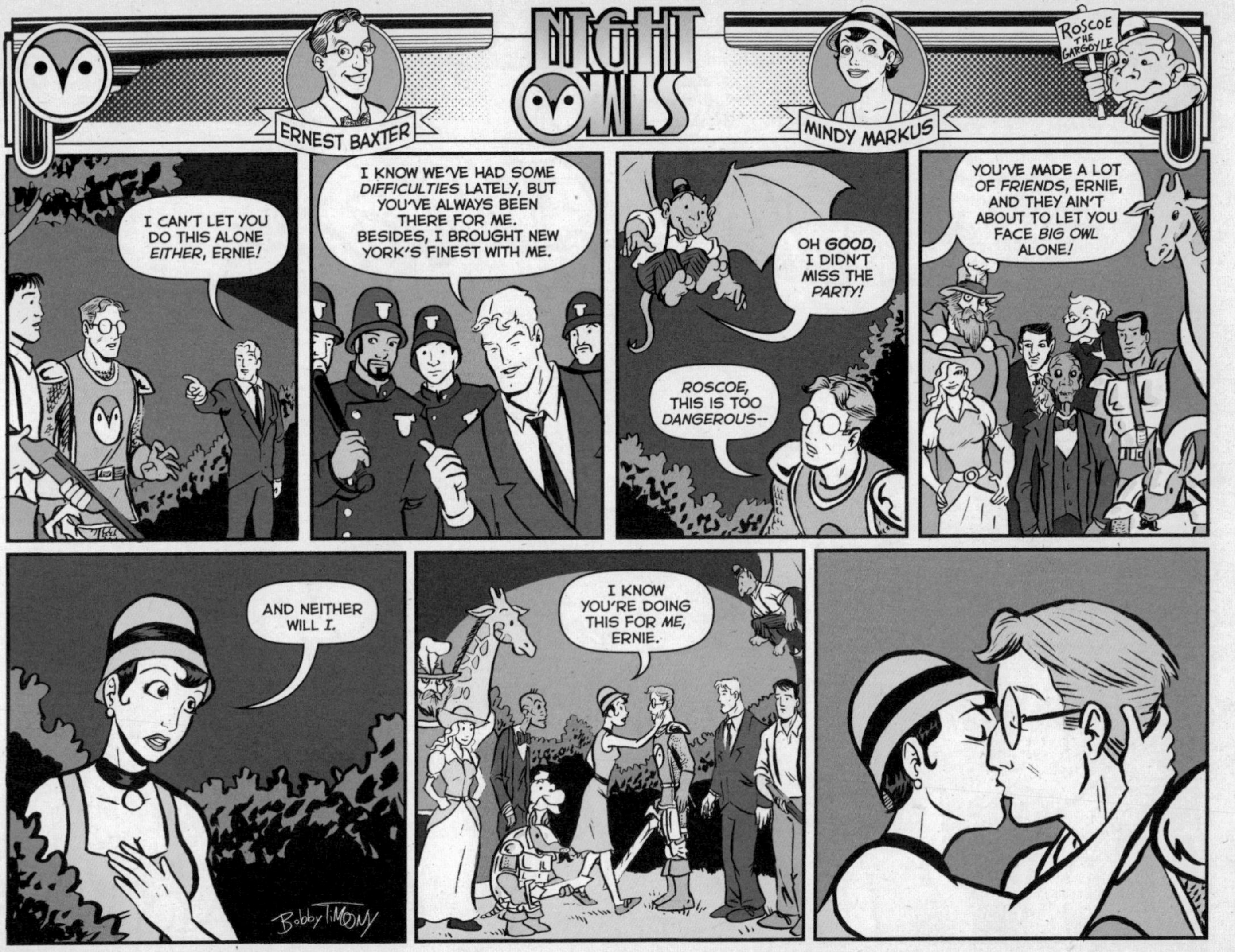
NIGHT OWLS
ERNEST BAXTER
MINDY MARKUS
ROSCOE THE GARGOYLE
I CAN'T LET YOU DO THIS ALONE EITHER, ERNIE!
I KNOW WE'VE HAD SOME DIFFICULTIES LATELY, BUT YOU'VE ALWAYS BEEN THERE FOR ME. BESIDES, I BROUGHT NEW YORK'S FINEST WITH ME.
OH GOOD, I DIDN'T MISS THE PARTY!
ROSCOE, THIS IS TOO DANGEROUS--
YOU'VE MADE A LOT OF FRIENDS, ERNIE, AND THEY AIN'T ABOUT TO LET YOU FACE BIG OWL ALONE!
AND NEITHER WILL I.
Bobby Timony
I KNOW YOU'RE DOING THIS FOR ME, ERNIE.

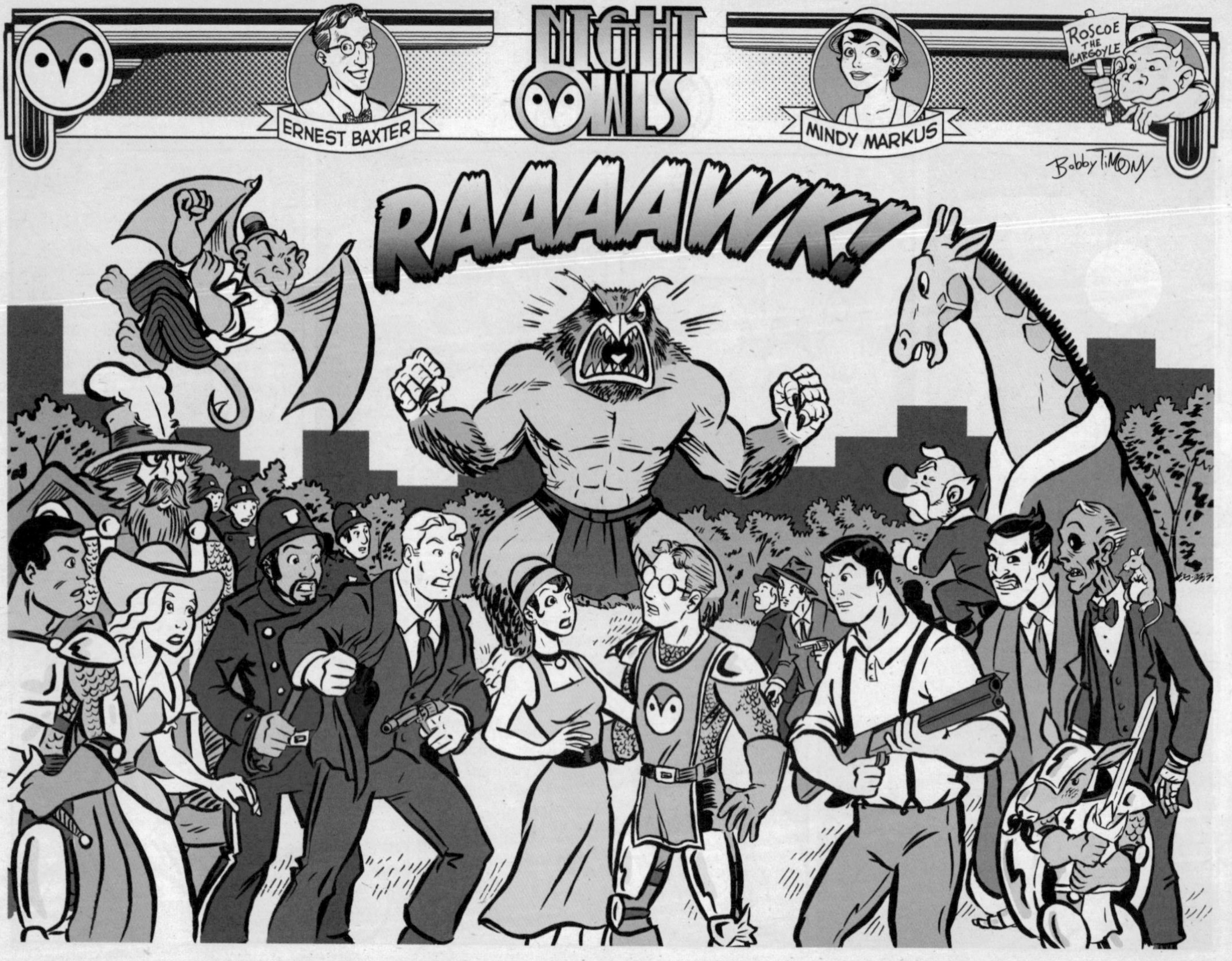

NIGHT OWLS
ERNEST BAXTER
MINDY MARKUS
ROSCOE THE GARGOYLE
Bobby Timony
RAAAAAWK!

Bobby Timony first came up with the idea for THE NIGHT OWLS while taking a class at the School of Visual Arts in New York City. His final assignment was to write and draw a complete 12-page comic. The very first panel of that project is strikingly similar to the header that eventually appeared at the top of every screen of the THE NIGHT OWLS webcomic!

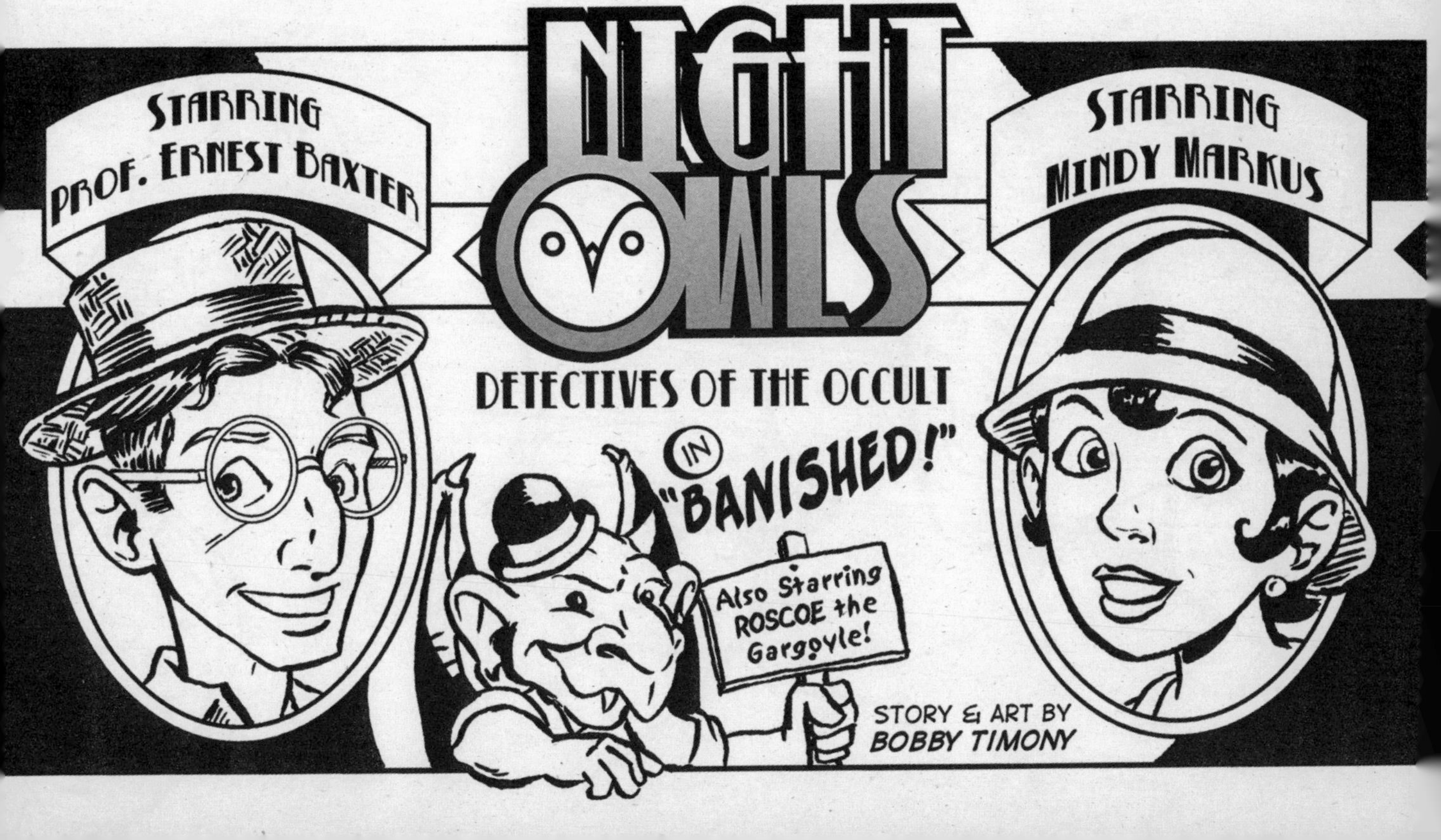

STARRING PROF. ERNEST BAXTER
NIGHT OWLS
STARRING MINDY MARKUS
DETECTIVES OF THE OCCULT
IN "BANISHED!"
Also Starring ROSCOE the Gargoyle!
STORY & ART BY BOBBY TIMONY

The final versions of THE NIGHT OWLS' brainy boss, Ernest Baxter, and scrappy flapper, Mindy Markus, haven't changed dramatically from Bobby's early attempts at drawing the characters, as some of his initial concept sketches here show.

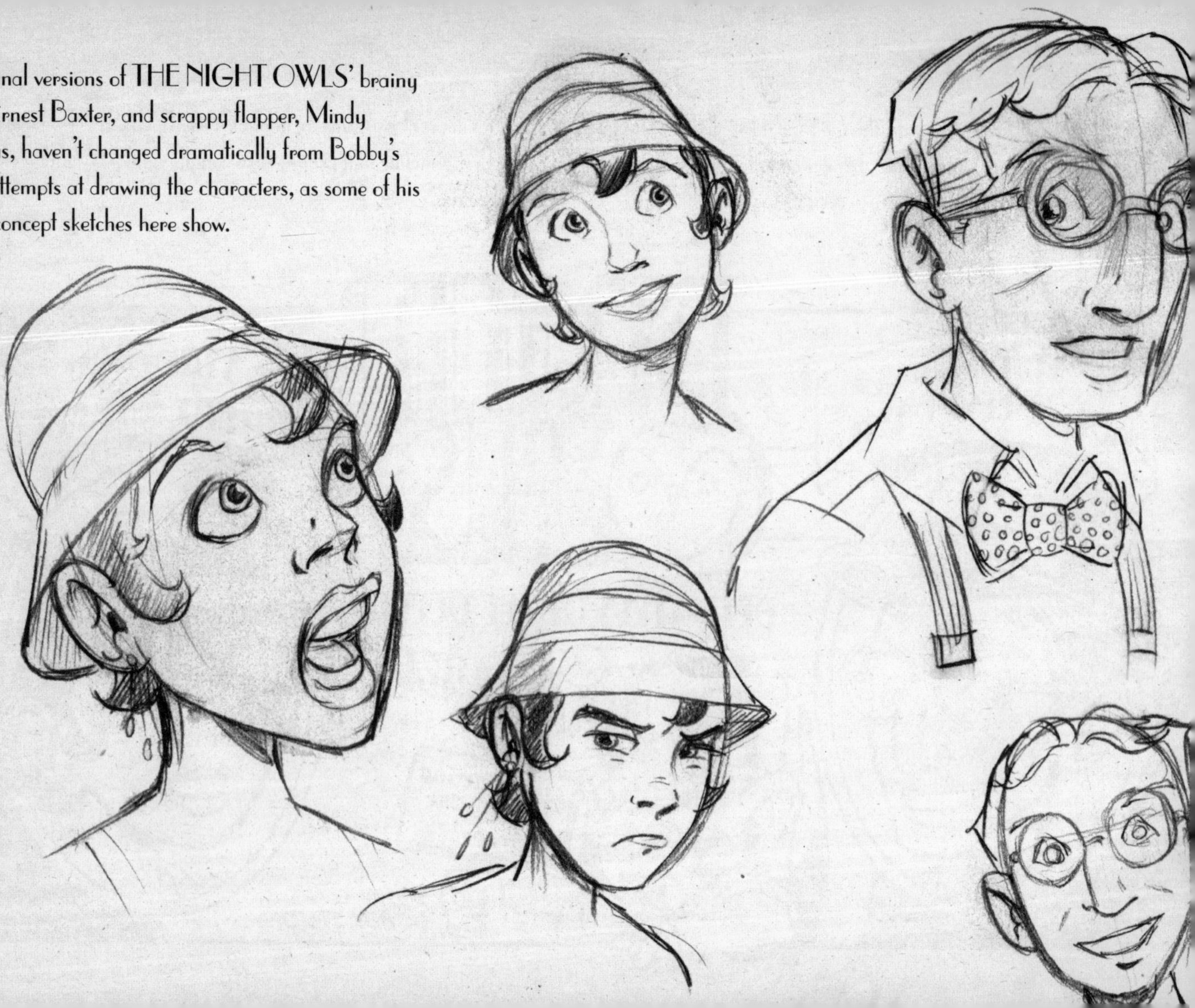

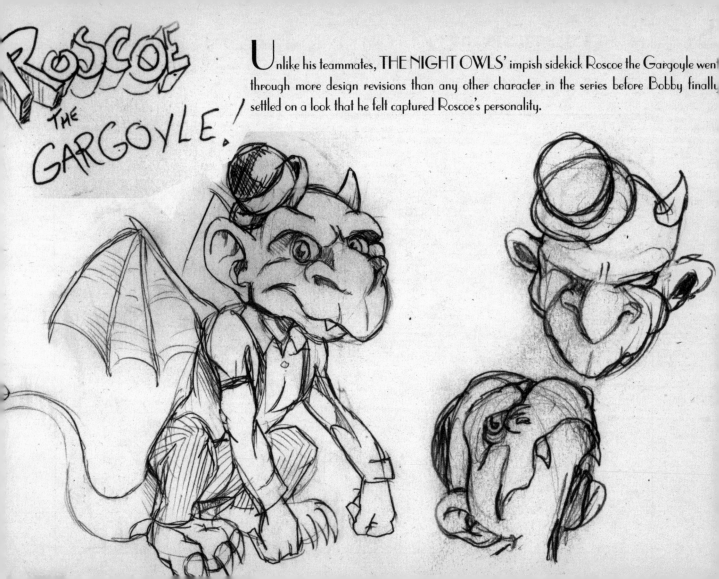

ROSCOE THE GARGOYLE!

Unlike his teammates, THE NIGHT OWLS' impish sidekick Roscoe the Gargoyle went through more design revisions than any other character in the series before Bobby finally settled on a look that he felt captured Roscoe's personality.

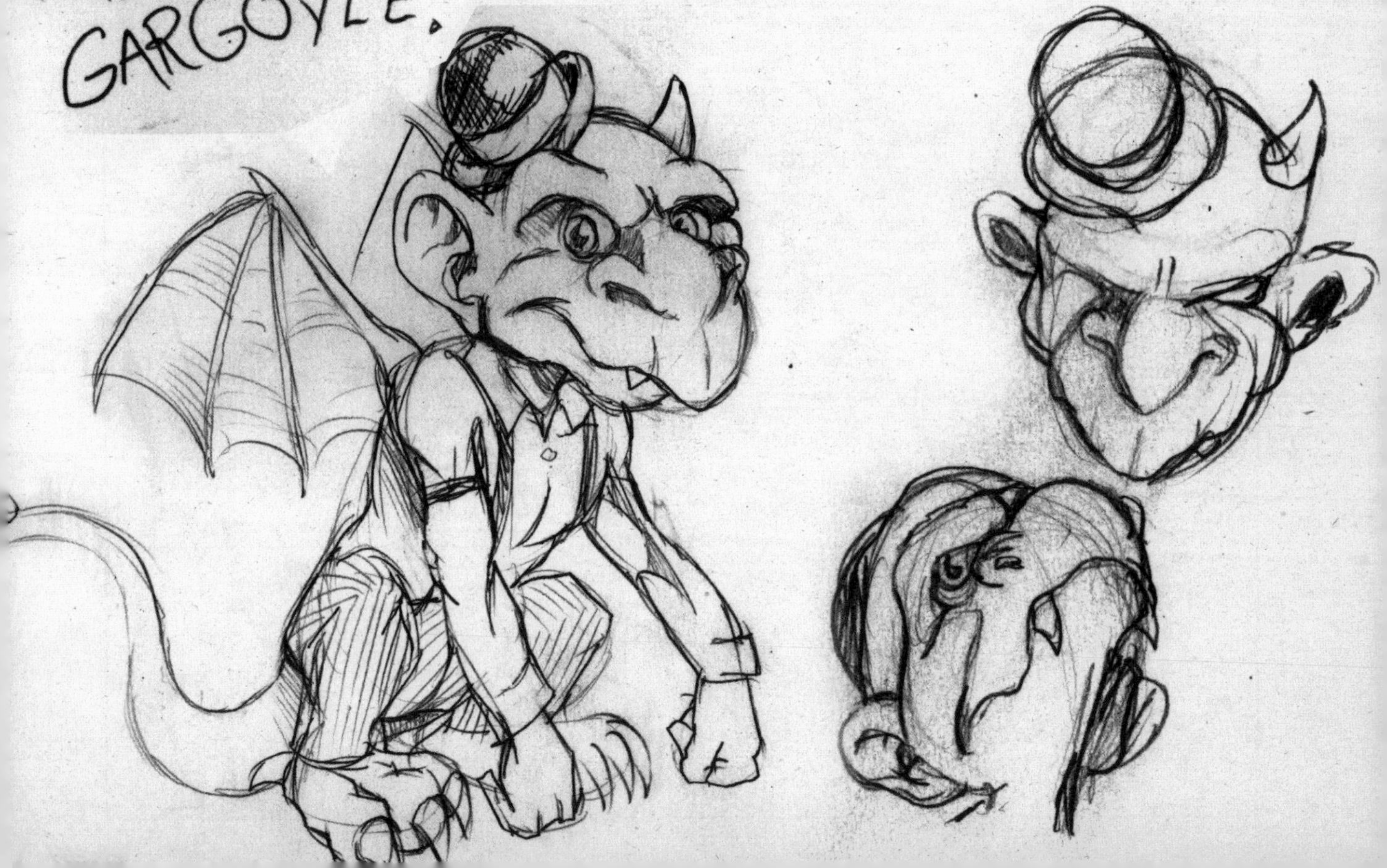

Shortly after finishing the class assignment for THE NIGHT OWLS, Bobby took part in a "24-Hour Comic Challenge" where he create a complete 24-page story in under 24 hours. With THE NIGHT OWLS still fresh in his mind, Bobby pencilled a short story about Erni Mindy, Roscoe and a strange, ghostly vigilante!

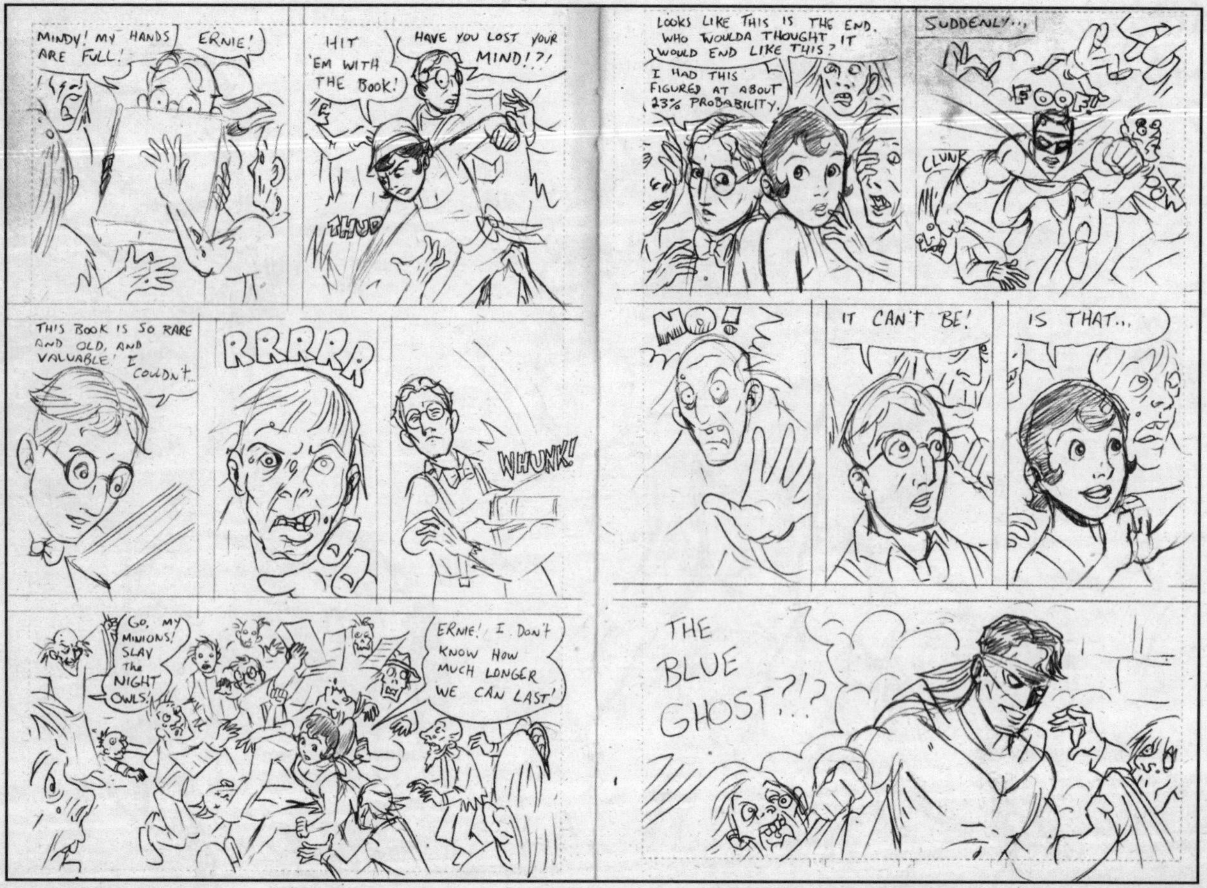

MINDY! MY HANDS ARE FULL!
ERNIE!
HIT 'EM WITH THE BOOK!
HAVE YOU LOST YOUR MIND!?!
THUD
THIS BOOK IS SO RARE AND OLD, AND VALUABLE! I COULDN'T...
RRRRR
WHUNK!
GO, MY MINIONS! SLAY THE NIGHT OWLS!
ERNIE! I DON'T KNOW HOW MUCH LONGER WE CAN LAST!
LOOKS LIKE THIS IS THE END. WHO WOULDA THOUGHT IT WOULD END LIKE THIS?
I HAD THIS FIGURED AT ABOUT 23% PROBABILITY.
SUDDENLY...
FOOF!
CLUNK
POW
NO!
IT CAN'T BE!
IS THAT...
THE BLUE GHOST?!?

While Bobby came up with the initial concept for THE NIGHT OWLS and provided the art for the entire series, it was twin brother Peter who took on the task of writing the story and jokes. However, Peter's usual process involved actually sketching his scripts! Seen here is Peter's initial sketch for the moment where Roscoe introduces his sister to Ernie and Mindy.

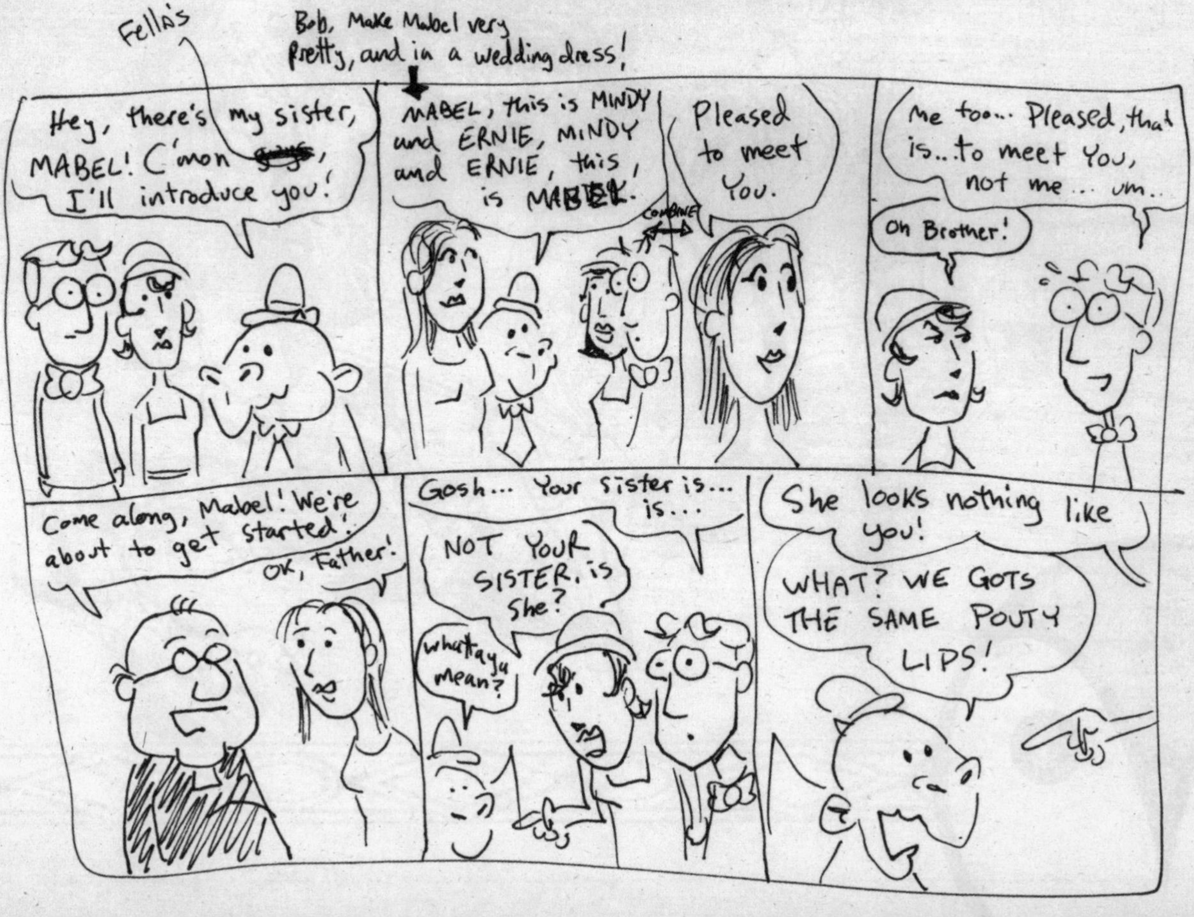

Fella's
Bob, Make Mabel very pretty, and in a wedding dress!
Hey, there's my sister, MABEL! C'mon ~~guys~~, I'll introduce you!
MABEL, this is MINDY and ERNIE, MINDY and ERNIE, this, is MABEL.
COMBINE
Pleased to meet You.
Me too... Pleased, that is...to meet You, not me... um..
Oh Brother!
Come along, Mabel! We're about to get started!
OK, Father!
Gosh... Your sister is... is...
NOT YOUR SISTER, is she?
whattayu mean?
She looks nothing like you!
WHAT? WE GOTS THE SAME POUTY LIPS!

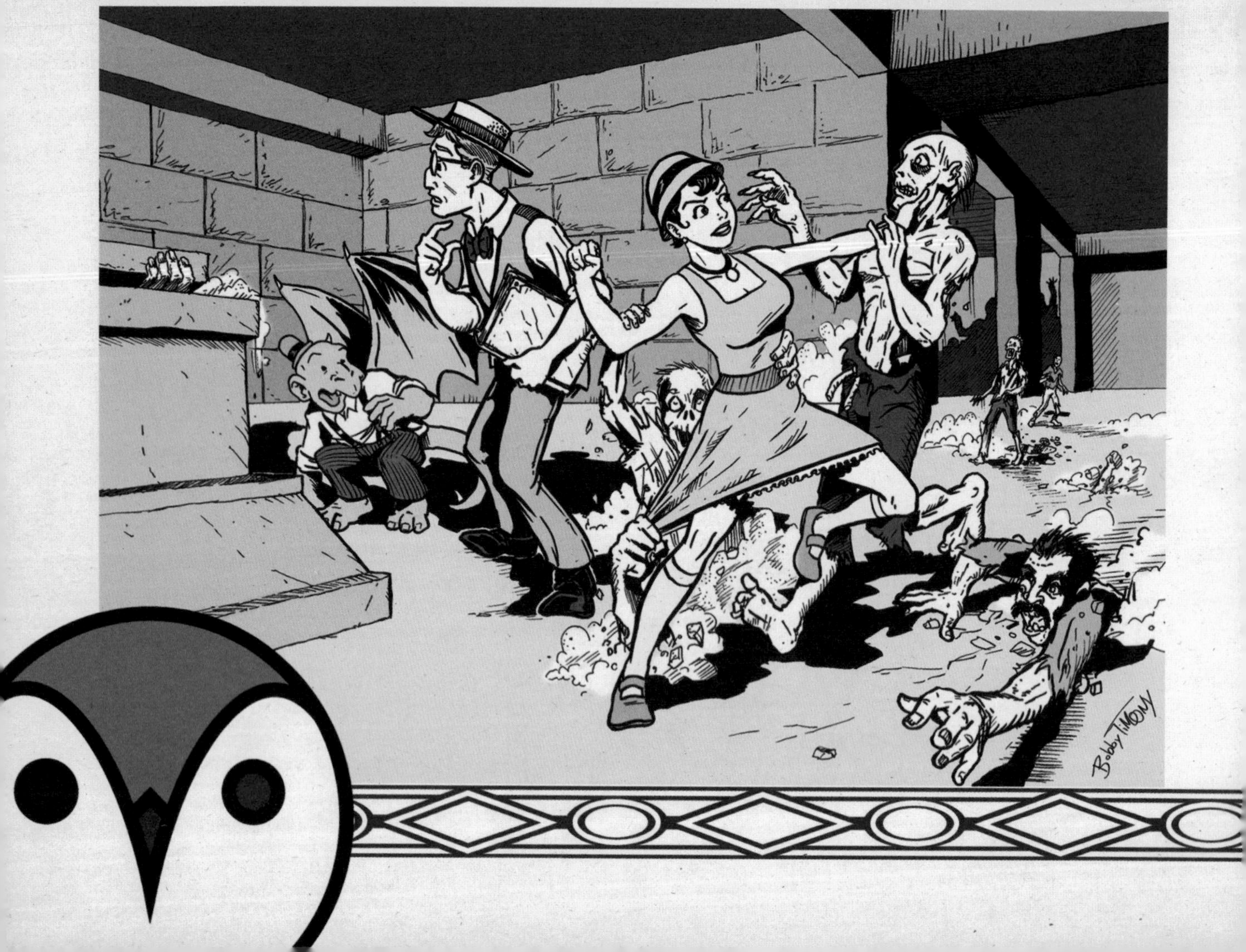
Bobby Timony

BIOS

PETER + BOBBY TIMONY

Peter and Bobby are identical twins, actors and carnival performers. THE NIGHT OWLS is their first published project. Peter has written scripts for independent films, one of which was shown in the Short Films Corner at the Cannes Film Festival. Peter's play KISS O' DEATH was performed Off-Broadway. He lives in New Providence, New Jersey with his wife Kerry. Bobby is a freelance storyboard artist for television commercials. He, his wife Danna, and their giant pet rabbit live in Brooklyn, New York.

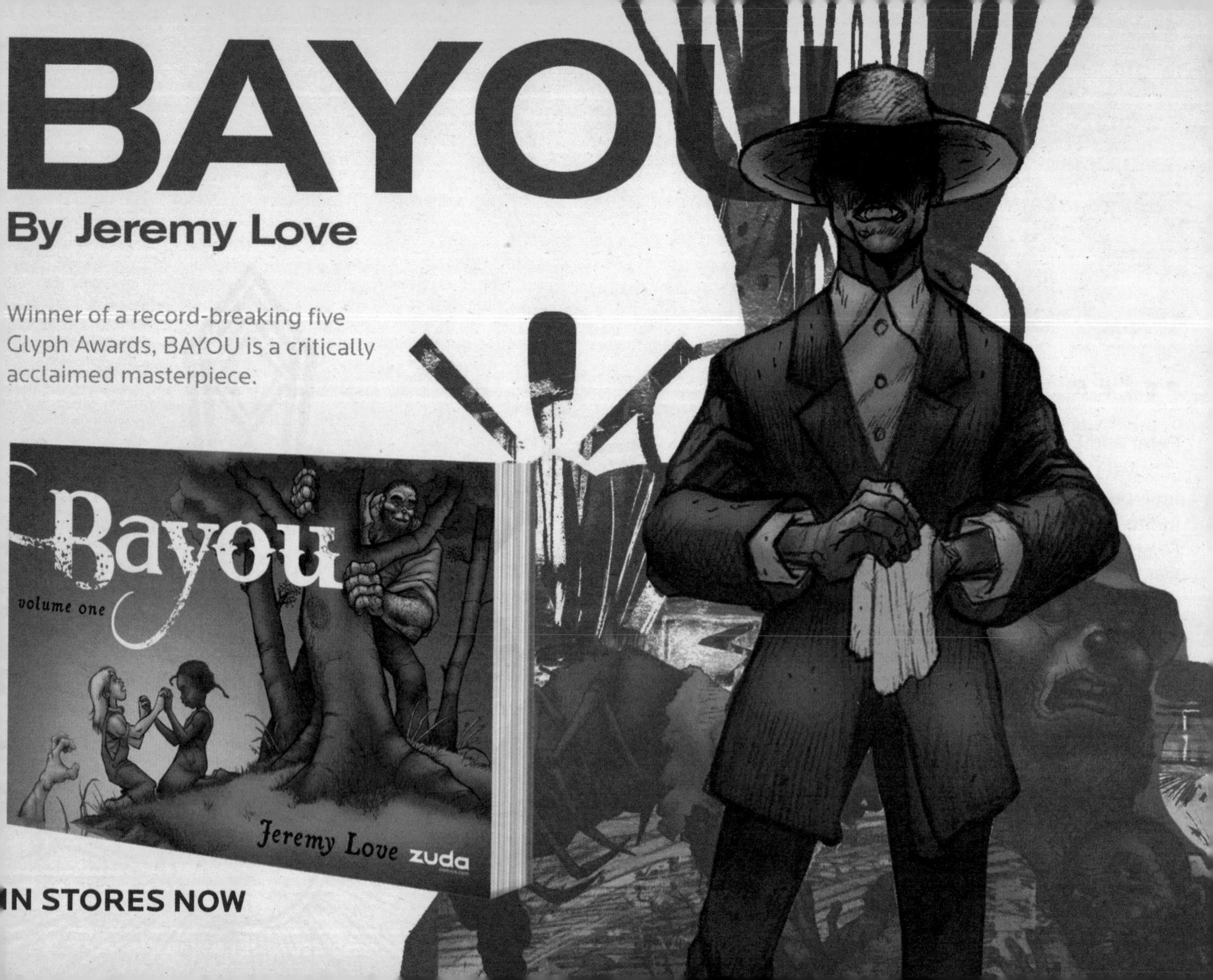
BAYOU
By Jeremy Love
Winner of a record-breaking five Glyph Awards, BAYOU is a critically acclaimed masterpiece.
Bayou
volume one
Jeremy Love
zuda
IN STORES NOW